BRITISH
TELEVISION
ADVERTISING
THE FIRST 30 YEARS

BRITISH TELEVISION ADVERTISING

THE FIRST 30 YEARS

EDITED BY BRIAN HENRY

CENTURY BENHAM
London

Copyright © The History of Advertising Trust 1986

All rights reserved

First published in 1986 by Century Benham Ltd
An imprint of Century Hutchinson Ltd
Brookmount House, 62–65 Chandos Place, Covent Garden
London WC2N 4NW

Century Hutchinson Publishing Group (Australia) Pty Ltd
16–22 Church Street, Hawthorn, Melbourne, Victoria 3122

Century Hutchinson Group (NZ) Ltd
32–34 View Road, PO Box 40–086, Glenfield, Auckland 10

Century Hutchinson Group (SA) Pty Ltd
PO Box 337, Bergvlei 2012, South Africa

Set in 11/13 Linotron Sabon
by Input Typesetting Ltd, London SW19 8DR
Printed and bound in Great Britain by
Butler & Tanner, Frome, Somerset

Designed by Roger Walker
Maps and drawings by Ian Isham

British Library Cataloguing in Publication Data
British television advertising: the first thirty years.
1. Television advertising—Great Britain—History
I. Henry, Brian
659.14'3'0941   HF6146.T42

ISBN 0–09–165800–4

CONTENTS

Foreword

LORD THOMSON OF MONIFIETH

LORD THOMSON OF MONIFIETH

Lord Thomson, who has been Chairman of the IBA since 1981, began his career as a journalist in Dundee in 1937 before wartime service with the RAF.

He was elected to Parliament as Labour Member for Dundee East in 1952 and held the seat for the next twenty years. During this time he was successively Minister of State at the Foreign Office, Secretary of State for Commonwealth Affairs (in which he succeeded another Chairman of the Authority, Lord Aylestone) and Chancellor of the Duchy of Lancaster.

Lord Thomson became a Commissioner of the EEC in 1973 and, on relinquishing this appointment in 1977, was elected Chairman of the Advertising Standards Authority, the body responsible for the regulation of non-broadcast advertising. Three years later he joined the IBA, initially as Deputy Chairman, succeeding Lady Plowden as Chairman on 1 January 1981

To be asked to write a Foreword to an important book is to be
paid a compliment: it can also on occasions be not a task but
a pleasure. On this occasion I find I am faced with three separate
but related pleasures resulting from three different points of contact −
with the publishers, with the subject matter, and with many of the
contributors.

Firstly, I write as President of the History of Advertising Trust. In
accepting the Presidency I was always hopeful that the work of the
Trust in trying to preserve, in a proper fashion, some of the remarkable
work which the advertising business has produced over the years −
and which is frequently passed over as mere ephemera − would also
result in the publication of scholarly historical work not only about
the creative content of advertising, but about its impact on our economic and social conditions. My happiness in seeing this history of
television advertising published may therefore be imagined, and in
recording this pleasure − and some small measure of pride − I must
sincerely congratulate the Trust in having brought this complex project
to fruition.

Secondly, as Chairman of the IBA, I have another obvious interest to
declare. I have been privileged to see many developments in broadcast
advertising during my chairmanship. To read the contributions to this
book by such distinguished professional participants in the IBA's own
history as Tony Pragnell and Peter Woodhouse is to increase one's
own understanding of the way that this most important advertising
medium has developed and contributed to the quality of British public
service broadcasting over the past thirty eventful years.

Thirdly, my interest in the whole subject of advertising was considerably sharpened, and my understanding of its mechanisms increased,
by my time as Chairman of the Advertising Standards Authority, and
the many stimulating opportunities that position gave me to meet
advertising people and gain an insight into the way they approached
their work. I am therefore very glad to see in print the incisive and
sometimes provocative words of Messrs David Bernstein, Winston

Fletcher, John Hobson and Tim Bell, giving their own perspectives to the history of the development of television advertising. Peter Rennie, writing from the standpoint of one of the major programme companies, reminds us of the considerable success of Independent Television in attracting a wide range of new products and services to the screen. This new business has contributed to the financial stability of the medium and at the same time increased the value of our service to the viewer.

Sir Ronald Halstead once started a presentation to an audience of young marketing people with the words, 'I am not in the advertising business and I only use it because it's cheaper than sending a salesman' – an opening that guaranteed their undivided attention. Here he has presented the advertiser's vital viewpoint. The advertiser's support for the television medium throughout its history, without at any time seeking to breach the statutory divide between advertisements and programmes, is something that broadcasters do well to remember.

From their positions of eminence in the research and production fields, Sir Bernard Audley and James Garrett have drawn upon their unrivalled experience of nearly the whole history of ITV, while my distinguished predecessor as IBA Chairman from 1967 to 1975, Lord Aylestone, has set down a personal memoir of that period of change and development. Students of the history of ITV will know that change and development are endemic to the business of broadcasting and the people who are fortunate enough to participate in it. The belief that there was once a golden age of tranquillity in the work of the IBA, of which some old Brompton Road hands talk most nostalgically, is – like all legends of golden ages – part of mythology.

Lord Briggs, the doyen of social historians, has moved from his monumental history of the BBC to write about the social effect of television advertising. He has done so in a way which will be invaluable, not only to readers of this book, but also to the many who will come after, eager to re-evaluate this ever-popular subject for their dissertations and other academic projects.

Finally, I must pay proper tribute to Brian Henry, not only for contributing so definitively the 'core' of the history contained in the book, but also for his skill as persuader, gentle arm-twister and sympathetic editor for all the other contributors. This is far from being his only achievement on behalf of the history of television. For a quarter of a century, as one of the longest-serving sales directors from the early days of the mid-1950s, he fostered the development and stability of Independent Television. Historians will find in the minutes of the ITCA and IBA's committees that he played a significant role, from the Pilkington to the Annan Commission and all the other inquiries in between, in the industry's response to all these external pressures. This book is proof of his success in these fields: I commend the book and its editor to you, the reader.

George Thomson

Introduction

BRIAN HENRY

Radio and, more especially, television have . . . become the prime instruments for the management of consumer demand. There is an insistent tendency among solemn social scientists to think of any institution which features rhymed and singing commercials; provides intense and lachrymose voices urging highly improbable enjoyments; offers caricatures of the human oesophagus in normal or impaired operation; and which hints implausibly at opportunities for antiseptic seduction, as inherently trivial. This is a great mistake. The industrial system is profoundly dependent on commercial television and could not exist in its present form without it. Economists who eschew discussion of its economic significance or dismiss it as a wicked waste, are protecting their reputation and that of their subject for Calvinist austerity. But they are not adding to their reputation for relevance.

J. K. Galbraith, *The New Industrial State* (1967)

Any historian of the advertising side of Independent Television in the first thirty years of its existence faces a daunting task. Many of the earliest written records of the industry are woefully incomplete and minutes and agendas of meetings, where they exist, seldom reflect the climate of the time or the long-forgotten pressures, political as well as financial, to which the participants were subjected.

Films of the early commercials have, in a great many cases, been destroyed and some of the programme companies, production houses and advertising agencies which once dominated the medium no longer exist. Some major television advertisers, too, have disappeared as a result of mergers and amalgamations and a number of well-known products which have survived into the 1980s have been disposed of by their original owners only to be re-launched, sometimes with greater success, by others.

But the very scarcity of material has been ample justification for further research and, indeed, for the publication of this history. There is at present no continuous record of television advertising in this country worthy to stand beside Bernard Sendall's monumental *Independent Television in Britain*, which covers the period only up to the first major upheaval in 1968 when new contractors were appointed.

No doubt one day Sendall's immensely detailed and authoritative work will be extended to embrace the subsequent phases but even then the advertising aspect is likely to remain secondary to the main theme of broadcasting *per se*. As Lord Hill once remarked when Chairman of the ITA: 'Television is all about programmes.'

Yet the initial public perception of Independent Television was, to a very large extent, conditioned by viewers' attitudes to television *advertising*. Certainly the original political opposition to ITV in the early fifties arose because it was feared that the demands of advertisers would very soon overshadow the needs of the audience. The contemptuous dismissal of the new service by some newspapers of the time as 'plug-TV' now has a ring of quaint absurdity after more than thirty years of public acceptance and support. But even the severest critics of the early days would now admit that the effect of Independent Television on the BBC – culminating in the advent of Channel Four in 1982 – has been beneficial, while on the ITV channels advertisers have never in practice sought to influence the content of programmes or the editorial independence of the programme makers.

The coming of ITV not only increased the vitality and range of the television medium as a whole. It also served to crystallize public attitudes to advertising itself. An ambiguous claim in a press advertisement seemed to gain an almost oracular power – as the BMA pointed out in their evidence to the Pilkington Committee in 1961 – when brought to life on the television screen. Such was the sheer impact of the new medium that, had a thoroughgoing system of advertising control not been foreshadowed in the 1954 Television Act, it would plainly have been necessary to invent one. The system of pre-transmission scrutiny of every advertisement – and currently some 10,000 new television commercials are submitted for advance clearance every year – has come to provide the audience with a unique form of consumer protection.

It was apparent soon after the opening of the service that television provided a range of benefits of far-reaching importance to the advertiser. Experience showed that once ITV coverage reached significant levels new products could be established in the market far more rapidly by television than by the use of other media. The effect of a TV campaign could be measured on an area-by-area basis and these areas, created in the early days by the coverage of a small number of VHF transmitters, could form an advertiser's sales territories and if necessary be treated as separate entities for test-marketing purposes. Thanks to an audience measurement service of high quality, advertising exposure was reported within two weeks of transmission and, as a result, campaigns were targeted with increasing precision and the minimum of wasted coverage.

It is no exaggeration to say that it was very largely television advertising from 1955 onwards which created the twin disciplines of scientific marketing and media planning, as several of the contributors to this volume have clearly demonstrated.

Despite the absence of many of the early records of the industry a further problem arose in the compilation of this book because of the many well-documented features of television advertising which it has proved impossible to explore fully or, in some cases, even to mention. I personally regret, for example, being unable (because of shortage of space) to describe in detail the imaginative marketing services which the contractors began to introduce over twenty years ago. These began simply enough by the offer on the part of the ITV stations of on-screen and point-of-sale promotional aids by which a retailer could support a manufacturer's campaign and maximize its effectiveness. I vividly recall TWW's pioneering work in this field.

By the end of the 1960s, however, the range of ITV's marketing facilities had been developed to such an extent that most ITV companies were offering their advertisers the use of auxiliary sales forces to sell advertised products to retailers in their areas and to ensure adequate stock levels. Much more recently, product distribution in a number of key multiple outlets has been guaranteed by some of the programme companies before a campaign begins on the air. As a result of this concentration on product marketing, in parallel with the sale of airtime, the TV companies have built up a knowledge of the structure of the wholesale and retail trade in their areas rivalling that of the most sophisticated manufacturers.

Nor has there been space to dwell more than briefly on the many original programmes of research which the contractors undertook over the years. The most ambitious of these studies was undoubtedly *The Londoner*, a massive survey of the population of Greater London and the Home Counties in which respondents were classified by personality variables, which was carried out by Associated-Rediffusion and published in 1963. One also recalls the measurements of relative advertising effectiveness carried out by ABC Television in their important Inter-Media Comparison research of the early sixties and the authoritative Granada Viewership Surveys which were issued at about the same time. The fierce competition for advertising revenue between the stations, which the critics of ITV's apparent airtime monopoly seldom acknowledge, has resulted in each company providing a comprehensive range of marketing and research services particularly suited to the structure and characteristics of its own area.

If it has been a pity, because of limitations of space, to have failed to mention some of the important by-products of television advertising in the historical section of this book, it has been a matter of much keener personal regret that the names of many figures who have contributed to the success of the medium have also had to be omitted for the same reason. The list is however a formidable one and to have singled out some and ignored others would, it seems to me, have been invidious.

It will, however, probably surprise many readers to learn that in an industry which is numerically small and usually thought to be dominated by extreme youth no less than seven sales directors of ITV companies have died during the period 1955–85. All made their own distinctive contribution to the success of Independent Television and their names deserve to be recorded: Alex Anson (Granada): Ron Blundell (Channel): Peter Cookman (Scottish): Peter Francis (Border): Peter Mears (Central): Philip Thomas (Wales West and North): John Wardrop (ATV). All are keenly missed by their colleagues.

It may well be thought that the history which forms the first section of this book concentrates over-much on the part played by my own company, Associated-Rediffusion, in the development of Independent Televison. There are, however, several reasons for this degree of emphasis. A-R was the first ITV company to be appointed and was awarded the all-important London weekday contract. Despite the unlikely antecedents of its principal shareholder, the British Electric Traction Company, in electricity supply and public transport in the days before nationalization, this background, when combined with many years experience of broadcast-relay services and publishing (the latter through the other major shareholder, Associated Newspapers) was to provide an unusually sound foundation on which to build a new system of broadcasting.

But, as with all companies, the eventual success of Associated-Rediffusion chiefly depended on the vision of a small group of people at its head. Pre-eminent among this group and Chairman throughout the entire fourteen years of the company's existence was John Spencer Wills. It was his determination and faith in the ultimate future of Independent Television – even after appalling losses and the withdrawal of Associated Newspapers – which were to ensure that A–R, and perhaps ITV as a whole, survived and, in the end, prospered.

There are frequent references in the history chapter to Captain T.

M. Brownrigg, the General Manager of A-R from the formation of the company in 1954 until his retirement at the end of 1963. It was Brownrigg who, knowing nothing whatever about either television or advertising (as he was the first to admit), was to set up the company, find premises in the old Air Ministry building, Adastral House, Kingsway, engage staff and ensure that the station was fully equipped and ready to go on the air less than a year after he himself had been appointed.

It may appear from the account I have given elsewhere that Brownrigg's attitudes and prejudices were firmly rooted in the past and that he operated in the manner of an Edwardian martinet and autocrat. All this was partly true. But in reality his quarterdeck manner, his tendency to dominate – at times to domineer, to name-drop incessantly and to deliver outrageous generalizations on almost any subject concealed an administrator of exceptional ability and a brilliant mind which grasped the unfamiliar problems of showbusiness and advertising with astonishing rapidity. His saving grace was an unquenchable sense of humour and the ability to laugh at himself.

Maurice Wiggin, the television critic of the *Sunday Times*, was shrewd enough to realize that the unique ethos of A-R, which he described as 'doggedly decent', was very much Brownrigg's own creation. And Brownrigg appropriated the same description for himself in a valedictory article which he wrote for *Fusion*, A-R's house magazine, when he retired. But this was to undervalue his own abilities, which were considerable. He imprinted his own personality on Associated-Rediffusion much as Reith had done at the BBC.

In the course of preparing a history of a complex subject one is bound to turn to many people for help and advice. My thanks are due, first, to all the contributors to this book who invariably responded sympathetically to editorial demands from me despite the fact that many of the authors also have to cope with other more important and urgent responsibilities. To them I am especially grateful.

Secondly, I would particularly mention Tony Pragnell, the former Deputy Director-General of the IBA, who has been a constant source of wise advice and guidance especially as regards the relationship between the broadcasters and government as well as the workings of the Authority under a succession of regimes.

There were, in addition, others I consulted for reminiscences and information, some going back thirty years or more, as well as for help in many other ways.

In this regard I am especially indebted to:

Bill Ambrose: Lady Anglesey: Lord Annan: Barry Barron: Lewis Breakspear: William Brown: Lord Buxton: Mike Chapman: Humphrey Chilton: Peter Cooper: David Coulson: Geoff Darby: Peter Davis: Sheila Diviney: Johanna Forsyth: Jo Gable: Joe Garwood: Archie Graham: John Guinery: Chris Hawes: Pat Hawker: Hugh Henry: Win Higenbottam: Carol Hibbert: Barbara Hosking: Sir Ian Isham: John Jackson: David Jarvis: Dick Johnson: David Lamb: Ronald Lane: Alex Letts: Barrie Macdonald: Kathy May: Leonard Miall: Kenneth Miles: Stuart Middleton: Roger Morgan: James O'Connor: Michael Parkin: Gabrielle Pike: Brian Rhodes: Nigel Rogers: John Salmon: Brian Sanctuary: Peter Scruton: Jack Smith: Tony Solomon: Ronald Stevens: Harry Theobalds: Howard Thomas: Philip Town: Boris Townsend: Ron Trainer: Peter Warren: Colin Webb: Robert Weir: David Wheeler: Colin Winchester: Piers Yeld: Muriel Young.

Finally, I am grateful to acknowledge the unfailing help and encouragement I have had from George Harrison, the Director of the History of Advertising Trust, and from Judy Slinn my researcher, who had the laborious task of verifying my personal recollections of the last thirty years.

But, above all, I must pay tribute to my wife, Jan, who has accepted with good humour and tolerance my total preoccupation with this project over many months.

ACKNOWLEDGEMENTS

The Editor and the History of Advertising Trust wish to express their thanks to the following whose help has made the production of this book possible:

The Advertising Creative Circle
The Independent Broadcasting Authority
The Independent Television Companies' Association

Advertisers:
Allied Lyons; Bass; Beecham Group; Birds Eye Walls; British American Cosmetics; Cadbury Schweppes; Elida Gibbs; Esso Petroleum; Gallaher; Kodak; Mars Confectionery; Martini & Rossi; Nabisco Brands; National Westminster Bank; The Nestle Charitable Trust; The Post Office; Rank Hovis McDougall; Richardson-Vicks; Rowntree Mackintosh; Spillers Foods; Van den Berghs; Whitbread.

Advertising Agencies:
AAP Ketchum; Bartle Bogle Hegarty; Boase Massimi Pollitt Partnership; Chetwynd Haddons; Collett Dickenson, Pearce & Partners; D'Arcy MacManus Masius; Davidson Pearce; Dorland Advertising; Foote, Cone & Belding; Grey Advertising; KMP Partnership; Lopex; Lowe Howard-Spink Campbell-Ewald; McCann-Erickson Worldwide; McCormick Publicis; Marsteller Little and Strodl; Ogilvy & Mather; The Royds Advertising Group; SSC & B. Lintas Worldwide; J. Walter Thompson; Valin Pollen International; Young & Rubicam.

In addition special mention should be made of the facilities which have been put at the Editor's disposal by the Television and Press Register for the recovery of commercials via their library and monitoring service.

The History

BRIAN HENRY

BRIAN HENRY (EDITOR)

Brian Henry was educated at Stowe and subsequently at Trinity College, Cambridge between the eras of the Apostles and *The Glittering Prizes*. He served in the RNVR during the Second World War and, at the age of twenty, navigated one of HM ships the ten thousand miles from Plymouth to the Philippines.

Beginning his advertising career in market research with the A. C. Nielsen Co., he moved in 1949 to the London evening newspaper *The Star*, where he became Advertisement Manager. He entered television in 1956 and was Controller of Advertisements of Associated-Rediffusion, the original London weekday station, from 1957 until he joined the board of Southern Television as Sales Director in 1961. He remained with Southern until 1981 apart from a break of two years when he was Director of Marketing of the Associated Newspapers Group during the launch of the new *Daily Mail* in 1971.

Brian Henry is the only person to have been Chairman of both the NPA and ITCA marketing committees, and he has also chaired the Advertising Association's Public Action Group and Finance Committee as well as the Television Consumer Audit and the Board of Advertising Education.

In the last few years he has been a director of Remploy and of a film production company

GROWTH OF COVERAGE OF THE ITV NETWORK

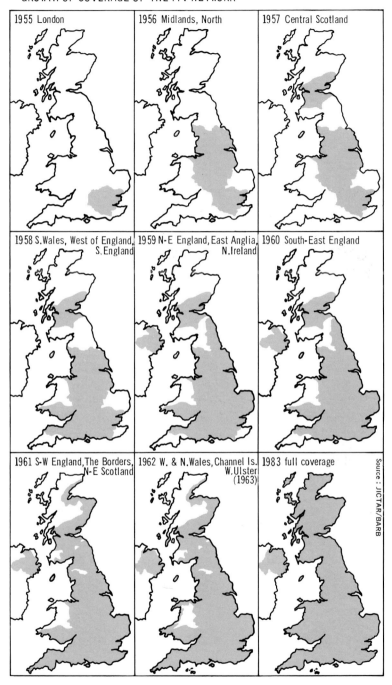

1955 London

1956 Midlands, North

1957 Central Scotland

1958 S.Wales, West of England, S.England

1959 N-E England, East Anglia, N.Ireland

1960 South-East England

1961 S-W England, The Borders, N-E Scotland

1962 W. & N.Wales, Channel Is. W.Ulster (1963)

1983 full coverage

Source : JICTAR/BARB

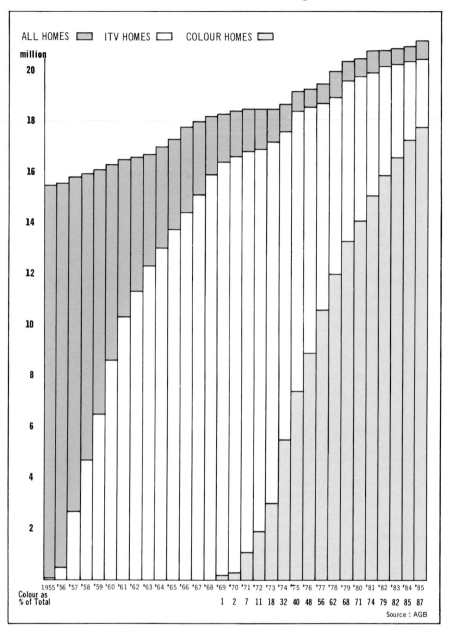

Chart 1. Growth of ITV and colour homes. The perceptive reader will notice that despite the superficial resemblance between this chart and the one on the right – both, for example, show the steady rise in the ownership of colour receivers since the late sixties – there is a considerable discrepancy between the total number of *sets* shown in Chart 1 and the number of *licences* in Chart 2.

It would appear from the figures that by 1985 some 1,900,000 (colour and monochrome) television sets were being operated without licences, an annual loss in revenue

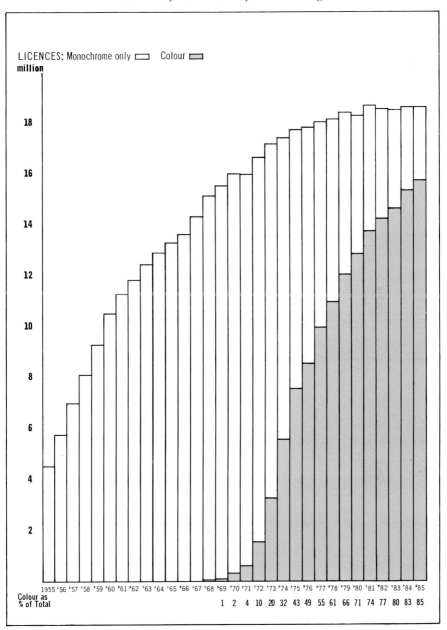

LICENCES: Monochrome only ☐   Colour ☐
million

Chart 2. Growth of television licences and colour penetration.

to the BBC (before deducting the costs of collection) of nearly £100,000,000.

It is worth adding however that a more effective licence evasion campaign which resulted in a reduction in the number of 'pirate' receivers would make no difference whatever to the finances of Independent Television. ITV does not receive any part of the licence revenue nor has it ever done so

PROLOGUE

A prediction from 1930

In one of those extraordinary flashes of insight which from time to time illumine the vision of twentieth-century novelists, Charles Morgan, writing in the *BBC Yearbook* for 1930, speculated on the possible future impact of the embryonic medium of television on the established arts. He wrote prophetically:

It is as yet too early to speak in detail of the probable effect on entertainment. It is not impossible that the time may come when, without leaving his armchair, a man may be a hearing and seeing member of the audience in any playhouse, cinema or concert hall throughout the world. If this power is ever brought to mechanical perfection, there is little reason, except the desire to be gregarious, that anyone but a few should go in person to any place of entertainment again; from which it follows that, for want of a local audience, theatres, cinemas and concert halls may be closed down and all entertainment be concentrated in studios supported by an international organisation of televisionists.

He went on to dwell on the obvious dangers if television were to be used as an instrument of political propaganda and concluded with a dire – though, as will be seen, unjustified – warning of the perils which lay in store if advertising were ever to be allowed on the air:

To leave the sources of entertainment in the hands of cynical money-makers is to imperil civilisation, and to imperil it more and more as the facilities of distribution increase. It is bad enough to give matches to an ignorant child; it is the last folly to give bombs to an evil one.

There is little doubt that for the next quarter of a century these views continued to be widely shared, if in a less extreme form, by almost all leaders of educated opinion in Britain, at least to the extent that they ever gave the subject serious thought. Parliament, the churches, the press, the teaching and other professions at every level – all were strongly opposed to any kind of association, particularly one of financial dependence, between broadcasting and the world of commerce and industry.

The purpose of this history of the first thirty years of television advertising in Britain is to trace the origins and developments of a service whose effects have been very different from those which its early critics foresaw, and whose benefits to the public (both as viewers and consumers) as well as to advertisers are now beyond question.

The first public television service

It is sometimes forgotten that Britain was the first country in the world to introduce a public television service. On 2 November 1936 the first BBC television broadcasts began, initially to only four hundred homes in the London area, from the Corporation's studio at Alexandra Palace. The transmission system, which was finally adopted on the recommendation of the Television Advisory Committee and was destined to remain unchanged for nearly thirty years, used the high-definition Marconi-EMI 405-line standard in one of the Very High Frequency bands of the broadcasting spectrum.

By 1 September 1939, on the eve of the outbreak of war, when television transmissions were suspended for nearly seven years, the number of sets receiving the service had risen to somewhere between twenty thousand and twenty-five thousand. There were no accurate viewing statistics at this stage nor, incidentally, was a separate licence required to operate a television receiver. The annual wireless licence fee, which had remained unchanged since 1922, stood at 10 shillings (50p).

The postwar years

It took nearly a year after the ravages and disruption of the Second World War to bring the BBC television service back into operation, and transmissions were not resumed until 7 June 1946. To help meet the increased cost of the service a combined radio and TV licence was introduced for the first time, at a cost of £2. As far as the future of broadcasting was concerned, the most urgent problem facing the Government was the question of the BBC Charter which was due to expire on 31 December 1946.

It was agreed to extend the life of the Corporation by a further five years, until the end of 1951, and in the meantime to decide whether or not to set up an inquiry into the whole future of broadcasting in Britain. The inquiry set up by the Government in 1949 under Lord Beveridge, the father of the welfare state, was to lead somewhat indirectly to the creation of Independent Television.

The Beveridge Committee

It is widely believed that all the members of the Beveridge Committee – except one – were totally opposed to any form of commercially financed broadcasting service. But this view is not entirely correct. Three members, including Lord Beveridge himself, expressed the opinion that a total prohibition of advertising might be reconsidered. 'Is there any decisive reason', they asked, 'why the most persuasive means of communication should not be used for this legitimate purpose?' But one member, Selwyn Lloyd, later Chancellor of the Exchequer and Foreign Secretary, went a great deal further. He declared that he deplored monopoly in any form, and went on to advocate the establishment for both radio and television of competitive broadcasting services which should be financed by sponsorship.

The Labour Government under Clement Attlee postponed a decision on the Beveridge Report, and it was not until 1952, after a Conservative administration had been returned to power, that the first steps were taken to introduce competition in broadcasting. Two important points, indicative of the Government's thinking, were expressed in the White Paper which was published in May of the same year:

The Government would be most unwilling to see any change in the policy of the BBC themselves towards sponsoring or accepting advertisements, and the existing restriction on commercial sponsoring without the consent of the Postmaster-General will be preserved. [Paragraph 5]

But at the same time Paragraph 7 gave some hopes for the future:

The present Government have come to the conclusion that in the expanding field of television provision should be made to permit some element of competition when the calls on capital resources at present needed for purposes of national importance make this possible.

By 1952 the issues seemed to crystallize around two questions: the undesirability of the continuing BBC's broadcasting monopoly and the possibility of additional television services being financed by advertising – probably in the form of sponsorship.

The abandonment of sponsorship

Two factors eventually caused the abandonment of plans for the introduction of a sponsored service. First, there was widespread criticism, on both sides of the Atlantic, of the inclusion of embarrassingly incongruous advertisers' announcements in the United States broadcasts of the Coronation service in June 1953. Secondly, the advertising agencies in Britain decided to support the use of 'spot' advertising which would be divorced from the content of the actual programmes themselves.

On 29 August 1953 the Postmaster-General, Lord De La Warr, was able to assure the House of Lords:

> There is a world of difference between accepting advertisements and sponsoring. The Government has made it clear that they envisage a system whereby the station and not the advertiser is responsible for the programmes.

Three months later the outline of Independent Television began to emerge in a further White Paper. While the BBC would continue to be 'the main instrument of broadcasting policy in the United Kingdom', the control of television 'should not remain in the hands of a single authority, however excellent it may be'. A separate public corporation with a life of ten years should be set up to oversee the additional service, operate the transmitters and appoint the programme companies who would provide all the material which was to be broadcast.

On advertisements the Government declared:

> 'In practice the fewer rules and the less day-to-day interference the better; the need would be for a continuing friendly and constructive contact between the corporation and the companies.'

In addition to 'spot' advertising it was felt that there should be scope within the new service for documentary films and shoppers' guides prepared by advertisers.

The debates and the Television Bill

The debates in both Houses of Parliament which followed the publication of the White Paper reflected passions which to a later generation seem incredible. Opening the debate in the Commons, the former Home Secretary, Herbert Morrison, warned portentously that this was 'to be one of the – if not the – most important debates since the war. On it depends the future thinking of our people and our standards of culture.'

The Television Bill was published on 4 March 1954 and sparked off the same kind of violent criticism received by the Government's proposals in the White Paper. Lord Reith, the pioneer and virtual founder of the BBC, compared the coming of advertising to the screen with the introduction into England of smallpox, the Black Death and bubonic plague. Lord Hailsham likened ITV to 'a Caliban emerging from his slimy cavern'. Lord Esher foretold of a descent into 'a planned and premeditated orgy of vulgarity'. In the Commons one of the bitterest controversies of the debate concerned the amendment to substitute the word 'Commercial' for 'Independent' in the title of the new 'controlling body', the ITA. Gilbert Mitchison, QC, the Labour Member for Kettering and something of a wit, pointed out however that a skunk would still smell extremely nasty even it were known as an independent raccoon.

A General Election was due to take place no later than 1956. Attlee made no secret of the fact that the Labour party, if returned to power, would abandon the whole notion of an Independent Television service. The opposition to the Bill was so intense and the debates so prolonged that the Government decided that there was no alternative but to employ the guillotine during the second reading and to proceed with the committee and report stages without delay. Lord Reith wrote in his diary:

20 July 1954 My sixty-fifth birthday. Sat in the House of Lords for twenty minutes, report stage of TV Bill. Absolutely nauseating; Jowitt asking courteously and cogently for a change in the title of the Independent Television Authority and De La Warr just feebly saying it couldn't be done and giving no reasons. And the three palsied old hags, Woolton, Swinton and Salisbury, yapping away on the front bench. I left in disgust.

The Bill received the Royal Assent ten days later, on 30 July 1954.

The first Television Act

Despite the hysteria and the forebodings which had arisen during the passage of the Bill, the resultant Act of Parliament, the Television Act, 1954, which brought ITV into being had been wisely drafted. Subsequent events have proved that it contained the essential safeguards which were needed to operate a service which was neither stifled by bureaucratic restrictions nor at the mercy of constant political and commercial pressures.

Its advertising provisions, which have scarcely been altered save in matters of detail in thirty years, were dealt with under three separate headings:

Section 4:
(i) Neither the Authority nor any programme contractor was to be allowed to act as an advertising agent.

(ii) The ITA must secure compliance with the rules within the Act and others approved by the Postmaster-General.

(iii) Nothing was to be included in any programme which might give the impression that it had been supplied or suggested by an advertiser (Section 4(6) – the 'no-sponsorship' clause; see Appendix B – Part II).

Section 8:

The Authority was to appoint a committee concerned with the standards of conduct in the advertising of goods and services and, in particular, those in the medical field. This committee was to draw up a set of principles to be followed in the acceptance of advertising and it was to be the duty of the Authority to secure compliance with these rules.

Finally, the Second Schedule of the Act (see Appendix B – Part I) laid down specific requirements as to the separation between programmes and advertisements, the total amount of advertising to be allowed, the placing of commercials, the approval of rate cards, the exclusion of political and religious advertising and the provision of facilities for local advertisers.

Little more than a year remained in which to set up the Authority, establish transmission facilities and appoint programme contractors if the new service was to begin in September of the following year. The two London companies, once appointed, had less than twelve months in which to find premises, engage staff and be fully prepared to go on the air.

Trade Test Transmissions. This caption was transmitted from the Croydon transmitter before the opening of Independent Television on 22 September 1955

1955

The Advertising Advisory Committee

The Television Act of 1954 had laid down that the Authority should appoint 'a committee representative of organisations, authorities and persons concerned with standards of conduct in the advertising of goods and services (including in particular the advertising of goods and services for medical or surgical purposes)' to advise it in the acceptance of advertisements in the new medium. On 14 January 1955 the Authority's Advertising Advisory Committee held its first meeting at the Arts Council's offices in St James's Square, London.

The reason for this somewhat unexpected venue was that the Chairman of the ITA, Sir Kenneth Clark, who presided over the Committee's first meeting, was also Chairman of the Arts Council of Great Britain. It was soon decided, however, that the AAC needed a permanent Chairman of its own. Accordingly Robert Bevan, Chairman of S. H. Benson and an advertising man of wide experience, was chosen to head this important committee and to follow the terms of reference which had been given it in the Television Act.

It had two main duties as defined by Parliament: first, to ensure that no misleading advertisments were transmitted, and secondly to draw up a series of principles which were to be followed in the acceptance of all television advertising. It was the responsibility of the Authority itself, however, to 'secure compliance' with the rules.

Less than five months later the first edition of the *Principles for Television Advertising*, embodying the first ground rules for the new medium, was published.

Hours of broadcasting and the 'Toddlers' Truce'

By March the Postmaster-General, Lord De La Warr, had decided that the hours of broadcasting for Independent Television should follow those of the BBC, with a maximum of fifty hours a week – thirty-five being allocated from Monday to Friday and the remaining fifteen at the weekends. In addition a small amount of extra time was granted for religious programmes and outside broadcasts. Finally, the Postmaster-General stipulated that television transmissions should cease between 6 and 7 pm every day to enable parents to put their younger children to bed without having to compete with the distraction of the television set. This so-called 'Toddlers' Truce', which the BBC already observed and which became the subject of much derisive comment in the press, was faithfully maintained until the first major extension in broadcasting hours took place in February 1957.

The Advertisement Committee formed

Two weeks after the inaugural meeting of the AAC, the programme companies (who did not yet have any kind of trade association) formed an Advertisement Committee to plan the practical aspects of a television service which was to be totally reliant on advertising for its existence. Captain T. M. Brownrigg, the General Manager of the London weekday station, Associated-Rediffusion, was elected to the chair. Others present at the first meeting included Charles Truefitt, also of A-R, Norman Collins, Richard Meyer and Lord Duncannon of the Associated Broadcasting Company (later to become ATV), and Cecil Bernstein and Victor Peers of Granada which, the following year, was to provide the weekday programmes in the north of England.

The principal topics discussed were the timing of the hours of broadcasting (within the limits defined by the PMG) which were agreed, as far as weekdays were concerned, as 10.30 am to 12.30 pm and 5 to 6 in the early evening. The main viewing period, it was decided, would run from 7.15 pm to closedown at 10.30. Surprisingly, considerable time was spent in discussing the implications of Paragraph 5 of the Second Schedule of the Television Act – the only clause which referred to advertising rates or 'tariffs', as the parliamentary draftsmen had called them. It had been made clear in the debates that the charges made to advertisers on television were to be entirely a matter for the programme companies, and that the Authority's responsibility would be limited to the approval of the 'detail, form and manner' of their publication. But the final paragraph of this section of the Act nevertheless seemed to provide a good deal of scope for rates to be increased on special occasions. It read:

'Any such tariffs may make provision for different circumstances and, in particular, may provide, in such detail as the Authority may determine, for the making, in special circumstances, of additional special charges.'

The members of the newly formed Advertisement Committee, particularly the representatives of A-R and ABC (whose companies were jointly to provide the programmes on the opening night of the new service), felt certain that public curiosity and the increasing momentum of their advance publicity would produce an exceptionally high level of audience on Day One, which would more than justify special rates being charged to advertisers. But what of other occasions? After some argument it was decided that the clause would continue to be used whenever programmes of 'wide national interest' were transmitted. In the event the provision to make special charges to advertisers for special programmes has seldom been invoked.

Those members with experience of advertising in other media, particularly Charles Truefitt, Advertisement Director of the Associated Newspapers group, publishers of the *Daily Mail*, *Sunday Dispatch* and *Evening News*, urged that effective safeguards should be provided to prevent a sudden withdrawal of business by advertisers. The trade association for the national press, the Newspaper Proprietors' Association, enforced a twenty-eight-day period of notice for cancellation of special positions in newspapers, defined as those which carried a premium above the normal scale (or run-of-paper) rates. It seemed to the Committee, however, that the problems arising from a last-minute cancellation of advertising in television would be even greater than in the press. Television had a fixed quota of programme time to fill and there was therefore no chance of reducing editorial and production costs at short notice. There was no equivalent in television of Fleet Street's 'downpaging' when advertising demand fell. It was therefore decided that all television bookings would be subject to a minimum period of notice of withdrawal of six weeks.

A new Postmaster-General

Early in April Dr Charles Hill, known to millions as the Radio Doctor, and subsequently Secretary of the British Medical Association and Parliamentary Secretary to the Ministry of Food, was appointed Postmaster-General. A month later he approved the rules which had to be drawn up by the Authority governing the amount and distribution of advertising time. Certain broadcasts – church services and appearances by members of the Royal Family, for example – were to be insulated from advertising. There was to be a minimum interval between consecutive commercial breaks. Advertising magazines and features – described in Parliament as 'shoppers' guides' and 'advertising docu-

An early meeting of the members of the Independent Television Authority at Prince's Gate. *Left to right* Jenkin Alban Davies, Dr T. J. Honeyman, Diana Reader-Harris, Sir Ronald Matthews (Deputy Chairman), Sir Kenneth Clark (Chairman), Sir Robert Fraser (Director-General), Dilys Powell and Sir Henry Hinchcliffe

mentaries' – were not to be transmitted between 7 and 10.30 pm. Most important of all, the total amount of advertising to be allowed in the day, which had not been defined in the Television Act, was to be limited to 10 per cent of broadcasting time or an average of six minutes in the hour. After carefully considering the question of the advertising quota, the Authority had concluded that more than 10 per cent of total broadcasting time would, in the light of American experience, defeat its own object because of the likelihood of adverse public reaction.

The first rate cards

In the remaining weeks leading up to opening night A-R and ABC issued their first advertisement rate cards. The board of Associated-Rediffusion had decided that their rates in peaktime, taking the well-established American sixty-second length as the standard, should be £1000 a minute. But shortly before publication it was thought that it would be a psychological mistake to offer advertising time in a completely untried medium for a four-figure sum, and the price was reduced to £975. ABC, the London weekend contractor, announced that it would go on the air with a rate of £950 a minute for Sunday peaktime, with a substantial reduction for Saturdays when it was expected that it would be more difficult to attract an audience.

Shorter commercials, it was decided, should not be charged pro rata to the sixty-second spots, and the thirty-second commercial (which was not to become the standard of measurement for several years) was priced at two-thirds of the minute rate. Two other features of the early rate cards deserve to be mentioned. Associated-Rediffusion prominently included a clause which undertook to give favourable future treatment to 'pioneer advertisers'. This undertaking was to prove troublesome years later, when advertising time on television was in heavy demand and the early advertisers were apt to claim the right to priority in the allocation of time in heavily demanded breaks in the most popular programmes.

Those who devised this clause were rightly concerned about the need to attract long-term forward revenue, and for this reason a variety of discounts were also announced, offering considerable cost reductions to advertisers who were prepared to place long-term contracts in advance. Following the established American practice 'series' discounts were offered to advertisers prepared to commit expenditure on a weekly basis throughout the year, and these discounts operated more generously the shorter the length of the spots in the series – thus offsetting, to some extent, the premium 'loading' on thirty- and fifteen-second commercials.

Finally, volume discounts were included so as to give an incentive to advertisers, particularly those with a multiplicity of products, to deploy the maximum sums of money in advance regardless of the spread of their expenditure.

Expenditure discounts, like the priority which was promised to 'pioneer advertisers', were later to result in many legal and commercial arguments between the programme companies and their advertisers. But in 1955 the need to secure future revenue was paramount. The programme contractors were committed to spending millions on studios, equipment, staffing and the making (and purchase) of programmes, when there was not yet the opportunity of cost recovery from networking. And in the summer of 1955 the appeal of these programmes to the public was largely unknown. The BBC had a well-established television network and three national radio channels which could be used to promote it. The effectiveness of television as an advertising medium was untried in Britain, and it was by no means certain that the public would accept the interruption of programmes by advertising and the invasion of their homes by salesmen who, according to some critics, would typify all that was most brash and blatant from across the Atlantic. It came as something of a surprise to discover on opening night that many of the commercials adopted the polite and informative tone of a Crown Film Unit documentary.

During July, two months before the London station opened, the programme companies decided to lengthen the cancellation period for advertisements from six to eight weeks in an attempt to introduce some further stability into their forward revenue, and the Advertisement Committee formed a 'small Copy Working Party' to preview advertisements before transmission. In the same month the BBC launched *Dixon of Dock Green*, a Saturday-night programme which was to delight the public and worry ITV programme controllers and airtime salesmen for the next twenty-one years.

Measuring the audience

It had not proved possible to set up a comprehensive system of audience measurement in the short time between the formation of the programme companies and their first air date in September 1955. Many advertisers, especially those with American connections, were known to favour the methods employed by the A.C. Neilsen Co. of Chicago which, for many years, had used an automatic recording device, the Audimeter, to measure radio listening and later TV viewing in the United States. Nielsen started in Britain with another advantage: many British advertisers already based their marketing decisions on the Nielsen Retail Indices, in which product sales were measured regularly by an accurate monthly audit at the point of purchase.

It seemed inevitable that, if the Nielsen Television Index were adopted by major advertisers, their agencies would be bound to purchase the data and that the programme companies would be obliged to participate in some form of joint contract if only to ensure access to the same information as their customers. The senior directors of the A. C. Nielsen Co. in Britain, Edward L. Lloyd, Justin Power and Graham Dowson, were all well known and highly regarded in the advertising business. In the light of their reputation and the renowned accuracy of the Nielsen data it seemed certain that their company would be appointed the research contractor for Independent Television.

The Nielsen regions. The regions shown on this map are those of the Nielsen Syndicated TV areas within which retail information has been regularly provided to Nielsen clients since the completion of the ITV network in the early sixties. Some ITV areas – Westward, Border and Grampian – are combined with the territory of the adjacent programme companies while ITV's coverage in Ulster and the Channel Islands is excluded. The boundaries between the Nielsen areas are drawn without overlap.

SCOTLAND

TYNE-TEES

YORKSHIRE

LANCASHIRE

MIDLANDS

ANGLIA

WALES, WEST
& WESTWARD

LONDON

SOUTHERN

Source : Nielsen

The Nielsen presentations

During June 1955, however, the Chairman of the parent company in Chicago, Arthur C. Nielsen himself, came to Britain and set up a series of four 'Executive Conferences' at the Dorchester Hotel, to which senior representatives of the major advertisers and their agencies were invited. The late Robert Silvey, then Head of Audience Research at the BBC, was present and said afterwards:

During visits to the States I had many times been assured with bated breath that whatever you thought about Art Nielsen you had to hand it to him as a Salesman so when I was invited to a luncheon at which the Great Man himself would give a Presentation, I looked foward to it with curiosity. Nielsen had set up his H.Q. in a suite of appropriate magnificence at the Dorchester. After a somewhat ponderously convivial lunch we were ushered into an adjoining room for the presentation. Nielsen's case was essentially simple and could have been effectively deployed in at most twenty minutes. It lasted fifty, though it seemed longer. Its protraction was achieved by the use of what I suppose would now be called a teaching-aid. By his side was a set of display cards on an easel. Each card bore one or two words – very occasionally three – presumably intended to drive home the Message. If my memory serves me, one bore the word, say, EFFICIENT, another SWIFT, another ECONOMICAL and another MOMENT–BY–MOMENT. A deferential aide stood by to whisk away each card as Nielsen's exposition disposed of its point. When we finally emerged, blinking, into the sunlight of Park Lane, I overheard one of my fellow-guests muttering grimly that after this experience of paralysing boredom not even the Archangel Gabriel would induce him to subscribe to this service.

Though the verdict of some of the programme companies and advertisers was somewhat less harsh than this, the majority of the audience went away antagonized and it seemed unlikely that the Nielsen Company would be chosen to provide the industry research service. Arthur Nielsen had, in any case, warned those present at the Dorchester that, even if the NTI were to become operative by January 1956 (four months after opening night), a contract would have to be signed by 11 July. As a temporary expedient a short-term agreement was signed by A-R and ABC with Television Audience Measurement Ltd (TAM) for the first four months of Independent Television. Meanwhile advertisers and agencies, through their trade associations the Incorporated Society of British Advertisers (ISBA) and the Institute of Practitioners in Advertising (IPA), negotiated a temporary contract with the BBC for the supply of audience research information, and it was not until the following year that a tripartite contract was signed with TAM to provide the main industry service.

Opening night

The opening night of Independent Television on Thursday, 22 September was marked by four simultaneous celebrations. Five hundred guests, drawn from a carefully selected list of the 'great and the good', including the Chairman and the Director-General of the BBC as well as many major advertisers, assembled at Guildhall where the Hallé Orchestra and the principal speakers were televised live. Nine hundred guests from the worlds of the arts and showbusiness were entertained at the May Fair Hotel, while a party for lesser mortals was held at the ITA's new headquarters at 14 Prince's Gate, Kensington. But undoubtedly the most uninhibited and enjoyable of the opening-night celebrations was that arranged by Associated-Rediffusion for its 'lower deck' staff at the Granville Theatre, Walham Green, which had been acquired to serve as one of the company's production centres for plays and advertising magazines.

Opening Night at Guildhall, 22 September 1955. Dr Charles Hill, the Postmaster-General (who was later to become successively Chairman of both the ITA and the BBC) inaugurates the new service

ASSOCIATED-REDIFFUSION LTD.

ASSOCIATED-REDIFFUSION LTD. is the result of the conjunction of two major enterprises in different fields of our national life : Broadcast Relay Service Ltd., with a long and valuable experience in sound broadcasting at home, in the Dominions and in the Colonies, whose Chairman and Managing Director, Mr. John Spencer Wills, M.Inst.T., is Chairman of the new company ; and Associated Newspapers Ltd., who have built and maintained an unrivalled pioneering tradition in newspapers, whose Managing Director, Mr. Stuart McClean, is Deputy Chairman.

Our General Manager is Captain T. M. Brownrigg, C.B.E., D.S.O., R.N. (retd.), who after a gallant and distinguished career as a naval officer, was the first general manager of the New Town of Bracknell in Berkshire, where he achieved a notable success in creating good relations between the local community and the newcomers.

Our controller of programmes and production is Mr. Roland Gillett, an Englishman who, after sixteen years in films both in Britain and in Hollywood and wartime service in the Fleet Air Arm, became one of the leading television producers in the United States.

On foundations which we know to be sure we are launching what we believe to be a pioneering enterprise. Ours is a venture which all concerned enter with zest, with pride in having so magnificent a chance, and with faith in our own capacity to create and sustain—in an entirely new field—a public service which will be second to none.

We are neither timorous nor apologetic about what we are undertaking from to-night onwards. We believe—with all the vigour and seriousness we possess—in the new policy which Parliament has approved, which we to-night have the honour to initiate.

We believe that television can and will prove to be one of the most significant and exciting developments in human communication—in education, in entertainment and in the visual arts—since the invention of printing.

Believing as we do in the principles of competition and free enterprise, it is by the methods of competition and free enterprise that we intend to develop Britain's new television service. We have neither the need nor the desire to imitate television in other countries ; and, in that spirit of rivalry which has been the breath and stimulus of life in Britain for centuries, we welcome competition and we shall strive, in everything we undertake, to give a far better service than our competitors.

That, in simple terms, is our task and our aim. " You can never plan the future by the past," said Edmund Burke. We know that we are facing the challenge of a new age. We know that we must adventure and explore. Television means the act of far-seeing. We shall try to create our contribution to to-morrow, we shall try to build to-day's bright window into the future, with to-morrow's methods and technique, and with to-morrow's aspirations, dreams, hopes and ideals. In the homes and by the hearths of to-day, with new vision founded on our traditional national values and faith, we shall strive to serve the Britain of to-morrow.

Associated-Rediffusion Limited

ASSOCIATED BROADCASTING CO., LTD.

The Associated Broadcasting Company brings to the field of independent television a Board of Directors whose combined experience in public service and entertainment is unrivalled.

A.B.C.'s Chairman, Prince Littler, has occupied a prominent place in the field of entertainment for many years and, among his other directorships, includes that of Moss Empires Ltd., Stoll Theatres Ltd., Associated Theatre Properties and many other theatre-owning and theatre-managing organisations.

A.B.C.'s Vice-Chairman, Norman Collins, a former director of the B.B.C.'s Television Service, has been in the forefront of the battle to bring independent television to Britain and has been closely associated with every stage of its development.

The Members of the Board of Directors and the Management Committee of A.B.C. include : the outstanding figure of the Variety world—Val Parnell ; Richard L. Meyer, a pioneer in independent television ; Harry Alan Towers, one of the foremost independent producers and distributors of radio and television programmes and Lew Grade—one of Britain's leading agents and an important figure in the entertainment field.

A.B.C. has been entrusted, initially, with the responsibility of providing the programmes for the London Station on week-ends and for the Birmingham Station, Monday to Friday. It is, therefore, the only independent television programme contractor with a programme responsibility which extends over the whole seven days of the week.

A.B.C. has predominantly turned to the field of experienced technicians and producers and numbers among its staff some of the many whose knowledge of television extends back to its earliest days in Britain.

Heading its Light Entertainment Department is Bill Ward, associated with many of television's best-known shows. Keith Rogers—another pioneer of television —heads the O.B. side ; and, in the initial stages, his responsibility extends considerably beyond the Outside Broadcast field.

Individual directors whose services are available to A.B.C. include Bill Lyon Shaw, Denis Vance, Desmond Davis, Henry Caldwell, Dicky Leeman, Leonard Brett, Stephen Wade, Cecil Petty and many more.

A.B.C. has converted Wood Green Empire—one of the largest suburban Variety Theatres—into one of the most modern and best equipped Television Theatres in the world. It is from here that many of the top Variety Productions of A.B.C. will originate.

In addition, through the interests of its Directors, A.B.C. will have available many of the best known theatres in London and the Provinces, including the London Palladium, whence will originate, each Sunday night a Variety highspot—SUNDAY NIGHT AT THE LONDON PALLADIUM. A.B.C. has recently acquired the British National Studios at Elstree—a fully equipped modern motion picture production centre where many of the television films which A.B.C. is presenting are being made. Through other Directors of A.B.C., the Company has a link with Highbury Studios and Nettlefold Studios—two other centres for the production of television films.

Many of A.B.C.'s major programmes will be produced for it by the Incorporated Television Programme Company Limited, with which Prince Littler, Val Parnell, Lew Grade and Harry Alan Towers are also associated. This Company, founded by public relations expert Suzanne Warner, adds further show-business strength through members of its Board, who include Hugh Beaumont, of H. M. Tennent Limited, Stuart Cruikshank of Howard & Wyndham Theatres, Phillip and Syd Hyams of Eros Films, John Schlesinger of the Schlesinger Organisation and Anthony Gishford of Boosey and Hawkes Limited.

The nerve centre of A.B.C.'s week-end operation is the modern control centre at Foley Street, London, within 200 yards of Museum Exchange—the nerve centre of the micro-wave and coaxial cable linking system of the G.P.O.

A.B.C. will also be developing a studio centre in Birmingham.

These are some of the personalities and facilities which together, will be ensuring that A.B.C. T.V. fills an important role in the pioneering and development of independent television in Britain.

Associated Broadcasting Company Limited

Two contrasting statements of aims and philosophy from the souvenir programme for the Opening Night at Guildhall, Thursday 22 September 1955

Some thirty minutes before Leslie Mitchell, who had also introduced the opening of BBC Television from Alexandra Palace in 1936, made the opening announcement inaugurating the new service, the Corporation struck a shrewdly aimed blow at the waiting audience. That day's episode of *The Archers*, the daily 6.45 pm radio serial with a regular following of over eight million listeners, featured the death in a blazing stable of Grace Archer who had been 'married' to Phil only the previous year. The impact of this entirely fictional event was comparable to the death of a much-loved public figure. The following day the *Daily Mirror* graphically reported:

On my way from Ashford to Dover I spoke to a number of people who were openly weeping for Grace Archer. I was travelling by car and as I passed through villages I saw people standing at their doors in tears.

I stopped again and again. Everywhere the story was the same.

In pubs, cafés and outside their doors people were crying over Grace Archer.

One family I spoke to on Romney Marsh were collecting flowers to make into wreaths and crosses to send to the funeral.

The first commercials

At 8.12 pm in the first 'natural break' in a star-packed variety bill the first commercials were broadcast. They were for Gibbs' SR Toothpaste (sixty seconds) and Cadbury's Drinking Chocolate (sixty seconds). Their appearance was accompanied by a polite cheer from the distinguished guests in Guildhall and feelings of intense relief from the sales staffs of A-R and ABC assembled in Television House.

But after the initial euphoria had worn off it seemed that their problems were only just beginning. Their rate cards had been written in the belief that at least 250,000 (or about 8 per cent) of the 3,175,000 homes in the London area would be capable of receiving ITV. The initial figures showed, however, that only 169,700 households had been equipped with the necessary converters and aerials to receive Channel 9 and, of these, some five thousand were temporarily out of action on opening night. The BBC, despite its radio onslaught earlier in the evening with *The Archers*, somewhat surprisingly opposed ITV's variety hour with its regular quiz *Animal, Vegetable and Mineral*, which hardly provided ITV with serious competition for the mass audience. The actual viewing record showed that ITV had obtained a TAMrating of 66 against 23 for the BBC, and that 11 per cent of sets were switched off in the maximum viewing period. More worrying was the cost to advertisers who, throughout the evening, had been charged a 50 per cent premium above normal rates.

Yet many advertisers had been determined to appear on opening night, whatever the cost both of the airtime and of the production of a filmed commercial. Sir Patrick Hennessy, Managing Director of the Ford Motor Company had been persuaded to use the talents of Karel Reisz and a then unknown twenty-three-year-old designer, Terence Conran, to produce a TV commercial long before the rest of the motor industry realized the full potential of the medium. But overwhelmingly the first commercials came from the fields of low-cost consumer goods – grocery products, toiletries, beer and petrol.

Prominent among the advertisers on Day One was Unilever, with products on the screen from Gibbs, Lever Brothers, Van den Berghs and Batchelors, an indication of the belief of the Anglo-Dutch giant in the potential of television to influence the spending habits of the house-wife. Unilever was to remain Independent Television's largest advertiser throughout the period 1955–85, despite the development of television advertising into almost every field of goods and services.

After the opening night, the responsibility for which had been shared between A-R and ABC, the normal programme pattern was established with ABC taking charge of the weekend service and A-R of the week-days. Within a fortnight ABC was renamed Associated TeleVision (ATV) to avoid confusion with Associated British Cinemas, which had been awarded the Saturday and Sunday contract for the Midlands and the North on 21 September, the day before the first contractors had gone on the air in London.

Girl With a Date, one of the earliest advertising magazines with which it was hoped to create a mid-morning audience, was presented by Muriel Young and Anne Valery. The programme was transferred to the evenings when all morning broadcasts were abandoned in December 1955 because of mounting financial losses

1956

It was clear by the end of 1955 that the early backers of ITV had been hopelessly over-optimistic about the ability of the medium to attract advertising revenue. In December morning transmissions had had to be discontinued because of low audiences, lack of advertising and the relatively high cost of programme production. Nor was the coverage of Independent Television growing in the way that had been anticipated. By January 1956 the number of homes it was reaching was still less than half a million, or little more than one in eight of the total number of households in the Greater London area which were within reach of the signal. It seemed clear that advertising rates would have to be reduced on both the weekday and weekend stations and that drastic steps would have to be taken to cut expenditure.

By July Associated-Rediffusion's losses had reached the staggering total of £2,700,000 and ATV, whose service had opened in the Midlands in February, was facing a severe financial crisis in both London and Birmingham. The rate cards, which the programme contractors had hoped would be regarded as sacrosanct, had become little more than the basis for initial negotiation. By the time Granada and ABC (respectively the weekday and weekend contractors) opened in the North of England Associated-Rediffusion had been compelled to announce an official 100 per cent bonus in London for all advertisers prepared to place business with the company between June and September and a further 50 per cent bonus to operate from mid-September until the end of the year. Unofficial discounts reached an even more generous level, and advertisers and agencies were able to recognize all the unmistakable signs of a buyer's market.

Apart from the problems of insufficient revenue to finance the service, sales directors of the television companies found that they had seriously underestimated the complexities of setting up and operating an all-company system which had to agree on the acceptability of advertising copy, the length and timing of commercial breaks (which had to coincide on all stations), the simultaneous networking of commercials and the recording and acknowledgement of future bookings.

One programme company continued until 1957 to note details of its forward sales in a large newspaper-style diary whose leaves still bore the legend 'front page solus', 'leader page 6" x 2 cols' and 'back page semi-solus'. Sales representatives, who did not yet enjoy the much more high-sounding titles of 'Sales Executive' or 'Sales Coordinator', were themselves able to enter (and erase) details of airtime which they and their colleagues had sold, reserved or optioned. As the day of transmission approached the 'diary' became increasingly dog-eared and illegible. Somehow or other the station's Traffic Manager had to decipher this much-amended information and produce a transmission schedule for his Presentation Department, which would then have to marry the details of advertising time sold with the equally complex running order and timing (to the nearest second) of the surrounding programmes.

Formation of the TPCA

It was apparent that many of the inter-company negotiations essential to the working of Independent Television could best take place under the aegis of a trade association although A-R, whose major share-holders had long experience of the inhibiting effect of trade bodies in transport and other public services, insisted that questions of prices and labour relations should not be dealt with on a formal industry basis. Accordingly, the Television Programme Contractors' Association was formed to deal with all other matters of common interest. A small secretariat was set up under an imperturbable and slightly pedantic Scottish lawyer, Laurence Parker, to plan the regular meetings, maintain records and service committees whose numbers and functions began to proliferate as the operation became increasingly complex.

At the outset the need for these committees mystified the rest of the advertising world. Advertisers and agencies complained bitterly about their inability to make contact with the heads of sales of the programme companies, who in many cases were spending twelve or more hours a week at industry meetings. But with revenue at stake in a federal system in which it was essential for all companies to work in concert it was impossible to delegate decision-making to inexperienced staff below senior-management level. Captain Brownrigg of A-R insisted on joining every industry committee and, while this gave him a unique overview of every aspect of a rapidly developing business, it proved frustrating in the extreme to his colleagues. As it was, most of the more important committees dealing with network programming and sales were attended by up to four representatives from each company, and it was not unusual for the members of a group from a single contractor to disagree openly between themselves in front of the others.

A joint approach to audience research

But there were occasions when the programme companies had to preserve a united front in their negotiations with outside bodies. One of the first of these concerned the vital question of audience research. A steering committee had been formed in November 1955 under Major George Harrison of the London Press Exchange, in the hope that all programme companies, advertisers and agencies would be able to agree on a common system of audience measurement. It was not, however, until the following March that agreement was finally reached and a one-year contract, to run to 30 June 1957, was signed with TAM on behalf of the TPCA (representing all the programme companies with the exception of Granada, who decided to use the Nielsen service), the IPA and the ISBA. After lengthy negotiations it was agreed that the contractors would meet 50 per cent of the annual cost of the basic research service, or £65,000 out of £130,000.

Associated Newspapers withdraws

In the same month the ITV set count, which now included the Midlands, reached one million, double the January total, and by September this figure had doubled again. Although the number of homes reached by Independent Television was growing to a point at which advertising in the new medium was no longer regarded as experimental, the level of revenue was still far below the cost of operation. The losses had been so great that Associated Newspapers, with a 50 per cent stake in A-R, decided during the summer to reduce their holding to 10 per cent by selling their interest to the other major shareholder, the British Electric Traction Company. Under the terms of a confidential agreement signed by Lord Rothermere, H.C. ('Harley') Drayton and John Spencer Wills, chairmen of Associated Newspapers, BET and Rediffusion respectively, Associated Newspapers undertook to continue to provide 'advertising support' and was entitled to retain up to four seats on the board of the company.

'Advertising support', which was to prove vital in the struggle to survive, included the services of John Clark, A-R's Television Advertisement Manager, his deputy Kershaw Smith and a number of other key staff including the Research Manager, R. M. Shields, who was later to become Managing Director of the Associated Newspapers Group. At board level the company was fortunate to have the services of Stuart McClean, an outstandingly able Deputy Chairman, as well as those of Charles Truefitt who, as already mentioned, became closely involved on the sales side and worked unremittingly to persuade a number of major advertisers to maintain their support during the first critical twelve months.

It was tragically ironic that Stuart McClean, whose vision and enthusiasm had played such a major part in obtaining the original contract for Associated-Rediffusion, should have been absent when AN decided to withdraw. He was, however, already fatally ill and, although he returned briefly during Southern Television's licence application (in which Associated Newspapers again figured prominently), he was to die soon afterwards in 1960 at the early age of fifty. Once Southern had been granted its contract Associated was obliged to relinquish its remaining 10 per cent holding in Associated-Rediffusion.

Establishing the sales departments

Because of their dual responsibilities in London and the Midlands a larger and more complex sales operation was developing at ATV under its first Sales Director, Patrick Henry, who, with his deputy, Anthony Jelly, had joined the company from the Odhams weekly colorgravure magazine *Woman* after experience with the Hulton Press, publishers of *Picture Post*. Hulton's, whose contribution to the marketing of media was far greater than that of any other publishing house, was to provide ABC Television with its Sales Director, George Cooper, his deputy, Bob Norris, and many other figures who were later to become prominent in market research, publishing and a number of leading advertising agencies. The high standards of statistical accuracy, design and all-round professionalism which Hulton's had developed in their sales promotional material were evident in all the printed literature which ABC and ATV sent to potential advertisers. Even their mailing lists owed their origins to Hulton's. Granada and Associated-Rediffusion began to develop a promotional style of their own, the former reflecting the individualism and social awareness of the Bernsteins, while the latter seemed closer to the establishment aura of the BBC.

It would be difficult to exaggerate the effect of this constant bombardment of the advertising community. Almost every week well-designed leaflets, brochures and market surveys arrived from the

Lord Rothermere agrees to recommend to the
Associated Newspapers Board and Messrs. Drayton and
Wills agree to recommend to the British Electric Traction
Board :-

(1) That B.E.T. will buy from Associated Newspapers
four-fifths of their interest in Associated-
Rediffusion Ltd. That interest shall consist
of all the money advanced through unsecured
loans, secured loans and shares, and money
owing by Associated Newspapers to Associated-
Rediffusion through firm commitments entered
into, with the knowledge and consent of
Associated Newspapers, prior to Saturday, the
11th August.

(2) That B.E.T. will pay therefor in cash the
nominal amount of that four-fifths interest,
less a discount of twenty-five per cent.

(3) That Associated Newspapers will not, merely
because of the reduction in their interest from
fifty per cent to ten per cent, withdraw their
advertising support of Associated-Rediffusion.

(4) That the transaction is subject only to the
consent of the Independent Television Authority.

(5) That Associated Newspapers will, if desired, leave
four representatives on the board of Associated-
Rediffusion.

(6) That the transaction shall be kept as private as
possible. *Rothermere*
3/9/56   *H. D. N...*
                  V. S. L... *30/Aug/56*
                                30/8/56

JSW/JMP
28.8.56

The vital clauses of the agreement by which Associated Newspapers withdrew from
Associated-Rediffusion in the summer of 1956 because of crippling financial losses

51

programme contractors in the advertising agencies and marketing departments of their clients. In addition, every seven days each IPA member agency which was a party to the TAM contract received a detailed minute-by-minute report of the audience figures for every programme and commercial broadcast in the previous week. Despite the vicissitudes of the new medium, advertisers were never allowed to forget its existence. This constant publicity throughout 1956 ensured that, when ITV turned the corner financially early in the following year, there was an awareness of the growing power and importance of television, and the realization that it was quite different from any other medium. More important: television advertising worked.

Renewed fears of sponsorship

Fears about the dangers of sponsorship had been repeatedly expressed during the parliamentary debates which preceded the passing of the

The advertisement from a programme page in *TV Times* for Friday 23 September 1955, announcing the transmission of the first of the Shell 3-minute John Betjeman commercials in the 'Discovering Britain' series.

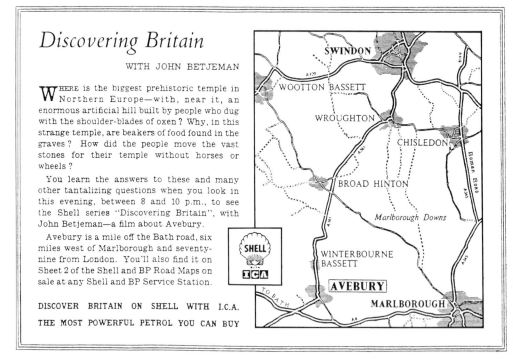

Discovering Britain

WITH JOHN BETJEMAN

WHERE is the biggest prehistoric temple in Northern Europe—with, near it, an enormous artificial hill built by people who dug with the shoulder-blades of oxen? Why, in this strange temple, are beakers of food found in the graves? How did the people move the vast stones for their temple without horses or wheels?

You learn the answers to these and many other tantalizing questions when you look in this evening, between 8 and 10 p.m., to see the Shell series "Discovering Britain", with John Betjeman—a film about Avebury.

Avebury is a mile off the Bath road, six miles west of Marlborough and seventy-nine from London. You'll also find it on Sheet 2 of the Shell and BP Road Maps on sale at any Shell and BP Service Station.

SHELL with I.C.A

DISCOVER BRITAIN ON SHELL WITH I.C.A.
THE MOST POWERFUL PETROL YOU CAN BUY

SWINDON
WOOTTON BASSETT
WROUGHTON
CHISLEDON
BROAD HINTON
Marlborough Downs
WINTERBOURNE BASSETT
AVEBURY
MARLBOROUGH

Avebury Stone Circle, Wiltshire. (Reproduced by kind permission of Shell UK Ltd)

The Shell series, *Discovering Britain with John Betjeman*. As far as can be traced there were twenty (or more) of these unique films, all three minutes in length, which were transmitted on Independent Television from the first Friday on the air (23 September 1955) until the temporary disappearance of branded petrol on 1 December 1956.

Some of the places visited were: Bradwell Lodge, Essex; Stourhead, Wiltshire; Heaton Hall, Manchester; West Wycombe, Buckinghamshire; Marlborough, Wiltshire; Wakefield Hall, Yorkshire; Haddon Hall, Derbyshire; Hardwick Hall, Derbyshire; Bolsover Castle, Derbyshire; Clifton Suspension Bridge, Bristol; Avebury Stone Circle, Wiltshire.

Typically, Betjeman chose far from obvious places, sometimes an archaeological site, sometimes a whole town, like Marlborough where he had been at school. But he seldom visited anywhere without pausing to remark upon an inconspicuous Tudor window, a Victorian-Gothic conceit, an unusual form of thatching which had diverted him on the way.

The scripts were all written and spoken by Betjeman himself with his own diffident yet curiously appealing delivery. His blend of scholarship and infectious dilettantism was always rare in a broadcaster. Now it has all but vanished.

Shell, which has always enjoyed a considerable reputation as a patron of the arts and artists, deserves to be congratulated on conceiving a use of television advertising – years ahead of its time – which did much to raise the standards of commercials and showed that a TV advertisement could be literate, gentle and scholarly. And still remain effective

Television Act in 1954. Section 4(6) had been deliberately included in the Act to ensure that nothing, apart from clearly recognizable advertisements, was broadcast which could give the impression that any material had been supplied or even suggested by an advertiser.

After several month's experience the Authority decided that an impression of sponsorship might be created if an artist appeared in a programme and an adjacent commercial, and ruled that a minimum separation of half-an-hour should be introduced between the two. In the same way it decided that advertising magazines and features must clearly reveal their purpose both in their method of presentation on the screen and their descriptive billing in the *TV Times*. The name of an advertiser could not be included in the title, even though all the products which were featured came from the same company.

The Suez crisis

The events in the Middle East during October and November were to have far-reaching repercussions for television advertising, even when the critical international tension which followed the Anglo-French landings at Suez had begun to relax. It was clear that after Colonel Nasser's nationalization of the Canal in October petrol supplies from the Middle East were likely to be at risk. On 4 November the programme companies reduced the cancellation period for petrol commercials from eight weeks to fourteen days and, when on 1 December the Government introduced the rationing of unbranded 'pool' petrol, all promotional activity among the oil companies had to cease immediately. Only one oil company continued to advertise in the six months which followed. Regent Oil (now Texaco) decided to produce a highly imaginative series of road-safety commercials which were screened at the times originally booked for conventional advertisements, and thereby gained itself a good deal of public approval.

Before the disappearance of the familiar brands of petrol from the market another oil company, Shell, had been responsible for an outstanding weekly series of three-minute commercials, using the unmistakable commentary of John Betjeman and entitled *Discovering Britain*. Each week Betjeman visited an historic house or archaeological site which he described in inimitable detail. The selling message was confined to the use of the Shell symbol at the beginning and end. Sadly, the campaign did not reappear when petrol advertising was resumed in May 1957. But by then the cost of a three-minute commercial on all stations every week would have been prohibitive.

1957

Independent Television, and particularly television advertising, were continually in the news in the early years of the new medium. Even when Beaverbrook Newspapers gave front-page prominence to the slightly sour comments of the chairmen of two major companies, Whitbread's and Waddington's, who alleged that their early television campaigns had been expensive and largely ineffective, there were many more who were able to claim completely the opposite. Publication of the revenue figures for the four programme companies on the air in 1956 was therefore eagerly awaited.

The contractors themselves were, however, reluctant to disclose the true state of their finances. That there had been heavy financial losses was beyond dispute. Most major advertisers knew that favourable deals could be obtained if they were prepared to commit significant sums to television on a long-term basis. But they were also conscious of the intense competition for revenue between weekday and weekend contractors in all three areas – London, the Midlands and the North. This duopoly had the effect of limiting, rather than increasing, their revenue, and the programme companies' ingenuity had not yet been put to work to devise the complex area expenditure-discount schemes which were to be introduced some twenty years later. Besides, there was some unease about the possible interpretation of the clause in the Television Act which stipulated that 'in the acceptance of advertisements, there must be no unreasonable discrimination either against or in favour of any particular advertiser'. Would a favourable arrangement with one advertiser be construed as 'unreasonable' discrimination as far as others were concerned? It was probably wiser not to put it to the test.

Captain Brownrigg certainly had no doubts on this score. As Chairman of the TPCA Advertisement Committee he was in the habit of laying down the law on the importance of selling only in accordance with the rate cards to the heads of sales of all companies, who had no alternative but to listen in respectful silence. Whether they followed his advice was impossible to discover, but every member of his own

O.O.M. 1/42

ASSOCIATED-REDIFFUSION

Office Memorandum
(O.O.M.)

SPRING WEEDING

1.   After the rain, cold and fog of winter,
enthusiasts tackle their gardens and, in order to
get a clear run of the year's work, the usual
practice is to use weed killers on the paths and
to dig up all the weeds and extraneous growths
in the beds.

2.   Similarly, now is the time for all good
secretaries to weed their files: to throw away all
papers which were of only passing interest and
to send to Central Registry files which should be
kept for reference, but these should be weeded
first.

3.   Over the year, extraneous growth has
sometimes taken root on the walls. A joke which
was funny last spring is faded and out of date
this spring. Now is the time to weed out one's
wall illustrations.

T. M. Brownrigg

30th January, 1959

One of Captain Brownrigg's many 'OOMs' (Official Office Memoranda). They covered
every conceivable aspect of the disciplines and routines in Television House – holiday
entitlement (always called 'leave'), completion of expense claims, use of company
transport, drinking on the premises and even the admission of pet animals to the
studios. Cats, for some reason, were allowed; dogs were prohibited. This particular
instruction related to the clearing out of old files and the removal of 'wall illustrations'.
Graffiti and pin-ups were, needless to say, strictly forbidden

company's sales department could personally testify to the ceaseless vigilance of the internal auditors at Associated-Rediffusion and the steady stream of Official Office Memoranda ('OOMs') which enshrined his instructions.

Eventually a monitored estimate of television revenue for 1956 was issued by the Legion Publishing Company, owners of Media Records Ltd, showing that the contractors had between them obtained just over £13,000,000 in the calendar year. But this figure took no account of discounts, local rates or any unofficial price reductions, and it is probable that true revenue had been overestimated by at least 50 per cent. Nevertheless, an apparent monthly income of over £1,000,000 served to put television in the front rank of advertising media.

The question of 'good taste'

Captain Brownrigg's strictures to the other companies were not confined to the operation of rate cards. In February he proposed that advertising for haemorrhoid remedies should not be accepted on television because it would be distasteful to viewers, and that toilet paper advertising should not be broadcast until after 9.30 pm on the assumption that only then would the audience have finished dinner! In fact, the majority of families – certainly those in the North and Midlands – had probably disposed of their main evening meal some three hours earlier. They were unlikely, in any case, to find anything incongruous or offensive in toilet rolls being shown close to food products on the television screen. After all, the same products were prominently displayed amongst the foods in grocery stores.

But Associated-Rediffusion itself insisted on an even more bizarre restriction of its own. Toilet rolls could only be shown on the London weekday station if they were wrapped or, as Brownrigg himself would probably have said, 'close-hauled'. Other companies threw good taste to the winds and allowed them to be shown 'running free'.

The end of the 'Toddlers' Truce'

Ernest Marples, who had been appointed Postmaster-General in January, abolished the 'Toddlers' Truce' on 16 February, and this removal of restrictions on broadcasting between 6 and 7 pm enabled the BBC to launch what was to become one of its most successful programmes – *Tonight*. Independent Television replied with its regional news magazines and peaktime, which had hitherto begun on most stations at 7.30, was eventually extended to include part, at least, of the additional transmission period. It seemed clear to the programme planners on both channels that if viewers could be captured between 5 and 7 pm they might well be persuaded to remain loyal for the rest of the evening. But television had to compete for family attention with many other activities at this time of day – mealtimes, homework and various comings and goings.

Schools broadcasting and advertising

In May, some months earlier than the BBC, Associated-Rediffusion as a result of the initiative of its Managing Director, Paul Adorian, launched its first television broadcasts for schools – to the accompaniment of widespread suspicion in the teaching profession. It was said that the use of television in the classroom could eventually make teachers redundant, and serious misgivings were expressed about the access which advertisers would gain to the impressionable members of a literally 'captive' audience. It was decided, however, that schools broadcasts would be 'insulated' from advertising in the same way as religious programmes.

On the other hand, although they carried no commercials around them, they 'earned' advertising time like any other programme. This valuable extra minutage could be transmitted at other times of day, including peaktime, provided that not more than eight minutes of advertising were broadcast in any single hour.

A long-term research contract

The audience research Steering Committee had worked well during the first year of the TAM contract, but a longer agreement was essential to introduce some continuity into the system and to give a measure of security to both the buyers and sellers of the data. In addition, Major Harrison was unwilling to chair a purely interim committee whose terms of reference were necessarily short-term.

It was decided to reconstitute the commissioning body as the Television Audience Research Advisory Committee (TARAC) and to ask the ubiquitous Captain Brownrigg to take the chair on the understanding that he would eventually be succeeded by representatives of the two other subscribing bodies, the IPA and ISBA. TARAC signed a contract with TAM for the supply of the industry audience measurement data, to run from July 1957 for a minimum of two and a maximum of five years. Granada, however, remained outside the agreement and continued its contract with Nielsen.

The case for betting advertising

Captain Brownrigg was convinced that Independent Television would greatly commend itself to the establishment (whose members, he claimed, considered ITV a largely working-class medium) if the programme companies were to televise horse-racing regularly during the afternoons as live outside broadcasts.

The first meeting he chose for this experiment was the St Leger, the oldest of the racing classics, which was run in September at Doncaster, far beyond the confines of Associated-Rediffusion's area. It had been agreed by the Network Committee that OBs, also often known as 'remotes', would normally be covered by the programme contractor in the area concerned. Not unnaturally, Granada and the ITA both complained in the strongest terms to A-R at this excursion into another company's area, but the broadcast took place as planned and, for the first time, starting prices were given over the air.

It seemed to Brownrigg that this undisguised encouragement to viewers to place bets made a good cause for the relaxation of the rule in the *Principles for Television Advertising* which expressly precluded any betting advertisements (including those for football pools) from being transmitted on Independent Television. He resolved to raise the matter with the Advertising Advisory Committee. Brownrigg presented the case persuasively in person, pointing out that OBs were costly and that camera crews were open to bribery because they could not fail to include some, at least, of the bookmakers' names on the screen. Suitably restrained advertising from the more reputable firms would, he declared, not only help to cover the cost of the broadcasts but would also avoid the temptation of corruption among the commentators and production staff.

But the AAC was not impressed by these arguments and the exclusion of all forms of betting advertising from television was confirmed. Some years later a well-known firm of turf accountants successfully submitted a 'Situations Vacant' advertisement to the Copy Committee but this was eventually rejected after a brief campaign because of the great prominence which was given on the screen to the telephone number, which was also used by the firm's racing clients.

Even in 1957 the work of the Copy Committee was beginning to increase in complexity and it was clear that a full-time staff would be needed to advise agencies, advertisers and production companies on the types of claims and on-screen portrayals which might cause problems. In November Audrey Gardiner, who had been Laurence Parker's secretary at the TPCA, was appointed to conduct these negotiations and she soon became the principal link with advertisers and agencies for copy matters. The more contentious issues were dealt with by the members of the Copy Committee under their Chairman, Alex Anson of Granada. It was he, too, who drew up a list of programmes, classified by type and duration, suggesting the distribution, number and length of the commercial breaks in each – bearing in mind that, although the maximum amount of advertising time had hitherto been determined by the Authority on a 'clock hour' basis, some account had to be taken in practice of the nature of the surrounding programmes. The Authority accepted these suggestions and based the guidelines in its formal control document *Advertising Rules and Practices*, first issued in 1958, on the criteria which the companies had suggested.

The year 1957 ended very differently from the way in which it had begun. Independent Television was now well established in the three major population centres of London, the Midlands and North, as well as the first regional area of Central Scotland. The appalling financial losses which, across the network, had amounted to no less than £11,000,000 in the first eighteen months, had been stemmed and all the stations were moving rapidly into profit. Their sales staffs were beginning to develop professional skills and a sound administrative system had evolved to process incoming business. The handwritten diary for recording bookings had been replaced by wall charts and visible-index recording systems like the Remington Schedugraph and Roneo Linedex which showed time sold, optioned and unsold for two years ahead – a measure of the confidence which the contractors now had in the future of their medium. To record bookings Granada installed a chain-driven roller-blind system, each 'leaf' of which (the size of a double-garage door) represented a single day of the week for a two-year period. A horizontal aluminium channel contained coloured perspex signals which covered the written details beneath.

The operation of these systems was laborious, but when updated they gave a unique view of the changing fortunes of each contractor. Some companies even photographed the summary information on the charts every week and circulated the prints to the members of their board. It was not until the advent of the computer in the late sixties that the visible booking systems were replaced, and when they went their disappearance was much lamented by sales and clerical staff alike.

1958

The second of the regional ITV companies to be appointed, that for South Wales and the West of England, Television Wales and the West (TWW), went on the air on 14 January 1958. With its arrival the total ITV set count for the first time exceeded five million.

The 'spot franchises'

The combination of a heavy demand for airtime and the limitation on hours of broadcasting (and therefore on advertising capacity) led a number of agencies to try to protect their clients by claiming that they had established 'spot franchises' in and around certain popular programmes. The one-hour Western *Wagon Train*, *Double Your Money*, *Take Your Pick* and *Val Parnell's Sunday Night at the London Palladium* invariably produced high ratings, and a number of major advertisers were prepared to pay fixed spot surcharges on top of peak-time rates to ensure that their commercials were transmitted within these and similar popular programmes. This once more raised fears of an appearance of sponsorship if, as frequently happened, the same products appeared in the same break in the same programme week after week. But this was not the only problem facing the sales departments of the programme companies when this occurred. Some agencies were quick to point out that to show favouritism to one advertiser at the expense of another in the allocation of the top-rated breaks could come perilously close to the 'unreasonable discrimination' forbidden under the terms of the Television Act.

It was common knowledge that the new booking systems which all the programme companies had now installed were capable of recording business for two years ahead, and by the end of the winter quarter of 1958 orders began to flood in for the whole of 1959 and even the early part of 1960. It was obvious, however, that many of these bookings were purely protective and had been made simply to ensure that when advertisers' budgets were finally approved a franchise had been established in the highest-rated programmes. Some agencies attempted

to retain these valuable spots even when the original advertiser relinquished them, and the contractors issued dire warnings about 'airtime
broking'. It was also apparent that just outside the eight-week period
was a constant 'creeping cancellation' of forward business, which
merely served to emphasize the speculative nature of orders for airtime
due for transmission a year or more ahead. The contractors took two
steps to help stabilize the situation.

On 1 May the TPCA (renamed the Independent Television
Companies' Association from the same date) announced that the
cancellation period would be extended from eight to thirteen weeks.
On the question of long-term bookings it was Alex Anson of Granada
who once again suggested a solution; all companies should open up
periods of airtime availability simultaneously at six-monthly intervals,
with the reminder that details of programme schedules would not be
made known until much later. Thus the two-year booking period
would eventually contract to eighteen months, which all companies
would extend on 1 January and 1 July each year. The problem of spot
franchises, if not at an end, was at least now contained in a more
manageable fashion.

Captain T. M. Brownrigg, CBE DSO RN (Retd), *right*, the first General Manager of
Associated-Rediffusion, with Jack Hylton, the company's adviser on Light Entertainment. Other advisers included Sir John Barbirolli (Music) and Sir John Clements
(Drama). Jack Hylton subsequently became a director of TWW, the first programme
company to be appointed to cover Wales and the West of England

In July Captain Brownrigg, somewhat to the surprise of the sales directors, relinquished the chairmanship of the ITCA Advertisement Committee, having held the appointment without a break since January 1955. He was succeeded by George Cooper, Sales Director of ABC Television, who brought to this key role in the industry a much-needed flexibility of outlook and a wide knowledge of media sales in both press and television. The relations between the programme companies and agencies and advertisers began to improve.

'Undetectable from live' – the coming of Ampex

But Brownrigg's dominating influence continued to affect another aspect of the programme companies' activities which was to have unforeseen consequences for advertisers. Early in 1958 a high-powered team arrived in Britain from the Ampex Corporation in California to demonstrate their new system of recording television material on two-inch magnetic tape. In the words of the manufacturer, the resultant signal was 'undetectable from live' in terms of both sound and vision quality, as the recording and immediate playback impressively demonstrated. Several of the programme companies and the BBC placed immediate orders for the equipment, which was already being successfully used by the US networks.

But Brownrigg and a number of others soon realized that if videotape were to be introduced on an unrestricted basis the film unions would be faced with the prospect of redundancies in the processing laboratories. In addition, once electronic editing of tape became possible the services of a number of technicians engaged in post-production work would no longer be required. Moreover, if videotape recording were to be treated as a more flexible substitute for film, then the trade unions would be likely to insist that the television production centres would have to be crewed with the same number of staff as were employed in 35mm film production.

Accordingly, a series of instructions were drawn up at Associated-Rediffusion which stipulated that videotape recordings were to be treated in all respects as 'live' transmissions. Editing was not to be allowed, 'fluffs' and other mistakes were not to be erased, no retakes would be permitted and all recordings were to be 'wiped' within twenty-eight days of taping. Finally, videotapes were not to be transferred from one programme company to another for later transmission. These restrictions were reflected in similar, if somewhat less officious, house rules in the other programme companies.

Commercials on videotape

So far no commercial production houses contemplated equipping them-selves with videotape recording equipment. At £25,000 per machine the cost of the new Ampex recorders alone was considerable, quite apart from the need for expensive electronic cameras and their associated control facilities. If, therefore, videotape were to be used for the production of commercials, it seemed that the work would have to be undertaken by the programme companies themselves.

One major advertising agency, McCann-Erickson, under its colourful and dynamic Chairman, Marion Harper, had established a reputation for pioneering the use of new technology in broadcasting. They had been the first agency in the United States to use videotape and at a later date were to be the first to employ a satellite to relay a commercial from America to Europe. They were determined to be the first agency to use videotape in Britain.

The client selected for this experiment was Carreras, manufacturers of a brand of cigarettes usually known just by their initials, DSB – 'Deeply Satisfying Barons'. The Chairman of the company, Sir Edward Baron, was brought to Television House by McCann-Erickson and interviewed on camera by the sports commentator Kenneth Wolstenholme, to the accompaniment of pack shots and a sales message. A few seconds later the commercial was played back exactly as it had been recorded. Sir Edward and the other guests were visibly impressed but it was not until the following year that a complete campaign on videotape (for Thomas Hedley's White Tide) was transmitted on the air.

The introduction of videotape, which rapidly revolutionized programme production, was to prove a much slower process as far as commercials were concerned. The programme companies had done a great deal to promote the use of live commercials, but with the rapidly escalating cost of airtime agencies were reluctant to risk the damage to their clients which could result from an obscured pack shot, an actor 'drying' on camera, the shadow of a microphone boom or any of the other numerous hazards of live production. Videotape could have provided the answer to all these problems had not the contractors, for reasons already explained, not insisted that the rules for taped programmes should also apply to commercials. In theory videotaped advertisements had the priceless advantages of immediacy, low cost and instant playback, but in practice the contractors' studios – certainly those in London – were heavily committed to live broadcasts, rehearsal and telerecording. If a studio happened to be vacant there was not always a director and crew available to man it at short notice, and attempts to introduce outside production teams to a programme company's premises would usually result in the threat of industrial action.

The more knowledgeable Directors of Television in the advertising agencies had serious reservations too about the lighting quality of commercials on videotape. There were severe limitations on the use of optical effects and animation, and in comparison with the best work on film, VTR commercials often looked crude. It was not until the sensitivity of cameras, recording equipment and tape itself had improved in the late sixties that the dominance of film for the production of commercials was broken.

'Opinion advertising'

The end of the year was marked by an imaginative use of television by a major national advertiser. Sir Isidore Gluckstein, Chairman of the caterers and food manufacturers, J. Lyons and Co., booked a two-minute filmed commercial on New Year's Eve, in which he addressed his customers, staff and shareholders to explain his company's aims of service to the public, low prices and consistent quality. This enterprising use of the medium was greatly admired, but the ITA was far from happy. If the technique was to develop it could amount to an 'invitation to invest' which, with the exception of Government stocks and National Savings, was expressly forbidden by the *Principles*. Not only this; the Authority well remembered Sir Bernard Docker buying time on television to appeal for public support in his battle for the chairmanship of the Daimler Car Company in 1956. Sir Robert Fraser declared at a meeting of the Standing Consultative Committee (the main policy-making forum for the contractors and the ITA) that in his view the only form of advertising which could safely be accepted in the light of the political provisions of the Television Act was the sort which was clearly designed to promote the sale of goods and services. Advertising designed to influence public opinion during a takeover battle or a campaign against nationalization on behalf of private enterprise – however well disguised – would in future be disallowed. The programme companies, on the other hand, argued that all advertising, even when designed to further the sale of well-known branded products, also served to enhance the reputation and general standing of the manufacturer in the public mind. The very use of familiar symbols and company names was designed to reinforce public confidence in those who had carefully promoted their own corporate identity, often over many years, by consistent and instantly recognizable advertising. 'Opinion advertising', as Fraser called it, was to present many problems of definition and interpretation over the next twenty years.

The growth in the number of advertisers using television continued to grow to such an extent, however, that by the end of 1958 Associated-Rediffusion was able to claim that the number of products it had carried on the screen had increased from 406 in the period March-September 1956 to 1166 in the corresponding period two years later. Other companies could report similar results. Meanwhile, the number of homes receiving Independent Television, which from August 1958 included those in the South of England, had risen to well over six and a half million. Further stations were planned in East Anglia, the West Country and the North-East, and ITV was already reaching nearly 50 per cent of the homes in the areas in which it was established and obtaining well over half the viewing audience. The next year was to provide a foretaste of the increasing dominance of the media scene by television which was to take place in the sixties.

1959

When Media Records issued its estimates of television advertising revenue for 1958 of £48,671,000, it appeared that there had been an increase of over 50 per cent in comparison with the previous year. In fact, the percentage increase was probably even greater because discounts, which could not be calculated by an outside monitoring service, were being steadily reduced. Nor could the value of surcharges for fixed spots, which were being paid with increasing frequency, possibly be estimated. Meanwhile the television companies continued to maintain complete confidentiality over their actual revenue.

The introduction of Contract Discount

Despite the self-evident buoyancy of the medium there were still problems for the contractors which it was thought could be solved by the offer of discounts in return for a guarantee by an advertiser of long-term expenditure. On 28 December 1958, but effectively from 1 January 1959, Associated-Rediffusion introduced 'Contract Discount', which replaced all other forms of expenditure incentives on the London weekday station. The new system was bitterly opposed by major advertisers, who took the view that the purchase of television airtime should, like other transactions in which they were involved, be subject to the usual benefits of 'bulk buying' without legalistic conditions. The leading members of the ISBA claimed that it was one thing to be asked to forecast their television advertising expenditure in advance but quite another to face legal penalties for non-fulfilment.

A-R insisted, however, that to obtain any kind of discount under the new system an advertiser should:

1 Guarantee the expenditure of a sum of money in advance.
2 Spend one-eighth of the total in July and August – the traditionally 'unpopular' months for advertising.
3 Only receive the percentage scale of discount related to the original guaranteed sum. Excess expenditure above this original 'bid' would be

subject to the original rate of discount even if the total would otherwise qualify for a higher scale.

4 Wait until the completion of a fifty-two-week period before receiving the discount which, subject to the other conditions, would vary from 5 to 10 per cent – a lower percentage than hitherto.

5 Sign a formal contract with legal penalties for non-completion. It was even suggested that Associated-Rediffusion would sue an advertiser in cases of default.

Among the advertisers who felt most strongly about the restrictions surrounding the award of contract discount were the oil companies who, as will be remembered, had faced a Government directive at the time of the Suez crisis to remove their branded products from the market and cease all promotional activity. They asked what would happen to an advertiser if the ITA, the ITCA Copy Committee or, more likely, a Government Department were to make a product or form of advertising unacceptable? Would all discount already earned by the advertiser be forfeited, or would A-R accept a *force majeure* clause in the contract? The answer, when it came, was even more unpalatable. Associated-Rediffusion said it would insist on the original expenditure commitment being fulfilled even though no advertising appeared on the screen.

In time all other companies were to adopt a less formal system of awarding discounts in return for an advertiser's guarantee of expenditure because the majority recognized the need for some degree of flexibility. For example, discounts were usually applied by the rest of the network at the time of transmission rather than being withheld until the end of the year and advertisers were allowed to move up (or down) the discount scales if the level of their expenditure changed. In other cases a degree of rate protection was given to discount-earning advertisers, so that when airtime rates were being increased at roughly six-monthly intervals those who had guaranteed their expenditure were protected, for a time, against the new prices. Not for the first time A-R had drawn the fire of criticism from agencies and advertisers in a way which was to result in complaints to the Pilkington Committee of their abuse of monopoly power and the pursuit of rigid sales policies.

Problems with Thornton Wilder

This year saw two advertising problems which, by coincidence, revolved around the work of the same American dramatist. In January the ITV network transmitted the 1944 feature film version of Thornton Wilder's *The Bridge of San Luis Rey*, the final scene of which was interrupted to accommodate commercials. Scores of outraged telephone calls were received by the contractors and questions were asked in Parliament of the Postmaster-General. The following morning the national press made the most of what they claimed was ITV's blindly insensitive pursuit of revenue at all costs. A meeting of sales directors was convened under Richard Meyer, a senior director of ATV, to draw up a more effective set of rules on 'natural breaks'.

In March another work by Wilder was at the centre of a further series of complaints, this time from advertisers. The network transmitted Granada's distinguished production of *The Skin of Our Teeth*, starring Vivien Leigh. Unfortunately, despite the high quality of the play and its cast it was only seen, according to TAM, in 356,000 homes nationally – a peaktime rating of 6. Most of the programme companies managed to find a formula to compensate advertisers for an audience level which, at the time, was unprecedented.

The problem of overbooking, which had so exercised the contractors a year earlier, seemed however to have eased and in January the cancellation period was reduced to its former length of eight weeks. In the same month Tyne Tees went on the air and the first complete campaign on videotape (for Thomas Hedley's White Tide) was broadcast on Southern Television.

The AAC and the Head of Advertising Control

Two important appointments which were made at this stage deserve to be recorded. The Chairman of the ITA's Advertising Advisory Committee, Robert Bevan, retired and was succeeded by Edward Glanvill Benn, a distinguished figure from the publishing world and Chairman of his family's firm, Benn Brothers, publishers of a large number of trade and technical journals.

Within the ITA itself the responsibility for advertising matters which had hitherto rested with the Secretary of the Authority, Anthony Pragnell, was transferred to a full-time specialist, Archie Graham, a senior civil servant with considerable sales experience from the Broadcasting Department of the Post Office. Graham, a shrewd and quizzical Scot, established excellent relations with agencies and advertisers without in any way weakening the links between them and the programme companies. His rulings, which were invariably delivered with great clarity, common sense and good humour, were not always popular, but the Authority and the contractors came to trust his judgement and his ability to explain the reasons for the decision to amend or reject an advertiser's claim or even an entire campaign.

The independent consultants

But neither Archie Graham nor the AAC was in a position to carry out the day-to-day pre-transmission examination of every individual commercial. Until the law was changed in 1963 this task had to be undertaken entirely by the Copy Committee, advised and assisted, as always, by Laurence Parker and Audrey Gardiner. It became increasingly apparent, however, that independent advice was needed in a number of technical areas in which only an expert was qualified to pass judgement. Commercials for medicines of increasing power and complexity began to arrive for transmission; and health claims, of whose basis laymen were largely ignorant, were also being made in the advertising of a number of food products such as dietary supplements and slimming aids.

The British Medical Association (which was already represented on the AAC) was approached for advice and their Secretary, Dr Derek Stevenson, agreed that the names of up to six eminent consultants would be suggested. In September the first of these experts to advise the Copy Committee, Dr A.H. Douthwaite, a senior consulting physician at Guy's Hospital, was appointed in the field of general medicine and Audrey Gardiner was made responsible for seeking his advice on the acceptability of medical products and their claims in television commercials. In November Dr K.A. Williams, a distinguished chemist, and Professor A.C. Frazer, an expert in pharmacology and human nutrition, were appointed with the same terms of reference.

The guaranteed audience rate card

Despite the fact that ITV continued to gain the major share of the audience against the BBC there were occasions when, as during the transmission of *The Skin of Our Teeth*, ratings fell well below the station average and the cost-per-thousand homes rose to a level which advertisers found unacceptable. As an experiment Associated-Rediffusion introduced on 22 June 1959 a summer rate card, which for the first time offered advertisers a guaranteed minimum audience and therefore a maximum cost-per-thousand, in this instance of 10 shillings (50p). In return the programme company required complete discretion on the timing (or slotting) of the spots in the package throughout the whole twelve-week period of the summer offer.

Initial reactions were mixed. Agency time buyers claimed that the guaranteed audience rate card took all the skill out of media planning and buying, and that it was also bound to ignore any of the criteria of audience composition. For instance, a product only of interest to women could be slotted into male-oriented sports programmes. Both agencies and programme companies felt that it might be unwise to put the responsibility for the measurement of viewing, and therefore the estimation of the results of the scheme in terms of revenue, in the hands of TAM, particularly as that company had now become the sole provider of the industry research service.

Nevertheless, this method of selling airtime had its attractions for the buyer as well as the seller. It was later refined to take account of broad audience categories – for example, housewives – and campaign periods were structured by date and time of day to meet the planning needs of the advertiser. From the contractor's point of view it provided a useful reserve of bookings which could be slotted into transmission schedules close to the airdate. Eventually these packages of airtime, which soon became known as Guaranteed Home Impressions (GHIs) or Guaranteed Homes Ratings (GHRs), became an important part of every company's rate card.

On 1 June the A.C. Nielsen Company, whose clients for the Television Index were now reduced to Granada and Southern Television, together with a small number of advertisers and agencies, took a 49 per cent financial interest in TAM. As a result TAM emerged as the sole research contractor.

In October Anglia and Ulster Television went on the air and the number of ITV homes, which had continued to grow steadily in the existing areas, reached eight million.

1960

Despite the addition of three new areas to the ITV network in 1959 (in which the level of set ownership was bound initially to be a good deal lower than elsewhere), Independent Television was, by January 1960, reaching 8,605,000 homes or 55 per cent of all the households in the areas in which it could be received. According to Media Records the value of advertising transmitted on ITV now amounted to over £1,000,000 a week and profits on all stations had reached unprecedented levels.

The amount of advertising on television

There had been no significant public criticism about the total amount of advertising transmitted on the air, but a number of Labour MPs complained from the Opposition benches to the Postmaster-General, Reginald Bevins, that the original intentions of Parliament were being ignored by the programme companies. It was alleged that the maximum allowance of advertising in the 'clock hour' which the ITA had authorized was actually beginning, in the wording of the Act, to 'detract from the value of the programmes' themselves. When fifteen-minute advertising magazines were transmitted, the critics alleged, the hourly total of advertising could reach as much as twenty-three minutes between, for example, 10 and 11 pm on weekdays. The Authority replied that admags (or shoppers' guides) had been deliberately excluded by Parliament from the advertising allowance and that, in any case, they all had a recognizable editorial content – even a storyline – which in cases like *Jim's Inn* and *What's In Store?* was popular with viewers. Nevertheless, the Authority was uneasy that the total amount of advertising on television was growing steadily. Sir Robert Fraser wrote to all the programme companies early in 1960:

Since the end of October, the monthly amount of advertising over the network as a whole has exceeded that of a year ago by 10 per cent in the month that showed the smallest increase, to 30 per cent in the month with the greatest.

The maxima for individual hours are at present eight minutes on weekdays and eight and a half minutes at weekends, the latter maximum being subject to the further rule that the average amount of advertising in peak hours must not exceed seven and a half minutes.

If the Authority felt that these maxima should be reduced, it seems likely that it will be wished to give effect to the changes in the autumn at the latest.

There seemed to be no alternative but to begin discussions with the Authority on the kind of reductions in the amount of advertising which would be acceptable.

Meanwhile, advertising rates were moving steadily upwards. In general, charges on the network as a whole rose by 20 per cent at the beginning of 1960, and not long afterwards further increases of a similar amount were announced to take effect in the autumn. Associated-Rediffusion warned, however, that if the amount of commercial time was to be drastically reduced by the ITA then a further price increase would be needed.

The introduction of pro rata rates

A-R was the first company to decide that the length of peaktime should be extended and that in all time segments the rates for longer commercials should be made pro rata to those for thirty seconds. This represented a complete and radical change in the price structure of television airtime. Since 1955 sixty seconds had been regarded as the standard for pricing purposes, with thirty-second spots being charged at roughly two-thirds of the minute rate. The effect of the introduction of pro rata rates was to increase the price of all commercials of more than thirty seconds by one-third, and by considerably more when the basic rate increases and segment changes were also taken into account. By September pro rata rates had been introduced on all stations, and inevitably a trend towards shorter commercials began.

The 'qualitative' advertising improvements

The summer of 1960, when the new rate cards were announced, was a time of many other important changes which were to affect Independent Television for years to come.

The negotiations with the Authority over the amount and distribution of advertising resulted in a number of so-called 'qualitative' improvements which led to the removal of 20 per cent of the commercial breaks within programmes. In theory this reduction in the number of 'natural breaks' did not necessarily involve any diminution in the total amount of advertising on the air. But there was already an upper limit of three-and-a-half minutes in the length of breaks at the end of programmes, and the Authority was also known to be moving towards a reduction in the hourly maximum from eight to seven and a half minutes. All internal breaks were removed from three weekly documentaries, some children's programmes and, rather strangely, from the twice-weekly fictional hospital series *Emergency – Ward 10*. Programmes of all types, of sixty to ninety minutes' duration, were restricted to two advertising intervals instead of three.

Had rates not been increased it is calculated that the network would have lost £10,000,000 a year as a result of these changes and one contractor, ATV, with a weekday contract in the Midlands and another at the weekends in London, would have forfeited as much as £2,250,000.

The appointment of further consultants

The problems of the Copy Committee continued to increase in complexity, and it became clear that further expert advice in the medical field was required. The list of consultants was increased by the appointment of Sir Derrick Dunlop of Edinburgh University and Sir John (later Lord) Richardson of St Thomas's Hospital to give advice to the companies (through the ITCA) on general medical matters.

The Pilkington Committee

But one event overshadowed all others in the summer of 1960 – the appointment of the Committee on Broadcasting under Sir Harry Pilkington. It was over nine years since the Beveridge Committee had reported, and decisions were now urgently required on a number of vital matters. Both the BBC and Independent Television claimed they needed another channel to cater for the needs of minorities, and advertisers believed there was sufficient advertising demand to finance a second commercial service. But little room remained in the VHF wavebands to provide satisfactory reception for another full national service. It seemed clear that any new channels would have to be accommodated in the Ultra High Frequencies, which would entail the replacement of transmitting and receiving equipment. But this was only one of the problems to face the Committee. Its main task was to consider the future of all broadcasting services in Britain.

Further reductions in advertising

In September the ITA decided that following the qualitative improvements which had been made earlier there should be a further reduction in the maximum amount of advertising to be allowed in the clock hour. While maintaining the daily average of six minutes in the hour, which had not been varied since 1955, the Authority had allowed a maximum of eight minutes provided the other rules on the length and distribution of breaks were maintained. As from 12 September, however, this hourly maximum was reduced to seven-and-a-half minutes, and this quota was further reduced to seven minutes from 24 December when the winter programme schedule for 1961 began.

There still remained one puzzling anomaly. All the rules on the advertising allowance which the Authority had issued in the early days had excluded Time Spots – seven-second commercials which were transmitted before and after the station clock and identifying symbol

The once-familiar station clock of the London weekday company, Associated-Rediffusion, before and after the transmission of which 7-second advertising 'Time Spots' were broadcast. The clock itself was always described as 'Mitch' in the company's programme schedules – after Leslie Mitchell, A-R's Head of Presentation

at the time of a programme change. Until July 1959 these Time Spots could total a further thirty seconds of advertising in the hour. At this stage, however, they had to form part of the total minutage, and on 1 January 1961 they were to be discontinued altogether, much to the disappointment of a number of advertisers who made use of this short but effective form of 'reminder' advertising. Among the programme companies the view was beginning to gain ground that the fewer the number of interruptions – station announcements, programme promotion, time checks and commercial breaks – the better. A glance at the minute-by-minute rating outline showed a certain amount of audience 'turbulence' when programme junctions occurred simultaneously on ITV and BBC, and the contractors began to commission 'switching analyses' from TAM to study the viewing behaviour of homes on the panel during and around prolonged breaks. It was evident from these analyses that some of the audience could be lost when the thread of programme output was broken.

The 'Kitchen' and 'Laundry' rules

The single largest category of advertising in the first five years of Independent Television had been washing and household cleaning products, mainly those brands manufactured by Unilever and Thomas Hedley. Both companies had developed a sophisticated and intensive use of television to the point at which they had virtually abandoned the use of other media. They were among the first advertisers to base their sales territories and product distribution on television areas, and every campaign schedule was the subject of detailed and exacting negotiation with their agencies and the programme contractors.

Not surprisingly, the ITV companies were acutely conscious of their degree of dependence on these two advertisers for a large part of their revenue, and in many cases assigned an experienced full-time sales executive to the task of servicing either Unilever or Hedley's; never, for obvious reasons, both. Each advertiser demanded a high degree of confidentiality in the handling of his own business, and the results of every campaign were subject to continuous weekly analysis and revision. Details of advance programme schedules (including those of the BBC) and rate cards were a matter of regular discussion between the sales directors of the ITV companies and the marketing departments of the two major advertisers.

This thoroughgoing use of the medium had a number of important consequences. Many marketing personnel who had been trained in the rigorous disciplines of Hedley's and Unilever eventually moved to other companies, in which they were able to apply their skills to developing the sale of many other products and services. Hedley's and Unilever had been among the first to recognize that the dramatic power of television to establish a brand, theme or slogan worked not only on the consumer but also on the retail trade. The TV contractors had cause to be grateful for the spread of this professionalism into new fields, which brought with it many new sources of revenue.

By the summer of 1960, however, there were signs that the similarity and sheer attack of much washing-product advertising were beginning to antagonize viewers. As the manufacturers themselves admitted, the very mention of washday in evening leisure time served to remind the women in the audience of one of the most disagreeable household chores. That fact was inescapable. Unfortunately, the two major advertisers had also discovered that a more subtle and oblique approach in their commercials was far less effective than straightforward demonstrations and claims to performance. Individual product improvements, particularly in synthetic detergents, might initially appear to be marginal but their cumulative effect on performance was none the less significant. From the manufacturer's point of view it was vital that in a capital-intensive industry every product advance, however small, should be promoted to the full. To succeed, washing products had to achieve rapid public acceptance and mass sales which meant that the use of television was essential.

Against a background of a total range of products on the screen which was still limited the repetition of a forceful sales message in one product field was likely to cause a certain amount of irritation to viewers, and in September the Authority decided to act. All the products in the washing and cleaning field were classified into 'A' and 'B' groups, the first consisting of those for cleaning clothes (washing liquids and powders, the 'Laundry' category) and the second, scourers, cleansers and the like (the 'Kitchen' Group). It was decided that not more than one product out of each group would be allowed to appear during each hour of transmission, though the rule was later relaxed to allow more than one product from the same group to be slotted within the hour provided that they did not appear in consecutive breaks.

Every contractor had the utmost difficulty in employing an equitable form of rationing in rescheduling airtime in the 'Laundry' field between the two principal advertisers, both of whom well knew the value of each commercial break. In the case of the 'Kitchen' group the situation was even more complicated because, unlike the 'A' category, which was dominated by the Hedley/Unilever duopoly, there were many more floor, bathroom and general-purpose cleaners, some produced by relatively small single-product companies. If a contractor's commitments to Unilever or Hedley were to be honoured, the products of a smaller advertiser could well be excluded altogether even when a certain amount of airtime remained unsold. Eventually the situation was resolved more or less to the satisfaction of all parties. But the Traffic Managers of the programme companies, who were responsible for the increasingly complex working of each station's booking system, had to apply yet another limitation to the slotting of forward business. The proliferation of these controls could often lead to delays in the processing of options and orders for airtime.

Further problems with washing products

As well as the Kitchen and Laundry rules, the Authority introduced further restrictions on the kind of claims and visual portrayals which could be used in washing-product commercials. The rapid growth of television coverage, often in places many miles from the transmitter, led to obvious variations in the quality of reception of TV commercials, and the ITA came to the conclusion that degrees of whiteness – certainly when shown side by side – could not be depicted with any kind of accuracy. Both major advertisers were adding fluorescers to their products to gain additional brightness but unless reception in the home was good and the set properly tuned this degree of contrast was not always clearly visible on the television screen. Side-by-side comparisons of whiteness were therefore disallowed. So were claims to absolute supremacy of performance, such as 'Daz washes whitest of all' and 'Persil washes whitest – and it shows.' Instead, so-called 'parity' claims (of equal excellence) were permitted, involving the Copy Committee and the ITCA staff in many hours of semantic disputation with the major advertisers and their agencies.

The introduction of fluoride toothpastes

Within a few months of the settlement of the washing product controversy both major manufacturers were to become involved in further negotiations to enable fluoride toothpastes to be advertised on television. Early in 1961 Thomas Hedley of Newcastle, owned since 1930 by Procter and Gamble of Cincinnati, decided to launch Crest, a fluoridated toothpaste which enjoyed phenomenal sales in the United States.

At the end of 1960 they had supplied voluminous evidence to the Copy Committee on the basis of their American experience to support the claim that the addition of stannous fluoride to dentifrice helped to resist tooth decay.

It had long been established that the existence of natural fluorides in the water supply led to a significant reduction in dental caries. Dentists on both sides of the Atlantic had also found that children's teeth benefited from the topical application of fluoride compounds in the surgery, but they were less certain that the same effects could be obtained from a toothpaste with a comparatively low concentration of a fluoride additive.

Stewart Ross, the British Dental Association's representative on the Advertising Advisory Committee, had been approached by Procter and Gamble and declared that he was inclined to accept the American Dental Association's 'ß' rating which had formed the basis of their claims in the United States. Professor Ronald Emslie of the Department of Preventive Dentistry at Guy's Hospital, who had been appointed dental consultant to the Copy Committee was, on the other hand, less impressed by the evidence. He stipulated that the US claims should be considerably modified before acceptance. Within a year, however, fluoride toothpastes were to be successfully launched on television by both Colgate-Palmolive and D. and W. Gibbs, in addition to Procter and Gamble.

1961

The closed-circuit sales conference

It had become commonplace for television advertising to be used to communicate with a company's sales force and the retail trade, but in January 1961 D. and W. Gibbs pioneered a new use of the medium. The sales staff of the company were gathered at the studios of the ITV companies throughout the country, which were linked on closed circuit to Television House in London where the Chairman and his colleagues were able to present their forthcoming TV commercials and marketing strategy for the coming year. Though the cost of studios and Post Office lines was not inconsiderable it was far less than that of summoning the entire sales team to one place and John Mann, Chairman of Gibbs, pronounced himself delighted. The experiment was later repeated with equal success by another Unilever company, Lever Brothers, in conjunction with the washing-machine manufacturers, Hoover.

Evidence to Pilkington

The year opened to the accompaniment of increasing activity by the Pilkington Committee. The first of a series of visits had taken place to the BBC, the ITA and the contractors, and a large number of outside bodies were beginning to assail Sir Harry and his colleagues with evidence, some of which was released simultaneously to the press. Joyce Grenfell, a member of the Committee, wrote:

There cannot be many organisations connected even faintly with broadcasting communication that were not included. Both the BBC and the ITA sent representatives from all departments and advisory bodies, those based in London and the regions. The arts, educational and religious bodies – mainstream and minority religions; technical interests, film interests, political, medical and trade union interests; associations of viewers and of listeners, workers in youth clubs, and of course, advertising interests – all were represented.

Under the latter heading the IPA, which had earlier complained to the contractors about what they considered a high-handed attitude towards those who financed the cost of the ITV service, said in their submission to Pilkington: 'The present monopolistic situation has, however, led to high costs (militating against the small advertiser) and short-comings in service, to the disadvantage of all.' They continued:

The Institute believes, therefore, that the interests of the public, as well as those of commerce and advertising, would best be served by increasing the number of efficient advertising media through the creation of an additional television advertising channel.

In addition to the need for a further channel, the IPA argued for an increase in broadcasting hours, the rejection of any form of sponsorship and an extension of spot advertising to radio.

The British Medical Association, which had formed a special committee, nineteen strong, to prepare its evidence, took an opposite view, however, and in doing so paid an unexpected tribute to the power of the medium:

Television has proved such a powerful medium of advertising, as it has for information and entertainment, that its accepted standards of advertising should, in the Committee's view, be re-examined. Many of the familiar arguments against advertising itself have been given renewed force by the novelty, the almost oracular power, of television as a medium. There is no question that an advertisement which appears two or three times during an evening's viewing, though its obtrusiveness and persistence may be exasperating, has a very great impact upon the people to whom it is aimed, probably much greater than a full-page advertisement appearing in the morning paper.

But they went on to say:

The Committee believes that the intrusion of advertising in commercially supported programmes tends to detract from their cultural value, and that if any fresh channel were made available it should be free from commercial control.

The BMA's view on medical advertising was succinctly expressed at the end of their memorandum to Pilkington:

The Committee is unanimously of the opinion that advertisements on television for drugs, medical treatments and preparations should be prohibited. But since this ideal is not likely to be achieved soon the

Committee recommends the setting up of a Committee, with doctors in the majority, to view all advertisements for such preparations. No advertisement for a drug or treatment would be allowed to be shown on television until it had passed the scrutiny of the Committee, which would examine it carefully and satisfy itself of the validity of the claims made or implied.

The Authority and the companies were equally dismayed at these strictures. After all, the BMA had been represented on the ITA's Advertising Advisory Committee since the latter's formation in January 1955. So were the Ministry of Health, the Pharmaceutical Society of Great Britain, and the Code of Standards Committee on the Advertising of Medicines and Treatments.

But not only this: the ITCA had itself approached the BMA to seek the names of medical experts who could be retained to scrutinize the claims in all medical advertisements before transmission. And the advice given by the consultants whom the BMA had nominated was regarded as mandatory by both the Authority and the companies. It was difficult to see what more could have been done.

But the problems of medical advertising were only just beginning. On 1 March, in a House of Lords debate, Lord Taylor of Harlow, a doctor and former Labour MP, launched a violent attack on the advertising of medicinal products on television. Like the BMA, he advocated a total ban of this category of advertising and claimed that the programme companies could well afford to lose the £5,000,000 revenue it represented out of their total income, which he estimated at £80,000,000 a year. A number of products were mentioned by name, mainly in the fields of analgesics, indigestion remedies, vitamin preparations and rheumatic salts. For the most part all were familiar, homely remedies commonly found in medicine cupboards throughout the country and freely sold over the counter without a doctor's prescription.

The Authority's Advertising Control Department and the Copy Committee met with ITCA's original consultant, Dr Douthwaite, and re-examined the scripts and films for no fewer than 184 medicinal products. New rules were drafted, disallowing the use of celebrities in medical commercials and forbidding any claims which might have the effect of delaying viewers from seeking proper medical advice. No products were actually banned but a number were withdrawn from television by the manufacturers and some were reformulated for introduction later. In other cases slogans which might be open to misinterpretation, such as Aspro's 'One degree under', were ruled out on the somewhat literal grounds that aspirin was an anti-pyretic and therefore could be expected to reduce temperature rather than raise it. Not for the first time the medical profession had sought to apply a precise and scientific judgement to a colloquial use of the English language. In any case, it is doubtful whether viewers felt they had been seriously misled by any medical advertising on the screen, and they probably missed the appearance of colourful personalities such as Gilbert Harding extolling the benefits of a well-known indigestion remedy. Not unnaturally, the proprietary medicine manfacturers felt they had been singled out for harsh treatment, and the programme companies ruefully took stock of their forward bookings which had been seriously depleted by the sudden withdrawal of a significant part of their business.

The third channel: the ISBA solution

In the same month as the House of Lords debate on medical advertising the ISBA, which was as anxious as the IPA to see competition among the programme companies for advertising revenue, announced an ingenious but complex plan for the allocation of a third television channel. In their evidence to Pilkington they proposed that four programme providers – the BBC and three separate commercial networks – should share each channel, two-thirds of each of which should be advertising-financed, and one-third remain dependent on licence revenue and run by the BBC.

If the ITV service were to be effectively trebled in this way two other important changes would have to take place. The number of ITV areas would have to be reduced and the hours of broadcasting, which had not been extended since 1957, would have to be considerably increased in order to make the system economically viable.

These recommendations found little favour with the members of the Pilkington Committee, who were opposed to any further extension of the commercial principle. There were certainly economic arguments in favour of enlarging some ITV areas and amalgamating others. Indeed, a number of bodies including several of the programme companies themselves had suggested as much to the Committee. But Pilkington had been impressed by the vitality and local ethos of regional television within the 'plural' framework originally devised by Kenneth Clark and Robert Fraser. The Committee saw no reason to put at risk much of the unique character of the system simply to satisfy the desire of advertisers for competition between the programme companies for their business.

'A Tax on Advertising?' – the Fabian view

The Fabian Society did not supply evidence to the Committee on Broadcasting but chose the time of the Pilkington inquiry to issue a provocatively worded pamphlet which drew attention to recent trends in advertising expenditure and, in particular, the impact of Independent Television on the national press and magazines. Having gone on to restate the familiar left-wing arguments against advertising – the need for consumer information as opposed to persuasion, the case for banning the advertising of socially harmful products (proprietary medicines and tobacco were cited), and the alleged cost of advertising to the consumer – the author recommended that all advertising should be taxed. The obvious place to begin was television. He wrote prophetically: 'What is clear at least is that a tax on TV advertising would be quite feasible, should do little harm either to the TV service or the advertisers, and would in effect tend to be a levy on the contractors.'

The introduction of Television Advertisement Duty

Less than a month after the publication of the Fabian Society proposals the Chancellor of the Exchequer, Selwyn Lloyd, announced the imposition from 1 May 1961 of a 10 per cent tax on television advertising, to be known as Television Advertisement Duty.

Reactions to this announcement were swift. Associated-Rediffusion issued an immediate press statement to the effect that they had been planning to make a major rate increase in the autumn but, in the light of the Chancellor's decision, they would obviously have to reconsider the position. By issuing this statement A-R ensured that, in their case at least, the duty would be passed on to advertisers in full and need not be absorbed by the programme companies at whom, many critics suspected, it had been aimed. The situation was not helped when the Chancellor appeared on television and, referring to his own minority report which had brought ITV into being at the time of the Beveridge inquiry, spoke somewhat surprisingly of the programme companies as 'biting the hand that had fed them'. It seemed that he, for one, expected the duty to be borne by the contractors.

Other companies were less emphatic than A-R in their reactions. ABC and Anglia reduced rates by 5 per cent for five months, while Tyne Tees and Scottish Television did so by the full 10 per cent, providing bookings were made non-cancellable. After some hesitation the remainder of the network followed A-R's example and added the duty to their rates in the form of a surcharge.

This brief account of the reactions of the contractors conveys nothing of the outcry which the imposition of TAD evoked among the agencies. Robert Bevan, now President of the IPA, wrote to the Chancellor on behalf of the Institute, complaining that by introducing the duty at less than three weeks' notice he would further weaken a large number of print media which had already lost revenue to television. If this was because advertising had proved more effective on television than in the press, advertisers would be likely to cancel press campaigns to meet the cost of TAD and more newspapers and magazines would be forced to close. *Picture Post, Illustrated, The News Chronicle* and *The Star* had all ceased publication during the previous year. Moreover, once the principle of taxing one form of advertising was established, it could be extended comparatively easily to other media.

But worse was to come. When the details of the scheme were published by the Board for Customs and Excise, the department responsible for the collection of the duty, it became clear that advertising agency commission would be allowed only on actual airtime rates excluding TAD. Thus, instead of obtaining 15 per cent commission on business placed on television, agencies discovered that their gross margin had been reduced at a stroke to 13.6 per cent. When on 26 July the Chancellor, under the additional economic regulators he had introduced in the Budget, increased TAD to 11 per cent, agency commission on TV expenditure fell effectively to 13.5 per cent. Unless an agency with the bulk of its billing on TV was able to obtain additional commission from the contractors, or fee income from its clients, it would be impossible for it to operate at a profit.

Despite the drastic effects on agency profitability which TAD created, the other alarming forecasts which the IPA had made to the Chancellor were not fulfilled. The tax on television advertising was not extended to the press, and in the event it became more profitable to an agency to place business in print than in broadcast media. When the Advertising Association's figures for expenditure by media in 1961–62 were published, they revealed a noticeable swing of expenditure away from television and back to the press.

'Presence' and 'Attention' research

While the Pilkington Committee was sitting and the companies were still grappling with the problems of Television Advertisement Duty, the results of two major television audience studies were released. In April and May the London Press Exchange, always in the forefront of media research, analysed the viewing behaviour of 1500 'non-working' housewives during the commercial breaks in London and the North of England. In June J. Walter Thompson carried out a similar examination of a much larger sample of some 20,000 housewives.

The two studies showed that there was a perceptible drop in audience when commercials were on the air, but the results of both research projects seemed to be contradictory as far as the relative values to the advertiser of 'middle' and 'end' breaks were concerned. A number of agencies and advertisers argued in favour of 'Presence' and 'Attention' factors being applied to the ratings for commercial breaks as a refinement of the TAM figures. But the problem was complicated by the inability of TAMmeters and Viewing Diaries to measure the presence of individuals in the room with any accuracy, and to record whether or not the TV screen was obtaining the undivided attention of each member of a family audience. Both presence and attention levels were also shown to be greatly influenced by the nature of the surrounding programme and the time of day it was broadcast. Some agencies made allowance for a reduction in audience during commercial breaks but attention levels among viewers proved impossible to measure.

The British Code of Advertising Practice

The Advertising Association, to which ITCA belonged, had begun work in 1960 on drawing up a voluntary code of advertising practice which it was intended should be applied to all media except Independent Television. Advertising on ITV had, of course, been regulated by statute since the beginning by the Television Act of 1954.

The programme companies were invited to join the Code of Advertising Practice Committee, whose early meetings were chaired by Leslie ('Bill') Needham, the Advertisement Director of Beaverbrook Newspapers and himself a member of the ITA's Advertising Advisory Committee. The CAP Code drew heavily on the wording of the AAC's *Principles for Television Advertising*, but ITCA suggested that CAP's rules should be strengthened by substituting the word 'must' for 'should' wherever possible, a suggestion which the other media owners received with little enthusiasm.

ITCA also argued in favour of a pre-publication check on all advertising being employed, as in the case of television, and for this purpose offered CAP the services of the ITCA consultants for a year, at the expense of the television companies. But both suggestions were rejected. The CAP Committee took the view that pre-publication scrutiny would be impossible with advertising appearing in several thousand publications, and pointed out that consultants were already retained by bodies such as the NPA, who were likely to play a leading part in the work of the new committee. Eventually, however, the operation of television and press copy control came closer together with the formation of the Advertising Standards Authority, the Advertising Standards Board of Finance and a greatly strengthened secretariat. The closeness of this relationship was ensured at a later stage by the *ex officio* appointment to the AAC of the Chairman of the CAP Committee.

1962

Advertising magazines

1962 was to be a year of important decisions for Independent Television, even before the publication in June of the report of the Pilkington Committee.

It seemed likely from preliminary discussions with members of the Committee that some sort of restriction would be placed on advertising magazines, which still remained outside the 10 per cent quota of spot advertising. In January, to clarify the position, the Authority issued a series of rulings embodying the description of admags which had been used in 1958 in the working document *Advertising Rules and Practices*:

Definition – An Advertising Magazine consists of a linked series of advertisements for different products or services. The advertisements may originate from one advertiser or from a number of different advertisers.
Content – The content of the programme as a whole must clearly and unmistakably reveal and serve its advertising purpose.

The wording used by the Authority clearly described the somewhat curious anomaly which admags represented. They were called 'programmes' in the rules, yet they had to be clearly distinguishable as advertising. In practice the ITA was inclined to look with greater favour on 'themed' presentations (such as magazines devoted to travel, fashion, motoring, Christmas presents or the products made or sold by one company) rather than those of the general interest variety. But airtime in 'themed' admags with their restricted formats had proved much more difficult to sell than in those without a specific subject. The Authority had also found that the slots (called 'participations' or 'mentions') in advertising magazines, could unwittingly give the impression that the products which were included had been selected on merit, especially if the presenters were acknowledged experts in their field such as Barry Bucknell on DIY, the Cradocks on cookery or Dr W.E. Shewell-Cooper on gardening.

While the new rules were being discussed by the companies and the ITA, the situation was further confused when the BBC launched its

Marks & Spencer made effective use of advertising magazines in conjunction with their major suppliers such as the Cotton Board, the International Wool Secretariat, Chemstrand and British Nylon Spinners. The fashion sequence in the admag used Marks & Spencer's own staff to model nylon nightwear

Fashion in the Making, transmitted in 1959, showed how M & S began as a 'Penny Bazaar' in Kirkgate open-air market in Leeds in 1884 and rapidly developed into an outstandingly successful nationwide retail operation.

consumer-service programme *Choice*, presented by the most authoritative presenter of all, Richard Dimbleby. Writing in the *Radio Times* the BBC's formidable Head of Television Talks, Grace Wyndham Goldie, said:

We have, in both sound and television programmes, over many years tried to assist the buyer by giving information which might be useful. Now we are taking this a step further in that the reports in *Which?* and *Shoppers' Guide* give names and prices, and in our reports we shall do so also.

The ITA had also been approached by the Consumers' Association (publishers of *Which?*) and the Consumer Advisory Council (publishers of *Shoppers' Guide*), on which the BBC programme was based, to see whether Independent Television would be prepared to broadcast a similar series. The programme companies, however, could see difficulties in recommending a 'best buy', especially when other products might simultaneously be condemned as being unsafe or overpriced. Admags and consumer-advisory programmes would, it was felt, fit uneasily into the ITV programme schedules.

The Authority finally decided that admags would be allowed to continue for the time being, but in a restricted form. No more than three a week were to be transmitted in any single ITV region, there would be no fixed proportion of 'themed' against 'unthemed' formats, and magazines shorter than ten minutes were to be abandoned. Particular care was to be taken with the storyline in cases such as *Jim's Inn* – which had celebrated its two-hundredth edition in March 1961 – so as to ensure that their advertising content was not overshadowed by their editorial ingredients which, under a long-standing title, could come to resemble those of a soap opera.

Despite these misgivings advertising magazines remained popular with viewers, who welcomed the regular appearances on the screen of familiar personalities such as Kenneth Horne, Sylvia Peters, John Slater, Doris Rogers and Jimmy and Maggie Hanley. From the point of view of the sales departments of the programme companies admags performed another useful function. A new advertiser who might be intimidated or confused by the complexities of film production could put himself in the hands of the programme company, in the knowledge that payment of a single rate for admag participation would cover all his airtime and production costs. Experienced producers such as Joan Kemp-Welch, Pat Baker and Alan Tarrant, working closely with their writers, could introduce a variety of seemingly unrelated products and services in a way which was natural and of intrinsic interest to viewers. Many major television advertisers of the 1970s and 1980s were first introduced to the medium through advertising magazines, and as a result the circle of companies on the air was steadily widened.

But advertising agencies were on the whole less enthusiastic about advertising magazines than were their clients. The larger agencies needed to employ a group of junior production executives, who often had to travel hundreds of miles to programme company studios to supervise admag participations. Television Advertisement Duty had to be paid on a notional airtime element (excluding the cost of production) in the rates. And at a time when total ITV advertising revenue amounted to about £80,000,000 a year, the income from admags did not exceed £1,600,000 or 2 per cent. There was clearly little immediate profit to be obtained by the agencies from advertising magazines unless the clients concerned could eventually be persuaded to become spot advertisers.

The advertising of cigarettes on television

Early in March the Royal College of Physicians issued its report *Smoking and Health*, which for the first time traced a significant statistical correlation in Britain between cigarette-smoking and the incidence of carcinoma of the lung, emphysema and bronchitis. The tobacco manufacturers were quick to point out that so far no 'causal relationship' had been established, but the demand grew in Parliament and the press for cigarette advertising to be restricted – particularly as far as children were concerned – in the one medium which was under direct statutory control.

After consultation with the programme companies and the AAC the ITA ruled that all tobacco advertising should be excluded from children's programmes and that all performers in cigarette commercials should be clearly over the age of twenty-one. A month later the manufacturers themselves decided to go further and to restrict all tobacco commercials to transmission after 9 pm, the time at which the period of so-called 'family viewing' came to an end. At the same time the Authority introduced a series of qualitative rules on the content of cigarette commercials, which were no longer allowed to connect smoking with social success and manliness or with the conventional heroes of the young. Nor could cigarette commercials portray the romantic themes and settings which had come to be associated with a number of well-known brands.

While the AAC was reviewing the changes which had been made to medicinal advertising since March 1961 the BMA issued a report on health education, acknowledging the improvements which had been made in this field of advertising on television. Glanvill Benn, who had been Chairman of the AAC since October 1959, decided to retire and was succeeded by Professor Daniel Jack, a well-known economist and Chairman of the Air Transport Licensing Board.

Publication of the Pilkington Report

It had become increasingly clear while the Pilkington Committee was sitting that its members were opposed to the financing of a broadcasting service by advertising but the principal recommendation in their report

– that the programme companies should hand over their entire airtime sales operation to the Authority – came as a surprise even to some of ITV's sternest critics. Such a fundamental change would have virtually destroyed the system and would have turned the contractors into a series of regional production units answerable to an all-powerful central planning Authority. In the light of this recommendation it was hardly surprising that the third channel, about which so many arguments had raged, should, in the view of the Committee, be awarded to the BBC.

But the other principal recommendations of the Pilkington Report were eventually to prove even more important. The Committee proposed that new television channels should be engineered on 625 lines in the Ultra High Frequency part of the broadcasting spectrum and that colour, when it came, should be confined to the 625-line UHF service. Advertising magazines, as the contractors had feared, were recommended to be discontinued and the Committee advised firmly against the introduction of any form of pay-television.

It was clear that the members of the Committee did not believe that the needs of the audience and those of advertisers could ever be satisfactorily reconciled. The effect since 1955 of competition on the BBC had, it was claimed, reduced rather than improved the quality of their programmes, while it was said that ITV had transmitted little serious material in peaktime. According to Pilkington, Independent Television had broadcast far too many American programmes, and the needs of the main regions of the British Isles, particularly Scotland and Wales, had largely been ignored.

It seemed that the Committee's recommendations on advertising were based largely on the submissions of a number of bodies whose views were known to be hostile. For instance, Pilkington took the view – without properly examining the evidence – that there were many misleading advertisements on television and that a significant number of commercials were deliberately designed to exploit human weakness. Too many advertisements, they claimed, featured children or were directed at them. The Report was issued on 27 June 1962 and Joyce Grenfell wrote afterwards:

That night we were bidden to dine with the Postmaster-General at the Savoy. After a delicious dinner Mr Bevins spoke and said that he didn't think our recommendations would be acceptable to the [Tory] Government. Harry [Pilkington] said they would do well to ponder the report for it was a serious and reasoned argument. It needed a courageous Government to face up to its recommendations.

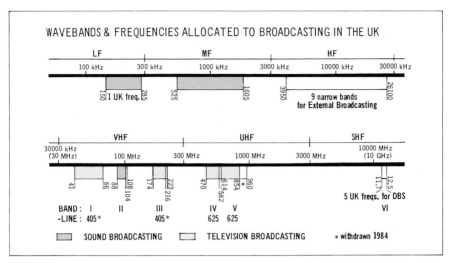

The broadcasting frequency spectrum.

The Government reacts

Less than two weeks after the appearance of the Report the Government made its views known in a White Paper. On the central question of whether the Authority or the companies should be responsible for selling the airtime it said:

The Government feels that the practical difficulties presented by these proposals have not been fully appreciated. So fundamental a change in the structure of Independent Television requires a most thorough examination, and the Government wishes to be satisfied that any new structure would remedy the defects it was designed to overcome and would not throw up equally serious difficulties of its own or deprive the system of those features for which it can fairly claim credit. Full account will be taken of the views which will be expressed in public debate and the Government will later submit to Parliament a statement of its own proposals for the future of Independent Television.

But the July White Paper cleared the air over some of the remaining issues on which a decision was urgently required. The Committee's recommendation that all future programme services should be operated on 625 lines in UHF was accepted. So was the view that the third channel (using the new waveband and line standards) should be awarded to the BBC. The aim would be to introduce the services in London by mid-1964 and to use the extension into UHF as the basis for the introduction of colour.

On the question of advertising, the Government accepted Pilkington's view that an hourly average of six minutes of advertising had proved reasonable and should therefore continue without being regulated by law. It was also agreed that advertising magazines should be abolished, that subliminal advertising should be prohibited, and that discussions should take place with the Authority on the vexed question of natural breaks. Finally, the Government undertook to reconsider the question of advertising in children's programmes and, at the same time, to give the ITCA's medical consultants statutory powers as a formally constituted panel.

The second White Paper

By the end of the year the Government had had the opportunity of hearing a wide range of views in Parliament and outside on the future of broadcasting. In the light of the importance of some of the other outstanding issues, the Postmaster-General's acceptance of Pilkington's recommendation to discontinue admags provoked a surprising outcry in both Houses of Parliament. Lord Brabazon of Tara, the veteran motorist and aviator, confessed in the House of Lords debate on the Pilkington Report to an affection for *Jim's Inn*, while several MPs declared in the Commons that advertising magazines provided a useful source of consumer information.

But the Postmaster-General's mind was made up. In the second White Paper on Broadcasting (issued on Christmas Eve 1962) he announced that admags would end on 31 March 1963. More important, the Authority was to be given a 'more formal and direct control' over all television advertising, and the AAC was to be strengthened by the inclusion of representatives of the public as consumers.

Despite the assurances from the IPA and the ISBA at the time of Pilkington that there was sufficient advertising revenue to finance a second commercial service, the Government remained unconvinced and in Paragraph 20 of the White Paper declared:

Second ITA programme
There is little evidence of a public demand for this. Furthermore the financial prospects of Independent Television may be less assured after 1964 when the existence of three television programmes instead of two will create more competition. The Government is not at present satisfied that in such a situation sufficient advertising revenue would be forthcoming adequately to sustain two commercial programmes. The Government still feels, however, that a second commercial programme may prove to be desirable in order to

Cooking with the Cradocks. Fanny and Johnny Cradock in an early advertising magazine. Note particularly the provision of gas, electricity and water supplies and the elaborately constructed set

allow full scope to Independent Television to offer more selection to viewers and to experiment. While the Government does not propose to authorise a second Independent Television programme in the near future, it does not dismiss the possibility of doing so later.

In fact it was not until nearly twenty years had elapsed after the publication of the White Paper that ITV was to be awarded a second channel.

Finally, despite the Government's doubts about the necessary revenue being available to finance the second ITV service, it was decided that provision should be made in forthcoming legislation for a substantial increase in the rental paid by each programme company to the ITA for its franchise. This increase would be designed to take account of the pre-tax profitability of each contractor.

The year 1962 saw the completion of the ITV network. The two smallest companies, Channel Television and Wales West and North (Teledu Cymru) went on the air in September. Their subsequent financial difficulties were later to underline the problem of polarization of advertising revenue in the major areas on which the Government had touched in the White Paper. There was more than a suggestion that, while there might be enough revenue to run two services in the main areas, the future for even a single service in the smallest regions might become precarious. The Government saw the rental as the best means of helping to redress this imbalance.

1963

At the beginning of 1963 Independent Television was able to claim that its coverage had reached 12,330,000 homes – nearly three out of every four in the areas of reception. The appointment of programme contractors had been completed in 1962, but additional transmitters were still needed to provide full national coverage and a decision was still awaited on the method of transfer of the existing broadcast services to 625 lines in UHF – Pilkington's main technical recommendation, which the Government had accepted.

The origins of the Television Consumer Audit

Television Advertisement Duty still bore heavily on the profitability of the advertising agencies, because commission continued to be allowed only on an advertiser's net expenditure, in other words on airtime rates excluding duty. In January, to help offset the impact of TAD, ATV extended a financial incentive which it had already used with some success in the previous year. In essence the scheme was a simple one. Any advertiser who reached a minimum qualifying level of expenditure on the Midlands weekday station was able to claim a 3 per cent discount in the form of a research allowance to be spent with the Schwerin organization. Thus a £100,000 campaign would provide a research budget of £3000, sufficient in 1962 to cover the cost of at least one major audience study. It was expected that advertisers would reimburse their agencies for the cost of this research and thereby help restore their commission from 13.5 per cent to the previous level of 15 per cent.

It had become increasingly clear, however, that there was a growing demand among advertisers for a regular measurement of the actual sales of products advertised on television, rather than for an evaluation of the impact or memorability of their commercials. Independent Television had been in existence long enough to provide a number of examples of instantly recognized – even well-liked – commercials for products whose sales, perhaps for quite extraneous reasons, had subsequently been disappointing. But no one could argue with actual sales and share-of-market figures.

In January the arrangements with Schwerin were ended and a new system of research, the Television Consumer Audit, was announced by ATV. It used a domestic audit carried out by a new company formed by Martin Maddan, Bernard Audley, Richard Gapper and Douglas Brown – all former directors of TAM and now known by the initials of the last three, AGB. The audit took place every seven days in a thousand representative homes in the Midlands ITV area, and measured the purchase and rate of consumption of a wide range of products, mainly branded foods and household goods, in thirty separate fields. The results of the research were made available free of charge to companies spending at least £10,000 on advertising with ATV.

The Television Consumer Audit, which had been born of the need to restore 'lost' agency commission, marked one of the most important developments in the marketing of television airtime. For the first time it provided the TV salesman with up-to-the-minute information on the effect of a client's advertising. The reactions of each advertiser's competitors in the marketplace could be studied; so could the effect of changes in pricing, advertising expenditure weights and marketing strategies throughout each product field.

It was not long before ABC Television, the weekend contractor in the Midlands, introduced a 50 per cent cost subsidy towards the cost of TCA research, provided the advertiser concerned extended his campaign to Saturdays and Sundays.

The new Television Act

It was essential that the Government's far-reaching plans for the future of Independent Television should now be embodied in legislation. Although some of Pilkington's proposals had been rejected, many had survived, and the original Television Act of 1954 (which was due to expire after ten years in 1964) needed to be replaced. The two White Papers of 1962 clearly showed that the Government considered the powers of the Authority to need strengthening in a number of important respects.

The Bill embodying all these changes was debated in both Houses of Parliament in February and March. Under its provisions the life of the Authority was to be extended until 1976 and the programme contracts, which were due to end in 1964, were to be replaced with new franchises whose duration was not to exceed six years.

As far as advertising was concerned, the Authority was to assume a 'more formal and direct control' over this aspect of the service. The medical consultants who had hitherto advised the ITCA were to become a formal Medical Advisory Panel responsible to the Authority. Their advice was to become mandatory while the Advertising Advisory Committee was to be strengthened by the inclusion of representatives of the public as consumers. The Chairman of the AAC was no longer to be allowed to have any interest, financial or otherwise, in the advertising business as such. There would therefore in future no longer be scope for the appointment of a distinguished figure from the world of advertising, such as Robert Bevan, to guide the work of the AAC.

Advertising magazines were not explicitly referred to in the Bill, the Postmaster-General having banned them with effect from 31 March 1963, but the Second Schedule included two clauses designed to prevent their being revived at some future date:

2   Successive advertisements must be recognisably separate.
3   Advertisements must not be presented in such a way that any separate advertisement appears to be part of a continuous feature.

Finally, Television Advertisement Duty was to be replaced by a major change in programme company rentals to a two-part system of charges, the first of which would more accurately reflect the profitability of each ITV area. The second stage of the rental, designed to provide 'additional payments' to the Exchequer, would be applied as a direct charge on 'net advertising receipts' in excess of £1,500,000. The scale of levy would rise progressively to a maximum of 45 per cent on an annual advertising turnover of £7,500,000 or more.

The Authority announces its plans

During the summer Lord Hill of Luton, the former Postmaster-General, was appointed Chairman of the Authority in succession to Sir Ivone Kirkpatrick who had been seriously ill since 1962. The Authority announced its plans for the important interim phase in the development of Independent Television from 1964 to 1967 during which the introduction of 625-line UHF transmissions was to take place.

The Authority wisely decided that there should be no change in the pattern of the franchise areas during a period of upheaval, and on 20 September advertisements for the new contracts appeared in the national press. Altogether twenty-two applications were received, eight from entirely new groups, including one from Beaverbrook Newspapers which had waged a continuous vendetta against Independent Television since the very beginning. The particulars of each contract which were sent to applicants contained for the first time details of the new and much increased ITA rentals, and although ATV at first threatened to refuse to complete its application unless the financial provisions of its contract were altered, all existing companies were reappointed, subject to certain conditions, in January 1964.

Advertising revenue and the Television Bureau

During 1963 the programme companies still showed great reluctance to disclose their actual advertising revenue figures and the critics of Independent Television continued to quote the Media Records assessment which was published every month on the basis of daily monitored reports. As in the early years of the medium when, as has already been seen, Media Records regularly overestimated ITV income by anything up to 50 per cent, these inflated figures continued to be published throughout 1963.

In September however the contractors decided to supply their total net revenues on a confidential basis every month to the accountants, Deloitte's, who would in turn issue an aggregate figure (but not for publication) to each company, which could then calculate its percentage share of total ITV income. When the year ended, the discrepancy revealed between the Media Records estimate and the true revenue was even bigger than had been suspected: Independent Television had actually obtained just under £63,000,000 in the year, while Media Records put the total at over £107,500,000– an overestimate of more than 70 per cent. Yet two years earlier Harold Wilson had claimed in the House of Commons that ITV was already taking over £80,000,000 in advertising revenue and was costing more to run than the BBC. With the forthcoming introduction of the new Treasury levy, based on annual net advertising receipts and payable every month, it seemed that the publication of actual revenue figures by the network could not be long delayed.

In the light of the new increased rentals and the award of a second television service to the BBC, a number of programme companies saw the need for a central bureau to promote television advertising to the business community; in March 1963 a working party of sales directors had been established for the purpose. ITV had plainly become a successful medium but its revenue had been exaggerated and three major advertisers, Unilever, Proctor and Gamble, and Beecham's, still provided a quarter of its total income. A significant loss of business had occurred when advertising magazines had disappeared, and it looked as if cigarette advertising would soon be banned. There was still confusion, too, among potential advertisers about the identity of the various programme contractors. All too often 'ATV' was identified with 'ITV', and film production was surrounded with a certain amount of mystique and the belief among non-television users that costs were prohibitive for all except the largest advertisers.

Those ITV sales directors who visited the United States in the early sixties found the original enterprising spirit of the British contractors had begun to stagnate in comparison with the vitality of the US networks. On the strength of their findings three companies – ATV, TWW and Southern – joined the American Television Bureau and found its confident and forceful approach to new business infectious and stimulating. Its President, Norman ('Pete') Cash, visited a number of ITV sales departments in London to persuade others to join, and, although some of the contractors considered that American methods could not be applied in the more conservative British market, the feeling was growing that a collective approach to the promotion of the sale of airtime in Britain could only benefit all companies. But it was to be another two years before a British Bureau of Television Advertising was formed and, in the meanwhile, no other companies decided to join the American TVB.

1964

TWW absorbs Wales West and North

Mention has already been made of the financial problems facing some of the smaller ITV contractors and it had been known for some time that Wales West and North was trading at a substantial loss. On 1 January 1964 the company was absorbed by its larger neighbour, TWW, which increased its advertising rates by 20 per cent to take account of the additional coverage it had gained.

Cigarette advertising: the US Surgeon-General's report

During the same month cigarette advertising once again became the subject of controversy with the publication of the report of the Surgeon-General of the United States on smoking and health. Its conclusions amplified the findings of the Royal College of Physicians two years earlier and the ITA again decided to refer the continuation of this form of advertising on television to the AAC.

At the outset the majority of members declared themselves in favour of a complete ban being imposed at once but the Authority pointed out that such a drastic step was properly a matter for Government action. The Committee was reminded that Independent Television already operated a series of strict rules on the content and timing of all tobacco advertisements. And it had to be remembered that the children and young people in the audience, whom these restrictions were designed to protect, were constantly exposed to the promotion of cigarettes in every other advertising medium. It was questionable, therefore, whether a ban on one form of advertising – however powerful – would actually result in any appreciable benefit to the nation's health. The Committee accordingly decided to await further Government action.

The Television Act, 1964

In March the 1963 Television Act was consolidated, with those parts of the original 1954 legislation that had been retained, as the Television Act, 1964. Under its provisions the Authority's *Principles for Television Advertising*, which had formed the basis of advertising control since 1955, were replaced by the more comprehensive *Independent Television Code of Advertising Standards and Practice*. In future it would be the statutory duty of the Authority to 'secure compliance' with the new rules.

A number of practical steps were needed, however, to put the new system of control into operation. A new body, the Joint Advertisement Control Committee (JACC), was formed to meet six times a year under the chairmanship of the ITA's Head of Advertising Control, whose membership was drawn from the Authority's advertising control staff, the ITCA and the Copy Committee. Arrangements were made for the Authority to receive the advice of the medical and other consultants and to take part in the daily closed-circuit preview and discussion of all new commercials. At the same time the Advertising Sub-committee of the Standing Consultative Committee, which had hitherto acted as the principal forum for discussion of advertising issues between the ITA and the programme companies, ceased to exist.

When the new programme contracts came into force on 30 July, all the proposals for the strengthened control of television advertising which Parliament had accepted had been embodied in legislation, and the new system which had emerged was fully operational.

The coming of BBC2

Neither the programme companies nor their advertisers were unduly concerned about the initial effect of the second BBC channel on ITV's share of audience. The Corporation had embarked on an explanatory campaign in 1963, using two appealing cartoon kangaroos, Hullabaloo and Custard, to symbolize BBC1 and its offspring, BBC2, and the manufacturers and retail trade had for over a year been vigorously promoting the sale and rental of dual-standard (VHF/UHF) receivers. But the public remained cautious and confused. As far as viewers were concerned, it seemed pointless to lay out large sums of money to receive an extra channel which might remain out of reach for several years.

The practical difficulties for the broadcasters of establishing the new service proved formidable. In the first place extensive engineering work needed to be done at the transmitters to provide the 625-line UHF service. For reasons of cost it was decided that this could be done only in stages, starting with the London station (Crystal Palace) on 20 April, the Midlands (Sutton Coldfield) on 6 December and the transmitters in Wales (Wenvoe) and Lancashire (Winter Hill) the following year.

The limited broadcasting hours of the new service, the numerous areas of poor or non-existent reception and the minority appeal of many of the BBC2 programmes all helped to make the growth of UHF coverage a painfully slow process. It was not until the introduction of colour on the main channels of BBC1 and ITV in 1969, following the duplication of both in black-and-white UHF, that the old VHF services began their rapid rundown. But the changeover was to present the programme companies with complex problems of coverage and audience measurement for the next twenty years.

Audience research

TAM was again appointed the official supplier of the audience-measurement service by the Joint Industry Committee for Television Advertising Research (JICTAR), which had now replaced TARAC and undertook to provide the data for three years, to coincide with the length of the programme company franchises, at a cost of £475,000 a year for the basic service.

Advertising rates and the ending of TAD

With the replacement of Television Advertisement Duty by the Exchequer levy, all companies made increases in their advertising rates roughly equivalent to the former TAD. The new rate cards came into operation on varying dates between 3 August (Granada) and 1 December (Southern).

Associated-Rediffusion changed its name to Rediffusion Television. Patrick Henry, ATV's Sales Director, resigned and was succeeded by two joint General Sales Managers, John Wardrop in London and Guy Spencer in the Midlands.

Publication of net revenue figures

In November the ITCA Advertisement Committee recommended that the confidential industry net revenue figures, which had been supplied to Deloitte's every month since September 1963, should be published at quarterly intervals. The annual figure for 1964 showed the industry total to be £74,433,162, a healthy increase of 18.3 per cent on 1963 but still far short of the £107,500,000 which Media Records had estimated a year earlier.

ITV and the Labour Government

Before the year ended a General Election had taken place. A Labour Government, with a narrow overall majority of five seats, had replaced the series of Conservative administrations which had been continuously in power since 1951 at the time when the Beveridge Committee, with one dissenting voice, had recommended against the setting up of any kind of commercial television system.

Life had not always been easy for Independent Television under the Conservatives. But the programme companies, and particularly their Sales Departments, had cause to remember the numerous attacks which had been made on many aspects of television advertising by Labour spokesmen since the service went on the air in 1955. And now one of the most articulate of these critics, Anthony Wedgwood Benn, had been given responsibility for broadcasting as Postmaster-General.

Yet ITV's popularity with the public seemed to guarantee that the whole structure would not be dismantled. At the same time it looked likely that political interference would increase rather than diminish and that further attacks, when they came, would be concentrated on the ways in which ITV obtained its revenue. The Sales Directors awaited developments under the new Government with interest tinged with a certain amount of apprehension.

1965

TCA extended to the major areas

The Television Consumer Audit, which had originally been introduced as a means of compensating the advertising agencies for the loss of commission resulting from the imposition of TAD, was now well established in the Midlands ITV area. But advertisers felt the need for similar information to be provided for the rest of the country, and to this end Audits of Great Britain had begun discussions with the four major contractors in 1964 with a view to extending the Audit to the remaining central areas.

In January ABC, ATV, Granada and Rediffusion held a well-attended presentation at the Hilton Hotel in London, at which the four major contractors and AGB announced the extension of the Television Consumer Audit to London and the North of England. The research reports for all three regions would be issued free of charge to advertisers who spent 75 per cent or more of their television appropriations with the programme companies operating in these areas.

This announcement was welcomed unreservedly by the several hundred advertisers and agencies who attended the presentation, especially when it was learned that more detailed special analyses of the data could be commissioned by advertisers for a comparatively small supplementary charge. The four programme companies themselves undertook to meet the £200,000 annual cost of the basic service, which would be provided by AGB.

The BBTA board formed

This was not the only concerted move made in 1965 to promote the use of television as an advertising medium. The discussions which had taken place among the programme companies during the previous three years to establish a central promotional body, and which had been suspended during the licence-application period, at last bore fruit. On 22 February the first board meeting of the British Bureau of Television

Advertising took place under the chairmanship of Anthony Jelly, Managing Director of Tyne Tees Television, who had been nominated by the ITCA Executive Countil.

The remainder of the board was made up of the sales directors of the four major contractors together with the sales heads of Southern, Grampian and Ulster Television. A sub-committee was formed to find a Managing Director who would be responsible for appointing the staff and setting up the company. It was planned that the Bureau's operations would begin by January 1966 at the latest.

The end of cigarette advertising

Discussions had been taking place for some months between the Ministry of Health and the Post Office about the desirability of banning cigarette advertising on television as the only medium already under statutory control. A ban in any other medium would have needed the enactment of special legislation.

Early in February the Minister of Health, Kenneth Robinson, said in reply to a question from Francis Noel-Baker in the House of Commons that he would shortly be asking the Postmaster-General to issue directions to the ITA, under Section 7 (5) of the Television Act, 1964, to bring cigarette advertising to an end 'when current contracts are completed'. Accordingly on 2 March Mr Benn told the Authority that all television advertising of cigarettes and hand-rolling tobacco must cease as from 1 August 1965. Cigars and pipe tobaccos, which had been more or less exonerated in the various reports on smoking and health, would be allowed to continue to appear on the screen.

When the ban was announced tobacco advertising formed the third largest revenue category on television; it was exceeded in financial terms only by washing products and confectionery. But the degree of dependence on cigarette advertising varied greatly by company – from 3 per cent to nearly 10 per cent of annual income. On the network as a whole its net value after all discounts amounted to £5,250,000 annually, or about 7 per cent of total ITV revenue.

Paul Adorian, Managing Director of Rediffusion and Chairman at the time of the Executive Council of the ITCA, said:

Bearing in mind that cigarette advertising on Independent Television is limited to times after 9 pm and that the style and content are subject to strict control, to say the least we are surprised that action by the Government to reduce cigarette smoking should be by singling out one medium of advertising rather than by tackling the matter at its source.

On the manufacturers' side Ronald Plumley, Chairman of Carreras-Rothman and a member of the Tobacco Advisory Council, said:

I believe that the restriction on advertising, either by law or the exertion of pressures, directed against the products of one industry introduces an unfair and potentially dangerous principle of discrimination in the relations of Government and industry in Britain.

But when the Minister of Health was asked from his own side of the House whether the Government's measures would be likely to cause redundancy in the tobacco industry, he replied: 'I rather doubt whether the intensification of the campaign [against smoking] will result in any sudden or dramatic drop in cigarette consumption.'

The Minister's forecast proved correct. There was no marked reduction in the smoking habit in the years immediately following the television advertising ban. But the manufacturers soon discovered that, without the immediate impact of television the launch of new brands, including those of low-tar content, became a good deal more difficult. Soon, as evidence of the harmful effects of cigarette smoking steadily mounted, they were to find pressures increasing for restrictions to be applied to their advertising in other media.

Changes in the Advertising Advisory Committee

In April the Advertising Advisory Committee received a report from the Consumer Council alleging that nineteen current television advertisements – all in the medical field – were in breach of the new Code. After an exhaustive examination by the Committee and the consultants, however, the original decision to accept all these commercials was upheld. But in view of the rejection of their complaints the Director of the Consumer Council, Dame Elizabeth Ackroyd, felt that she had no alternative but to resign from the Committee.

Having completed his four-year term of office, Sir Daniel Jack, the AAC's Chairman, retired and was succeeded by Sam Howard, former Chairman of ICI Pharmaceuticals.

The choice of a colour system

In December the Postmaster-General announced that the German Phase Alternation Line (PAL) system would be used for the transmission of colour television when it was introduced in Britain, in preference to the American NTSC and French SECAM which had been tested alongside it by the Television Advisory Committee.

1966

The BBTA begins operations

In January 1966 the British Bureau of Television Advertising began operations under its newly appointed Managing Director, Nigel Rogers. He had for many years been the widely respected Media Director of the advertising agency S.H. Benson, which had recently merged with Mather and Crowther to form Ogilvy, Benson and Mather (later Ogilvy and Mather). The Bureau was established in the same building as the ITCA at Knighton House in Mortimer Street, London, and among the first members of staff to be appointed were Tim Pepper, who had been a Marketing Manager at TWW, and Dorothy Moncrieff, who came from the British Film Institute. The Bureau staff eventually grew to eleven.

Colour date announced for BBC2

In March the Postmaster-General announced the starting date of the colour service on BBC2 as being 'towards the end of 1967'. To the disappointment of the contractors there were apparently no plans for the introduction of colour on BBC1 and ITV, and the possibility of there being a second channel for Independent Television seemed more remote than ever.

The March Election

At the end of the month the Labour Government, which had been handicapped by its slender margin of seats over the other parties, was returned to power with a convincing overall majority of ninety-seven in the second General Election in less than two years. Edward Short (later Lord Glenamara) was appointed Postmaster-General in succession to Tony Benn, who was transferred by Harold Wilson, to the new Ministry of Technology.

One of the most urgent problems facing the Government was the menace of rising inflation, and on 20 July the Prime Minister introduced a complete six-months' 'freeze' on incomes, prices and dividends, to be followed by a similar-length period of 'severe economic restraint'.

One television company, Anglia, had already announced a rate increase of 12.5 per cent which it had intended to put into effect in the autumn. In the light of the Prime Minister's announcement, however, reinforced a month later by the statutory powers which the Government had assumed under the Prices and Incomes Act, Anglia had no alternative but to withdraw its new rate card. The remainder of the companies decided that they would have to leave their rates unchanged at least until the end of the year. Granada however went further and announced that even when the 'freeze' had ended they would make no immediate rate increase.

The future shape of Independent Television

Meanwhile the Authority had extended the programme companies' contracts, which were due to expire in mid-1967, to July 1968, and just before Christmas announced that seven-day programme companies would thereafter be appointed everywhere except in London. The North of England, which had hitherto formed a single ITV region – 'Granadaland' – would be divided into the two separate areas of Lancashire and Yorkshire. As a result of these changes there would in future be fifteen companies operating in fourteen areas: one more of each than there had been before.

1966 had proved to be a difficult year for Independent Television. In comparison with 1965 revenue had increased by less than 3.5 per cent, at a time of rapidly rising costs, to a total of £85,825,169. In terms of the set count the landmark of fifteen million homes had been passed as long ago as March and numbers were still growing. But in a further White Paper issued by the Government in December the idea of a fourth service received another discouraging setback:

However it were allocated, a fourth television service would make large demands on resources. The three main services of television already provide a large volume of programmes of various kinds and the Government do not consider that another television service can be afforded a high place in the order of national priorities.

Moreover, before deploying the last frequencies certainly available for television for many years to come, the Government would need to be satisfied that the case for committing them to any new service had been fully established.

It was decided that the way in which the existing 405-line VHF services were to be converted to 625-line UHF would have to await the recommendations of the Postmaster-General's Television Advisory Committee.

1967

The year opened in a flurry of activity on several important fronts. BBC2 began transmission of the first of a number of major drama series to capture the public imagination – and, incidentally, the last of its type to be made in black-and-white. *The Forsyte Saga* was shown to an unusually large audience on the new UHF service and was swiftly repeated to over eighteen million viewers on BBC1. It began to look as if the competition which the ITV contractors had fully expected to face from two complementary BBC services was at last beginning to gather momentum.

The changeover to UHF

The Postmaster-General at last announced a decision on the method of changeover from VHF to UHF. It was decided, on the advice of the TAC, that BBC and ITV would share the same Ultra High Frequency transmitter sites, and that the well-tried but obsolescent 405-line VHF service would be phased out by duplicating transmissions in black-and-white on 625 lines in UHF. It was hoped that as a result colour would be made available on both the new UHF services within three years.

This announcement cleared the air, at least as far as the manufacture and sale of television receivers were concerned. Once the primary services of BBC1 and ITV were duplicated in the Ultra High frequencies, the need for dual-standard reception capability would disappear and the trade could concentrate on making and selling UHF-only sets. But even if the problems of the changeover were coming to an end in the television factories and showrooms, they were bound to increase on the ground in terms of audience measurement and definition of markets with the creation of two non-coincident areas of reception of each company's transmissions.

Within a fortnight of the PMG's announcement the Authority began to invite applications for the new programme contracts which were to run from 30 July 1968 for six years or 'the introduction anywhere in

the country of a second ITA service, whichever is the less'. All applicants were warned of the hazards of the duplicated service in Paragraph
11 of Part II of the contract particulars:

(ii) No guarantee can be given that, when the Authority starts to
broadcast on 625 lines in UHF the programmes which it is broadcasting
on 405 lines in VHF, the UHF area in which a contractor's programmes are
broadcast will coincide with the VHF area, nor can it, in the case of UHF
stations which cover the area of more than one contractor, be taken as
certain that the allocation of such stations to contractors in UHF will be
the same as corresponding stations for VHF, even though the stations occupy
the same sites.

The applicants were further disconcerted to discover that the
contract particulars only listed the proposed 405-line VHF stations for
each contract area (some of which still remained to be built), and
a disturbing qualification was added to the polar diagrams of each
transmitter's coverage:

The maps indicate 405-line coverage only, on the specified technical
standards, not the actual extent of viewing either of the contract station
or of outside stations overlapping parts of the contract area.

Finally, to provide an indication to the Authority of the ability of
each company to introduce UHF and colour broadcasts in its studios
and technical areas, two key questions were asked:

17   How far is the applicant at present 625-line and colour 'capable'?
What remains to be done to make complete arrangements for the
introduction of 625-line and colour broadcasting? How much would it cost?
18   From the date of a colour service beginning in the contract area(s)
for which the applicant is applying, how much colour programming would
the applicant originate, and to what extent, and at what speed would this
increase?

It was clear that a considerable amount of detailed engineering and
studio research would have to be rapidly undertaken by any group
hoping to obtain a licence from 1968 onwards, at a time when it
was impossible to forecast the period of recovery of the large-scale
investment which would be required. To make matters even more
complicated (because of the delayed decision over the UHF conversion
process) the Authority had been unable to announce the siting and
power of the UHF stations or any reliable timetable within the six-
year contract period when the new transmitters would be introduced.
It seemed that the entrance fee to the network for would-be contractors
would be formidable and several of the groups came to the conclusion

that colour advertising, when it was eventually introduced, would need to bear a heavy surcharge on the lines of the premium which was applied to colour space in the press. They could, however, draw some consolation from the reminder in the contract particulars that:

'The charges to be made for advertising time are a matter for the programme contractors, subject to the provisions of Paragraph 7 of Schedule 2 of the Television Act, 1964.'

Lord Hill announces the new contracts

If the plan for the start of the new contracts in July 1968 was to be followed perilously little time remained for the completion of applications. Yet by the closing date on 15 April no fewer than thirty-six had been received for the fifteen contracts. Interviews with all the applicant groups followed over the next two months, and on Sunday, 11 June, in the conference suite at 70 Brompton Road, the Chairman of the Authority, Lord Hill, made the momentous announcement of the award of the new licences.

Four new companies were to be appointed, two of them at the heart of the network in London. Thames, London Weekend Television and Harlech were to replace Rediffusion, ATV (in London) and TWW. Granada's five-day licence in the North was to be changed to a seven-day franchise in Lancashire and the immediate surrounding area and an entirely new group, the Yorkshire Television consortium, was to provide the service in the North of England east of the Pennines. In the Midlands ATV's weekday franchise was to be extended to include the weekends. With the exception of TWW, whose Chairman, Lord Derby, later refused the offer of a 40 per cent stake in the new Welsh company, Harlech Television, all the regional companies were to be reappointed.

Although the first half of 1967 had been dominated for the contractors by the nerve-racking ritual of the licence applications, a number of other developments were taking place simultaneously which were to have important consequences for their advertising revenue.

The Monopolies Commission report on soaps and detergents

In April the Monopolies Commission issued a detailed report on soaps and detergents, whose main advertising medium, since 1956 at least, had been television. It had been claimed that the high level of promotional activity in this field had increased the monopoly power of the two dominant protagonists, Unilever and Procter and Gamble, had effectively prevented entry into the market of smaller competitors, and had unnecessarily increased prices to the consumer. The two major manufacturers replied convincingly and in detail to all the charges which had been made, but the final report recommended that two brands should be launched (or at least relaunched) by each company with minimal advertising support. Wholesale prices should be reduced by 20 per cent and selling expenses, including advertising, should be cut by 40 per cent. The Government accepted the Commission's findings, which the manufacturers accepted under protest.

JICTAR *invites tenders for industry research*

On the audience research front, JICTAR signed a one-year contract extension with TAM at a reduced figure of £465,000 and announced that applications were invited for a new industry research contract for the six-year period of the new programme franchises starting in July 1968.

Control of television advertising rates

By 30 June the statutory period of 'severe economic restraint' had ended but the Government made it known that all proposals to increase television advertising rates would be referred to the Department of Economic Affairs, a clear indication that some form of price control would continue.

Colour begins on BBC2

It had been expected that the BBC would not begin colour transmissions until the autumn, but on Saturday, 1 July some seven hours of broadcasting took place in colour, mostly of the tennis championships from Wimbledon. Colour transmissions continued on a limited scale on BBC2 throughout the summer but by November, the original date intended for its introduction, some eleven hours of programmes a week were being broadcast in colour.

ITN *begins* News at Ten

On 3 July, to the accompaniment of some reservations from the programme companies, ITN introduced Britain's first half-hour television news programme, *News at Ten*, presented by Alastair Burnet and Andrew Gardner. ITN's operation, which had been highly praised by the Pilkington Committee, gained greatly in editorial scope and authority from this move, and once a regular and loyal audience for the new format had been established some of the companies were able to include the period between 10 and 10.30 pm within peaktime.

The centre commercial break in *News at Ten* became sought after by advertisers needing a selective audience, but the Authority supported the Editor-in-Chief of ITN, Sir Geoffrey Cox, when he asked that topical newspaper and magazine commercials should not be transmitted in the middle of the new programme. To have allowed publications with a topical content, often related to that of the day's news, to appear in this particular break could have blurred the distinction between advertising and editorial.

Lord Aylestone appointed ITA Chairman

Lord Hill had been Chairman of the ITA since July 1963, and the announcement of his appointment by the Prime Minister to the chairmanship of the BBC was greeted by all-round amazement and a certain amount of protest within the Corporation. Lord Aylestone, a former Labour Chief Whip and Lord President of the Council, was appointed Chairman of the Authority in his stead.

AGB gains the JICTAR contract

On 1 November JICTAR, replacing TAM after thirteen years, announced the appointment of AGB as the research contractor for the six-year period 1968–74. It was decided that there should be a period of parallel working by AGB and TAM in the months before the new contract began.

TCA extended to the first regional station

On the same date Southern Television joined the Management Committee of the Television Consumer Audit, and a panel of five hundred reporting households was set up in the South of England so that five-area reports could be produced by the TCA from 1 January 1968.

1968

1968 marked a watershed in the development of Independent Television. Even before the beginning of the new programme contracts in July, many features of the system which had become familiar since 1955 had disappeared.

When the year opened nearly sixteen million households were able to receive Independent Television, but many of the programme companies' staffs were already on the move to the new contractors, and projects of all kinds were having to be abandoned or transferred to successors. Three examples illustrate the many changes of direction which had to take place.

ABC Television, which had provided the ITV service at the weekends in the North and Midlands since 1956, had taken delivery of an IBM 360 series computer installation which it intended to operate in its London offices in Hanover Square to handle all its advertising bookings. But Rediffusion, ABC's partner in the new London weekday station (Thames Television) was already in the process of installing a Univac 1050 machine in Television House, Kingsway, which was to be Thames's first headquarters. ABC's computer and the accompanying software had to be sold back to the manufacturers.

Rediffusion, which had been responsible for the ever-popular *Double Your Money* and *Take Your Pick*, important parts of the weekday network schedule since 1955, had been told by the Authority at the time of the licence applications that these programmes would not be allowed to continue in the new contract period. Other programmes such as *The Life and Times of Lord Mountbatten*, work on which had started at Rediffusion, had to be transferred and completed by Thames in the form of one-hour instead of half-hour instalments.

In the meantime both the BBC and Independent Television faced the heavy capital outlay needed to finance transmissions in colour, and at the beginning of the year the Government authorized the first combined colour TV and radio licence which was established at £10. It was expected that the newly increased licence fee and the growth of colour reception would be sufficient to meet the foreseeable costs of the BBC.

Independent Television was, in comparison, at a distinct disadvantage. The Authority had made it clear to all applicants for the new licences that the studio costs of 625-line and colour origination in UHF would have to be borne entirely by the contractors themselves. In addition, the costs of the service at the transmitters, which the Authority intended to meet initially out of reserves, would be passed on to the companies in the form of increased rentals. But the timetable for the introduction of colour was now becoming clear and the ITA said that it hoped to bring the colour service to all regions provided a start was made in the main areas in the autumn of 1969. The programme companies began to work towards the latter date, in the hope that the Government's price controls would not prevent them from increasing their advertising rates to help meet the cost.

With the relaxation of statutory price controls in June the new Prices and Incomes Board (which had succeeded the previous Department of Economic Affairs) made television advertising rates the subject of an 'Early Warning' system which, because of the change of licences, affected the existing contractors but not the new companies. Yorkshire Television, for example, which issued its new rate card in April, had a temporary advantage over the adjacent areas of Tyne Tees and Anglia, whose licences had been renewed in their existing areas and whose old and new rates could therefore be compared. On the other hand, had the ITCA not accepted the 'Early Warning' system on behalf of all companies there was a danger that a prolonged investigation would have taken place through the PIB. As it was, the 'Early Warning' procedure was intended to last for two years, until March 1970.

The beginning of the new contracts

The new contract period for Independent Television began to the accompaniment of a series of problems, many of which were completely unforeseen. Within a few days of the start of the new service a major union dispute put the entire network, with the exception of Channel Television, off the air. An emergency service was mounted from ATV's small London studios in Foley Street, which were manned by non-union and management staff from all companies. Thames and London Weekend, under their Sales Directors George Cooper and Guy Paine, ran a temporary but effective seven-day network sales operation which charged £4000 for sixty seconds up to 7 pm and £7000 for the remainder of the evening but the revenue it produced, though valuable, was only a fraction of what had originally been estimated.

Although the dispute ended on 18 August the delay in forward programme production – which the strike brought to a complete stand-still – had serious consequences for the following autumn and winter schedules, quite apart from the immediate financial losses which occurred during the summer period. To make matters worse, the BBC chose the summer to launch a number of new programmes including *Dad's Army*, which soon proved popular. Meanwhile, a serious situation was developing in audience measurement.

There had been unavoidable delays in installing the new Setmeters, with which AGB replaced TAMmeters, and the increased sample of reporting homes seemed to be behaving quite differently from those on the old TAM panels. It was obvious, too, that viewers greatly missed the regular appearance on Independent Television of *Double Your Money* and *Take Your Pick* – two programmes which the ITA particularly deplored. By September ITV's share of audience was down to less than 50 per cent in the London, Scotland, Southern, Tyne Tees, Wales and West, Anglia and Westward areas. In October it dropped still further, and the BBC claimed that, when the figures for their two channels were combined, ITV's share of total viewing had fallen to a mere 40 per cent. The programme companies began to wonder whether the traditional channel preference which they had enjoyed had gone for ever.

An increase in broadcasting hours

John Stonehouse, who had been appointed Postmaster-General in the last few weeks of the old contract period, announced an increase in the amount of broadcasting time allowed for BBC1 and ITV of 180 hours a year, together with a further fifty hours of outside broadcasts to begin with the autumn programme schedules in late September. This now only served to intensify the contractors' problems.

Preparations for colour

Throughout the autumn the programme companies continued to complete their plans for the introduction of colour on ITV, the date of which was now only a year away. A joint working party was formed with the IPA to consider colour film and videotape standards and a strong case was made by the agencies for the gradual replacement of 35mm by 16mm for filmed commercials, with the sub-standard gauge being the only one to be used for colour from the date of its introduction. In the end, however, it was felt that a move towards 16mm would bring with it a loss of optical quality which most advertisers considered vital for clarity and product recognition on the screen. The more pressing problem was that of airtime rates and the extent to which they would bear a surcharge for colour.

The contractors considered three possible courses of action: first, to apply a surcharge of 5–10 per cent to existing advertising rates for the transmission of colour commercials, but to delay doing so until the level of colour reception reached an equivalent percentage of homes in the area concerned. As an alternative some thought was given to the imposition of a handling charge which would be applied to all colour commercials – regardless of reception capability – as soon as their transmission began. Finally, an increasing body of opinion in the programme companies favoured embodying the cost of colour in all airtime rates, without attempting to reflect the enhanced value to the advertiser of the new dimension which would be given by colour to both programmes and commercials.

In the end it was this latter view which prevailed and in January 1969, at an important seminar on colour advertising held by the BBTA for 830 delegates at the Royal Garden Hotel in Kensington, the following cautiously worded statement was issued:

> The BBTA cannot speak for individual programme companies but we understand that – in the initial stages of the availability of colour – programme companies do not expect to operate any additional airtime charge for the use of colour.

The financial results for 1968

Despite the arrival on the scene of the new contractors in the summer, and a penetration of ITV into 90 per cent of all homes by the end of the year. the revenue figure of £100,000,000 proved as elusive as ever. The two-week interruption of the service in August had, as has been seen, affected the production of many forthcoming programmes. It was impossible to calculate whether ITV's apparent serious loss of viewers in the late summer and autumn was traceable to changes in the audience measurement system or to a genuine resurgence of competition from the BBC.

By any previous criterion, however, the financial results for the year were disappointing. The revenue of £98,758,770 showed an increase of only 7.8 per cent on the total for 1967, and this at a time when greater investment was required from the companies in programmes and capital equipment than at any time since 1955. There were already signs that the Exchequer levy, which was still based on turnover, was proving an insensitive regulator of profitability.

1969

When the BBTA seminar, *Colour '69*, took place in January little more than 1 per cent (170,000) of ITV-receiving homes were equipped with colour receivers. The plans to introduce the service at the transmitters were, however, well advanced and it was hoped that, unlike the phased launch of BBC2 in UHF five years earlier, the ITV colour service would be in operation by the end of the year in the London, Midlands, Lancashire, Yorkshire, Scottish and Southern areas. The plan was to launch colour simultaneously in the four central areas on Saturday, 15 November – the same date as colour was introduced on BBC1.

But the plan involved the biggest technical change ever to take place in broadcasting history when, on the night of 7–8 September, scores of line-standards converters were moved from the ITV studios to the transmitters to enable the existing programmes to be broadcast in 625-line UHF under the elaborate duplication process which had already been agreed. The changeover proved smooth and uneventful and viewers who continued to receive ITV programmes on the older single-standard sets were unaware that any change had taken place. Once this hazardous operation had been completed the way was clear to launch trade test transmissions in colour three weeks later. When high-quality colour pictures were received in dealers' showrooms throughout the London, Midland and Northern areas, it was obvious that the initial trials had been an outstanding success.

The beginnings of demand-led rates

In February the programme companies decided to publish advertising revenue figures for the ITV network on a monthly, rather than a quarterly, basis and thereby provided agencies with the essential means of assessing the relative strength of demand for airtime every month on a station-by-station basis. Admittedly, each company's exact share of total ITV revenue was still largely unknown at this stage, but most experienced time buyers were able to calculate the proportion each station had obtained by comparing the turnover figures shown in a number of contractors' annual reports with the monthly industry revenue totals.

Once obtained, this information could be used to give an indication of the extent to which discounted airtime was likely to be available. A station with a consistently high share of network revenue was unlikely to offer many concessions. On one with a low share – relative to its coverage – bargains could usually be obtained by persistent negotiation.

But, in general, television rate cards in 1969 were still based on the conventional structure of time segments, which had been devised in 1955 and in which the charges payable by advertisers were based on the twin factors of audience delivery and demand. The two were, incidentally, usually unrelated. Indeed, a number of stations with consistently high ratings invariably obtained a disappointing share of national revenue. Carried to its logical conclusion, this argument might suggest that by scheduling a few more unpopular programmes a company would automatically increase its share of network revenue. But this presupposed that most advertisers planned their television campaigns so as to achieve an equal number of 'impacts' (measured in rating points) in each area, and overlooked the importance of marketing factors such as above-average levels of employment, personal expenditure, home ownership and other indications of affluence. It was hardly surprising that companies with low ratings, or in areas where the viewers seemed to prefer the programmes of the BBC, laid greater stress on the value of the market they covered than on the viewing habits of their audience.

Computer-based sales

By 1969 a number of programme companies had turned to computers to process much of their sales information. The installations for the purpose, whether in-house or operated by an external bureau, were initially used to produce advance transmission schedules, sales statistics, invoices and financial data in a 'batch' mode. As has already been mentioned these systems replaced the former visible charting systems which had to be manually maintained and updated. Similar installations were being introduced in the agencies to produce orders, campaign schedules and statements for dispatch to clients.

On 7 March 1969, however, Southern Television announced the first on-line real-time computer service to process advertising bookings. Its introduction was not without its problems. Sales executives and their assistants took some time to become familiar with the new procedures to handle options, bookings and cancellations, but it rapidly became clear that the speed and capacity of more advanced machines would alter the whole basis on which airtime was bought and sold. The visual-display unit gradually became the sole source of information on airtime availability for the sales groups in companies which introduced real-time data processing in the 1970s.

Surcharges, discounts and pre-empt rates

Thus, by the end of the sixties, three seemingly unrelated factors had combined to set the scene for the introduction of sales methods which were to dominate advertising on Independent Television for the next fifteen years. They were, first, the disclosure of monthly revenue figures from which each company's strengths and weaknesses, in sales terms, could be calculated by the buyer of airtime; secondly, the continuation of Government-inspired price controls, whether statutory or voluntary, which prevented rates from being increased fully to reflect the level of demand; and thirdly, the advent of real-time computer systems which alone could cope with a constantly changing price structure. All three factors, when seen against the background of a fixed supply of airtime which was governed by limited hours of broadcasting, and therefore could not be expanded, led to the introduction of the controversial 'pre-empt' rate structures which were eventually to be adopted by all the ITV companies.

In 1968 the new London weekday contractor, Thames Television, had introduced the first 'pre-empt' rate card in which discounts and surcharges could be applied to all rates according to demand. The percentages of both were set at three levels – 10, 20 and 30 per cent above and below 'standard' rates – and it was made clear in the rate card that a spot booked at any level up to the so-called 'superfix' surcharge of 30 per cent could be displaced by a booking at a higher rate. Thus, both buyer and seller had to estimate in advance the likely level of demand in order to calculate the price required for the airtime with the breaks in the most popular programmes commanding the full F3 (+30 per cent) surcharge. Conversely an increasing level of discount enabled the programme company to claim wider discretion in the slotting of bookings at less than 'standard' rates. In a typical early 'pre-empt' rate card a 10 per cent discount would be applied to run-of-week bookings, 20 per cent for run-of-month and 30 per cent for run-of-campaign. The payment of the various surcharges entitled the agency to select a particular commercial break subject to possible pre-emption, save in the case of the maximum rate.

Collapse of the mast at Emley Moor

On 19 March the Authority's 1265-foot tubular-steel aerial mast at the Emley Moor transmitter, at the time the tallest in Europe, collapsed because of storm-force winds and the weight of ice which had accumulated on the cables supporting the structure. As a result Yorkshire Television lost nearly all its coverage only nine months after the company had gone on the air. A temporary VHF aerial was put up in a matter of days to provide a service for Sheffield and the surrounding area but it was several weeks before it was possible to provide a more powerful signal for the remainder of the region, using a much larger mast which had to be brought in sections from Sweden and re-erected on the site.

The revised Advertising Code issued

In April the Authority issued the second edition of the *Independent Television Code of Advertising Standards and Practice*. It embodied references to three important pieces of legislation which had become law in 1968 – the Trade Descriptions Act, the Medicines Act, and the Children (Performers) Regulations.

Airtime rates and price control

By May the ITV network was once more in severe financial difficulties. IBA rentals had been increased in April, and the addition and replacement of equipment for the introduction of colour in the autumn were proving even more costly than had been estimated. Those contractors who had been on the air before 1968 had been unable to increase their rates for over two years and the majority felt that if a price increase were impossible because of continued Government controls the ITA should be asked for an extension of the hourly advertising allowance from 7 to 7½ minutes between 6 and 11 pm every day. But the Authority did not find it possible to agree to this proposal.

It was clear from discussions with the Director of Broadcasting at the Post Office, however, that companies which could show a significant increase in their coverage and operating costs might be allowed scope to increase their rates. Under the 'Early Warning' procedure, applications to do so had to be submitted via the Post Office to the Department of Employment and Productivity and the submissions which were made during the remainder of the year eventually enabled limited rate increases to take place early in 1970.

The Ministry of Posts and Telecommunications

On 1 October the Post Office became a public corporation. The Postmaster-General, John Stonehouse, was made Minister of Posts and Telecommunications with continued responsibility for broadcasting.

The cost of problems with copy

The strengthened system for the control of the content of television advertising which had been introduced in 1964 was expected to have a serious impact on ITV revenue, especially if similar restrictions did not apply in other media. But one major campaign was rejected in 1969 very largely on the basis of the original rules in the 1954 Television Act. The decision to do so involved the proposal to advertise *The Bible Today* which was to be published every week in partwork form. It seemed to the ITCA Copy Committee that acceptance would be difficult, in view of the fact that some years earlier the ITA had been advised by their lawyers that advertising for the *New English Bible* would be unacceptable on television in the light of the clause in the Television Act which expressly forbade any advertising 'directed towards a religious end'. *The Bible Today* had to be rejected for the same reason – a decision which cost the network some £1,000,000 in lost advertising revenue.

Modifications, resulting in further losses, also had to be made in the claims for margarines whose ingredients were high in polyunsaturated fats. This was because of the lack of unanimity at the time in the medical profession about the connection between the consumption of animal fats and the incidence of cardio-vascular diseases. The members of the Medical Advisory Panel ruled that no reference to polyunsaturates could be allowed in television commercials, a decision which was not reflected in the advice received by the CAP Committee. As a result, advertising for margarines which contained specific or implied health claims was transferred to the press.

A number of advertisers, too, were beginning to feature BBC programmes, characters and themes in their commercials, and ITCA issued the first of a series of warnings to agencies and advertisers to the effect that TV advertisements based on well-known BBC series would not be permitted, for the understandable reason that publicity thereby given to programmes on the Corporation's channels would be likely to damage ITV ratings and therefore harm advertisers. But the application of this rule led to additional losses of revenue.

Colour on ITV at last

On Saturday, 15 November the ITV colour service opened as planned in London, the Midlands, Lancashire and Yorkshire, and on 13 December was extended to Central Scotland and the South of England. The ITA was confident that, now that a start had been made, the coverage of the colour service could be completed in the rest of Britain before the end of 1972.

But the appeal of the new service was not great enough to offset the reverses in advertising revenue which were continuing to take place. In December the ITV companies collectively obtained £1,000,000 less in advertising income than in December 1968, and the final twelve-month total showed a reduction of 1.2 per cent on the figure for the previous year.

1970

The formation of STAGS and Trident

When the year began the financial problems of the network seemed no nearer solution. During 1970 the increasing costs of two separate sales departments led on 1 May to the formation of a joint company, Scottish Television and Grampian Sales (STAGS), to handle airtime sales for the two ITV contractors north of the Border.

A more fundamental amalgamation took place in the north of England because of the decision to reallocate a powerful new UHF transmitter, at Bilsdale in the North Riding, to Tyne Tees rather than to Yorkshire Television as had originally been intended. It was expected that when the new transmitter went on the air early in 1971 the effective coverage of Yorkshire Television would be considerably reduced and, in the light of the already difficult revenue situation, a joint management company, Trident Television, was formed which would provide a number of facilities, including a joint sales department, for both companies.

The PIB investigation

The troubled finances of the industry as a whole were once more to be subjected to scrutiny as a result of the Government's decision in March to ask the National Board for Prices and Incomes (the PIB) to examine the costs and revenues of Independent Television, excluding the operation of the Exchequer levy.

Reduction of the levy

It had already been recognized that the levy had been one of the principal factors in creating the deepening financial crises which faced the ITV companies, and on 1 April the majority of the scales of payment were modified to reduce the burden to the network as a whole by £6,000,000 a year.

ORKNEY

SHETLAND

The Independent Television Network
1985

Inverness
● Aberdeen

NORTH SCOTLAND

SKYE

Ft.William

MULL

Dundee
Perth ●

CENTRAL SCOTLAND
● GLASGOW
● Paisley
EDINBURGH

Hawick ●

Londonderry

ULSTER
BELFAST ●

ISLE OF MAN

Dumfries ● **BORDER** NEWCASTLE

Carlisle ● S.Shields
SUNDERLAND

NORTH-EAST
Darlington ● Hartlepool
MIDDLESBROUGH

Scarborough ●

● Douglas

Barrow-in-Furness

York ●

Blackpool ● BRADFORD HULL
● Preston LEEDS
NORTH-WEST ● Huddersfield
Bolton ● ● Oldham **YORKSHIRE** Grimsby ●
LIVERPOOL ● MANCHESTER
Birkenhead ● SHEFFIELD Lincoln ●
ColwynBay Chester ● Chesterfield
STOKE-ON-TRENT
DERBY ● ● NOTTINGHAM Cromer ●

Peterborough ● Norwich ●

WOLVERHAMPTON ●
Dudley ● Walsall ● LEICESTER
BIRMINGHAM ● COVENTRY **EAST OF ENGLAND**
EAST & WEST MIDLANDS ● Cambridge

Northampton ● Ipswich ●
Milton Keynes

WALES & THE WEST Gloucester ● Luton Colchester ●
Swansea ● Oxford ● Harlow
● Rhondda Basildon
CARDIFF ● Newport Swindon ● **LONDON** ●
BRISTOL Reading ● Slough Southend-on-sea ●
Basingstoke ● Guildford Margate ●
Maidstone
SOUTH & SOUTH-EAST Dover ●
SOUTHAMPTON
Exeter ● Havant Brighton
Bournemouth ● PORTSMOUTH Hastings ●
SOUTH-WEST Poole ●
PLYMOUTH ● Weymouth
Torquay

Isles of Scilly

CHANNEL ISLANDS

© BARB 1985

i

Cadbury's Smash 'Martians' (Boase Massimi Pollitt).

Heineken 'Electric Tennis' (Collett Dickenson Pearce).

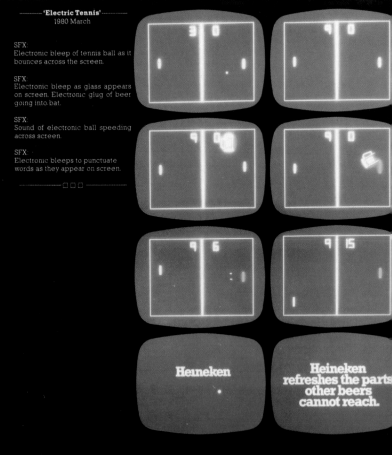

'Electric Tennis'
1980 March

SFX:
Electronic bleep of tennis ball as it bounces across the screen.

SFX:
Electronic bleep as glass appears on screen. Electronic glug of beer going into bat.

SFX:
Sound of electronic ball speeding across screen.

SFX:
Electronic bleeps to punctuate words as they appear on screen.

□ □ □

Heineken

Heineken refreshes the parts other beers cannot reach.

Top: Babycham (Saatchi & Saatchi).

Parker Pens 'Finishing School' (Collett Dickenson Pearce).

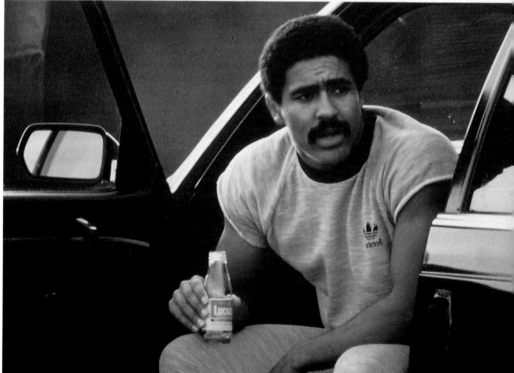

Top: Ribena (D'Arcy MacManus & Masius).

Lucozade Daley Thompson (Ogilvy & Mather).

Top: Fiat Strada 'The car made by robots' (Collett Dickenson Pearce).

Rowntree's Yorkie (J Walter Thompson).

Top: Brooke Bond PG Tips 1981 (Davidson Pearce).

Brooke Bond PG Tips 1957 (Davidson Pearce).

The development of a brand: *Cadbury's Milk Tray* 'And all because the lady loves Milk Tray' (Leo Burnett).

The development of a brand: *Cadbury's Flake* (Leo Burnett).

In April the colour-set count began to show a significant increase when the figure of 300,000 colour-receiving homes was reached. In the same month Harlech Television changed its name to HTV to avoid the impression of Welsh dominance in a company whose responsibilities covered the West of England as well as Wales itself.

The June General Election

In June the Labour Government, which had been in office since 1964, was replaced by a Conservative administration under Edward Heath with a majority over all other parties of thirty seats. Christopher Chataway was appointed Minister of Posts and Telecommunications, and it was decided that the forthcoming PIB Report which had been commissioned by the previous Government would, when completed, be addressed jointly to Robert Carr, the new Secretary of State for Employment, as well as to Mr Chataway. Any change in broadcasting policy would, it was felt, be likely to have implications for employment in a number of industries.

The definition of ITV areas

During July JICTAR issued a new map of the United Kingdom, using the definition of ITV areas which the BBTA had evolved in 1967 when the Bureau's first marketing manual had been produced in an attempt to remove some of the existing uncertainty as to the extent of each company's coverage. The area outlined on the BBTA maps followed the boundaries of Administrative Districts in order to simplify the task of advertisers in achieving product distribution to coincide with areas of television reception. This move had the effect of stabilizing a situation which was rapidly becoming even more complex.

In the early days of VHF transmissions, areas of reception had initially been defined by signal strength using a measurement of 250 μV/m (250 microvolts per metre). This line was later replaced by one drawn as a result of boundary and overlap surveys, commissioned from TAM or AGB, which defined areas of reception on the basis of whether 15 per cent or more of homes in the places surveyed were able to receive the signal of an identifiable ITV transmitter. This method, however, produced areas of considerable overlap between adjacent stations, a problem which was further magnified as a result of the programme of UHF station construction which began in the mid-1960s and was to continue for the next twenty years.

It must be explained that 98 per cent of the population could be covered satisfactorily in VHF with no more than forty-seven transmitters. To provide comparable coverage in UHF needed at least fifty main transmitters and 450 local relay stations, the sites for all of which had to be selected at suitable points stretching from the Channel Islands in the south to the northern limits of the network in the Shetlands. To meet the planned timetable of station building, a new transmitter was at one stage being added to the network every week.

Once the decision had been taken to transfer Britain's entire television broadcasting system from VHF to UHF by the duplication process the problems of overlap were bound to proliferate. As the UHF set count increased, the figure for VHF reception fell, and it was not unusual for a household to transfer its viewing from one ITV company to another if the UHF signal showed a noticeable improvement on previous VHF reception. Some homes were able to enjoy reception from two or even three sources. But again, in the initial stages of UHF a temporary signal strength line (of 70 decibels) was used to describe the limits of reliable reception until it could be replaced with the results of an official boundary and overlap survey.

The PIB inquiry

The National Board for Prices and Incomes became acutely aware of the problems of television coverage at an early stage of their investigation into the costs and revenues of Independent Television. Taking the JICTAR figures for January 1970, they noted that, while the total net coverage of ITV was 16,500,000 homes, the collective total for all companies was 17,710,000. But the total national overlap factor of nearly 7 per cent (equivalent to 1,210,000 homes) disguised the problems of individual companies, whose set counts were liable to contain 10 per cent or more of households already covered by another contractor.

Ignoring this difference between 'gross' and 'net' coverage, the PIB noted that there was a close correlation between the number of homes covered and a company's share of total ITV revenue. The figures they used are shown in the table opposite.

The PIB also noted the levelling off in television advertising which had occurred in the late 1960s – the result, it was claimed, of a loss of confidence among advertisers and agencies. In the year before the Report was published the press was seen to have improved its advertising revenue by 10 per cent, while revenue in television, which

Area	Company	Homes share %	Revenue share %
London	Thames	25.2	14.5 ⎱ 26.1
	LWT	25.2	11.6 ⎰
Midlands	ATV	15.5	13.6
Lancashire	Granada	14.7	12.7
Yorkshire	YTV	10.8	9.4
Southern England	Southern	7.3	8.1
Wales and the West Country	Harlech	7.3	7.0
Central Scotland	Scottish	7.0	6.4
North-east England	Tyne Tees	5.0	5.0
Eastern England	Anglia	6.8	4.6
South-west England	Westward	2.7	2.4
Northern Ireland	Ulster	1.8	2.0
English/Scottish Borders	Border	1.0	1.0

Programme companies shares of coverage and revenue 1970

Source: NBPI

continued to rely on the food, drink and tobacco industries for half its income, had remained more or less static. The increasing purchasing power of the major food retailers, who had not yet become large-scale television users in their own right, had forced many manufacturers into below-the-line activity – discounts, promotions and sales incentives of all kinds – largely at the expense of above-the-line advertising on television.

The PIB felt that the award of an additional commercial channel, whether it were run by the existing contractors or not, would only serve to exacerbate ITV's financial problems, but they saw possibilities in an increase of broadcasting hours which would be capable of attracting additional revenue without adding proportionately to operating costs. The regional system had clearly led to the creation of a certain amount of spare production capacity.

Finally, the PIB criticized the variable structure of television rate cards, overlooking the fact that ITV's pricing system had very largely been created in response to the numerous price controls which had been applied throughout most of the previous decade.

It is fashionable to dismiss the reports of Royal Commissions and Boards of Inquiry as a convenient method by which a Government can pacify its critics and avoid taking a radical course of action. Nowhere is this more true than in broadcasting circles, where it is widely believed that the findings of a succession of investigative bodies have invariably been ignored. Yet the truth is that, while a committee's central recommendation has often been rejected – as in the case of Beveridge, Pilkington and Annan – other equally important features of their reports which have received comparatively little publicity at the time have come to be adopted, almost by stealth, and have exercised a profound influence over the way in which the broadcast media have developed. And so it proved with the PIB Report of 1970, to which the ITV companies reacted with a good deal of indignation.

Their sales departments had been criticized for their unwillingness, or inability, to forecast revenue, for their lack of direction and formal training, and each company's over-concentration on its own market share rather than on the overriding need to enlarge the revenue of the whole industry. Yet at heart most contractors knew these criticisms to be well founded and over the next few years all were to take positive steps to develop those sides of their business which, they privately admitted, had been neglected.

Above all, the PIB clearly saw the need for stability in the industry, especially in the light of the upheavals which had followed the withdrawal of a number of licences in 1968. They said:

To bring this [stability] about we consider that the ITA should institute an early warning system for unsatisfactory performance; it should, over the life of the contract, give a contractor two warnings before deciding that a contract should not be renewed. Under such an arrangement any contractor falling below the standards held to be desirable, and thereby jeopardising his prospects of a renewed contract, would be informed and given the opportunity of correcting the situation. Correspondingly, a contractor not under warning would have a presumption that his franchise would be renewed.

Unfortunately, in referring the question of the costs and revenues of Independent Television to the National Board for Prices and Incomes the Government had specifically excluded the workings of the Authority from the terms of the inquiry.

Temporary withdrawal of 'pre-empt' rates

The discounted rates which all companies included in their charges to advertisers became known during the autumn as 'cost regulators', particularly among those agencies which prided themselves on their ability to buy airtime at below station average costs-per-thousand.

Following the criticism which had been made of the 'pre-empt' system by both the PIB and their customers, all ITV companies withdrew this form of offer from their rate cards and substituted 'early booking' discounts which were designed to ensure that as much business as possible was placed in advance. This helped to increase the level of sales over the Christmas period in what had been a difficult year.

Retirement of Sir Robert Fraser

In October Sir Robert Fraser, who had been Director-General of the ITA and the chief architect of Independent Television since 1954, retired at the age of sixty-six. He was succeeded by Brian Young, who had previously been Director of the Nuffield Foundation.

Changes at London Weekend

During November Arnold Weinstock resigned from the board of London Weekend Television and the shareholding of his company, GEC, was taken over by Rupert Murdoch who became a director of the company. The Advertisement Director of the *News of the World*, Bert Hardy, was appointed to take temporary charge of the sales side of London Weekend.

There had been many changes in the senior management of LWT since the resignation in September 1969 of Michael Peacock, who had been Managing Director, and the Programme Department Group Heads. These moves affected the Sales Department throughout 1970. Guy Paine, the company's original Sales Director, became Deputy Chief Executive under Dr Tom Margerison, and the Sales Department was run in turn by Peter Golsworthy and Desmond Pryor. By the end of the year all four had left the company.

1971

1971 was to prove a much more successful year for Independent Television than the troubled twelve months which had just ended.

End of pre-notification of rate increases

In January notification was received from the Minister of Posts and Telecommunications that, with the ending of price controls, no further advance notice of rate changes would be required by the Government. All companies announced sorely needed rate increases, to take effect in the spring. Thames Television, which in common with all other contractors had withdrawn 'pre-empt' rates six months earlier, reintroduced three pre-emptive scales and cancelled its early booking discount.

New licence fees for the BBC

The BBC, too, was able to strengthen its finances when on 1 February the Minister announced an increase in the colour licence fee from £10 to £12, and the abolition of the radio-only licence. The cost of black-and-white television reception was increased at the same time to £7.

Colour reception

By January the ITV set count had reached 16,860,000 homes, and colour receivers formed 4 per cent of the total. It is interesting to note that, if a surcharge had been applied to airtime rates for colour advertising on the basis of a 10 per cent colour penetration figure (as some of the contractors had suggested in 1968), a premium at this level would have produced no additional income for the network until 1972. With the advantage of hindsight it seemed clear that the decision to embody the cost of colour in the general level of advertising rates had been the right one despite the subsequent effect of Government price controls. This course of action had had another advantage: a colour premium would have discouraged advertisers – who were already facing steep increases in the cost of production of commercials in colour – from using the medium.

In fact, by the summer it was estimated that colour commercials formed no less than 85 per cent of all those transmitted on Independent Television. Agencies, production companies and not least the contractors themselves had successfully overcome the problems of providing an acceptable monochrome picture from a colour film or videotape, and it was confidently expected that over the next five years colour reception would reach over half the audience. In the interim, the manufacturers' own forecasts published by BREMA estimated that the number of colour receiving homes would have grown to 1,500,000 by the end of 1971, and 2,600,000 a year later.

Two new major transmitters opened

On 15 March the 500kW Bilsdale transmitter, carrying the programmes of Tyne Tees Television, came into operation, followed two months later by the equally powerful Belmont station, in Lincolnshire, providing the Anglia signal. Had it not been for the joint Trident operation with Tyne Tees, Yorkshire Television would have found itself encircled by the considerable encroachment from the companies to the north and south of its area.

That to the south, Anglia, the total number of whose ITV homes now exceeded that of any other regional company, was able to establish the East of England as a recognizable marketing area and had engaged Peter Battle from Southern Television, no stranger to the problems of overlap, as its Sales Manager under John Margetson.

Further changes at London Weekend

The major reorganization was completed at London Weekend Television when, on 8 March, John Freeman, formerly British Ambassador in Washington and High Commissioner in India, and a distinguished journalist and broadcaster, became Chairman of the company. Ron Miller, who had handed over to Peter Battle at Anglia, became Head of Sales and London Weekend's revenue steadily began to improve.

The CBI 'Initiative'

Before Parliament rose for the summer recess the Chancellor of the Exchequer, Anthony Barber, announced his plans to raise the growth

British Television Advertising

To: The President
Confederation of British Industry

UNDERTAKING

_____

1. We give this undertaking to the President of the Confederation of British Industry in respect of the twelve months ending 31st July 1972.

2. We undertake to do our utmost:
 (i) to avoid raising prices of products/services supplied in the United Kingdom;

 (ii) to limit any unavoidable increase in any of our prices to 5% and if possible less;

 (iii) where, in exceptional circumstances or for reasons beyond our control, a larger or earlier increase is imperative for a particular product/service, to limit the weighted average of price changes over the whole range of related products/services to 5%, and if possible less;

 (iv) to time any unavoidable price increase to be distant at least twelve months from any previous price increase; or if this is not possible at least eight months from any previous increase and at a maximum rate proportional to an annual rate of 5%.

3. This undertaking will be read in conjunction with the notes appended and in particular note (c).

4. If as the year proceeds we find that conditions beyond our control seriously impair our ability to adhere to this undertaking, we will notify the Director-General of the CBI and will discuss our difficulties with him or his officials before taking action.

Signed .... Date...

Company ....

The CBI 'Initiative'. The President of the CBI, Sir John Partridge, wrote to all members of the Confederation on 26 July 1971, inviting them to sign this undertaking not to increase prices by more than 5 per cent in the year ending 31 July 1972. The ITV companies received a similar approach through the Advertising Association

NOTES TO UNDERTAKING

(a) Although this undertaking is not conditional on any compact with the Trade Unions, we look to them for a positive response to it.

(b) The progress of the policy to which this undertaking relates will be reviewed not later than March 1972, and this review will take into account the growth of the economy and the trend of pay settlements.

(c) It has to be recognised that the cost of many imported items and much indigenous produce fluctuates, sometimes violently, according to market, climatic or other conditions that are beyond our control. Where such costs are a major proportion of total costs it is impossible to undertake not to reflect them in prices. This particularly applies to edible materials which are the basic commodity of food manufacturers, to various metals and other basic raw materials.

(d) The clauses of the foregoing undertaking cannot all have application in the cases of capital goods or operations of a "one-off" kind, or goods for which the cycle of manufacture and delivery greatly exceed the currency of this undertaking. Clauses 1, 2(i), 3 and 4 however apply and all such goods will be priced in accordance with the spirit of this policy.

(e) Changes in quantity or quality or product specification in the direction of either increased or reduced value will be regarded as relative price changes.

(f) Percentage limitations on price increases will be calculated on price excluding purchase tax or excise taxes that do not enter significantly into costs.

(g) Goods or services priced in currency denominations so small that the minimum price increase for individual items must exceed 5% are excluded from the limitations imposed by clause 2(ii) of the undertaking but, wherever the range of products allows, such price increases will be brought within the ambit of clause 2(iii).

(h) Price increases notified to customers before the date of commencement of the undertaking although becoming effective thereafter are excluded from the price limitation clauses of the undertaking.

rate of the Gross National Product to 4–4.5 per cent in the year ending July 1972 as part of a Government programme of reflation. Among the measures to be adopted were cuts in Purchase Tax, the abolition of hire purchase restrictions (both of which helped to stimulate the sale of television sets) and more generous capital allowances.

The Confederation of British Industry had noted with growing concern the way in which pay and prices had been leapfrogging each other in turn at a time when the profits of member companies were continuing to decline. The CBI felt that it was vital that, if the Chancellor's measures were to succeed, some form of self-imposed price control should be introduced. Accordingly, on 15 June the President of the CBI wrote to the two hundred largest member companies in the Confederation, strongly suggesting that industry in the private sector should take a lead. The response was encouraging, and a further letter from the President was sent to all members inviting them to sign a written undertaking that they would do their utmost to avoid making any price increase of more than 5 per cent during the year ending 31 July 1972. Inevitably these letters were received by a number of major television advertisers who were not slow to remind the contractors that in many highly competitive fields their TV budgets formed a significant part of their marketing expenditure. The question was asked: would the contractors, none of whom were members of the CBI, support the 'initiative' and so help to hold down costs?

The following month the television companies received a copy of the CBI's letter through the Advertising Association to which the ITCA belonged. But by the time this was received the companies had already published details of their autumn rate increases with pre-emptive discounts and surcharges. ATV announced however that it would continue to employ a non-pre-emptive system and would continue to maintain its conventional rate structure.

Plans for extra hours and ITV2

During the summer the ITCA continued to make plans for additional broadcasting hours (which had been recommended in the PIB report) through a working party specially appointed for the purpose. The unanimous view was that a programme schedule should be established of continuous transmissions from midday onwards rather than for isolated experiments to be made in the early morning.

Other working parties had been established within the ITA and among the companies to make plans for an additional commercial channel confidently designated as 'ITV2'. Meanwhile, a powerful campaign was being mounted by a group known as TV4, made up of independent producers, journalists, trade unionists and film makers.

The Authority's plans for ITV2

The Authority examined the three possibilities: a competitive service provided by new contractors under the ITA, a general service independent of both the Authority and the BBC, and a fourth specialized (possibly educational) channel. As a result the Authority came down heavily in favour of a complementary service being furnished by the existing contractors in their own areas under the ITA's general direction and control.

Many possible methods of selling the airtime were examined, some surprisingly close to the formula which was finally adopted ten years later for Channel Four.

On the programme side there was however a major difference between the ITV2 proposals and those which eventually came into being in 1982. In 1971 the Authority envisaged a joint Programme Planning Board being formed, under an ITA chairman, to ensure that the joint programme planning of both services was fully complementary. This they preferred to the idea of a separate company being created for the new channel, albeit with directors of the ITV1 companies on its board. The Authority sent its recommendations to the Minister of Posts and Telecommunications in December 1971.

Some other views on the fourth service

The ISBA made its official views known at an early stage of the TV4 debate and argued that in the first instance hours of broadcasting should be extended and the levy removed. The ISBA believed that, once these essential changes had been made, a competitive service could be set up by a new group of programme companies under either the existing Authority or a new public board. Some advertisers took the view however that each existing contractor should be given a second franchise in another part of the country in order to ensure competition in both sales and programming terms in every region.

Outside the advertising business a clamour of contradictory recommendations arose. Some claimed there was scarcely enough talent available to supply three television channels, let alone a fourth. Others argued in favour of greater 'accountability', 'open access', 'grass roots' television and the University of the Air. Peter Cadbury, Chairman of Westward Television, declared that the new service should be provided free to viewers, and carry no commercials so as not to harm the advertising revenue of the smaller contractors.

It was left to Brian Young, Director-General of the Authority, to remind the warring factions of the aims which had guided the ITA in its submission to the Minister:

The Authority's interest is solely that of improving the service, and it bases its proposal that there should be a second Independent Television channel upon the wider range of programming which could then be broadcast. ITV1 has had marked success in providing programmes that are attractive. An ITV2 would unquestionably enlarge the range available to the audience as a whole. It would also benefit sections of the total audience who have particular interests which cannot often be catered for, at least in peaktime, within the confines of a single service.

The Select Committee on Nationalized Industries.

Even before the Authority's ITV2 submission had been sent to the Minister, the Government announced that Sub-Committee 'B' of the all-party Select Committee on Nationalized Industries was to report on the workings of the Independent Television Authority. The ITA had not been investigated by the Prices and Incomes Board in 1970 when the costs and revenues of the programme companies were being studied. But inevitably, the SCNI was bound to cover old ground in that both inquiries had to examine the relationship between the companies and the Authority, and both had to take account of the essential part which advertising played in financing the cost of the service. The SCNI, whose report faithfully recorded the exchanges which took place between the members of the Committee and those who gave evidence to it between December 1971 and April 1972, proved to be the more thoroughgoing investigation.

ITV revenue exceeds £100,000,000

The final advertising revenue figures for the year showed the biggest annual percentage increase since 1964. Revenue had exceeded £100,000,000 for the first time and had surpassed the figure for 1970 by nearly 15 per cent.

1972

The decision on ITV2 postponed

The Minister gave the answer to the ITV2 proposals more quickly than the Authority and the programme companies had expected. Despite the strength of the arguments both had put forward in favour of the increased scope which would have been provided by a separate, complementary channel, a decision to set up an additional ITV service was indefinitely postponed in a statement issued by the Minister, Christopher Chataway, on 19 January. Instead, all restrictions on broadcasting hours were unexpectedly removed, and the hitherto mandatory religious 'closed period' on Sundays between 6 and 7.30 pm was abandoned.

The increase in broadcasting hours

Much work had already been done by the working parties which had been studying the various alternatives for extending broadcasting hours, but none had envisaged complete freedom being given to Independent Television after seventeen years of restrictions. In addition the Authority stipulated, after having made ambitious plans to include many serious special-interest programmes in the abortive ITV2 schedules, that at least 40 per cent of any increase in the existing service should be devoted to 'balance' material of an educational, informative or artistic nature. It seemed clear that if new material of this order (rather than a diet of feature films and repeats) was to be provided for the extra hours, the earliest date by which an extended schedule could be introduced would be the autumn. In the event the extra hours were not taken up until 16 October after existing daytime commitments to televise the Olympic Games, Party Conferences, the TUC Conference and mid-week golf had been discharged.

The crisis at the power stations

Early in January a series of labour disputes interrupted the electricity supply at the power stations. The ITCA wrote to all agencies promising that in the event of transmitter failures, or the more likely widespread breakdown of reception in the home, requests for compensation for lost advertising would be sympathetically considered.

The power crisis of 1972 formed a landmark in relations between the television companies and their customers. For the first time a joint Advertising Liaison Committee was formed by the ITCA, IPA and ISBA to consider requests for the postponement or cancellation of advertising, and this Committee continued to meet until the immediate problems had been overcome in March. By this date, however, there was a formidable backlog of unplaced advertising; the Authority there-fore authorized a temporary increase in the hourly advertising allow-ance, from 7 to 7½ minutes for a six-week period from 13 March to 30 April, provided the daily quota was not exceeded.

Cancellations and postponements

Even after the strike was over the problems of cancellations and post-ponement of advertising within eight weeks of transmission still remained, and during March the ITCA formed a permanent committee, under Ron Wordley, Sales Director of HTV, to deal with this conten-tious subject on a confidential basis. In theory, all requests for cancel-lations involving more than one programme company had to be referred to the Cancellation Committee and reasons given in writing to support the case. But the contractors did not always see cancellations in the same light. Some took the view that a booking was only accept-able, and therefore could only be cancelled, on a designated *product* basis. Other companies allowed bookings to be made in the name of an *advertiser*, thus enabling an agency to transfer a cancelled booking to another product from the same manufacturer. But this stratagem, it was argued, could lose the programme companies revenue, especially if the substitute was part of a campaign already destined for television at a later date. As usual, it was the most heavily demanded stations which insisted that the letter of the law should be obeyed and, by the time an answer to a request for cancellation had reached the advertiser via his agency, it often appeared that the ITV companies were behaving with dictatorial unconcern.

The problems of the advertiser were intensified when the Cancel-lation Committee asked for details of new product launches in terms of formulation, stock levels, distribution and the like in order to arrive at an informed decision. Information of this sort could be valuable to a competitor, and its disclosure – often with reluctance – led to a certain amount of bitterness in the relationship between the TV companies and their clients.

Eventually a number of the contractors introduced financial penalties for the cancellation of business at short notice and the Cancellation Committee disappeared. But the uneasy feeling remained that financial penalties might be circumvented just as easily as the cancellation rules.

A change of Minister

On 7 April Sir John Eden, Minister for Industry at the DTI, succeeded Christopher Chataway as Minister of Posts and Telecommunications, an appointment which was to last until the change of Government in March 1974 and the transfer soon afterwards of responsibility for broadcasting to the Home Office.

Formation of an overseas sales company

During June a number of the programme companies, led by Trident, announced the formation of a joint company under the title Central Independent Television Advertising Sales (CTS), to promote the sale of airtime on ITV to advertisers in Europe. The companies concerned were Trident (Yorkshire and Tyne Tees), Granada, STAGS (Scottish and Grampian) and the Midlands contractor, ATV. Offices were opened in London, Paris and Frankfurt.

Unlike the BBTA, to which all companies belonged and which had been limited to a predominantly research and informational role, CTS was required to perform a specific selling function on behalf of its members. There was no doubt that a great deal of business was to be gained from the rest of Europe. By 1972 every contractor had made a number of successful overseas sales visits, and all the ITV companies usually attended the annual conferences organized on the continent by *Admap*, the Association of British Travel Agencies (ABTA), the European Society for Opinion Surveys and Market Research (ESOMAR) and the Market Research Society.

In the same month as the formation of CTS Britain signed the Treaty of Accession to the EEC, with a view to full membership of the Community on 1 January 1973. It seemed that there could not have been a better time to launch a joint ITV sales operation.

CTS recorded a number of sales successes and undoubtedly paved the way for the whole network, as well as its own member stations, to gain business from European sources, particularly national export bodies and trade bureaux. But knowledge of the unique features of Independent Television was shaky and confused among the majority of European advertisers. Having patiently explained the relationship of the fifteen programme companies with one another and with the Authority, the sales staff of CTS had to admit that a number of important ITV stations, including both those in London, were outside their remit. This either added to the confusion in Europe or stimulated sales of airtime on behalf of non-members.

The challenge of new business

During the summer of 1972 the programme companies continued to examine new sources of revenue. The BBTA had built up considerable resources in terms of research material, including a comprehensive library of films and videotapes, and was making regular presentations in a number of fields – retail stores, the automotive trade, fashion and finance. But its efforts, thorough and professional though they were, were inhibited by the terms of reference it had been given. The member companies were reluctant to give the Bureau a specific selling role, believing that a disproportionate amount of business would be channelled into a limited number of companies, especially if the advertiser concerned decided to select a single test marketing area. The BBTA itself found it invidious to recommend one ITV area at the expense of another, and the feeling among the companies was that the Bureau was better employed in publishing its excellent marketing manuals, bulletins and occasional papers – the latter dealing with individual product fields – on behalf of the whole network.

Despite the apparent monopoly in airtime sales enjoyed by every contractor – except in London – the competition between the companies for new business was intense. Each sales director found himself devoting an increasing proportion of his department's budget to commissioning research surveys and marketing manuals for his own area. In some cases special New Business groups were formed by individual contractors, while in others each sales group was given precise new business targets in addition to its ongoing responsibilities for revenue from existing sources. There was bound to be some duplication of effort in the process but the general belief was that the more new business activity was seen to take place the better.

But budgets for the purpose were clearly not inexhaustible and, if a choice had to be made between expenditure on BBTA and an additional outlay on a company's own sales effort, the latter – which was capable of producing immediate results in revenue terms – usually won. The outcome for Nigel Rogers and his colleagues was bound to be discouraging, especially when it was remembered that the original cost of the Bureau had been set at £250,000, a figure which, in the event, the companies had not been prepared to meet. The total annual cost of the BBTA never exceeded £160,000 and it was felt that the division of the Bureau's costs, strictly in relation to Net Advertising Receipts After Levy (the so-called NARAL formula), worked in favour of the smaller companies. A major contractor with, say, a 14 per cent NARAL share of revenue would have to contribute over £22,000 to the Bureau, while a small station could derive a disproportionate benefit for less than £4000 a year. Its methods of funding and ambiguous terms of reference eventually combined to bring about the demise of the BBTA in 1974. But for the time being the pursuit of new business continued through the efforts of both the Bureau and of the individual companies.

Mail order and direct-response advertising

Inevitably, one of the untapped fields to which the contractors turned their attention was that of mail order – not yet known by its more respectable-sounding title of direct marketing. The figures showed that this category of advertising had been worth £12,575,000 to all media in 1971 but that only £400,000 (or 3.1 per cent) of the total had been spent on television.

Direct-response advertising was not without its risks. As well as a high degree of advertising activity, this field of business had been marked by no fewer than twenty major bankruptcies in 1971, and every newspaper and magazine was able to quote examples of shoddy merchandise and long delays in delivery of products which readers had ordered and paid for. If Independent Television was to enter this area, extensive safeguards would have to be provided and methods of ordering devised which were both knave- and foolproof. It seemed that the answer was for the programme companies to employ a facilities house to which stocks of goods and cash could be entrusted, and to launch the scheme only when an adequate protective system was in place.

ITA becomes the IBA

On 12 July the Independent Television Authority was made responsible for Independent Local Radio in addition to ITV. Its name was accordingly changed to the Independent Broadcasting Authority (IBA).

Report of the SCNI issued

On 27 September the Select Committee on Nationalized Industries, which had been appointed in November 1971 to examine the workings of the Authority, published its report. Its advertising recommendations were brief and to the point:

1   The provisions of the Act concerning natural breaks should be more strictly observed, particularly in feature films and the longer documentary programmes.

2   Provision should be made to broadcast official health and safety announcements in peaktime and the Authority should discuss the means of doing so with the Central Office of Information.

3   The Authority should initiate networked discussion programmes in which the consumer associations could test products and answer the claims of advertisers.

4   The Authority should consider 'bunching' advertisements in blocks of up to thirty minutes in the same way as Switzerland, Italy, West Germany and Holland.

Even more important was the recommendation that no fourth channel should be allocated until a wide-ranging examination had taken place into the whole future of broadcasting – a recommendation which was to lead to the appointment of the Annan Committee.

The programme companies, particularly those who had given evidence to the Select Committee, felt that yet another official inquiry had failed to grasp some of the basic features of Independent Television. This view was shared by the IPA and the ISBA, and it was decided to put forward a joint paper to the Minister, Sir John Eden. A working party for all three bodies was formed under the chairmanship of Brian Henry, Marketing and Sales Director of Southern Television. The SCNI's more extensive comments on programming and relations between the companies and the Authority were prepared by a small working party of the ITCA Council consisting of Ward Thomas and Peter Paine (Trident) and Aubrey Buxton (Anglia).

The advertising working party pointed out that nowhere did the Act define 'natural breaks', that the selection of 'advertising intervals' was invariably the responsibility of a senior programming (rather than a sales) executive among the ITV companies, and that the number and duration of breaks had in any case been steadily reduced since 1955. As for the Central Office of Information (CoI) films, it was pointed out that airtime to the value of £20,000,000 had been given to the Government since 1955 without charge to the taxpayer. If, on the other hand, there were evidence of a paid-for campaign in other media, there was no reason why time on the air should be made available for nothing.

The working party noted that some members of the SCNI had visited the United States in the course of the inquiry and had been impressed by the so-called 'fairness doctrine' of the Federal Communications Commission, the essence of which was that the broadcaster should make an equivalent amount of airtime available to answer an advertiser's claim. But this was very different from allowing the consumer associations to discuss advertisers' claims on the air. The representatives of the ITCA, IPA and ISBA felt that products were best tested (and reported on) in print, and drew attention to the fact that the Government had just decided to appoint a Minister for Consumer Affairs who was probably in a much better position than the broadcasters to make a decision on the most effective means of protecting the shopper.

The proposal for the block system of advertising provoked the greatest discussion and the longest reply. Briefly summarized, the following points were made. First, the Committee had overlooked the fact that those countries who used the thirty-minute block system all relied on obtaining a share of licence income in addition to advertising revenue. Secondly, thirty unbroken minutes of commercials a night could only accommodate one-third of the current amount of advertising on ITV. Finally, the need for other sources of finance would inevitably lead to an intolerable increase in the licence fee, not to mention the problems of trying to satisfy the demands of advertisers after the loss of two-thirds of the advertising allowance. The working party's paper ended:

We find it very difficult to understand why the Select Committee has recommended the creation of a half-hour advertising period which is likely to prove as intimidating to the viewer as it would be unattractive to the advertiser. We believe, moreover, that the Committee's recommendation contains one of the many fallacies in the Report in the assumption that it is advertising, as an integral part of the programmes, which has led to the drive for maximal audiences. The BBC with both its services – especially BBC1 – has for many years broadcast competitively against ITV despite the fact that it carries no advertising on any of its channels. The pressure of competition is now such that the Corporation frequently obtains more than 50 per cent of the total viewing audience and this is achieved by a combination of ruthless cross-promotion, by publicising BBC [television] programmes on radio, by contriving simultaneous programme junctions on BBC1 and 2 and, above all, by the employment of every available skill and resource of programme production to achieve the maximum level of audience.

The Minister seemed to be more impressed with these arguments than with the recommendations of the Select Committee, though it is only fair to add that two of the SCNI's recommendations were to reappear in the report of the Annan Committee. But they fared no better in 1977 than they had done in 1972.

Sir Hugh Greene's Granada lecture

On 16 October a large audience assembled in Guildhall to hear Sir Hugh Greene, the BBC's Director-General in the period of revolutionary change in the Corporation from 1960 to 1969, deliver the Granada Lecture on *The Future of Broadcasting in Britain*. Some of his conclusions were as surprising to the senior ITV executives in the audience as they were to his former colleagues.

He paid a generous tribute to the quality of many ITV programmes, mentioning several by name, and dwelt at some length on the demoralizing effect on all who worked in the medium of the numerous inquiries which had been commissioned by successive Governments to examine every aspect of broadcasting. But he singled out one report in particular for unstinted praise:

What gave me a certain amount of malicious pleasure is that the Pilkington Report, so much derided by many Conservatives on its appearance, is now regarded as being, what it always was, the most important piece of work on the purposes of broadcasting which has appeared in this or any other country.

He went on, to the increasing astonishment of his listeners, to declare that in his view the case for the fourth channel being given to Independent Television had been soundly made, provided the Authority were to sell the airtime and plan the programmes exactly as Pilkington had recommended.

Turning to the subject of audience research, he urged that consideration should be given to the setting up of a joint system of audience measurement for BBC and ITV on the lines adopted some years later under the joint Broadcasters' Audience Research Board (BARB). But one aspect of audience research in Independent Television seemed to trouble him unduly:

The influence of TAPE, Mike Firman's Television Audience Programme Evaluation system, which claims to be able to forecast how many people are going to watch each and every programme, 'has increased, is increasing and ought to be diminished'. I use the words of the Dunning motion on the personal power of George III. There is a danger that TAPE might influence programming more than the IBA. Such mechanical methods of judging programme values are bound to have a bad influence on quality and militate against enterprise and experiment.

No one connected with Independent Television expected Mike Firman, the Managing Time Buyer of the advertising agency Masius Wynne-Williams and long regarded as the scourge of media salesmen, to be indicted within the historic walls of Guildhall by a former Director-General of the BBC, or that he would be compared with the demented monarch who had supposedly lost the American colonies.

The TAPE research

The TAPE service had begun innocently enough as a by-product of Mike Firman's encyclopaedic knowledge of cinema films in terms of their box-office record and the popularity (or reverse) of their settings, plot, stars and other ingredients, to each of which he gave a numerical value. This information had been carefully amassed in the Media Department of Masius Wynne-Williams for several years and, when suitably refined, enabled a Predicted Audience Rating (known as a PAR score) to be arrived at. There was no doubt that the TAPE method could usually predict the size of audience of any feature film against known opposition, though it was less reliable in forecasting the popularity of one-off live programmes. But the TAPE research was bought and used by a number of the programme companies as a guide, at least, to effective programme scheduling.

There was, however, some substance in Sir Hugh's criticism of TAPE, more especially as it was known to be closely allied with the media-planning side of a major advertising agency. A few years later the TAPE service was divorced from the Masius Wynne-Williams operation, and Mike Firman formed a separate company which eventually expanded its service to North America and Australia.

Publication of a new IBA Code

At the end of October the Authority published a new advertising Code to embody the rules which were to apply in future to radio as well as television. But at the same time a number of other changes were made, arising from the mass of case law which had developed since the previous edition.

In particular the rules to prevent an appearance of sponsorship being created by identifying advertisements with certain programmes were strengthened. The term 'news flash' was disallowed, ITV programme characters and settings could not be used in commercials, and great care would in future have to be taken not to connect an advertisement with a televised sponsored event. Private investigation agencies were added to the list of prohibited classes of advertising until such time as the Government had introduced a system of licensing for such organizations.

1972 in retrospect

The year had shown a considerable increase in ITV advertising revenue to £134,161,914, an improvement of 23.4 per cent on the figure for the previous year. But the CBI 'initiative' had ended in July and once again prices of all goods and services were beginning to advance steadily as the signs of inflation began to reappear. On 6 November the Government imposed a compulsory ninety-day 'freeze' on prices, pay, rent and dividends.

It had been a year of decision for Independent Television. Sir Hugh Greene had urged in his Guildhall speech that long-term plans for the future of broadcasting should be made for the period up to 1985 and it was becoming clear that a more comprehensive inquiry than those of the PIB and the SCNI was needed to plan the way forward, as the members of both bodies had recognized.

The year had also seen the passing of two pioneers of Independent Television – both, as it happened, from the same company, ATV. In September the deaths occurred of Richard Meyer and Val Parnell, both of whom had been closely concerned with the setting up and successful development of one of the two original programme companies.

1973

By 1 January 1973 Independent Television coverage had grown to 93 per cent of all the homes in Britain and the set count had reached 17,191,000. The coverage of colour, after four years of rapid growth, now exceeded three million homes.

ORACLE announced

In April the IBA, which had carried out much successful research and development work into digital transmission systems, initially for international line-standards conversion, announced the advent of an important new secondary broadcasting system. The normal 625-line UHF picture contained a number of field-blanking lines whose use had hitherto been confined to the transmission and reception of test signals for engineering purposes. But two of these lines could be used to carry much more complex additional information in the form of a full-screen multicoloured display which could be received on a domestic television set once it had been equipped with the necessary decoder. Plainly this development, which became known as ORACLE (Optional Reception of Announcements by Coded Line Electronics), had enormous possibilities for carrying continuously updated news and information. The BBC, too, had been working along parallel lines and the following year announced CEEFAX ('see facts'), which used similar digital techniques. Meanwhile the programme companies began to consider the possibilities of using ORACLE for the transmission of topical advertising.

More problems of coverage

The history of Independent Television since 1955 and the various official inquiries which had taken place into the workings of the service had clearly illustrated the importance of carefully planned signal coverage to the wellbeing of the system. By 1973 the regional framework, which had had to be adapted to the complexities of the conversion to UHF, still broadly followed the pattern which Kenneth Clark and Robert Fraser had devised in the mid-fifties.

Yet, as we have seen from the periodical effects of recession, the system had to depend in the final analysis on the economic survival of every company in terms of its ability to attract advertising revenue to a recognizable marketing area. Roughly two-thirds of ITV's income was obtained by the five central contractors in London, the Midlands, Lancashire and Yorkshire. That left the remaining third (amounting to about £50,000,000 in 1973–4) to be divided unequally among ten companies whose size, in terms of coverage (excluding the smallest of all, Channel) varied from 175,000 homes (Border) to Southern Television with ten times that number. And, as the PIB had pointed out, there was always a close correlation between a company's coverage and its advertising income.

Experience showed that many advertisers would redeploy their television expenditure in a time of recession in a way which could penalize the smaller ITV companies, especially if the areas on the fringes of the network contributed only marginally to the sales of their products. It was not unusual for an advertiser to cancel or reduce the weight of his campaign in the five smallest areas if the major contractors made a steep increase in their advertising rates at short notice.

The key factors in determining the true extent of each contractor's marketing area were the choice of sites for transmitters and the way in which each was allocated to a particular company's service. Some examples will make the social and marketing problems clear.

Many of the sites on the west coast of Scotland north of the Clyde, including the medium-power 20kW transmitter at Torosay on the Isle of Mull which fed a number of relay stations, were allocated to Scottish Television rather than to Grampian because of the difficulty of establishing a reliable signal path from one of the latter's other transmitters. Thus viewers in the Oban area received a service which was primarily designed for the Forth/Clyde valley rather than the more appropriate programmes radiating from Aberdeen and intended for the Highlands and Islands. In terms of marketing, this transmitter allocation meant that products advertised on STV needed to be distributed on the west coast as well as in the Central Scotland area if viewers and retailers were not to be alienated.

Further south, the Cumbria and Lake District area was divided. The northern part was serviced by Border Television from Carlisle, while Kendal and the Furness peninsula, usually regarded as an integral part of the Cumbrian area, received their signal from Manchester.

But these were minor marketing problems compared with those which occurred around the Yorkshire area. The allocation of the powerful Bilsdale transmitter to Tyne Tees had led to the formation of Trident Television, as a result of which the majority of the advertising carried by the company was booked to appear on Tyne Tees as well as on Yorkshire. But some campaigns still remained which advertisers wished to confine to a single area, and within JICTAR there was incessant pressure on Trident to agree to a boundary survey to establish the limits of coverage of Bilsdale. It was known that the Tyne Tees signal from this transmitter could be received in Harrogate, York and even Hull, but how did the homes in these places divide their viewing loyalty? If, on the other hand, the campaign were booked to appear on Trident as a whole, then it seemed advisable for the products advertised to be distributed as far north as the Scottish border. But this stimulus of consumer demand in the remote parts of the area could lead to resistance from the retail multiples, who were growing in importance and beginning to dictate the choice of media to manufacturers.

During the sixties and early seventies few of the major multiples had been prepared to gear the distribution of products which were advertised on television to those of their branches which fell within the coverage of the ITV companies which a manufacturer had selected for his campaign. The television regions seldom coincided with the geographical structure of the retail groups or with the delivery radius of their own transport. Indeed, their depots and warehouses were sometimes located outside the boundaries of the television area (or areas) in which many of the retail outlets they served were located.

The store groups themselves did not become major television advertisers in their own right until the late seventies. But when they did so their patterns of product distribution began to come into line with the ITV areas which the majority of manufacturers had adopted for sales purposes some twenty years earlier. As a result, the marketing departments of the major multiples began to make use of TCA and Nielsen TV area data which had originally been designed to meet the needs of manufacturers.

Every ITV company faced similar problems of definition of the markets it covered. If the overlap battle was lost, the consequences could be measured not merely in terms of viewership but in actual revenue if, as often happened, the advertiser concerned employed marketing criteria in apportioning his advertising expenditure between contractors.

The Committee on Broadcasting Coverage appointed

On 4 May the Minister of Posts and Telecommunications appointed a committee, under the chairmanship of a distinguished former diplomat, Sir Stewart Crawford, to consider the whole question of broadcasting coverage. Submissions were invited from interested parties who wished to make a case for improved coverage or for the transfer of their service from one signal source to another. The Committee on Broadcasting Coverage began to address itself to some of the complex social problems of television reception which have been described earlier.

ITV2: the Authority's further submission

In July the IBA made a further submission to the Minister in the light of a number of suggestions which had been put to it since the original plans for ITV2 had been drawn up at the end of 1971. The arguments in favour of a complementary (rather than a competitive) service were developed, and the Authority pointed out that minority or specialized programmes deserved to be shown at times of maximum audience availability – in other words, in peak, rather than in off-peak, time. But scheduling along these lines would only be possible if two or more channels under a joint programme-planning system were allocated to Independent Television.

The Authority saw, too, the scope for additional programmes being supplied to ITV2 by the regional companies and outside producers, somewhat on the lines suggested by those who had argued in favour of a National Television Foundation with a separate channel of its own.

Responding to the IPA and ISBA, who had urged that the new channel should not be handed over to the existing contractors, the Authority emphasized:

It should be clear, however, from all the Authority has said that, in proposing ITV2 it is not seeking to see the existing programme companies made more powerful or more prosperous. Neither of these ends is in any event likely to occur. The degree of coordination required in a two-channel service, and the Authority's consequent proposal for a Programme Planning Board, would lead to a development of the Authority's role and to a system in which it played a larger part in planning the networked part of the output.

The Authority apparently believed that the opposition of advertisers to their proposals for ITV2 arose solely from the high profitability of the existing programme companies. Their submission continued in the same vein:

So far as prosperity is concerned, the allocation of the fourth channel to ITV2 is likely to bring no greater financial profit to the existing programme companies than would either its allocation elsewhere (except perhaps for a predominantly popular purpose) or a decision not to allocate it to anyone. If the existing programme companies had to provide programmes for a second service, their financial surpluses would be reduced, in spite of increased advertising revenue, both by their additional programme expenditure and by the additional rental which the Authority would need for additional transmitter development. It is in any event now an established feature of the ITV system that Government has the powers to appropriate sums over and above a reasonable return on capital arising from the operation of the public franchises which television contracts represent.

There had, it is true, been objections over the years from advertisers and agencies to the large profits some contractors had made, but most critics also recognized the high level of investment required from shareholders and the risks of non-renewal of short-term contracts. The real worry among advertisers arose from the prospect of an extension of monopoly if the sale of airtime on the new channel were to remain in the hands of the existing companies – an argument which did not strike the IBA with full force until the finalization of plans for Channel Four in 1980.

The ITCA proposals

The Authority's ITV2 proposals to the Minister were followed by those from the companies. These envisaged the formation of a separate company, the shareholdings in which would be held by the contractors, and a complementary programme service being provided on the lines proposed by the IBA but with a major guaranteed quota of material coming from outside independent producers.

The ITCA declared that:

A complementary (but not competitive) fourth channel is unlikely to be self-financing. It would be subsidised by the ITV companies; directly from ITV1 and ITV2 advertisement revenue, and indirectly, from surplus studio production resources.

The effects of the fuel crisis

The last quarter of the year was dominated by the consequences of the deepening fuel crisis. On 6 October fighting had again broken out between Egypt and Israel, and ten days later the Arab oil producers announced a major cut in all oil supplies until Israel withdrew from the occupied territories. At home Phase III of the Government's counter-inflation policy began and, because of the compulsory pay restraints which it imposed, the National Union of Mineworkers declared a ban on all overtime working.

There followed a series of emergency fuel-saving measures which had an immediate impact on Independent Television. In December all television transmissions closed down on alternate evenings at 10.20 and 10.30 pm, a 50 mph speed limit was introduced and, on New Year's Eve, a three-day working week began which was to last until 8 February 1974.

As a result of the Government's control of prices, the turn-of-the-year rates on all ITV stations were the same as those for the previous year and yet, despite all these problems, revenue for the year as a whole showed an increase of nearly 20 per cent on the figures for 1972. Indeed, the companies estimated that in the final quarter of 1973 as much as £10,000,000 worth of advertising business had failed to be accommodated because of the pressure of demand.

1974

The purchase of the James Bond films

On 7 January the ITV network announced the purchase for £850,000 of six James Bond films which had already earned £20,000,000 at the box office in Britain alone. One cinema owner described the sale as 'not only killing the golden goose, but also auctioning off the eggs' and it seemed clear that when films such as *Dr No* and *From Russia with Love* were eventually scheduled they would enjoy exceptionally large television audiences.

AGB reappointed

AGB was reappointed on 19 January by JICTAR to continue to supply the industry research service for a further three years, to the end of July 1977. For the first time BBC2 data was to be included in the weekly reports, in view of the fact that coverage of the BBC's second channel had reached 90 per cent of all ITV homes.

Industrial disputes and the General Election

The industrial action which had begun with the NUM had now spread to ASLEF and the power workers. It seemed that the Conservative Government could no longer survive after a ballot among the mineworkers had revealed 81 per cent in favour of strike action. On 10 February a complete stoppage of coal production took place, followed less than three weeks later by a General Election and the resignation of Edward Heath. A minority Labour Government took office and Britain returned to a five-day week. Anthony Wedgwood Benn was once more made responsible for broadcasting as Minister of Posts and Telecommunications in Harold Wilson's second Labour administration.

The consequences of the widespread industrial disputes continued to affect the advertising revenue of Independent Television long after normal broadcasting hours were resumed on 8 February. In addition to the non-production of many goods which were normally nationally advertised, for several months there were acute shortages of tinplate, glass, paper, board and plastics for packaging, which affected many other products. A number of advertising campaigns, in particular those for gas and electricity, were cancelled completely. Many new product launches were abandoned and the joint liaison committee of the ITCA, IPA and ISBA was re-formed to deal with an unprecedented series of cancellations which affected all companies. The financial situation became so bad that one contractor, Channel Television, warned that it might be forced to close.

In its Budget on 26 March the Government announced severe credit restrictions and increases in income tax. It was plain that 1974 was going to be an exceptionally difficult year for all advertising media.

The Home Office and broadcasting: the Annan Inquiry

Tony Wedgwood Benn's reappointment as Minister of Posts and Tele-communications proved short-lived. On 29 March responsibility for broadcasting matters was transferred to the Home Office under Roy Jenkins, and a fortnight later the Home Secretary announced that Lord Annan (who had been nominated earlier to head a similar inquiry which had been abandoned at the time of the 1970 Election) would become Chairman of a committee 'to consider the future of the broadcasting services in the United Kingdom . . . and to propose what constitutional, organisational and financial arrangements and what conditions should apply to the conduct of all these services'.

The IBA Act, 1974

The financial crisis of 1974 only served to emphasize the insensitivity of the Exchequer levy which had been applied to each company's advertising turnover, regardless of profitability, since July 1964. On 23 May the Independent Broadcasting Act became law, changing the future basis of calculation of the levy from one on revenue to one on profits.

The new system came into operation a month later and the Act made clear that for levy purposes profits were to be determined by the deduction of 'relevant expenditure' from 'relevant income', two phrases which were later to prove somewhat ambiguous. But the Government's intentions were clear enough; to exact 'additional payments' from two-thirds of all profits arising from a contractor's television activities, exempting only a small 'free slice'. Diversification into other fields suddenly began to look attractive.

The IBA's plans for 1976–79

In April the Government announced that the life of both the Independent Broadcasting Authority and the BBC would be extended from 1976 to 1979. With the removal of at least some of the uncertainty surrounding the future of the medium, the IBA was able to outline its plans for this three-year period.

No change was contemplated in the regional structure of Independent Television, despite the talk of mergers in the 1960s. On the contrary, it was felt that some companies, notably HTV and Southern, might well, given the possibilities of local coverage in UHF, be able to provide more in the way of different programmes for the separate parts of their areas. But the IBA did not consider that the additional advertising revenue generated in this way would be sufficient to meet the cost of a full dual service. There might also be scope for minor changes in transmitter allocation between companies, but this would have to await the recommendations of the Committee on Broadcasting Coverage (the Crawford Committee).

In conclusion the Authority considered that the companies' existing franchises should be extended to 1979 rather than be readvertised, subject only to a detailed review of each contractor's performance taking place in 1974–75. Thereafter it was felt that a good case had been made for contracts being awarded on a 'rolling' basis, provided means could be found to avoid them ending simultaneously.

The Belmont transmitter reallocated

At the end of July the Belmont transmitter, which had carried the Anglia programmes in UHF since 1971, was transferred to Yorkshire Television, and the ITV set count and boundaries of both areas underwent considerable changes. The reallocation of Belmont reduced the amount of geographical overlap between the Trident and Anglia areas, but not without causing considerable protest from viewers in Lincolnshire and around the Wash who had grown accustomed to receiving local programmes from Norwich.

But the Authority had decided, on the basis of the needs of the majority served by the Belmont transmitter, that Yorkshire Television was likely to provide the more appropriate service. The area known as the East of England, which had stretched almost as far north as Scarborough, was reduced to a region confined mainly to East Anglia.

Price control and advertising rates

In 1973 the previous Government had established the Price Commission under Sir Arthur Cockfield as an important part of its machinery for controlling inflation and the Commission continued to operate under the new Labour administration. It was made clear that the prices of goods and services could only be increased on the basis of rises in 'allowable costs' in a predetermined period for a given unit of output.

But in the case of television, which made one product – programmes – and sold another – airtime – it proved difficult to decide exactly how 'units of output' should be measured. Unlike almost all other industries, where production costs were directly related to output, it was self-evident that television programme costs had little to do with the size of audience offered to advertisers. Indeed, some of the more expensive programmes were transmitted to relatively small numbers of viewers in extreme off-peak time.

After some deliberation, the Price Commission finally agreed that it would be satisfied to accept cost increases which had occurred between 30 April 1973 and 15 July 1974 if they were set against each £100 of advertising revenue obtained in the same period. The results were revealing: costs in some companies were shown as having risen by as much as 30 per cent, with an average for the industry as a whole of around 20 per cent. These cost increases formed the basis of new rate cards which were issued during the summer to take effect in most cases in mid-September. The amounts by which rates were increased, however, varied widely between stations from 9 per cent to as much as the full 30 per cent.

The programme companies hoped that the rate increases in the second half of the year would produce signs of recovery from the financial setbacks which had beset Independent Television, especially during the period of industrial unrest during the first quarter.

Closure of the BBTA and CTS

Much remained to be done to regain sales revenue for the network. During the summer a short but effective campaign devised by the BBTA to promote television advertising had taken place on the air. But already a number of the larger programme companies were beginning to question the cost-effectiveness of the Bureau in the light of their own financial contributions which, on a share of revenue basis, could amount to £20,000 a year or more for a major contractor.

During October it was finally decided to close the Bureau as far as its active promotional role was concerned and to maintain a small revenue-forecasting and information service under the management of the ITCA. In the same month those companies which had pooled their European activities under CTS decided to close down their sales operation on the continent.

As far as the BBTA was concerned it could look back on a record of considerable achievement in its eight years of existence. It had given 1350 presentations, many of which resulted in business and all of which created interest and publicity for the medium. Its maps and manuals had become the accepted standard for marketing purposes, and its case histories and bulletins were cited by other media, particularly the national press, as examples of the most effective way to establish the right climate for effective selling.

But it was the smaller contractors who missed the Bureau most keenly. They had come to rely on the BBTA to supply a wide range of research and charting facilities which, unlike the larger companies, they could not afford to provide for themselves.

But the view was gaining ground that more revenue would be produced for Independent Television if the companies acted competitively and were seen to be doing so. After nearly twenty years the need for education in the use of the medium seemed to have diminished, and the power and effectiveness of television were universally acknowledged in almost every field.

Retirement of Archie Graham and Laurence Parker

October marked the end of an era with the retirement of two Scotsmen, both of whom had made a notable contribution to the success of Independent Television. Archie Graham retired as the Authority's Head of Advertising Control, to be succeeded by Peter Woodhouse, while Laurence Parker, General Secretary of the ITCA, was followed on his retirement by Mary Lund, who joined the Association from the National Coal Board. In November the Advertising Association awarded Archie Graham its highest honour, the Mackintosh Medal, for services to the industry.

The Crawford Committee report

If the numerous local special-interest groups which had given evidence to the Committee on Broadcasting Coverage had hoped to obtain a wholesale transfer of stations from one area to another, most of them were to be disappointed when the Committee's report was issued in November. Instead, the Crawford Committee upheld the recommendation which the Television Advisory Committee had made (and successive Governments had accepted) that the provision of complete national coverage of BBC1, BBC2 and Independent Television in 625-line UHF colour was more important than the setting up of additional services or the realignment of transmitters.

The Committee expressed concern that nearly 700,000 people, especially in Scotland and Wales, still remained out of reach of the original 405-line ITV service in VHF, and that the manufacturers were already running down the production of VHF receivers and components. It was therefore considered essential that Phase I of UHF coverage, down to communities of one thousand people, should be completed without delay and that Phase II, covering smaller groups of five hundred to one thousand, should begin as soon as possible despite the relatively high cost per viewer of providing the service in remote areas.

On the vexed question of the transfer of the Belmont transmitter to Yorkshire, the Committee noted that arrangements had already been made to provide viewers whose affinities lay with the East of England with a daily news service from Anglia via this transmitter. On the more general problem of which service should be provided in a population centre in an overlap area – the examples of Dundee, Swindon, Weymouth and Reading were cited – the Committee recommended:

We think that when deciding on the allocation of a transmitter in such cases the IBA should be guided by the wishes of the majority of the people served by the transmitter, so far as they can be ascertained, rather than by an attempt to provide a uniform service from a single programme company. Where the decision has the effect of bringing the town within the areas of two programme companies both should give it appropriate editorial coverage.

But undoubtedly the most far-reaching of the Crawford Committee's recommendations related to the provision of a fourth television channel in Wales, in which Welsh-language programmes were to be given priority. Such was the diligence of Plaid Cymru, the Welsh Language Society, the University of Wales Committee on Broadcasting and various other highly articulate and persuasive bodies that the Committee was convinced that the new service should be set up in the Principality in advance of a decision being taken as to the allocation of any fourth service elsewhere in the United Kingdom. The programmes should be provided by HTV and the BBC, though it was left to the Government and the Annan Committee to work out the details.

Inevitably, Crawford's bombshell was to lead to a further inquiry, the Siberry Committee, and to a further financial burden being imposed on the rest of the Independent Television network.

The outlook at the end of 1974

Despite the autumn rate increases, advertising revenue for the network as a whole showed a reduction of over £10,000,000 on the figure for the previous year – a drop of 7.2 per cent. But the ending of the levy on turnover was already beginning to restore profitability among the companies, and the colour-set count was approaching a total of 7,500,000 homes in spite of the Government's severe restrictions on consumer credit. Lord Annan had completed the formation of his Committee in July and visits were already taking place to the IBA, the BBC and the programme companies.

Most companies had emerged from the Authority's review of performance successfully and it was possible to make plans for the next four years with reasonable certainty now that stability seemed to have been restored to the industry.

1975

Penalties for cancellations

Early in 1975 three programme companies decided to leave the ITCA Cancellation Committee, the forum at which joint decisions were taken by the network on the acceptance of airtime cancellations within eight weeks of transmission. Since 1955 the cancellation problem had – for understandable reasons – often soured relations between the programme companies and their advertisers, and the work of the Cancellation Committee, to which those Sales Directors who served on it devoted much negotiating time and effort, was frequently misunderstood or misinterpreted, as has been seen earlier.

From a contractor's point of view, the withdrawal of business at short notice often resulted in the creation of short-term availability of airtime which could not be resold because money from other advertisers had already been committed elsewhere. The complete abandonment of the cancellation rules would therefore have led to heavy losses of revenue even in a fully sold situation. It was evident that the TV companies needed some means of protecting their forward business.

Advertisers, on the other hand, argued that decisions to cancel TV bookings at short notice were seldom taken lightly, and some pointed out that their contracts were, in any case, placed with individual companies and not with the ITCA. They failed to see why a cancellation, which was often no more than the unavoidable postponement of a campaign, could not be dealt with – like the original booking – on an individual station basis.

For all these reasons Thames, London Weekend and Westward decided to reduce their cancellation periods from eight to six weeks, and to allow cancellation even within six weeks of transmission provided that the advertiser concerned paid a penalty charge of 20–40 per cent of the cost of the airtime which he wished to relinquish. Eventually a similar policy was adopted, with variations, by the rest of the network.

The companies' evidence to Annan

During March the ITCA submitted its evidence to the Annan Committee. Recalling the central recommendation in the Pilkington Report of 1962 (which thirteen years later still found some supporters), that the Authority should be made responsible for the sale of airtime and programme planning while the companies should simply become production units, the ITCA argued its case forcefully.

In any broadcasting system reliant solely on advertising for its finance, the making of programmes and the sale of airtime should, in the view of the companies, be indivisible. A national sales operation – whoever ran it – would produce far less revenue than fifteen separate sales departments all competing for business. Indeed, the independence of the companies, in both the sales and the programming sense, lay at the heart of the regional system which even Pilkington had commended. And it was not only in television that a decentralized sales operation had been found to produce more revenue than any monolithic national system. The companies pointed out that a similar form of devolution had been recommended by the McKinsey organization for the International Publishing Corporation in 1967, and by the Economist Intelligence Unit – also in 1967 – as well as the Prices and Incomes Board, which reported on the national press in 1970.

The history of the previous twenty years had above all shown the need for financial strength among the programme companies. This strength could, the companies were convinced, best be ensured by retaining a series of lively and completely separate sales operations.

Despite the Pilkington Committee's suspicions there was no evidence after twenty years that advertisers had ever influenced the ITV programme schedules or the content of individual programmes. The high standards of television advertising, particularly in terms of its stringent copy controls, had been beneficial to all media. In fact, the Advertising Standards Authority and the Code of Advertising Practice, which operated an increasingly effective self-regulatory control in other media, owed their existence very largely to the television system.

The ITCA evidence continued:

Although television has grown rapidly into the most powerful advertising medium in Britain, early misgivings about this method of funding a television service have not been realised. Today there is no evidence of general public concern.

Yet by reason of its effectiveness television has tended to draw the fire of those who are critical of advertising in all its forms. Advertising remains an emotive word to a small but influential minority, while to the public at large television commercials, like press and poster advertisements, have been at best a source of information and amusement and at worst a matter of indifference.

Perhaps the most telling comparison in the sections of ITCA's evidence devoted to advertising was the index of the cost of a thirty-second commercial in peaktime on all stations. At constant prices this was shown to have fallen by 16 per cent in the eleven years since 1964. It would be difficult in the light of these figures to claim that the programme companies had abused the apparent monopoly they had been given.

It seemed from the subsequent interviews that the members of the Annan Committee found these arguments convincing.

The real cost of television advertising. The table below, which was included in the ITCA's evidence to the Annan Committee, shows the total cost at current and constant prices of a 30-second commercial in peak viewing time on all stations between 1964 and 1974. Despite the allegation that the programme companies had set out to exploit their monopoly power the figures reveal that in eleven years the real cost of the most heavily demanded advertising time actually fell by 16 per cent

Year	Network 30 sec peak time rate	at 1964 prices	at 1964 prices index
	£	£	£
1964	4,772	4,772	100
1965	4,994	4,821	101
1966	5,039	4,742	99
1967	5,407	4,844	101
1968	5,537	4,698	98
1969	5,528	4,690	98
1970	6,055	4,844	101
1971	6,701	4,873	102
1972	7,057	4,440	93
1973	7,060	3,838	80
1974	8,037	3,994	84

Lady Plowden succeeds Lord Aylestone

In April Lady Plowden, a distinguished educationalist and a former Governor of the BBC, succeeded Lord Aylestone as Chairman of the Independent Broadcasting Authority.

Wage and price restraint

On 11 July the Chancellor of the Exchequer, Denis Healey, announced a statutory limit of £6 a week on pay increases until 1 August 1976 and a further strengthening of the controls on the cost of living through the Price Commission.

Two important changes in television advertising rates were caught by the Government's price restraints. On 9 July HTV had submitted a new rate card to the Commission using the recognized 'allowable cost increase' formula but, for the first time, embodying Exchequer levy in the claim. Not altogether surprisingly, this latter item was disallowed, but HTV decided to lodge an appeal and the case was eventually decided in the company's favour in March 1976. There was no reluctance on the part of the other contractors to share in HTV's legal costs because the way was now open for rate increases to be made in a way which no longer penalized an efficient company.

In advance of the successful HTV appeal, however, the network made plans to schedule *Dr No*, the first of the James Bond movies which had been bought from United Artists in 1974. It was obvious, not least to advertisers and agencies, that a feature film of such massive box-office appeal, even if it dated from 1962, would achieve an exceptionally large audience on television. Invoking the clause in the IBA Act which entitled them to charge special rates for special programmes, the contractors notified the Price Commission that they proposed applying surcharges, varying from 35 to 62 per cent, to their basic rates. All were disallowed and, when the film was eventually transmitted on 28 October, every available second of time on all stations was sold at maximum rates. As expected, *Dr No* was seen by a huge audience of twenty-seven million people – a figure which might have been even higher had there not been freak atmospheric conditions which affected television reception in some areas during the programme.

Partly as a result of the success of *Dr No*, the advertising revenue of Independent Television during October exceeded £20,000,000 for the first time in a single month.

Discussions on joint audience research

Throughout the summer discussions took place between the programme companies and the BBC on the possibility of devising a joint system of audience measurement for both services. The Corporation had for many years used an aided-recall technique in which several thousand interviews took place every twenty-four hours to establish the audience to the previous day's television programmes on all three channels. The contractors, agencies and advertisers, on the other hand, had relied since 1955 on a combination of meter measurement and viewing diaries derived from a representative cross-section of households in every ITV area. The results from the two forms of measurement frequently varied, but they were designed to produce different data – the BBC concentrating on individuals and ITV on homes. Five years were to elapse before a joint system of audience research was established to satisfy the needs of all parties.

Area boundaries: the ISBA map

Another more pressing problem of audience research confronted JICTAR. Following the passing of the Local Government Act in 1972 there had been a drastic reduction in the number of administrative districts in England and Wales in 1974 and in Scotland a year later. The boundaries of the original administrative areas had, for all practical purposes, hitherto formed the limits of the regions of Independent Television, but with the formation of larger areas this method of definition of coverage was no longer practicable. It was clear that areas would have to be split between contractors, and that AGB would have to carry out an Establishment Survey to discover actual reception conditions on the ground.

To complicate matters still further population data, which were derived from the 1971 census, were based on the old districts. Another census would not take place until 1981, when the new larger regions would form the framework for measurement. Without the BBTA, whose operations had ended in 1974 and whose maps and tables had been widely accepted for the definition of ITV areas, there was likely to be a move on the part of advertisers to draw lines of their own on the map – if only to determine their sales and distribution areas in relation to television coverage.

In October the ISBA announced that Guy Batham of Lever Brothers had been commissioned to produce a series of maps of television marketing areas, eliminating overlap between regions and arriving at a set count for each company derived from these somewhat arbitrary criteria. The members of the ISBA hoped that, once 'discrete' marketing areas were established, it would be possible to produce compatible information for other media – press, posters, radio and cinema – on a similar basis.

Meanwhile JICTAR, through its Technical Sub-committee, had commissioned AGB to investigate ITV reception capability within the many disputed administrative districts which the reorganization of local government had created.

Agency credit and commission

In the early years of Independent Television the ITCA had awarded commission of 15 per cent to those advertising agencies whose names appeared in the list of agencies recognized by the Newspaper Proprietors' (later Publishers') Association. It soon became clear, however, that television needed a separate system of its own. By the early sixties procedures had been set up for applications to be received and recognition granted by a formally constituted ITCA Agency Recognition Committee, whose membership consisted of five ITV Sales Directors together with a permanent secretary. Agencies were recognized and commission awarded on a two-tiered system – nationally to those who met minimum criteria of television billing and numbers of accounts, and locally to those who concentrated their clients' TV expenditure on one station which was prepared to vouch for the applicant's creditworthiness.

By December 1975 the whole system needed to be reviewed. The Office of Fair Trading had brought all commission systems throughout the commercial world under scrutiny, while in the advertising field a number of media specialists had been formed which concentrated solely on media planning and buying and whose operation bore little resemblance to that of the so-called 'full service' advertising agency. Delays in payment of accounts and the prospect of bad debts were beginning to affect the cash flow of all media owners.

Accordingly, John van Kuffler of the accountants Peat, Marwick, Mitchell and Co. was asked to prepare a report for the ITCA Marketing Committee. He recommended that for their own protection the television companies should separate the award of commission from the granting of credit and that they should be prepared to register their recognition agreements with the Office of Fair Trading. A detailed review began of the payment record and financial status of every agency with whom the contractors did business.

Experimental advertising on ORACLE

By December ORACLE, Independent Television's secondary transmission system on teletext, had undergone successful field trials. Experimental advertising now began from the editorial suite at London Weekend Television, using a total of 200 pages (soon to be expanded to 800) for editorial and advertisements. Though the transmissions were confined to the London area and the response time comparatively slow, ORACLE obviously had considerable possibilities as a supplementary medium whose advertising content could be as rapidly updated as its news. A company, ORACLE Teletext Ltd, was formed and Technical, Editorial and Marketing Committees established to set up a service which was eventually intended to cover the whole country with a regional as well as a national service.

The revenue for the year

The revenue for the year showed a marked recovery after the reverses of 1974. With a total of £176,523,201 the figure represented an increase of 18.3 per cent on that for the previous year.

1976

ITV reaches 96 per cent of all homes

The coverage of Independent Television was, by January 1976, reaching almost all of the population, and when the year began the set count was 18,620,000 or 96 per cent of all homes. The 8,906,000 colour sets included in this figure were to be found in 48 per cent of all the homes receiving ITV.

The 'Gold Star' packages

In January London Weekend Television announced the introduction of a new form of airtime 'package' which represented a development of the Guaranteed Home Impression rates which had been considerably refined since their introduction some eighteen years earlier. The packages, based on selected highly rated programmes, guaranteed the advertiser a total of sixty homes' ratings, with cost increases and reductions being applied for variations above and below this figure.

There was obvious scope for this form of selling during further transmissions of the James Bond films and when ITV broadcast major live sporting events or programmes such as the *Royal Variety Show*. The Price Commission, which had earlier rejected special rates being charged for advertising around *Dr No*, seemed to find nothing objectionable in the practice of payment by audience delivery providing discounts were applied if the package failed to reach its target.

Late payment

At the end of January the chief accountants of all companies were asked to notify the ITCA of delays in payment for advertising transmitted in December 1975. The figures showed that some 36 per cent – over £6,600,000 – remained outstanding. The companies agreed to keep track of delays in payment, and in cases of persistent slowness to warn agencies through the ITCA of the risk of loss of recognition.

HTV and the Price Commission

In March the HTV appeal to include Exchequer levy as an allowable cost as the basis for their rate-increase proposals, which the Price Commission had rejected earlier, was upheld in court. At the same time the Commission changed the base for its calculations, as far as the ITV companies were concerned, from cost per £100 of sales turnover to a more logical cost per 100 hours of broadcast-output formula.

Margarine and health claims

Following a further report by the Royal College of Physicians, in which 'low fat' margarines were pronounced 'safer' than butter, the consultants on the Medical Advisory Panel agreed that references to polyunsaturates would in future be allowed in television commercials provided no health claims were made or implied. Since 1969 no reference to polyunsaturates had been allowed on television, and seven years later the medical profession was still divided in its attitude towards the consumption of animal fats and its connection with heart disease. But Van den Bergh's, the manufacturers of Flora, considered that an important advance had been made in permissible claims and swung more of their advertising budget into television.

The new research contract

As a result of the extension of all the programme franchises to July 1979 it became possible to invite applications from research companies for a new JICTAR contract. The specification from 1977 onwards was based on a one-year 'rolling' appointment with one year's notice of termination on either side and a maximum duration of five years – in other words, until July 1982 at the latest. Eight applications were received but, after detailed examination by JICTAR, AGB, who had held the contract since 1968, was reappointed.

The basis of the contract had been altered to allow for the setting up of a fourth channel, as well as for the possibility of a joint ITV/BBC audience measurement system being established within the five years.

In the meanwhile JICTAR carried out a test of unmonitored viewing diaries in the Yorkshire Television area to discover whether individual viewing habits could be reliably measured without additional verification being provided by Setmeters. When the results were examined, it was found that self-completion diaries were not a reliable guide to patterns of viewing in a multi-channel situation with two BBC services and a number of different ITV signals being received in the various parts of the test area. It looked as if meter measurement, supported by diaries, would continue to be the standard for some years to come.

Agency recognition and the late-payment surcharge

It was now clear that all media owners' agency-recognition agreements would have to be registered with the Office of Fair Trading, and on 21 June, the ITCA's documents were formally delivered to the Director-General. The revised form of application for recognition now required agencies to provide their latest audited accounts together with evidence that the company was legally constituted and had a paid-up capital of at least £20,000.

In October the companies introduced a financial penalty of 2 per cent for delays in payment which was to be applied from the 25th of the month following transmission, and a further 2 per cent, calculated on a day-to-day basis, was to be applied for every month thereafter. The severity of this penalty provoked an outcry from the advertising agencies – who might themselves be in difficulty because of delays in payment by their clients – and the surcharge was reduced to 1.5 per cent with a further 1 per cent to be applied from the 10th of the subsequent month.

'Television Costs: a Few Facts'

The year had proved to be a seller's market for television. Despite the success of the Montreal Olympics on the BBC in the summer and the increasing popularity of BBC2 programmes throughout the year, the demand for airtime was such that the final ITV revenue figure of £230,806,620 showed an increase of nearly 31 per cent on the total for 1975 – itself a record.

But by the autumn there was a groundswell of complaints against the programme companies, and the November issue of *Admap* contained an important article by Harry Henry, then Visiting Professor of Marketing at the Cranfield School of Management, which put these complaints in perspective. The critics of the programme companies had claimed that ITV ratings had been on a downward trend for some time, and that share of audience was being steadily lost to the BBC. The contractors, it was alleged, had refused to invest in programming to arrest the decline but had nevertheless gone ahead and increased their charges to advertisers even faster than the rate of inflation. When these rates proved unacceptably high it was said that several of the programme companies deliberately undersold their advertising minutage to keep the price up and so harden the market.

Harry Henry attacked these arguments with wordy gusto. He showed that the number of ITV homes had increased by over 11 per cent since 1970 and, apart from the usual seasonal variations, that average hours of viewing were much the same as three years earlier. Of course rates had risen steeply during the period, but when indexed against the number of homes reached it could be shown that the increase was actually *less* than the rise in the Retail Prices Index. When the figure was further refined to take account of the growth in colour reception and the extra value which colour undoubtedly added to an advertiser's commercials, the comparison looked even better. As far as artificial hardening of the market was concerned, since when had any manufacturer been compelled to sell *all* the goods which he produced?

These arguments were too much for Ian Spear, then Media Director of Ted Bates. He replied to Harry Henry's article in the next issue of *Admap* with a broadside of his own entitled 'Television Costs – a Few More Facts':

Perhaps an academic can blandly dismiss the recent drop in audiences to ITV programmes as nothing more than part of a cyclical trend . . . But it is of acute concern to the practitioner particularly when it coincides with massive increases in the rate card price of airtime.

He went on to quote the rises in actual costs of campaigns for his own agency's clients and the drop in ratings in peaktime – as opposed to the figures for 'all hours' which Harry Henry had used. Where Ian Spear and Professor Henry seemed to agree was in their admission that television rates were very much the creation of demand. But it was Harry Henry who had the last word. In a parting shot in *Admap* he concluded:

Maybe if Mr Spear concentrated his attention on the job for which he is paid he might do better, and be better able to maintain for his agency's clients an acceptable level of cost-effectiveness and fulfilment of the advertising task – if he knows what these academic phrases mean.

1977

By January the number of households receiving Independent Television in colour had reached 10,607,000 – a coverage of 56 per cent of all ITV homes. The growth to ten million sets and beyond represented the fastest increase in colour-reception capability of any country in the world.

The Annan Report published

Undoubtedly the most important event in broadcasting during the year was the publication on 24 March of the report of the Annan Committee. It was a tribute to Lord Annan's patience and skill as a conciliator that the Committee, whose members covered a wide spectrum of opinion, was able to reach a unanimous view on almost all its recommendations. Not that there had been any shortage of submissions. Some 750 organizations and individuals had supplied the Committee with written evidence varying in length from a single page to long and closely argued documents of considerable complexity. At the end of an exhaustive report, the style of which was widely praised on all sides for its elegance and clarity, the Committee gave its conclusions in no less than 174 recommendations.

The advertising side of Independent Television emerged from the inquiry with little substantial criticism. The Pilkington recommendation that the Authority – rather than the programme companies – should sell the advertising time was once more re-examined, and this time decisively rejected.

'The IBA could not be expected to match the marketing efforts and expertise of the eager beavers in commercial companies who knew their regions intimately.'

Nor did the Committee object to spot advertising and the use of natural breaks, though some members (as in the Select Committee on Nationalized Industries of 1972) thought that experiments should take place to schedule advertisements in blocks on the European model. Natural breaks were thought to be, on the whole, responsibly chosen, and it was noticeable that complaints about the incongruity of advertising within programmes now seldom arose because of improvements in presentation and the reduction of the number of commercial breaks which had taken place some years earlier. The Committee nevertheless recommended that the IBA should not hesitate to reduce the number of breaks in those programmes 'in which such breaks might be inappropriate', and went on: 'The IBA must examine its reason and aesthetic sense and be prepared to exercise them more frequently.'

It was, however, in relation to advertising in children's programmes that the Committee made its strongest recommendation. It urged, on a majority vote, that advertisements should be excluded altogether from all children's programmes and from intervals between them. The same majority was in favour of prohibiting commercials for products or services of interest to children being screened before 9 pm.

As far as rate cards were concerned the Committee formed the view, despite some reservations by Professor Hilde Himmelweit, that the preemption process by which late bookings at premium rates could displace lower-priced spots was the most practicable means of accommodating advertising in periods of high demand. The report put the position clearly:

Since the upper limit of the supply of advertising is fixed, a flexible pricing system is the best way to tap the demand and provide the maximum revenue for ITV. Programme contractors should be able to exercise their commercial judgement in selling advertising by offering packages and rates which will allow them to sell cheaply during difficult periods and sell dear when the demand is greatest. Programme contractors ought to be able to exercise their ingenuity and acumen to attract advertisers to their own regions in competition with the advertising sales departments of other companies. Given the need for flexibility in order to attract revenue, most of us concluded that it was not practicable to stipulate a fixed structure for the companies' rate cards.

The Committee had spent a good deal of time examining the system of copy control exercised by the IBA and was told by the ISBA and IPA that the mechanisms were 'too tough' and that the Authority was sometimes too legalistic in its approach. But Annan commented: 'On this point, the advertisers' representatives failed to bring tears to our eyes.'

The Committee concluded the section of its report devoted to advertising with a subjective view, in which for the first time aesthetic considerations began to creep into its otherwise well-balanced judgement on the effectiveness of television copy control:

The quality of advertisements is an important element in the quality of a good public broadcasting service. We are far from suggesting that all advertisements are vulgar, ineffective and badly made. Some are a pleasure to watch; some are highly amusing, and the zany quality of others is enchanting. British advertisers frequently win awards at international festivals and presumably some advertisements lead to satisfying up-turns in the fortunes (financial or otherwise) of those whose products or interests they exist to promote. Yet the public needs to be more aware of the continuing battle against poor advertising. We believe that the IBA's Code of Advertising Standards and Practice should be more readily available to the public so that they can know more about the rules which govern television advertising and which aim to maintain the highest standards.

Perhaps the members of the Committee, who had done their work so conscientiously, had finally allowed their own sensitivities to colour their attitudes toward the values and needs of the marketplace. After all, it was hardly to be expected that a group of people, drawn for the most part from a highly educated elite, would find that all television commercials, with their need for directness and simplicity in their approach to the mass audience, invariably appealed to their own tastes.

The replies to the Annan Report

As far as the advertising recommendations of the Annan Committee were concerned, both the companies and the Authority felt that the verdict had, for the most part, been a fair one. But they resolved to point out the dangers of accepting the Committee's views on advertising to children.

By the end of June both the ITCA and the Authority had sent their comments to the Home Secretary. The ITCA reminded Merlyn Rees that the proposed removal of advertising from children's programmes had not had the support of all members of the Committee. The majority view had, moreover, been coloured by some largely irrelevant American research which appeared to show that children's enjoyment and recollection of what they saw on television were reduced if the programmes were interrupted by commercials. British research, on the other hand, showed that children's viewing – even among four- to nine-year-olds – was concentrated solidly on adult programmes. In the case of ten- to fifteen-year-olds children's programmes claimed less than 12 per cent of their viewing. The removal of commercials from children's programmes would therefore do little or nothing to 'shield' them from advertising. Children of all ages were, in any case, exposed throughout their daily lives to advertising in a wide variety of other media, most of which were far less responsibly controlled than television. When it came to Annan's recommendation that products 'of particular interst to children' should not be advertised until after 9 pm the ITCA thought the term almost impossible to define. It might include confectionery, but what about clothes or breakfast cereals?

In the Fleming Memorial Lecture which he gave in April, shortly after the publication of his Committee's report, Lord Annan had referred to a loss of revenue of £15,000,000 if advertising were removed from children's programmes. But this, the companies said, was a considerable under-estimate.

The Authority took the same robust line but concentrated on what they considered was the Committee's dismissal of parental resilience and children's common sense. Children's covetousness was more likely to be stimulated by the sight of goods in shop windows and in the hands of their friends than by carefully controlled television advertising. Neither the IBA's film on copy control, which had been shown repeatedly on television, nor the recent parliamentary debates had elicited any complaints on this score. As for the loss of over £15,000,000 in advertising revenue if the breaks in children's programmes were removed, the Authority believed that this could have a disastrous effect on the budgets available for programme production, not to mention the loss to the Exchequer in the form of reduced income from the levy.

At the end of their comments to the Home Secretary, the Authority conceded that children's programmes of up to thirty minutes in length – the majority – should no longer carry an advertising break. Commercial breaks between two children's programmes, which the Committee had also wished to see discontinued would, however, continue to be allowed. Like the ITCA, the Authority also found itself unable to define products 'of particular interest to children', and accordingly declared the proposal of post-9 pm transmission of this type of advertising unworkable.

The AA conference on advertising control

On 10 May the Advertising Association held an important conference at the IBA on the advertising control system which was attended by leaders of the medical, legal and other professions. Both Lady Plowden, Chairman of the IBA, and the Rt Hon. George Thomson, who had recently been appointed Chairman of the Advertising Standards Authority, spoke of the effectiveness of the parallel statutory and self-regulatory systems of control. Lady Plowden quoted the tribute to the television system made by the Annan Committee:

> We consider that on the whole the procedures of the IBA for vetting advertisements stand up well to criticism and yet are not too onerous on the advertisers. We recommend that the statutory requirements on advertising should be retained.

She concluded:

> I believe broadcast advertising provides shoppers with a useful and unique service of information and suggestion – one which nourishes trade, helps employment and increases prosperity. I believe that advertising is a very good way of paying for broadcasting and I am glad Lord Annan agrees with me about this. I believe, too, that British creative standards are high and getting higher all the time and that advertising can be a very attractive addition to our programmes. But all this depends on an effective system of advertising control. Such a system, mature and sensitive enough to satisfy an increasingly sophisticated and educated public, could not have been created overnight. Such a system is not just code wording, conditions and committees, it is a matter of feeling and intent. It is the result of long experience, hard thinking and learning by mistakes. It is the result of cooperation, understanding and goodwill between advertisers, advertising agencies, viewers and listeners, consumer groups, the Government and the Authority.

'Per item' rates

During the year a number of the companies introduced a new feature to their rate cards to attract direct-response advertising to television in a way designed to ensure that the cost of the airtime to the advertiser was geared entirely to the resultant sales of his products. Most direct-response advertisers who relied primarily on press advertising had for many years 'keyed' their advertisements, so that the response from individual publications could be accurately measured by the inclusion in the address or on a coupon of an identifying code (OBS2 – second *Observer* advertisement; DT1 – first *Daily Telegraph* advertisement, and so on). A number of advertisers had also used spaces in the regional editions of the *TV Times*, with or without television support, in the same way.

Although the power of television as an advertising medium was universally acknowledged there were obvious difficulties in tracing the immediate response to a TV campaign, despite the fact that many advertisers had used box and telephone numbers and simplified addresses on the screen. In addition, several of the programme companies had installed in their studios banks of telephone-answering machines to which a special number was allocated. These were used particularly by holiday advertisers to gather names and addresses for the distribution of their brochures.

The 'per item' method of calculating the cost of television advertising had, however, been used effectively by a number of stations in the United States. The PI rates in Independent Television were made available to direct-response advertisers who were able to satisfy the programme company concerned that the product to be advertised was not available through normal retail outlets, and who were prepared to disclose the actual sales figures resulting from the campaign. A cost per item having been agreed between the television company and the advertiser, the sale of the airtime was negotiated on the basis of a small initial transmission charge, augmented afterwards by an additional sum based on the number of units of the product which had been sold. The contractor concerned usually reserved the right to select the dates and times of transmission of PI spots at his discretion.

From the station's point of view the scheme had a number of advantages. Spots at PI rates could be used to fill unsold time and the sources of the contractor's revenue could be widened; and the direct-response advertiser, accustomed to calculating his marketing costs within precise limits, was assured that his advertising outlay would be related entirely to sales. On the other hand, the majority of advertising agencies disliked PI rates and the scope they gave to a contractor to create an artificial seller's market in the same way as, it was alleged, a heavy quota of local advertising could be employed to 'harden the market'.

There were difficulties, too, in policing the PI system of airtime sales. It was not always possible to ensure that the products concerned were available only to post and telephone customers, and there were administrative problems in handling goods and cash through a facilities house. Conventional retailers, many of whom had now become considerable television advertisers in their own right, did not disguise the fact that they considered that many direct-response advertisers offered inferior products with minimal customer service. PI rates were to remain a contentious issue between the television companies and their customers for the next eight years.

Sales trends for the year

During the summer the programme companies, whose revenue was now running between 15 and 25 per cent ahead of the 1976 level, announced autumn rate increases in accordance with the Government's 'allowable costs' formula. In most cases standard rates were increased by around 15 per cent but additional pre-emptive surcharges were introduced, of amounts ranging up to 45 per cent.

Despite these increases, agencies and advertisers began to express misgivings about the possibility of airtime being rationed during the last quarter of the year. By the end of December it was clear that ITV revenue had risen by almost the same percentage as in 1976, when the figure had shown an increase of nearly 31 per cent. The 1977 total of nearly £300,000,000 proved to be 29.9 per cent up on the revenue for the previous twelve months.

The new technology: teletext and satellites

On 30 August the board of ORACLE decided that the time was ripe to announce the launch of a teletext system of editorial and advertising. It was to take place on 1 October, with continuous transmissions from 9 am to 10.30 pm.

The inaugural press conference, held at Thames Television's Euston studios, was told that the companies intended to introduce a separate service in Scotland within two years and to extend the regional system rapidly to all the other areas by 1982. The costs and revenue of the system would be divided in proportion to each contractor's share of total ITV income, and eventually each company would set up its own facilities for editorial and advertising purposes. The quota of advertising would be set at 15 per cent of the total number of editorial pages.

In September the World Administrative Radio Conference (WARC) meeting in Geneva decided on the national allocation of channels for television transmissions by satellite. Every country – even those as small as Andorra, the Vatican and Monaco – was allocated five national channels in the Super High Frequency wavebands. Unfortunately the programme for the launch of the first European Orbital Test Satellite, OTS-1, suffered a setback because of the failure of the NASA launch vehicle. It was decided that the next attempt would be made using the European Space Agency's Ariane rocket from French Guiana.

Revisions to the IBA Advertising Code

Just before the end of the year the IBA issued the fifth edition of its Code of Advertising Standards and Practice which allowed member firms of the Stock Exchange to advertise for the first time. The ban on slimming clinics was lifted, provided their treatments were based on proper dietary control, and lotteries sponsored by local authorities were allowed to appear on the screen despite the continuation of the long-standing ban on betting advertising. Finally, the Medical Advisory Panel further relaxed their rules on references in margarine commercials to polyunsaturates, although specific health claims were still prohibited.

John Wardrop and Guy Spencer retire

The record of important events of 1977 would not be complete without recording the simultaneous retirement from ATV at the end of the year of John Wardrop and Guy Spencer. Both had remained with the company throughout the twenty-two years since 1955, and had run its Sales Department with considerable success since the departure of Patrick Henry, ATV's first Sales Director, in 1964. Many of their original colleagues had gone on in the interim to become managing directors of other ITV companies, and it was fortunate that Peter Mears, who succeeded the Wardrop and Spencer duo, could, like them, claim over twenty years' unbroken experience with the same company.

1978

New-length commercials

There had been many occasions since 1955 when the possibility of changing the lengths of commercials on television had been discussed between the contractors and marketing, media and creative people among their customers. By the beginning of 1978, however, pressure to make a change was increasing because existing formats were, it was claimed, restricting creative freedom and making time buying unnecessarily difficult. The majority of opinion seemed to favour dropping seven-, fifteen- and forty-five-second spots, and the adoption of the so-called 'metric' lengths of ten, twenty, forty and fifty seconds while retaining the existing thirty- and sixty-second time lengths. But, as it was essential for commercials to be interchangeable between stations, it was recognized that it would be preferable for all companies to make the change simultaneously and after a long period of notice to allow existing films and videotapes to run their course.

The ITCA Marketing Committee formed a small working party of Ron Miller (LWT) and Mike Hutcheson (Ulster), under the chairmanship of Brian Henry (Southern), to examine the whole question of commercial lengths and to make recommendations to the rest of the network. The working party noted that both London companies had had some success in allowing single advertisers to combine specially made twenty- and forty-second commercials which were charged as a single sixty-second spot. In other cases the twenty-second commercial was an extended version of one of fifteen seconds, while the forty-second spot might be a cut-down adaptation of one of forty-five seconds. Either way the favourable price for sixty seconds, which escaped the cost-loading which was applied to shorter commercials, proved an attraction to advertisers. Yet some of the contractors were not so sure. A trend towards longer commercials, the time in which might be filled with a miscellany of shorter spots from a single advertiser could, they thought, present slotting problems and would certainly lose premium revenue on a heavily sold station.

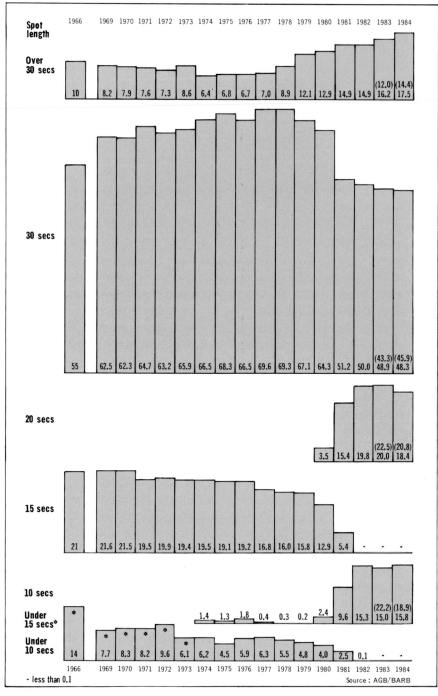

Spot length	1966	1969	1970	1971	1972	1973	1974	1975	1976	1977	1978	1979	1980	1981	1982	1983	1984
Over 30 secs	10	8.2	7.9	7.6	7.3	8.6	6.4	6.8	6.7	7.0	8.9	12.1	12.9	14.9	14.9	(12.0) 16.2	(14.4) 17.5
30 secs	55	62.5	62.3	64.7	63.2	65.9	66.5	68.3	66.5	69.6	69.3	67.1	64.3	51.2	50.0	(43.3) 48.9	(45.9) 48.3
20 secs														3.5	15.4	19.8	(22.5) 20.0	(20.8) 18.4
15 secs	21	21.6	21.5	19.5	19.9	19.4	19.5	19.1	19.2	16.8	16.0	15.8	12.9	5.4	-	-	-
10 secs / Under 15 secs*							1.4	1.3	1.8	0.4	0.3	0.2	2.4	9.6	15.3	(22.2) 15.0	(18.9) 15.8
Under 10 secs	14	7.7	8.3	8.2	9.6	6.1	6.2	4.5	5.9	6.3	5.5	4.8	4.0	2.5	0.1	-	-

- less than 0.1

Source : AGB/BARB

CHANNEL 4 ( )

Distribution of commercial lengths; percentage share of all spots

It seemed preferable, once agreement had been obtained among all the programme companies, to introduce new commercial lengths in which each spot was individually priced and in which the loading on shorter commercials was preserved, with charges for spots longer than twenty seconds remaining pro rata to the thirty-second rate.

It came as a surprise, therefore, when on 30 January Thames announced a reduction in the prices of forty-five- and sixty-second commercials to 140 per cent and 170 per cent of the standard thirty-second rate – a cut of 10 per cent and 30 per cent respectively. It seemed that Thames intended to encourage the production of metric-length commercials which the London weekday station would continue to schedule in a composite form to fill a one-minute spot. The rest of the network, however, decided to maintain its conventional rate structure until a general move was made to announce new commercial lengths on all stations.

During April and May the IPA and ISBA, both of whom were in favour of new-length commercials, produced their own ideas on the way in which the price structure of metric-length spots should be arranged. Both proposals were based on a reduction in the premium charged for commercials of less than thirty seconds, and it seemed clear that there would have to be considerable negotiation before the new lengths were introduced. Agencies and advertisers claimed that few campaigns would be replanned with shorter commercials, and that thirty-second spots (which at the time formed by far the majority of all those transmitted on the network) would continue to predominate indefinitely. In fact the trend towards thirty seconds had been climbing steadily upwards over the previous ten years. In 1966 only 55 per cent of all commercials had been of thirty seconds, while 35 per cent had been of shorter length. By 1976 the number of thirty-second spots had increased to 66.5 per cent, while those of less than this length had fallen to 26.9 per cent. If the introduction of metric commercials were to reverse this trend, it was clear that the contractors could only gain in revenue terms provided the premium on the shorter spots remained.

ISBA *unique marketing areas*

In February the ISBA, which a year earlier had produced a map of the ITV areas whose boundaries had been drawn to eliminate overlap, issued a series of tables of marketing data for each region under the title *Area Information 1978*. The contractors, however, continued to use JICTAR information to plan their programme coverage and as the basis for the marketing manuals which they issued. The net coverage of each station had not yet assumed critical importance in the setting of expenditure levels, by reaching which an advertiser could qualify for special discounts based on a station's 'net homes percentage' formula.

European liaison: James O'Connor appointed

The programme companies continued to keep in touch with television advertising developments in Europe and it became increasingly obvious that ITCA needed an adviser, experienced in international committee work and knowledgeable about television, to represent them at EEC, Council of Europe and other meetings when broadcast advertising was discussed. It was agreed that James O'Connor, who had recently retired as Director of the IPA after twenty-five years, was the ideal candidate and he was appointed European Adviser to the programme companies on 1 July. At once the flow of information from the continent began to improve. The companies were given early warning of impending legislation from Brussels and of moves which were being made among powerful consumer lobbies throughout Europe.

Among the most disturbing series of restrictions known to be in preparation were those contained in the EEC Draft Directive on Misleading Advertising, which was intended to apply to all media. It was agreed that the main opposition to its new and far-reaching restrictions should be coordinated through the Advertising Association, as the federal body to which the ITCA and all the other advertising trade associations belonged. Further representations would be made through the European Advertising Tripartite (EAT).

ITV Facts and Figures

Whatever their views about the disappearance of the BBTA, all companies felt the need for a single publication of the kind for which the Bureau had formerly been responsible, containing basic information about Independent Television. In July *ITV Facts and Figures 1978* was issued.

It listed details of each company's senior sales management, its research and marketing facilities and production requirements, together with coverage and set-count information for every ITV area. The publication, which was much welcomed by advertisers and agencies, is now updated and issued every year by the Marketing Services department of the ITCA.

The White Paper and the IBA Act

The Government, which had now had time to consider the numerous views which had been expressed following the publication of the Annan Report a year earlier, outlined its plans for the future of broadcasting in a White Paper issued in July. Annan's recommendation that the fourth channel should be run by an entirely new body, the Open Broadcasting Authority, was accepted, and it was thought feasible for it to be financed by a combination of spot and block advertising. The IBA would, however, be given responsibility for pay-television and cable services. The Government noted with approval that the IBA had already decided to remove advertising breaks from children's programmes of thirty minutes and less, but did not accept Annan's more radical recommendation to eliminate all advertising from programmes addressed to children. It was intended that, where appropriate, legislation would be introduced in Parliament to give effect to these proposals, and to extend the IBA Act and the BBC's Charter into the 1990s.

In the meantime more immediate legislation was passed, extending without change the Independent Broadcasting Authority Act (which was due to expire on 31 July 1979) to the end of December 1981. It seemed certain to the programme companies that the Authority would have little alternative but to extend their franchises until the same date.

Advertising by charities proposed

The Annan Committee had expressed the hope in its report – without making a formal recommendation – that the Authority would consider relaxing the rules in its advertising code to allow charities to advertise. A working party (WOPAC) had been formed in November 1977 under the IBA's Deputy Director-General, Anthony Pragnell, to examine the subject and make recommendations.

Unfortunately, the charities who gave evidence to the working party were not unanimous in their views. As at the time of the passage of the 1954 Television Act, the belief still prevailed that there was a fixed 'pool' of funds for charitable purposes. It therefore followed that, if television advertising were to be allowed, the larger charities, who were better able to afford a television campaign, would be bound to benefit at the expense of the smaller institutions. Nevertheless the working party decided in its report, issued in September, that the ban on charitable advertising should be lifted, subject to suitable safeguards for an experimental period, and the position reviewed after three to five years.

The Government did not however take an immediate decision and the outcome was not made known until after the General Election in May 1979. When the new Government came to power the Home Secretary, William Whitelaw, decided that no change should be made to the rules, and charitable advertisements continued to be restricted to announcements of flag days, special events and lotteries.

Television advertising reaches £1,000,000 a day

Expenditure on television advertising had continued to rise during the year, and when 1978 ended the total revenue of the network was seen to have reached £363,004,836 – an average of almost £1,000,000 a day – and an increase of 21 per cent on the record figure for 1977.

1979

The 'winter of discontent'

When 1979 opened there were already signs that the onset of serious economic problems would soon force the Government to seek a further mandate from the electorate. The OPEC countries had announced that they would make four separate increases in oil prices during the year – a move which was bound to affect the cost of almost all goods and services and make the continuation of wage restraint an impossibility. The trade unions were already becoming restive in the light of the limitation of wage increases to a maximum of 5 per cent.

The troubles came to a head when over two thousand oil and petrol tanker drivers stopped work, followed shortly afterwards by stoppages throughout the whole of the road haulage industry. Workers in a number of vital public services withdrew their labour and all these industrial disputes coincided with weather of exceptional severity. When retail stock levels began to decline alarmingly a number of manufacturers and retailers were forced to cancel their television advertising. By the time the lorry drivers' strike had ended at the end of February, cancellations across the network amounted to £9,000,000.

After a vote of confidence in the Government had been defeated – admittedly by only one vote – at the end of March the Prime Minister, James Callaghan, decided to go to the country.

The General Election and its aftermath

The General Election took place on 3 May and a Conservative Government under Margaret Thatcher was returned to power with a majority over all other parties of 43 seats. William Whitelaw was appointed Home Secretary and, at the opening of Parliament on 15 May, the Queen's Speech contained a clear indication of the new Government's policy and the way in which it would affect Independent Television.

Statutory controls on prices and wages were to be abolished. The Price Commission was to go. The IBA (rather than the Open Broadcasting Authority recommended by Annan and supported by the previous Government) would be given the responsibility for the fourth television channel, and an early start was to be made on a separate service in the Welsh language using the new channel.

Production costs: the interim Equity agreement

With the abolition of price controls by the Government advertisers expected early announcements to be made of rate increases. However, before any new rate cards had been issued they were confronted with major increases in the production costs of TV commercials as a result of a new agreement for the employment of artists.

On 1 February the actors' union, Equity, concluded an interim agreement with the IPA and the Advertising Film and Videotape Producers' Association (AFVPA), the effect of which was to increase the minimum scales of payment, which had admittedly not been changed for over twenty years, by 250 per cent. Much of the increase was represented by repeat fees and, as might have been expected, more contracts were negotiated with artists on the alternative 'buy-out' basis for a single lump sum.

Some advertisers warned that they might be forced to reduce the number of artists in commercials and turn instead to animation and pack-shot techniques of presentation. Certainly the days of large casts in commercials seemed to be at an end.

But artists' fees were only one of a number of elements in the total budget for a television commercial. The cost of all these elements had been steadily increasing, despite the years of price control which were just ending.

Nor could the television contractors remain entirely indifferent to the rising production costs facing advertisers. When one of their clients set his advertising budget he seldom differentiated between expenditure on airtime and that on film or videotape production. Advertising appropriations were not inexhaustible, and the use of more expensive commercials would inevitably limit his outlay on airtime.

The table opposite shows the production cost of television commercials over the ten-year period 1970–80, expressed in monetary terms and as a percentage of the total cost of transmission charges and production.

Despite the concern which had been expressed by advertisers at the ever-rising costs of production, the figures for most years showed a fairly constant relationship with total TV expenditure of somewhere

	TELEVISION PRODUCTION COSTS 1970–80	
Year	*Production costs* *£ million*	*Proportion of airtime* *+ production cost*
1970	13	10.4
1971	15	10.5
1972	18	10.2
1973	21	10.0
1974	27	10.3
1975	28	11.9
1976	35	11.4
1977	45	11.3
1978	56	11.6
1979	63	13.4
1980	70	10.1

Source: Advertising Association

between 10 and 11.5 per cent. It appeared that it was only during the years of recession – when expenditure on airtime fell – that the percentage figures for production rose steeply above this level.

The fourth channel: conflicting views

Despite the fact that the Government had made it known that the Authority was to be made responsible for the fourth channel, no decision had so far been announced as to whether the service was to be run by the existing contractors or provided by newcomers. The majority of advertisers had, however, campaigned from the time of the Annan Committee for a competitive system and, at the annual general meeting of the ISBA in July, their President, Sir Adrian Cadbury, once more returned to this theme.

The argument was a simple one: advertisers were themselves facing intense competition at home and abroad and their profit margins were under pressure. Television was a vital medium to them in most consumer markets and it was firmly believed that a new channel, whose rates and sales practices were competitive with those of the existing service, would at least help to stabilize marketing costs. It might even reduce them.

From the contractors' point of view, however, it was extremely doubtful whether enough advertising revenue existed – or could be generated in the short term – to finance two separate services in every area. If, as a result of competition for revenue, programme companies were forced to amalgamate, most of the unique regional flavour of Independent Television would be lost.

The Authority and the ITCA continued to stress the importance of putting the interests of the viewer ahead of those of the advertiser. Competition for advertising revenue and the demands of advertisers for a mass audience could only lead to an increasing similarity in the output of two competing ITV services and to a drastic reduction in programme budgets. The quality of Independent Television could best be maintained if the programmes on the fourth channel were complementary to those of ITV1. It seemed that these views were making some headway with the Government.

The trend of revenue

Some of the advertising which had been cancelled during the previous winter had undoubtedly been regained – perhaps as much as £6,000,000 out of the £9,000,000 which had originally been lost. The latest revenue figures for June 1979 showed an increase of 36 per cent on the figure for the same month in 1978.

The major companies announced rate increases to take effect on 3 September averaging 15 per cent which one leading agency, Young and Rubicam, claimed were insufficient to avoid some form of airtime rationing. At the same time, Y. and R. recognized that for the central contractors to increase rates by a larger amount might militate against the renewal of their licences and would certainly lead to higher wage demands from the trade unions in television.

The regional companies, however, moved their rates upward by much greater percentages, varying from 28 to 45 per cent, to take effect during the second half of September.

ITV's longest strike

The financial buoyancy of the network was destined to be short-lived. On 23 July the principal union in Independent Television, the ACTT, which had made a claim for a 25 per cent wage increase, rejected an offer from the companies of 9 per cent. They were soon joined by NATTKE and EETPU in a series of one-day strikes. The situation deteriorated rapidly and, at 6 pm on 10 August the entire network went off the air.

On the assumption that the dispute might be settled at short notice each company continued to produce daily transmission schedules and, where possible, assembled film and tape commercials for immediate transmission. But hopes of an early resumption of the service soon faded and, despite the convening of the joint liaison committee with the IPA and ISBA to deal with the cancellation and postponement of advertising, it soon became clear that a number of agencies were facing serious financial problems. The situation became so critical for those heavily committed to television that the programme companies suspended their late-payment surcharge and made arrangements for the settlement of outstanding accounts to be deferred.

By the time the strike ended on 19 October – after nearly eleven weeks off the air – it was estimated that Independent Television had lost between £90,000,000 and £100,000,000 in advertising revenue and the agencies at least £13,500,000 in commission. And the dispute left a legacy of bitterness among those who worked in the industry. Viewing loyalties to Independent Television had been disturbed, if only temporarily. Forward production had been brought to a complete standstill and the introduction of many new programmes had had to be delayed, in some cases until well into 1980.

Other developments during the strike

But many other developments, some with far-reaching consequences, continued to take place while Independent Television was off the air.

The Post Office launched Prestel, to the accompaniment of a good deal of over-optimistic publicity. Lord Thomson of Monifieth, Chairman of the Advertising Standards Authority since March 1977, was appointed Deputy Chairman of the IBA to succeed Lady Plowden when she retired as Chairman at the end of 1980. The Authority held the first of many public meetings in the hope of discovering what the man and woman in the street thought about Independent broadcasting. The five-hundredth IBA transmitter went on the air and the Royal Television Society held its annual convention at King's College, Cambridge. The latter event was chosen by the Government for the announcement of its plans for the structure of the fourth channel.

Channel Four: the Home Secretary's announcement

The Home Secretary, William Whitelaw, gave the opening address and with it the *coup de grâce* to the Open Broadcasting Authority.

I am convinced that not only would the creation of an Open Broadcasting Authority, directly dependent on the Government for funds, be potentially dangerous; it is also unnecessary to achieve what we want. The experience and ability of the IBA if used to the full, the money, equipment and skills of the ITV companies and the talents of the independent producers, can be harnessed to provide a different and worthwhile service on the fourth channel.

As to who was to sell the airtime – the all-important question from the advertiser's point of view – the Home Secretary went on:

The main source of funds for the Fourth Channel will be spot advertising, though block advertising and sponsorship may be permitted. I know many people in the advertising world would like to have another source from which they could purchase advertising time on television. Having looked at this with particular care, the conclusion I have reached is that competitive advertising on the two channels would inevitably result in a move towards single-minded concentration on maximizing the audience for programmes with adverse consequences for both of the commercial channels and, before long, for the BBC. This is not a criticism of the television companies: I do not believe they could prevent it if they tried and still remain viable.

Despite the inescapable logic of his argument, the Home Secretary's announcement was received with dismay by the majority of agencies and advertisers. They were already reconciled to the fact that there would be no competition – in the advertising sense – in Independent Television before 1982. But it now seemed that the airtime monopoly which the contractors enjoyed might continue until satellite and cable systems began to replace conventional broadcasting in the 1990s.

Channel Four: coverage and organization

It had been decided at an early stage of planning the coverage of the new channel that a lesson must be drawn from the opening of BBC2 in 1964. The Corporation's second channel had been introduced in London and the Midlands in the first year, followed by Lancashire and South Wales in Year 2. Quite clearly, a 'slow-burn' opening of a commercially financed service might well prove fatal to the new channel, and the Authority accordingly advocated a 'big bang' start being made simultaneously in all areas.

On 29 October the IBA reported that by November 1982 – the projected date for the launch of Channel Four – 82 per cent of the population nationally would be able to receive the new programmes. But the signal would not reach this percentage of homes in every area because of the time needed to carry out the necessary engineering work at each of the transmitters. The service would be likely to open with less than 70 per cent coverage in some areas, but it was hoped to make up the shortfall within two years.

Airtime on the new channel would be sold by the contractors in their own areas and they would retain the revenue. Channel Four would, however, be run by a separate company whose board would be appointed by the Authority. The finance would be provided by the ITV companies in the form of subscriptions, calculated in roughly the same proportions as their IBA rentals, so that the resources for the programmes on Channel Four would not be directly dependent on the surrounding advertising.

Nor would Channel Four be a programme maker in the accepted sense. It would acquire and commission its material from a variety of sources, including the ITV contractors and independent producers, and was expected to be on the air initially for some forty-five to fifty hours a week.

Channel Four: advertising

The IBA made their plans for the sale of advertising time on the fourth channel known in a long statement which they issued on 12 November. It began by analysing the uncertain economic climate and the way in which the revenue for two national television services might be expected to grow, recognizing that, although Channel Four would not be self-supporting for several years, its only source of finance would be the *combined* income of the two channels. The operating cost – at 1979 prices – was likely to be within the range £60,000,000-£80,000,000 and the programme companies, five-sixths of whose surpluses already went to the Government in levy and tax, would inevitably be faced with declining profitability for some time. But the statement continued with a memorable sentence:

Nevertheless, we should not wish to see the Fourth Channel as a permanent pensioner of ITV1: for the continuing health of the IBA's television services we should hope to see the Fourth Channel in due course adding between a fifth and a quarter, in real terms, to the total advertising revenue earned by the programme contractors.

The key to the success of the new channel would be the extent to which it would be able to attract additional advertising revenue by offering advertisers access to specialized audiences at an economic cost.

But the Authority also considered that:

The addition of a second channel carrying advertising. . . should relieve some of the tensions that have arisen between those who sell and those who buy advertising time on television. The Authority recognises, however, that some advertisers had hoped to have competitive selling of time, and that they will be disappointed that the needs of good broadcasting rule this out.

A desire for competitive selling is not necessarily linked to an expectation that such competition would result in a lowering of advertising rates. The advertisers' expressed concern is more that the programme contractors' position should not permit the imposition of arbitrary conditions governing the sale of advertising time. It is a matter on which advertisers and agencies have strong feelings.

The Authority accordingly concluded its statement with a promise to consider the prohibition of two practices which would otherwise be likely to bring these feelings to a head:

1 Making the sale of airtime on ITV1 conditional on the purchase of airtime on Channel Four.
2 Linking discounts between the two channels.

Two positive measures were also likely to be adopted:

1 The requirement that each company should publish separate rate cards for ITV1 and Channel Four.
2 That an Advertising Liaison Committee should be formed at which senior representatives of the Authority, the companies, the IPA and ISBA should meet regularly in order to improve relationships and discuss matters of common interest.

And there might, in the Authority's view, be a place for such a Liaison Committee with only a single channel.

The new contract period: advertisers' views

The cryptic reference in the Authority's outline of its plans for the fourth channel to the possible place for an Advertising Liaison Committee, even with a single commercial channel, arose directly from a paper which the ISBA had submitted to the Authority in October. By then it had become clear that the contractors' monopoly of airtime sales was likely to continue after the new contracts began in 1982.

The paper listed a number of alleged abuses of monopoly power, most of which were said to have occurred since the replanning of the network in 1968:

1 The operation of the ITCA Cancellation Committee.
2 The deliberate restriction of the sale of airtime to harden the market.
3 The absence of any reliable means of verifying after transmission that correct commercials had been broadcast.
4 The price differential which continued to be applied to commercials of less than thirty seconds.
5 The absence of prior consultation with advertisers before changes in sales policy were made by the contractors.

The view of the contractors was that almost all of these grievances were best dealt with on an individual company basis rather than by the full network, let alone the IBA. For example, the Cancellation Committee had already been abandoned by three companies, and its operation during the recent road-haulage strike – which the ISBA had singled out for special odium – had tried to take account of the problems of individual advertisers in a sympathetic and efficient way.

The subject of verification of transmission of commercials had been discussed by the contractors and advertisers for years, but the necessary electronic equipment to identify each film or videotape off-air was only just becoming available. The contractors took the view that errors occurred infrequently and that it would be better to instal the equipment, which was still untried and expensive, after the new contracts began.

But the ISBA's chief hope for the new contract period was that there should be a return to the divided franchises (of the kind which had existed before 1968) in the North and Midlands in order to introduce an element of competition for revenue, at least in the major areas. They went on to suggest that the division should be on a three-day and four-day (rather than a weekday/weekend) basis, but that in London competition for revenue should take place between three (rather than two) contractors.

The paper ended with a plea for a committee to be formed at which advertisers could air their grievances to the Authority. It seemed that there would be no shortage of items for the agenda.

'Metric' commercials announced

In November Thames Television announced that it would accept so-called 'metric' commercials from 7 January 1980. Other companies hesitated to make a similar move, especially at short notice, because provision would have to be made to accommodate 'old'- and 'new'-length commercials side by side. On the other hand, the number of metric spots would begin to proliferate only after they had become acceptable on all stations. After much discussion, the balance of opinion at the ITCA Marketing Committee was in favour of introducing metric commercials on the rest of the network within the next three years, but to delay the phasing out of fifteen- and forty-five-second spots until the new contracts began on 1 January 1982.

Revenue in 1979

The year had proved to be the worst for industrial disputes since ITV had begun twenty-four years earlier. In the light of the difficulties created by stoppages in many industries it was surprising that the reduction in the advertising income of Independent Television had not been greater: when the year ended the revenue for the network was seen to have fallen by only 4.5 per cent below the total for 1978.

1980

The first metric rates

Thames Television had been the first company to accept 'metric' commercials within a sixty-second spot for an experimental period, and it was the same company which announced separate rates for the new-length commercials as a permanent part of its rate card. On 7 January ten- and twenty-second spots were introduced on the London weekday station, at 50 and 80 per cent respectively of the cost of thirty seconds, thus preserving the price loading on shorter commercials. The rates selected fell either side of those for fifteen seconds which, since the early sixties, had been set at between 65 and 70 per cent of the thirty-second rate by all stations.

Applications for the new contracts invited

On 24 January the IBA announced the specifications for the new programme contracts which were to operate for the eight years from 1 January 1982 to 31 December 1989. The contract particulars were detailed and lengthy, but the features likely to be of greatest importance to advertisers were:

1 The offer of a separate contract for a breakfast-time service.
2 The creation of two further dual regions in the Midlands and South in addition to the existing well-established division into two sub-areas of Wales and the West of England.
3 The transfer of a number of transmitters between areas and the construction of others.

The Committee on Broadcasting Coverage (the Crawford Committee) had not recommended the reallocation of any transmitters from one area to another when it reported in 1974, despite the many submissions it had received from interested parties. But by the time the Authority came to announce particulars of the new contracts nearly twenty thousand people had attended IBA public meetings and over

7500 had been interviewed in the course of a major research survey.

As a result of 'taking the public mind', as the Authority termed it, it had been decided that a number of transmitters would be reallocated as follows:

1 The five southern Lakeland relays from Lancashire (to be known in future as North-West England) to the Borders.
2 Four relays along the Pennines from Lancashire to Yorkshire.
3 The main transmitter at Bluebell Hill (between Chatham and Maidstone) from London to the South (to be known in future as South and South-East England).
4 The Marlborough relay from the South to the West of England.

All these changes were important to the viewers and the companies affected. But the transfer of Bluebell Hill from London to the South was to alter the whole balance of power between major and regional stations.

Changes to rate cards

A number of contractors issued new rate cards during the first quarter of 1980. In so doing they established features of airtime selling which marked a radical departure from the practices which had grown up over the previous twenty-five years.

Two major companies, Thames and Trident, announced the ending of volume discount, though the first-named later abandoned its plans to do so. The Thames scheme had been intended to provide an incentive for pre-payment in place of the former straightforward percentage reductions on an advertiser's total expenditure. Trident, however, resolutely maintained its stance, facing considerable protests and the withdrawal of some of its business by advertisers.

Anglia introduced the first 100 per cent fixing charge for its highest-priced spots (which were totally protected against pre-emption) but, at the same time, increased discounts on its lowest rates in order to introduce greater price flexibility. STAGS, representing Scottish and Grampian Television, decided to gear its rates to those of the whole network on the basis of its 'net homes' percentage of 8.36 per cent, so that the cost of advertising in its area would automatically increase if rates went up elsewhere. London Weekend, facing the unique problems of the only station on the air with a two-and-a-half-day franchise, announced a 66 per cent rate increase for advertisements cancelled within five days of transmission, but offered concessions for long-term expenditure commitments to the station.

Its weekday counterpart, Thames, introduced a discount of 2½ per cent for agencies who were prepared to settle accounts by the first working day of the month following transmission, and a number of contractors began to include metric commercials, including forty- and fifty-second spots, in their rate cards.

A new Broadcasting Act

A new Broadcasting Bill was published in February. It extended the life of the Authority to 1996, formalized arrangements for the fourth channel, and set up a Broadcasting Complaints Commission (on the lines which the Annan Committee had recommended) to act as a single forum for complaints about both Independent Television and Local Radio, and the BBC.

It was interesting to note that the Commission's terms of reference would allow it to deal with complaints about advertising, as well as programmes, insofar as Independent Television and local radio were concerned. The Bill received the Royal Assent in November.

The new licence applications

The short period between January and May proved exceptionally difficult for every programme company. The closing date for all licence applications had been set by the IBA at 9 May, and the senior managements of every contractor, often assisted by teams of outside consultants – architects, engineers, and accountants – were working long hours, including weekends, in providing answers to the Authority's exhaustive questionnaires and preparing for the final IBA interviews. Similar activity was taking place – with a good deal less at stake – among newly formed applicant groups, whose members almost invariably included senior staff who were still ostensibly working for the existing contractors. An air of uncertainty and mounting insecurity descended on the entire industry for, while the whole future of every company hung in the balance, the service had to be maintained in a rapidly shrinking franchise period for which programmes had to be planned and made, schedules prepared and airtime sold with every appearance of confidence and normality.

It was difficult to improve relations between the programme companies and their customers, which had been steadily deteriorating, at a time when advertisers and agencies had the uneasy feeling that not only the game but whole teams and many of the leading players might change completely in less than two years. Only the new rules seemed certain.

There were altogether forty-three applications for the new licences – eight for the breakfast-time contract and thirty-five for the conventional franchises, including those from the existing incumbents. Three franchise holders were relieved to find themselves unopposed, while one area, South and South-East England, attracted no fewer than six applicants (originally seven).

The rest of the year was devoted to a series of final public meetings, one in each area and two in the case of the dual regions, culminating in the IBA interviews which began on 22 October and ended on 11 December. Towards the end of this period the Authority announced that the names of the new contractors would be made known on 28 December 1980 – a Sunday and chosen, like the day of the previous announcement, 11 June 1967, so as not to affect share prices on the Stock Exchange.

The closure of the VHF service announced

On 20 May the Home Secretary announced plans for the closure of the original 405-line VHF network over a four-year period beginning in 1982. As a result, the boundaries of the ITV areas, some of which still included pockets of VHF reception, would, for all practical purposes, be based solely on UHF coverage when the new contracts began.

At the same time, the extension of the UHF service to communities of fewer than five hundred people was announced, notwithstanding the high cost of providing the four television channels (BBC1 and 2, ITV and Channel 4) in remote and often mountainous areas where reception was difficult. It was calculated that the cost of supplying the signal to each viewer in London was 5p a head, while in the smallest rural communities it was as much as £85 a head – a cost ratio of 1700:1.

The Channel Four company formed

Meanwhile the structure of the fourth channel was rapidly taking shape. At the end of May Edmund Dell was appointed Chairman of the new company and Sir Richard Attenborough Deputy Chairman.

Nine consultants who later became directors, four of them from the ITV contractors, were selected and Jeremy Isaacs, a distinguished figure in the industry with long experience at Granada, Associated-Rediffusion, Thames Television and the BBC, was appointed Chief Executive. Premises for studios and offices were acquired in Charlotte Street on the site of the old Scala Theatre.

The Advertising Liaison Committee

The Authority had been persuaded that a forum was needed for the discussion of advertising issues between themselves, the programme companies, advertisers and agencies. Plans for the formation of such a body had been included in the statement of the IBA's future policy which had been issued in November 1979. On 27 June the inaugural meeting of the new Advertising Liaison Committee took place at 70 Brompton Road, under the chairmanship of Lord Thomson.

It was decided that the terms of reference of the new body would be ratified at its next meeting in October. They were:

1 To consider matters of principle relating to commercial relationships which might be raised by the participating bodies.
2 To improve liaison and communications on advertising matters between advertisers, agencies, the ITV programme companies and the IBA.
3 To examine ways in which outstanding differences might be resolved.
4 To provide any guidance, advice and information which it might consider helpful to all who were involved in the Committee.

Joint ITV/BBC audience research

Suggestions had repeatedly been made for many years that there should be a single form of audience research for both the BBC and Independent Television. The former Director-General of the BBC, Sir Hugh Greene, had advocated it in his Guildhall lecture in 1972, somewhat to the surprise of his listeners. Discussions had been held on the subject between the programme companies and the BBC, culminating in the test of unmonitored diaries, as an alternative to meter measurement, in the Yorkshire area five years later. But the Annan Committee had been particularly emphatic on the subject because of the unnecessary cost of two systems and the frequent differences in their figures for the same programme. As the Annan Report expressed it:

The achievement of a common system should not be regarded as an ideal, but as an essential requirement on the broadcasting organisations. It is unedifying to see each organisation attempting to justify the widely conflicting figures in its own favour. In pursuit of their ideal system, both sides are placing too much emphasis on maintaining a refinement and accuracy which is beyond what the eventual figures are worth.

It went on:

We recommend therefore that the BBC and ITCA at once devise a combined system of assessing audience ratings for all broadcast channels. This system should be capable of accommodating the measurement of audiences for the new services we have recommended. A degree of inaccuracy in the figures resulting from this system is inevitable, but at the same time it must not be so wildly at variance with what an Authority has good grounds for believing is the size of the audience that it will not be accepted throughout the industry as a fair standard. We make no recommendation concerning the running of the system but we express the belief that there should be one body responsible for carrying out the measurement of the sizes of audiences on all broadcasting outlets.

After the publication of his committee's report on broadcasting coverage, Sir Stewart Crawford had been asked in 1978 to head an ITCA/BBC inquiry into the way in which a controlling body should be set up to operate a unified audience research service. His subsequent recommendations had been accepted by the programme companies and the Corporation.

When it came to the appointment of a Chairman for a permanent joint body Sir Stewart was once more the obvious choice, and on 21 July 1980 the formation of the Broadcasters' Audience Research Board (BARB) was announced under his chairmanship. At its first meeting, two days later, it was agreed to set up a joint system of audience measurement for both services with effect from July 1981. In the meantime JICTAR signed a one-year agreement with AGB, based on the existing specification, at a fixed price of £1,154,000, to cover the period until the changeover.

But advertisers and agencies declared themselves less than satisfied with the new arrangements under BARB. They had not been consulted during the early discussions with the BBC and, being excluded from the board of the new body, their representation was confined to

---

BBC television regions. Once a joint ITV/BBC audience research system had been established BBC data had to be tabulated in accordance with the Corporation's area boundaries, which differ from those of Independent Television

ABERDEEN ■

SCOTLAND

GLASGOW ■ ■ EDINBURGH

■ STUDIO CENTRES

NEWCASTLE ■

NORTHERN
BELFAST ■
IRELAND

NORTH EAST

Isle of Man

NORTH WEST
LEEDS ■
MANCHESTER ■   NORTH

BANGOR ■

MIDLANDS ■
NORWICH ■

WALES   BIRMINGHAM ■

EAST ANGLIA

CARDIFF ■
BRISTOL ■   LONDON ■
WEST   SOUTH   SOUTH EAST
SOUTHAMPTON ■

SOUTH WEST

PLYMOUTH ■

Channel Islands

Source : BBC

membership of the subordinate Audience Measurement Management Committee (AMMC).

Since the publication of the Annan Report, however, the emphasis of audience measurement had been placed increasingly on the requirements of programme planning in meeting the needs of the viewing public. Had the new unified system of research been designed primarily to satisfy the demands of advertisers it is doubtful whether the BBC, several of whose senior executives were known to be opposed to sharing a system with Independent Television, would have agreed to participate. In its evidence to Annan the Corporation had stressed the importance of regular measurement of audience appreciation of programmes, a matter which was not of primary concern to advertisers and agencies, and the IBA and some of the companies had taken a similar line. And successive Broadcasting Acts since 1963 had stipulated that qualitative audience research should be carried out in Independent Television.

BARB was therefore, as the name implied, designed to be a policy-making research body for the broadcasters with two important operating committees, the AMMC and the Audience Reaction Management Committee (ARMC), reporting to it. The former was to provide the vital datum points of audience size, while the latter body, which included the IBA in its membership, would deal with questions of audience appreciation.

The Advertising Advisory Committee

On 1 August Professor Aubrey Diamond was appointed Chairman of the IBA's Advertising Advisory Committee on the retirement of Professor Royston Goode, who had occupied the chair of the AAC since July 1976. Aubrey Diamond, Professor of Law and Director of the Institute of Advanced Legal Studies in the University of London, was a leading authority on consumer protection, a field of increasingly complex legislation and control directly relevant to the work of the AAC.

The new contractors announced by the IBA

The chairmen of all the groups which had applied for the new licences were summoned by the IBA to Brompton Road on Sunday, 28 December to learn their fate. Southern and Westward heard that they were to be replaced by Television South and Television South-West respectively. Trident Television was told it would no longer be allowed to control Yorkshire and Tyne Tees, though the Authority said it would be prepared to consider a joint arrangement between the two companies for the sale of airtime. TV-am, as opposed to AM-TV, was awarded the contract for a national breakfast-time service to start in 1983.

All other contractors were reappointed subject to a number of conditions relating to changes in such matters as majority shareholdings, local representation, programme coverage, and the individual responsibilities of certain chairmen and managing directors. ATV would have to find a new name more indicative of its area.

Despite the total security which the Authority had managed to preserve for many months, some of this information appeared to have leaked out to a number of radio programmes including *The World This Weekend* on BBC Radio 4 at midday. But these reports probably arose from nothing more sinister than the unmistakeable demeanour of the various applicants seen leaving the IBA building during the morning. The full announcement had to await the IBA's press conference, presided over by Lady Plowden, at 5 pm the same day.

The new licence announcements: the aftermath

To the majority of those working in Independent Television the announcement of the new licences was accompanied by feelings of undisguised relief. Much of the uncertainty which had surrounded the future was removed. Job opportunities would undoubtedly improve with the increase in the number of employers and the expansion of the service.

From the management point of view plans, many of which had been in preparation for a year or more, could at last be progressed towards completion and orders to suppliers confirmed. Most important, those members of companies' staffs who had been covertly at work on behalf of the successful applicants for the new licences were now obliged to identify themselves. If the precedents of the change of contracts in 1968 were anything to go by, the vast majority of those working for Southern and Westward, the companies which were to lose their licences at the end of the following year, would be protected by the offer of re-employment from their successors.

But the transition was not going to be easy. If key staff were to leave for more rewarding openings elsewhere only a new company or one whose licence had been renewed could hope to attract replacements.

On the sales side many people who considered they had been held back by years of Government-inspired salary restraint began to make overtures to the new companies. It was a period of offers and counter-offers, of hesitancy and divided loyalties in whose light it was exceptionally difficult to maintain the confidence of advertisers and agencies whose expenditure alone supported the entire system.

The announcement of the new licences had one unexpected consequence. The relationships between the contractors and their customers, which, as the Authority had observed first-hand at the meetings of the newly formed Advertising Liaison Committee, had reached an absolute nadir in 1980, actually began to improve. For the second time in recent memory the full import of short-term ITV franchises and the risk of dismissal began to make its impact. Many of the programme companies' sternest critics reflected that it was scarcely remarkable if the contractors had pursued policies which had, at the time, seemed opportunistic and unyielding, if even a highly regarded and professional operation could be brought abruptly to an end with neither a note of warning nor the chance of appeal.

The revenue for 1980

Despite all the prevailing uncertainty and upheavals, the advertising revenue for 1980 showed the largest increase of any year since 1955. The total of £529,311,243 represented an improvement of 52.6 per cent on the strike-bound 1979 figure.

1981

The pattern of television ownership

When the year began Independent Television was reaching nearly twenty million homes – 97 per cent of those in the country – and colour was being received in three out of every four ITV households. But other forms of in-home entertainment were beginning to appear which would soon compete for the viewer's attention and complicate audience measurement. Nationally, 21 per cent of all homes – more in some areas – were using more than one television set and could therefore be expected to divide their viewing. The number of homes with video-cassette equipment still remained small, at 2 per cent nationally, but the figure was expected to rise sharply over the next few years. Clearly the audience-measurement system would soon have to take account of these competing forms of viewing activity.

LWT introduces an early payment discount

In January London Weekend Television announced the introduction of a 2½ per cent discount, on the lines already adopted by Thames, for agency accounts which were settled by the first working day following the month of transmission.

IBA developments

Three important developments took place under the aegis of the IBA. Lord Thomson, who had served as Deputy Chairman for the fifteen months since October 1979, became Chairman of the Authority in succession to Lady Plowden, who retired. The new Broadcasting Complaints Commission, which was to cover both Independent broadcasting and the BBC, held its first meeting, and the Channel Four Television Company came into being as a wholly owned subsidiary of the IBA.

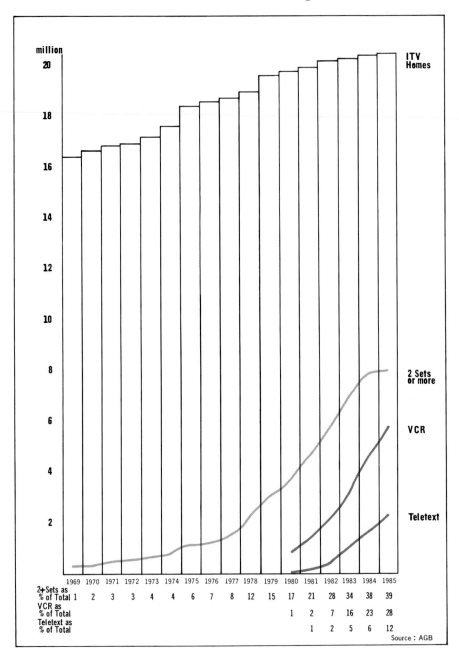

	1969	1970	1971	1972	1973	1974	1975	1976	1977	1978	1979	1980	1981	1982	1983	1984	1985
2+Sets as % of Total	1	2	3	3	4	4	6	7	8	12	15	17	21	28	34	38	39
VCR as % of Total													1	2	7	16	23	28
Teletext as % of Total														1	2	5	6	12

Source : AGB

Ownership of more than one set, VCR equipment and teletext in ITV homes 1969–85

ORACLE

The IBA had for some time been discussing with the companies a code of rules, for both editorial and advertising material on teletext, in order to comply with the requirements of the 1980 Broadcasting Act which specifically referred to this form of transmission. The Code, which was approved by the Home Secretary, was issued in May and divided into two parts – A, which applied to all teletext transmissions, including purely editorial matter, and B, which concerned advertisements only.

The rules in Part A extended the familiar programme requirements of the Broadcasting Acts to teletext but in a shorter, simplified form. Standards of good taste, decency, accuracy and impartiality were to be observed, and references to religion and charitable matters severely limited. There was a brief 'no-sponsorship' clause and another excluding the use of subliminal methods of communication.

But the rules on advertising presented some new problems. If advertisements on ORACLE were to have a reasonable chance of being seen, a facility must be provided to integrate advertising with editorial material, either by use of a 'trailer' or 'pointer' elsewhere in the system, or in the form of a composite page. The Authority agreed that fractional pages should be allowed, provided the advertisement occupied no more than 15 per cent of the total page area and was displayed in a different colour from the editorial part of the text. Products such as medicines, alcoholic drinks, tobacco and matches would not be allowed to appear on pages addressed to children. Full-page advertisements must again be clearly labelled to distinguish them from editorial, and the total amount of advertising in this 'solus' form must not exceed 15 per cent of the total number of pages in the system at any one time.

Given this maximum quota of advertising, regulated by realistic and flexible rules, the programme companies were hopeful that they would be able to recover the costs of establishing the ORACLE system within five years, and eventually be able to move into profit. It was, however, essential that ORACLE should have a Sales Department of its own, and during the year Humphrey Metzgen, a former senior marketing executive from Times Newspapers, was appointed Sales Controller of the new service. He attended meetings of the ITCA Marketing Committee to ensure close liaison with all the programme companies, whose support was essential. Plans were made to issue a rate card during the summer and to transmit the first paid-for advertisements from 1 September 1981.

The initial ORACLE rates for one week's transmission of a full-page nationally were set at £400, with £300 being charged for fractional advertisements booked to appear on specified pages. Discounts were applied to the cost of regional campaigns and to those booked to appear for four or more weeks consecutively.

When the service opened, 180,000 homes were capable of receiving ORACLE transmissions – a similarly modest figure to ITV's set count on opening night in 1955. But it was expected that ORACLE's coverage would grow with similar rapidity as an increasing number of set manufacturers and rental companies came to include teletext decoders as a standard part of the circuitry of their receivers and as the system became more widely known.

Direct Broadcasting by Satellite

During May the Home Office published its first report on Direct Broadcasting by Satellite in the form of a discussion document; it also reviewed a number of options which seemed to be available at the time. They revolved around the two alternatives of choosing either an early start date for a limited service in 1986–87 or delaying the introduction of a more ambitious system to 1990. The BBC and the Granada Group favoured making an early start, with two national UK channels being financed on a subscription basis. The IBA, on the other hand, said it wished to see Channel Four, which was not yet on the air, firmly established before the opening of a DBS service in 1990.

The Home Office had also examined forecasts which had been made of possible DBS advertising revenue, all of which were extremely pessimistic at least for the initial years. Audiences to DBS broadcasts would be likely to be small and difficult to measure and at the outset advertising income would be insufficient to finance the operating costs of £10,000,000 a year for even a rudimentary service of fifty hours a week. A service comparable with that of ITV or BBC would cost many times this amount and self-evidently would need other sources of finance.

Throughout the report the Home Office emphasized that any DBS channels which were eventually authorized should not be allowed to undermine the existing BBC and IBA services.

Taking all these factors into account, the future of Direct Broadcasting by Satellite looked decidedly gloomy.

The Advertising Liaison Committee

A number of features of programme company rate cards continued to trouble advertisers and agencies. Those most often referred to at meetings of the new Advertising Liaison Committee included:

1   Share or 'parity' schemes in which an advertiser would earn discount only if he spent a minimum percentage of his television budget with the station concerned. The required minimum figure was often based on that station's net coverage of ITV homes.

2   The cancellation rules.

3   The pre-emption rules. Agencies claimed that the period of notice given by contractors for the pre-emption of bookings should be the same as that required by the programme companies for cancellations.

4   The operation of 'per item' (PI) and local rates, both of which were considerably lower than other charges in the rate cards. They could be used, it was alleged, to increase a station's advertising minutage and therefore harden the market.

The majority of members of the ALC felt that these and a number of other complaints would best be satisfied if a set of principles could be agreed between all parties and used as the ground rules in the day-to-day sales operation. By the end of 1981 eight general principles, which may best be summarized as follows, had been agreed by which the contractors undertook to:

1   Use their best endeavours to sell the maximum permitted amount of airtime irrespective of the rate involved.

2   Define cut-off points after which spots would no longer be liable to be pre-empted.

3   Give reasons in writing when cancellations were refused.

4   Give more advance information to enable advertisers and agencies to judge the probable state of the airtime market. The contractors, however, declined to publish their past monthly revenues on a station-by-station basis, which was the guide to the level of demand which advertisers wanted.

5   Provide more information in advance of any changes being made in terms and conditions or in the structure of their rate cards.

The Principles Governing the Sale of Airtime, like many other 'Heads of Agreement', concealed in their somewhat bland and nebulous simplicity years of acrimony and misunderstanding. Yet the new rules were far from innocuous and represented a real step forward in the relationships between the contractors and their customers. As in most prolonged negotiations, there had been concessions on both sides. All present at the ALC recognized that the Principles, like the rules governing the content of television advertisements, were not immutable. They were expected to become more specific especially after Channel Four and the new breakfast-time service had come on the air.

Plans for breakfast TV and Channel Four announced

On 17 June the Authority announced that TV-am, which had been awarded the contract for a national breakfast-time service, would go on the air in May 1983. Like all the other programme contracts, TV-am's franchise was expected to last the full eight years, so that Peter Jay's consortium would continue to provide the early morning service until 1990. The Authority decided to delay the opening of breakfast TV so as to allow Channel Four to become established from the autumn of 1982 and to lessen the impact on the revenue of Independent Local Radio.

The first year's operating budget for Channel Four of £104,000,000 would be raised from the newly appointed contractors in broadly the same proportions as their ITV rentals.

TSW takes over from Westward

On 1 August Television South West replaced Westward Television some five months before the end of the latter's contract. Harry Turner, who had been Westward's Sales Director since September 1973, assumed similar responsibilities at TSW.

The end of 1981

On 1 December the Home Secretary announced an increase in the cost of a colour television licence to £46, and for black-and-white to £15, in order to provide much needed additional revenue for the BBC.

At the end of the year the STAGS and Trident operations came to an end, though a joint sales arrangement was to continue between Yorkshire and Tyne Tees Television under the Link operation.

Lord Windlesham left his position as Managing Director of ATV (which was to become Central Independent Television on 1 January 1982) and was succeeded by Robert Phillis, who had been Managing Director of the *TV Times*. Derek Palmar, Chairman of the Bass group of companies, became Chairman of Yorkshire Television in place of Sir Richard Graham.

Southern Television, which had provided the Independent Television service in the South of England since August 1958, broadcast its final programme on New Year's Eve. The transmission ended with the star of the company's familiar compass symbol growing ever smaller on the screen until it finally vanished into the firmament.

Revenue for the year

The last year of the old contracts proved to have been a successful one in terms of advertising revenue and showed an increase of 15.5 per cent on the total for 1980. The combined figure for all stations amounted to £611,236,286.

1982

The start of the new contracts

When the new programme contracts began it was not expected that the overall coverage of Independent Television would have increased significantly above the figure for January 1981. But within the new total of 20,151,000 homes it was known that a number of other important changes were beginning to take place. Colour penetration had risen to 15,718,000 or 78 per cent of all homes. Ownership of second sets was up to 28 per cent and videocassette recorders were now owned by 7 per cent of households.

With the transfer of the Maidstone (Bluebell Hill) transmitter from London to South and South-East England, and the announcement that the Tunbridge Wells relay was also being awarded to the South, the TVS set count had grown significantly to a figure approaching two million or 10 per cent of the network.

Some of these changes were recorded by the ISBA in a new edition of its manual, *Area Information 1982*, and reflected in the accompanying maps of ITV areas which once again eliminated overlap. For the first time a marketing survey, which would be widely used by advertisers, was based on the preliminary results of the population census of 1981, which had shown a number of significant changes from the 1971 figures.

Satellite television

Meanwhile a number of developments were taking place in the satellite field. In January Satellite Television Ltd (SATV) was set up with plans to launch an English-language programme service, financed by advertising from April 1982. Robert Kennedy was its Managing Director. SATV would initially make use of the European Orbital Test Satellite (OTS) for an experimental period of one year, with the possibility of a further extension. Thereafter SATV hoped to obtain access to a channel on the first European Communications Satellite (ECS–1).

On 4 March the Home Secretary announced that, following discussion of the paper on the subject which had been published in 1981, he proposed that two DBS channels on ECS–1 should be awarded to the BBC and a start made in 1986.

On 26 April SATV began its service with two hours of programmes a night. They were received initially in Norway, Finland and Malta, and Switzerland was added in July. But coverage was still small and reception confined to the cable networks which redistributed the signal.

Cable services

Of even more immediate importance than possible DBS channels were the opportunities for a large number of additional terrestrial services being provided on cable. The Government's Information Technology Advisory Panel (ITAP) had been asked to prepare a report and recommendations on the scope of cable services of all kinds, initially for the Minister for Information Technology, Kenneth Baker, and later for submission to the full Cabinet.

In a refreshingly frank and straightforward report the Panel noted that existing cable services in Britain were declining in importance and that unless action were taken quickly the market could be dominated by overseas systems and equipment. A Government decision should therefore be announced by mid-1982, recognizing that cable was the best means of distributing programmes from satellites, that entertainment channels and interactive services should be provided, that a supervisory authority with the minimum statutory powers was needed, and that private enterprise could be relied upon to provide the necessary finance. On the subject of advertising the Panel said:

The introduction of cable systems carrying advertising channels would offer advertisers a wider choice of medium, and would establish direct competition to off-air commercial services. It would also reduce the audience to commercial TV. ITV companies could thus be faced both with competition for TV advertising and a reduction in the rates they could charge, because of reduced audiences. This could force a cut in programme expenditure and consequently a decline in the range and quality of output.

On the other hand, the introduction of cable systems would enable far more firms to participate in TV advertising. These might either be firms with a local customer base, for whom national or regional advertising is irrelevant, or with a specialised market, who would wish to advertise on channels directed to that market. . . . But it is not clear that the introduction of cable systems would necessarily have a large effect on the advertising revenue base of off-air commercial TV services.

On balance, the Panel felt that cable services in Britain would rely predominantly on subscriptions rather than on advertising for their finance. Clearly a more searching examination of the numerous options which the ITAP had examined was required, and on 6 April a fuller inquiry was commissioned from a small committee of three under the former Cabinet Secretary, Lord Hunt of Tanworth. The programme companies, both through the ITCA and on their own account, gave evidence to the Hunt Committee. So did advertisers and agencies, through the ISBA and IPA.

Considering the magnitude of the issues and investment involved, the Committee was given an absurdly short time within which to make its report. Subsequent events were to prove the Government's plans to usher in the new technology by means of an entertainment-led consumer revolution to have been premature and insufficiently researched. As it was, the Committee followed the instruction it had been given in the Home Secretary's terms of reference and delivered its report on 28 September, just twenty-seven weeks after it had begun its work.

Its examination began with two dangerously naïve deductions. The first was based on the relationship, seldom a constant, between Gross National Product and advertising expenditure. The Committee noted that in 1960, advertising in all media had reached 1.43 per cent of GNP. If this ratio had been reached in 1980 (when it had actually dropped to 1.32 per cent), then an additional £200,000,000 would have been spent on advertising. And if the percentage had risen to the United States figure, advertising would have benefited by as much as £500,000,000. The second fallacy in the report was based on the belief that new advertising media invariably created their own sources of finance. Put both factors together and it seemed that there was plenty of advertising money to finance cable.

The Committee ended its necessarily brief and superficial review of the advertising prospects for cable with the words:

As we have already said we consider it very unlikely that the full potentiality of cable expansion could successfully be achieved without advertising revenue. We also believe that advertising on cable will have some positive benefits. Accordingly we recommend that it should be allowed.

The advertisers' view

In their submission to the Hunt Committee the ISBA argued strongly in favour of advertising being allowed on all cable channels as an essential and integral part of the service. It would not damage the revenue of other media, as some had claimed, and it was essential that the programme companies were excluded from any investment in, or control of, cable services. For this reason it was desirable that copy control of cable advertisements should be exercised through the ASA/CAP machinery (used by non-broadcast media), rather than through the usual IBA/ITCA pre-transmission scrutiny.

Thames Television and the Office of Fair Trading

In July one of the leading advertising agencies, the J. Walter Thompson Co., formally complained to the Office of Fair Trading about the operation of an incentive-discount scheme on Thames Television. This scheme gave an agency that guaranteed a predetermined proportion of its TV expenditure to the station the facility of buying airtime at one level below the customary rate. It will be recalled that Thames Television had for some years operated a complicated multi-stage pre-empt rate card.

The OFT referred the matter to the Authority, which issued a carefully worded reprimand based mainly on the fact that the Thames incentive scheme had not been disclosed in the company's rate card. But the hue and cry raised other issues.

Incentive schemes on Thames – and by implication those on other stations – would in future have to be shown by the contractors concerned to be free of the taint of 'unreasonable discrimination', in the words of the original Television Act which had seldom been invoked since 1955 but still remained in force. The Director-General of Fair Trading said that the OFT would examine the operation of television incentive schemes in general to see whether they seemed to be operating *prima facie* against the public interest.

Link Television ends pre-emption

On 13 September Link Television, the sales operation which serviced both Yorkshire and Tyne Tees Television, announced the ending of pre-emption on both stations. Trident Television had not been afraid to adopt a line of its own when it had brought volume discount to an end in 1980. The abolition of pre-emption by Trident's successor was widely welcomed but it was some time before other contractors made a similar move.

Fees for artists in commercials on Channel Four and TV-am

All the forecasts which had been made for Channel Four and TV-am showed that audiences were unlikely, in general, to reach the levels of the majority of those for other ITV transmissions. The IPA therefore proposed reduced fees for artists appearing in commercials on the two new channels, a view supported by the majority of advertisers.

Equity, the actors' trade union, however, took the view that the fees ought to be the same as those already paid for appearances in commercials on ITV1. After all, there were already a number of programmes on the existing channel which obtained low ratings, and commercials appearing around those programmes reached audiences which were no higher than those expected for Channel Four and TV-am. Payment of artists' fees had not hitherto been geared to a box-office principle of audience size.

The contractors stood aloof from this dispute because the engagement of artists for commercials was entirely a matter for the agencies, production companies and ultimately the advertisers themselves. If, on the other hand, the dispute resulted in a deadlock, then an embargo by Equity on commercials for Channel Four and Breakfast TV could have an immediate effect on the revenue of the contractors and therefore the very survival of the new channels.

It was clear that the negotiations between Equity and the IPA were in imminent danger of complete breakdown when the air date of Channel Four was only a month away.

Channel Four revenue figures

While these negotiations were going on, the IPA and ISBA asked the contractors to disclose separate revenue figures for ITV and Channel Four, the previous decision not to publish ITV revenue by companies having been confirmed. The view of the ITCA was that global figures only, showing the combined ITV and Channel Four revenues, should be published.

Channel Four and S4C

On 1 November the Welsh fourth channel (Sianel Pedwar Cymru – S4C) opened, followed twenty-four hours later by Channel Four itself. The IBA's transmitter-conversion programme had been consistently ahead of schedule and, instead of the 82 per cent coverage originally promised by the Authority, on opening night the new service proved to be within reach of 87 per cent of the population.

ORACLE regional service in London

ORACLE had now developed a regional service of advertising and editorial pages in Scotland and, since February 1982, the Channel Islands. During November a regional service opened in London.

A new Director-General of the IBA

On 12 November John Whitney, former Managing Director of Capital Radio and founder of the Local Radio Association, was appointed Director-General of the IBA. He succeeded Sir Brian Young, who retired at the age of sixty.

Revenue for the year

When the year ended the figures showed a percentage increase almost as great as that for the previous year. At £697,079,051 the revenue of the network was up by 14.1 per cent on 1981.

1983

The Equity/IPA dispute

When the year began, the dispute between Equity and the IPA over the rates of payment for artists appearing in commercials on Channel Four and TV-am had not been resolved. The union proposed that for the first six months of 1983 a temporary arrangement should be made at 50 per cent of the ITV1 rate, but the IPA rejected this suggestion.

The programme companies, whose Channel Four revenue had been severely affected by the dispute, were allowed by the IBA to redistribute advertising minutage on ITV1 in order to gain up to two additional minutes between 6 and 10.30 pm each day as a temporary compensation for loss of revenue. But it was difficult to see what could be done to help TV-am when it went on the air in February.

During January the 1983 subscription for Channel Four was announced by the IBA at £123,000,000, approximating to 18 per cent of ITV1 revenue. In the light of the Equity dispute it was obvious that all stations would have to subsidize Channel Four heavily to meet the subscription figure.

The start of breakfast television

It had originally been planned that TV-am should go on the air in May but, after hearing that the BBC intended to start its own breakfast-time programmes at an earlier date, the opening of ITV's *Good Morning Britain* was moved forward to 1 February. The BBC replied by announcing that its breakfast programme would begin on 17 January, thus gaining a precious two-week start on Independent Television.

TV-am opened on 1 February to the accompaniment of considerable publicity, not all of it favourable. When the viewing figures were issued at the end of the month it became clear that the BBC had established a 2:1 lead over ITV in the first four weeks of early-morning transmissions.

The following month the situation deteriorated further as a result of serious disagreements within the company. Peter Jay, Chairman and Chief Executive of TV-am, resigned on 18 March, to be replaced temporarily by Jonathan Aitken, who was in turn succeeded by his cousin, Timothy, on 14 April. By this time all the members of the so-called Famous Five who had so impressed the IBA at the time of the licence application – David Frost, Michael Parkinson, Angela Rippon, Anna Ford and Robert Kee – had left the company. When a new Editor-in-Chief, Greg Dyke, was appointed from London Weekend Television at the beginning of May TV-am's share of the viewing audience had fallen to 15 per cent of the BBC's figures.

Cable television: the White Paper

Debate and speculation had continued since the publication of the Hunt Committee's report on cable in September 1982, and on 27 April the Government issued its White Paper, *The Development of Cable Systems and Services*, outlining a number of steps it intended to take even before legislation had been drafted and debated. In the first instance it announced that it was prepared to offer ten to twelve pilot licences for cable services covering 'identifiable and self-contained communities of not more than 100,000 homes' for a period of twelve years.

In the longer term the White Paper envisaged the appointment of a supervisory Cable Authority which would award franchises and licences in areas of up to 500,000 homes on the basis of competitive bids. It would be obligatory for each cable operator to provide all existing BBC and IBA sound and radio services, and to be able to accommodate all five DBS channels.

On advertising the White Paper said:

A wider range of advertising will be possible on cable than on independent broadcasting. With appropriate safeguards some sponsorship will also be permitted. Cable advertising which is analogous to ITV and ILR advertising will be restricted to the amounts allowed under IBA rules. Classified advertising and channels wholly or mainly devoted to advertising will be excluded from this limitation.

So it appeared that, while conventional advertising on cable would be limited, like that on ITV, to 10 per cent of total transmission time, classified advertising, which the programme companies hoped to attract to ORACLE, would be allowed in addition.

On 26 November the new Home Secretary, Leon Brittan, announced the granting of licences to eleven consortia for the provision of the first pilot cable services in Aberdeen, Belfast, Coventry, Croydon, Ealing, Glasgow, Guildford, Liverpool, Swindon, Westminster and Windsor. It was calculated that the cables would 'pass' only a million homes in these places and that an investment of £300,000,000 (at 1983 prices) would be required. It looked as if it would be some time before cable services presented any kind of a threat to Independent Television in either audience or advertising terms.

Developments in audience research

During March BARB discussed the replacement of self-completion diaries, from which information on individual viewing behaviour had been obtained for many years, by either a push-button system or an electronic viewing diary. At this stage the companies preferred the latter because of its ability to record guest viewing and the use of battery-operated portable sets. The BBC, IPA and ISBA, however, favoured the simpler but less flexible push-button meter by which each member of a household could record his or her viewing. This method was eventually adopted as the basis of the Enhanced Measurement System (EMS) which was introduced in December.

An important change was also made to the definition of ITV coverage, which still relied on the 15 per cent density of reception line. As a result of the virtual completion of national coverage in UHF the continued use of this form of definition created an overlap factor of nearly one-third (32 per cent). In the light of this figure the programme companies agreed that area boundaries should in future be drawn on the basis of 'preference' rather than simply 'ability' to view.

Signs of recovery at TV-am

The first signs of recovery began to appear at TV-am during July, when the station's share of audience returned to 32 per cent. By August the figure had climbed to a majority share of 52 per cent against the BBC's *Breakfast Time*, partly, it is true, because of the success of *Roland Rat* in capturing a large children's audience during the school holidays, but also because of other on-screen improvements which had been introduced.

On the sales side Tony Vickers, who had been widely expected to join TV-am when the company was formed, was appointed Sales Director from Link Television on 1 July. It began to look as if the revenue figures which had appeared in many of the original licence applications would at last be attainable. In November Fleet Holdings acquired 20 per cent and Kerry Packer a 10 per cent investment in the station.

Direct-response advertising

On 1 September the IBA, after further discussions on the subject at the ALC, decided to place restrictions on the transmission of 'per item' (PI) advertising. These spots would no longer be transmitted between 6 and 10 pm and bookings would be confirmed only after the deadline for pre-emption, so as to widen the availability of airtime for other advertisers.

DBS contracts: the Home Secretary's announcement

In the same month the Home Secretary announced that legislation would be introduced before the end of the year to enable the IBA to issue contracts for DBS channels, with a provisional starting date in 1987-88.

Revenue for the year

The eventual increase in revenue for the year showed a return to the high percentage level which had been seen regularly before the change of contracts in 1982. Revenue for 1983 was 18.5 per cent up on the previous year's figure and now stood at £824,310,721.

November in particular had been phenomenally successful. In this month the network obtained a record total of £96,645,272 – the highest monthly figure ever reached throughout the thirty years from 1955 to September 1985.

1984

The 1984 Establishment Survey

By the beginning of 1984 the full extent of growing competition for viewing time was revealed with the results of the Establishment Survey. The penetration of colour-set ownership had now reached 85 per cent of all the 20,464,000 homes covered by Independent Television; 38 per cent of homes had more than one set, 23 per cent had portables, while 6 per cent were able to receive the ORACLE and Ceefax teletext services. Nearly one in four homes – 4,678,000 – had VCR equipment.

ORACLE regional service opens in all areas

In January ORACLE announced that the number of field-blanking lines, which provided the necessary capacity for teletext transmissions, was being increased from four to six. As a result the response times of the system improved, and in April it became possible to provide a regional service for both editorial and advertising purposes in all fourteen areas of Independent Television.

Satellite services and the ITV contracts

In May the Government announced its plans for a three-channel Direct Broadcasting Satellite service to be set up in 1987 in place of the two-channel BBC-only service which had been planned for 1986 and abandoned on grounds of cost. It would use the British Unisat system provided by British Telecom, GEC-Marconi and British Aerospace.

The BBC and ITV would be given one channel each, while a third would be awarded to a consortium consisting of Thorn-EMI, Granada TV Rentals, S. Pearson, Virgin Records and Consolidated Satellite Broadcasting – described as the 'Third Force'. The total cost, at current prices, was expected to amount to £560,000,000 over seven years.

If the existing ITV contractors were going to recoup their share of this massive investment in the satellite programme, it was obviously essential for their contracts to be extended beyond the existing expiry date of 31 December 1989. The IBA said that if the programme went ahead along the lines described it would not expect to readvertise the contracts before 1989 at the earliest, and that the existing contractual arrangements would therefore be likely to remain undisturbed until 1997.

The report of the Adam Smith Institute

On 4 May a report was published which was to prove the opening salvo in a debate of increasing acrimony about the fundamental question of the way in which the broadcasting services of Britain should be financed. The Adam Smith Institute issued its *Omega Report*, which left the reader in no doubt where its sympathies lay. It declared:

If television is to have a healthy future in Britain then it must move towards the demands of its audience. Logically, the only possible way this can occur is by moving away from the television licence fee to other forms of finance. . . there can be little future for a system which discriminates against the paying viewer in favour of the decisions of the bureaucrat.

The report, couched in the trenchant style of an eighteenth-century pamphleteer, described the orthodox view of 'quality' broadcasting as 'elitist' and dismissed the BBC's 'commercial virginity' as self-deception of a high order in the light of the publicity the Corporation allegedly gave on the air to its own records, books, computer systems and sponsored events. In addition, it was claimed, BBC programmes on all channels were 'studded with advertising plugs' for a wide range of goods and services from other sources.

The report went on to urge that the prohibition of the advertising of cigarettes, betting and other banned categories of advertising on ITV should be removed forthwith, and BBC1 and *Breakfast Time* allowed to carry commercials. BBC2 should be financed by a mixture of cross-channel subsidy, public subscription and sponsorship.

The VHF wavelengths in Bands I and III, which had formerly been used by BBC1 and ITV and which the Government had foreseen as ideal for re-engineering on 625 lines to provide two further television services, should, according to the Adam Smith Institute, be allocated to radio. The IBA should be replaced by a more 'commercially aware' body on the lines of the American Federal Communications Commission.

The findings of the *Omega Report* found favour with a number of advertising agencies who were also preparing a case for advertising to be allowed on the BBC.

The new audience-research contract

In January AGB began to phase in the new Enhanced Measurement System (EMS) which was intended to replace the earlier Setmeters by September. The new meters could record viewing on up to four receivers through a Remote Detection Unit (RDU), and the main meter itself could be activated to record the viewing of up to eight individuals via a push-button handset. The old tapes and diaries were done away with because the meter acted as a data-storage unit which could be scanned at night and the information transferred automatically to AGB's central computer via a normal telephone line.

When the first reports appeared they showed an immediate improvement in ITV ratings, suggesting that a great deal of previous viewing had gone unrecorded. But there were a number of other factors at work to increase audience levels, including the greater appeal of programming and the rising total of unemployed, for whom TV offered a form of low-cost entertainment.

An important part of the new audience-measurement equipment for homes on the AGB panel was the RDU, a 'slave' of the main meter, which was able to record viewing on up to four subsidiary sets provided they were mains-powered. It was planned to use a modified RDU to record viewing via a VCR. The IPA and the ISBA were, however, opposed to the inclusion of 'time shift' viewing to recorded programmes within the total audience figures because of the tendency of viewers to 'zap' through recorded commercials.

The end of the Equity/IPA dispute

A vote among Equity members on 18 September at last led the union to accept a revised offer of fees for artists who appeared in commercials on Channel Four and TV-am. The rates were agreed at 55 per cent and 37 per cent respectively of the ITV1 rate.

With the ending of the dispute on 1 October, and the all-round improvement in ratings to Channel Four, the programme companies looked forward to much-needed revenue increases from this source. TV-am was already experiencing an increase in revenue.

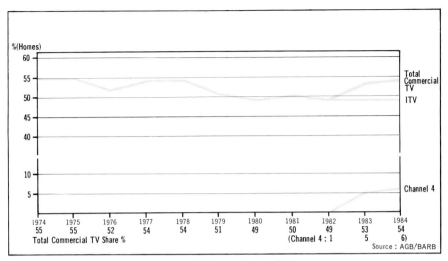

Share of viewing to ITV and Channel Four, 1974–84

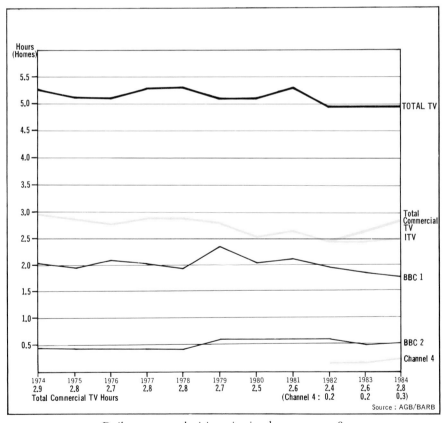

Daily average television viewing hours, 1974–84

Revenue and advertising minutage

The revenue for the autumn, however, proved disappointing. October's figure showed only a 1 per cent improvement on the total for October 1983, while November, which at one stage had been expected to be the first month to reach £100,000,000, in the event recorded a fall of 3 per cent to £93,800,000.

The concession which the IBA had given the contractors, to enable them to redistribute their daily advertising allowance to gain an extra two minutes a day between 6 and 10.30 pm to help compensate for the effects of the Equity dispute on the revenue of Channel Four, was now withdrawn. One minute of advertising was removed on 29 October and the remainder on 25 November.

December's revenue showed a slight improvement, with an increase of 3 per cent on the same month of 1983. But the year as a whole, bearing in mind the results in the first six months, was only 10.7 per cent up, at £912,265,807.

Separate sales on Yorkshire and Tyne Tees

The joint sales operation for Yorkshire and Tyne Tees, Link Television, came to an end on 31 December and the two companies went their separate ways for the first time in over twenty years.

1985

The BBC licence fee

The BBC licence fee of £46 for colour television and £15 for black-and-white, which had been established three years earlier, was already overdue for revision when the year began. The BBC had argued that cost inflation in broadcasting was already running well ahead of the increase in retail prices, and that if they were to maintain their existing services a licence increase of 50 per cent was needed if the new fee was to remain at the same level for a further three years. The Corporation began a publicity campaign with the slogan 'The BBC – the best bargain in Britain'.

The lobby for the BBC to accept advertising was, however, already gathering momentum. Just before the Christmas recess eleven Conservative MPs had tabled a motion in the House of Commons calling for the complete abolition of the licence fee and for the BBC to be allowed to take advertising on at least some of its radio and television channels. And although a private member's bill for the same purpose was defeated by 159 votes to 118, it was clear that a major controversy would bring matters to a head within a few months.

The Dallas affair

On the face of it there seemed little connection between the financial predicament of the BBC and the renewal of the purchase of its most successful imported soap opera, *Dallas*. But the attempt by Thames Television's Managing Director, Bryan Cowgill, a former BBC Channel Controller, to outbid his former employers by offering double the price for the new series – without consulting the other ITV companies – merely served to highlight the Corporation's financial problems. Eventually, after six months of acrimonious exchanges and the involvement of the chairmen of both the BBC and the IBA, Bryan Cowgill tendered his resignation and was succeeded as Managing Director of Thames by Richard Dunn. As a result of the *Dallas* affair the informal agreement between the BBC and the programme companies not to outbid one another for programme purchases was referred to the Office of Fair Trading.

Channel Four

The audiences to Channel Four continued to improve and by January had reached an 8.6 per cent share; 74 per cent of the ITV audience was viewing Channel Four at least once a week and 90 per cent at least once a month. In January, however, the IBA announced that the subscription for Channel Four, which was borne by the contractors under their franchises, would be increased by 15.8 per cent to £161,000,000, a figure still well ahead of its estimated revenue.

Four of the companies decided that a joint Channel Four advertising rate was needed which, with a generous allowance towards commercial production costs, would attract additional advertisers towards the channel. Early in the year London Weekend, TVS, Anglia and Central Television, covering between them half the network, announced special rates for the period 1 March 1985 to 31 January 1987.

On 3 June Giles Shaw, Minister of State at the Home Office, disclosed that Channel Four's revenue had reached 11.1 per cent of the ITV figure in the first quarter of 1985 compared with only 4.6 per cent in the corresponding period of 1984.

Revenue in 1985

The downward trend of revenue which had begun the previous November, however, continued into 1985. In January the figure fell by 2.2 per cent, with a larger drop of 7.6 per cent in February. Even when allowance was made for the fact that the February of 1984 (a Leap Year) had included an extra day, the drop was still 4.7 per cent. The March figure showed a fall of 5 per cent and the first quarter of the year an overall reduction of 4 per cent.

The Peat, Marwick report on the BBC

The financial problems of Independent Television, which had led to the curtailment of a number of plans for expansion, were reflected in the situation of the BBC. In March the accountants Peat, Marwick, Mitchell and Co. produced a report for the Corporation which advocated a greater use of independent producers (in a similar way to

Channel Four), the sale of some assets, an improvement in management information and the use of outside contractors for a wide variety of services. It appeared that the Corporation would have to make savings of £65,000,000 a year and that there might be up to four thousand redundancies.

The Chairman and Director-General claimed that the BBC had emerged creditably from the investigation, but one of the consultants from Peat, Marwick who had taken part said that two hundred pages of their report (which had not been published) contained a number of critical comments and that their findings had, in some cases, been distorted.

New licence fees and the Peacock Committee announced

On 28 March the Home Secretary announced an immediate increase in the colour-licence fee to £58, and to £18 for black-and-white. At the same time a Committee was appointed, under Professor Alan Peacock of Heriot-Watt University, to examine the future financing of the BBC by advertising, sponsorship or other alternative means. It was hoped that the Committee would make its recommendation by the summer of 1986, and written evidence was invited by 31 August 1985.

Plans for 'SuperChannel'

The original 'Club of 21' (consisting of the BBC, ITCA and the so-called Third Force), which had hoped to provide a Direct Broadcasting by Satellite service, decided early in the year to abandon their plans largely on grounds of the high cost of the British Unisat system which the Government had stipulated. In the light of the appointment of the Peacock Committee, and the possibility that the BBC might eventually be financed by advertising, it seemed that these plans might have to be shelved indefinitely.

The programme companies, however, saw scope for a European satellite service to be known as SuperChannel (which might be carried on ECS–3) being launched by Independent Television. It would broadcast existing ITV material, including news, from 6.25 am until early the following morning. The service, which would be made available free throughout continental Europe, would be financed by advertising. It was hoped that a start could be made by October 1986, and the signal received by master aerials and distributed on cable to an estimated ten million homes. Meanwhile the Government decided that the original DBS contracts would be readvertised.

Schools broadcasts and Channel Four

It had been hoped during 1984 that schools broadcasts, which had been transmitted on ITV during the mornings since 1957, would be moved to Channel Four in the autumn term of 1985 and general programmes introduced in their place from 9.30 am onwards on ITV1. An early change was, however, out of the question in the light of the revenue situation. The transfer of schools programmes was finally postponed until the autumn of 1987 after tentative plans had been abandoned for a start in 1986.

TV-am

The audience to TV-am continued to improve and its increasing dominance over the BBC's *Breakfast Time* began to be reflected in its advertising revenue. It was now regularly achieving a sales figure of between £1,300,000 and £2,700,000 a month and was expected to produce at least £28,000,000 in 1985. By June TV-am was regularly obtaining two-thirds of the viewing audience against the BBC.

ITV revenue improves

Apart from April, when revenue again fell – by 0.15 per cent – the next few months began to show a steady improvement on the figures for 1984. May was 7.9 per cent up on the previous year, June by 0.7 per cent and July by 10.1 per cent. In August the double-figure increase was maintained at 11.67 per cent while in September the improvement was one of 12 per cent. Agencies began to revise their estimates for the year as a whole.

Changes among the Sales Directors

The last two years had witnessed an almost complete change of sales directors among the television companies. Peter Rennie had retired from Granada at the end of 1984 and had been succeeded by Nick Phillips from the Beecham Group. Harry Turner had become Managing Director of TSW and was succeeded by Pauline Shuker, while Jonathan Shier had gone from Scottish Television to follow Tony Logie (who had been appointed Sales Director of Sky Channel) at Thames.

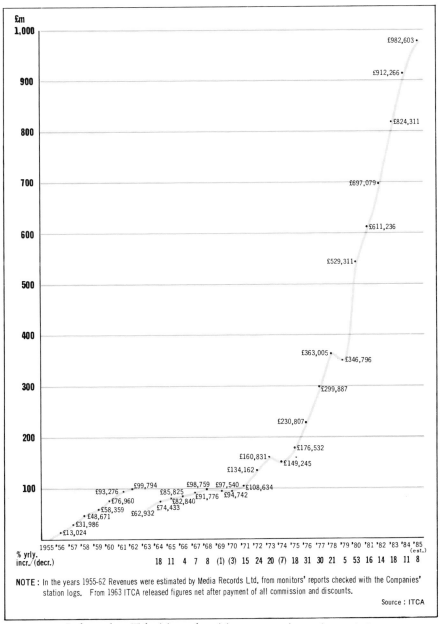

£m

| £982,603 · |
| £912,266 · |
| · £824,311 |
| £697,079 · |
| · £611,236 |
| £529,311 · |
| £363,005 · |
| · £346,796 |
| · £299,887 |
| £230,807 · |
| · £176,532 |
| £160,831 · |
| · £149,245 |
| £134,162 · |
| £99,794 |
| £98,759 £97,540 · £108,634 |
| £93,276 · |
| £85,825 |
| · £76,960 |
| · £91,776 · £94,742 |
| £82,840 |
| · £58,359 |
| £74,433 |
| £62,932 |
| · £48,671 |
| · £31,986 |
| · £13,024 |

1955 '56 '57 '58 '59 '60 '61 '62 '63 '64 '65 '66 '67 '68 '69 '70 '71 '72 '73 '74 '75 '76 '77 '78 '79 '80 '81 '82 '83 '84 '85
(est.)

% yrly.
incr./(decr.)   18 11   4   7   8 (1) (3) 15 24 20 (7) 18 31 30 21   5 53 16 14 18 11   8

NOTE : In the years 1955-62 Revenues were estimated by Media Records Ltd. from monitors' reports checked with the Companies'
station logs.   From 1963 ITCA released figures net after payment of all commission and discounts.

Source : ITCA

Independent Television advertising revenue in ooo's 1956–85
(see Appendix K p. 511)

Pre-emption and new sales methods

The pressure from advertisers on the contractors to end pre-emption still continued, and it was interesting to note that some companies had refrained from using this method of selling on Channel Four. Border, Granada, TSW and TVS all made their Channel Four bookings non-pre-emptible, while London Weekend did not employ pre-emption on either of its channels.

When Anglia announced, several months in advance, that it intended to abandon pre-emption altogether on both channels from 1 January 1986, a number of other companies began to consider reverting to a conventional rate structure. In a rising market pre-empt rates had helped to maximize revenue, but this form of selling had involved a disproportionate amount of prolonged negotiations both for the ITV sales departments and the advertising agencies. After six years without price controls the programme companies were beginning to feel that another kind of rate structure was needed.

The new generation of sales directors was already examining different methods of airtime selling designed to enable advertisers to target their campaigns more accurately to specific sectors of the television audience. Thames Television announced that, in future, sales executives' responsibilities would be allocated by target markets, identified by types of audiences rather than by categories of advertising or other more familiar systems of delegation.

Developments in ORACLE

ORACLE was reaching 2,800,000 homes by the end of September and could claim an average daily page 'traffic' of nearly two million viewers. Its classified advertising revenue had increased from 2 per cent to 20 per cent of its income. ORACLE was expected to provide an important ancillary medium which could be used in conjunction with the improved direct-response facilities which the contractors were beginning to introduce, especially in the financial area where advertising restrictions had recently been relaxed.

The end of the first thirty years

But undoubtedly the biggest question which remained unresolved at the end of the first thirty years of Independent Television was whether or not the BBC was to be allowed to derive its income, in whole or in part, from the sale of advertising.

The Royal Television Society Convention, held once again in September in Cambridge, had been devoted to 'Television in the 1990s'. Both the formal proceedings and the televised debate on the subject showed the overwhelming majority of those who worked in broadcasting to be strongly opposed to the introduction of any form of advertising on the Corporation's channels. So were most of the 474 submissions which Peacock had received up to the end of August, though subsequent research and written evidence seemed to reflect the opposite view. The issue was not, in any case, likely to be resolved until the end of 1986.

The first thirty years of Independent Television ended, therefore, as they had begun, in an atmosphere of uncertainty and considerable apprehension for the future. ITV had been introduced only ten years after the Second World War at a time when the public which would provide the audiences, and the business community which was expected to supply the advertising revenue, were both conditioned by shortages, rationing and regulation. It was inevitable, too, in the 1950s that in broadcasting the scarcity of television channels would create the need for supervision and control by central authorities ultimately answerable to Parliament. Above all, the potentialities of television as an advertising medium were largely unexplored and unknown. Indeed, it was by no means certain that ITV, being totally dependent on advertising revenue, would actually survive.

The world of the eighties had, by contrast, witnessed a social revolution against the background of swift and complex technical advances which brought in their train universal television coverage and the possibility of an almost unlimited number of programmes being made available by cable and satellite. As an advertising medium television had, at the end of its first thirty years, established its pre-eminence, as a result of its sheer effectiveness, in almost every field of products and services. Yet the financial problems of the programme companies persisted even in a state of virtual advertising monopoly. It seemed that the broadcasting institutions themselves, as well as their sources of finance, would in the next thirty years be likely to undergo changes no less radical than the technical developments which have formed the background to this long and eventful history.

Wise Hindsight

PETER RENNIE

PETER RENNIE

Educated at St John's School, Leatherhead, Peter Rennie later saw service in the Royal Navy, principally in the Adriatic in minesweepers. At the end of the Second World War, and after training at RADA, he went on the stage. In 1952 he became Radio Controller at J. Walter Thompson. In 1954, while at JWT, he set up and headed, arguably, the first television time-buying unit in the UK.

In 1962 he joined Granada Television as Deputy Sales Director. He became Sales Director in 1967, since when he has served on a number of industry committees. Within ITCA he was Chairman of the Copy Committee for two years and of the Marketing Committee for a total of five years.

It was in his capacity as Chairman of the Marketing Committee that Peter Rennie made the initial approaches to the BBC from which stemmed the Broadcasters' Audience Research Board (BARB), of which he is a director.

He retired from Granada Television in February 1985 and today acts as Marketing Consultant to the Granada group

WHEN I was invited to write a chapter covering the period since the publication of the Annan Report I was tempted to take the advice of Voltaire: 'Mind your own business and cultivate your garden.' There can be little doubt that this period – the first half of the eighties – has witnessed more turbulence and more change than any other in the thirty years of ITV's history. Nevertheless, I have exceeded my brief by starting at the point when the previous franchises were granted because of the impact of those changes on Granada and on our sales and marketing activities.

Up until 1968 Granada had operated the weekday franchise for both Lancashire and Yorkshire, and was in competition with ABC at the weekends. ABC also operated on weekends in the Midlands against ATV on weekdays. ATV held the weekend franchise in London. A fuller description is contained in another chapter, but these few details serve to illustrate the odd nature of the contracts held by Granada, ABC and ATV. From a financial viewpoint Granada's original franchise generated a much larger share of network revenue than that which was to follow – the seven-day franchise for the North-West region – but what it did, for the first time, was allow us genuinely to represent an identifiable marketing region with distinct characteristics, most of which proved uniquely exploitable. Previously it had been extremely difficult to construct a compelling case for two very different and often disparate regions which, in any case, we only represented for five days per week. It is said of Lancashire and Yorkshire that the only thing they have in common is the M62; in our day, even that wasn't true.

We were fortunate to be one of the founding sponsors of the Television Consumer Audit which was started on the initiative of ATV who, like Granada, recognized the need to acquire robust and dynamic data about their new market. Today TCA is taken very much for granted, but from 1970 it did much to revolutionize the work of our sales departments and the views of many of our clients.

It was the first service to use ITV regions as a basis for marketing data. It was the first to measure actual consumer purchases in the home rather than through retail outlets. It was the first to be set up and heavily subsidized by a media owner with a view unambiguously to inform and to influence its clients. Few would deny that a great deal of today's marketing expertise was, if not generated, at least stimulated by the arrival and exploitation of TCA data.

The constituents of the quiet revolution which was to follow were legion. From where Granada stood, the most significant was the decision to switch signal standards from VHF to UHF. The good news was that the medium was to be hugely enhanced by the gradual introduction of colour on UHF (see Charts 1 and 2, pages 24 and 25); this surely was the least heralded and most fundamental event of the decade, and one which the companies never quite found the right moment to promote. Television had always been the most compelling medium, but it was colour which finally gave it the edge over all other media. Consider for example the enhancement which colour brought to *Brideshead Revisited* on the one hand or, more prosaically, to the instant identity of Kellogg's cornflakes or Boot's No 7.

The then ITA acknowledged that the shallower pattern of the UHF signal would reduce the range of the signal from existing transmitters and that it would need to be compensated by the construction of a number of booster transmitters. Consequently, with the sole (and to us, disturbing) exception of the North-West region, the transmission areas were all enlarged; this in turn led to a considerable increase in the degree to which one area overlapped another. In 1972 only one-fifth of the homes in the UK lay within overlap areas; by 1982 they had risen to almost one-third. It was a slow, insidious change brought about by the process of television-set replacement (from monochrome VHF to colour UHF). Its effect on Granada demonstrated itself in a long-drawn-out decline in our franchise area, accompanied by a parallel fall in share of network revenue.

Another side-effect of what was generally called the 'overlap problem' was that it became increasingly difficult for manufacturers to continue to use the ITV map for the purposes of distribution and market analysis. The ISBA called for discrete transmission areas. The television companies, while conscious that a problem existed, refused to allow their individual transmission areas to be tampered with. From the impasse which followed there emerged an ISBA marketing map which, by means that the companies regarded as arbitrary and unsatisfactory, eliminated overlap altogether.

In the meantime the process of transfer from VHF to UHF was complete. VHF transmissions were dropped and, with the prospect of relatively little further change to the shape of things, in 1983 the companies faced up to the problems posed by the conventional method of area definition which had served us well in the past but which was no longer adequate. The overlap problem had to be resolved.

By agreement with the ISBA and the IPA, and after a good deal of close cooperation, a formula was thrashed out in 1984 which used 'preference to view' data as a means to refine the traditional 15 per cent criterion. This formula would serve to realign every transmission area and to reduce the proportion of homes in overlap to 18 per cent (see Table 1).

TABLE 1: PROPORTION OF TV HOUSHOLDS IN OVERLAP			
%	1972	1982	1984
London	27	36	29
Midlands	38	49	30
North-west	18	46	29
Yorkshire	47	74	28
Central Scotland	14	16	8
Wales	30	54	33
South	42	59	44
North-east	28	67	19
East	78	56	56
South-west	37	30	19
Border	25	41	30
North Scotland	49	45	22
Ulster	—	—	—
Network	20	31	18

Source: JICTAR/BARB

It is to the credit of the medium, but at considerable cost to its management, that television is seen to be so important, so central to contemporary civilization, that it is almost constantly the subject of official inquiry. Considering the periods covered by the Pilkington, Annan and Hunt inquiries – and now Peacock – and adding to those the statutory reviews and renewal of contracts, there have been very few years in which some trauma, some sword of Damocles, has not hovered over the industry. If heart or lung disease, one-parent families or drug abuse had enjoyed the same critical attention, it is possible that the public good would have been better served.

Be that as it may, the granting of a seven-day franchise – at least in the view of the television companies' clients – is tantamount to the award of a monopoly. It is the contention of the companies, of course, that they do not have a monopoly in the sense that all other media compete with TV and vice versa. It is an argument which does not appeal to those of our clients who are heavily or totally committed to television, but the monopoly theory is diminished by the fact that, since the early seventies, the companies have been successful in broadening the base of their revenue by the acquisition of a whole new raft of business which they have wrested from the competition – principally from Fleet Street.

Some of the marketing data which follow and which plot the changing pattern of expenditure across the seventies are derived from advertisers' expenditure on Granada. However, they can be said to reflect the pattern of events across the network quite closely.

In 1970 there were virtually no colour sets, no daytime or breakfast-time broadcasts, no VCRs, no Prestel, ORACLE or Ceefax, no fourth channel, no video games, and only 22 per cent of homes had a second set. Between the three channels we broadcast 7280 hours per annum, with BBC2 penetration at only 37 per cent of homes. Fifteen years later, all four channels have blanket coverage, colour is in 84 per cent of homes and more than one-third of them have at least two television sets.

In 1985 the four channels (including TV-am and *Breakfast Time*) transmitted approximately 22,500 hours – an increase of 309 per cent in the choice offered to an increasingly discerning public – and average hours viewed per day increased by 10.8 per cent from 4.6 hours to 5.1 hours (excluding breakfast-time transmissions). At the same time the universe (individuals four years old and over) has increased by 5.4 per cent from 48.4 million to 51 million. The average monochrome transmission of *Coronation Street* in autumn 1970 was delivered to 7.5 million homes, while in 1985, in colour, it was delivered to more than 9 million homes. *The Mousetrap*, now in its thirty-third year, would need to run, to full houses, for a further sixty-four years before achieving the coverage of just one transmission of *Coronation Street*.

Only in 1974, due to the oil crisis, and in 1979, the year of the ACTT dispute, did revenue actually decline (see Chart on page 235), the average annual current price increase over the fifteen years being 18 per cent. In reality, after inflation, the picture is somewhat different; revenue in each of the years from 1974 to 1977 was less than in 1973, and the average real annual increase is less than 6 per cent over the whole period. Seen against the changes in size and quality already described, ITV would appear to have given extremely good value.

There is no doubt that the companies became accustomed to a regular pattern of growth in the sixties and early seventies but we were brought abruptly to our senses by the effects of the oil crisis in 1974-75. It became obvious that we were too dependent on a relatively small number of products – in 1973 it amounted to 1585 on Granada – and the companies started to set about the task of broadening the base of their business.

As evidence, the share of revenue derived from the top ten product categories on Granada in 1974 (see Table 2) gives a clear indication of the shifts in emphasis across the subsequent ten years. The variance, after allowing for inflation at 249 per cent, is shown in the last column, the station increase after inflation being 54.5 per cent (or 4.9 per cent per annum).

TABLE 2: TOP TEN PRODUCT CATEGORIES ON GRANADA

Place 1974	Category	1974 share %	Place 1984	1984 share %	Revenue Growth current prices%	Variance 1974 prices
1	Food/beverage	28.8	1	21.9	+ 308.5	+ 17.0
2	Alcohol	8.9	2	7.8	+ 374.1	+ 35.8
3	Toiletries	8.0	7	4.8	+ 223.1	− 7.4
4	Confectionery	6.8	5	5.0	+ 296.3	+ 13.5
5	Laundry	5.4	9	4.0	+ 300.1	+ 14.6
6	Leisure	3.7	4	6.6	+ 874.3	+179.1
7	Publications	3.5	—	3.5	+ 432.7	+ 52.6
8	Retailing	3.3	10	3.8	+ 513.0	+ 75.6
9	Cosmetics	3.2	—	2.1	+ 250.5	+ 0.4
10	Medicinal	2.9	—	2.1	+ 289.8	+ 11.7
—	Motoring	2.1	3	6.7	+1644.6	+399.7
—	Financial	1.5	6	4.8	+1670.9	+407.3
—	Household	2.1	8	4.1	+ 956.9	+202.7

Source: Granada Television

What emerges from this ten-year snapshot is that the traditional supporters of television continued to patronize the medium, but that there are now 38 per cent more individual products (up from 1582 to 2188) absorbing the additional airtime which has become available. Of the five markets which performed above station average, three were newly into the top ten.

Food and beverages predictably held top place, with total real expenditure up from 17 per cent, but the category share fell from 28.8 to 21.9 per cent. Despite the fact that the market had changed significantly, with the decline of some traditional beers and the development of lagers and wines, alcohol as a category stayed in second place. Share declined by a point, but net revenue rose 35.8 per cent from the same number of products.

Toiletries were down from no. 3 to no. 7; just as many brands were advertised, but their total net expenditure fell by 7.4 per cent – the only category in this analysis whose expenditure increase was less than inflation.

Confectionery, despite being up 13.5 per cent in 1984, lost one place in the top ten; its share over the intervening years had been a consistent 5-6 per cent. The same can be said of laundry products, whose share declined by 1.4 percentage points; they dropped from no. 5 to no. 9 on revenue, which was up 14.6 per cent.

Leisure products, in response to increasing affluence, nearly doubled their share from 3.7 to 6.6 per cent, and showed a real increase of 179.1 per cent. Publications, both Fleet Street and partworks, held their share at 3.5 per cent but dropped out of the charts despite a 52.6 per cent net increase. Retailing, at no. 8 in 1974, just stayed in at no. 10 with a 75.6 per cent increase. Interestingly – and reflecting the hugely changed structure of the retail business – this growth came from a market consisting of fifteen fewer clients. Cosmetics, at no. 9 in 1974, also dropped out of the charts, with revenue up just 0.4 per cent from four fewer products, as did medicinal products, up 11.7 per cent from three fewer products.

And so we turn to what the DJs refer to as 'new entries'. Household products (broadly defined as white goods, small electrical and kitchen equipment) came in at no. 8; they increased in number by no fewer than fifty-seven, doubled their share and showed a real increase in revenue of 202.7 per cent. Motors and motoring came in at no. 6, with an additional eighty-nine products across the years and real revenue up by 399.7 per cent.

The star performer, and the product category which still holds out the greatest promise for the future – and which has demonstrated clearly the pulling power of television – was financial services. Seventeen 'products' were advertised with us in 1974, sixty-five in 1984; their real expenditure quadrupled at 1974 prices, and at current prices rose by no less than 1670.9 per cent.

Channel Four has been an extremely important element in the development of new advertising markets. The very fact that Channel Four was required to accommodate the interests of minority audiences, to cater for people whose tastes had previously been overlooked, meant that the range of commercial contact would be enlarged. And so it has proved. Television is now used by managements which previously had believed it to be either too large for them or environmentally unsuitable.

The arrival of Channel Four was, to those who thought seriously about it, a means to make ITV all things to all men. Others hoped that it would serve simply to increase supply and to reduce costs. Today, it stands on its own merits; no cost regulator, but a medium to be reckoned with.

Channel Four and TV-am both suffered the misfortune of being launched against the background of an industrial dispute. It was made doubly distressing by the fact that it was not their fight – they were simply the unwitting victims.

The reasons which lay behind the compromise which is Channel Four are for another chapter – or another book – but the decision to offer ITV the sales franchise was greeted with dismay by the ISBA. To their mind, our perceived monopoly had been not only renewed but enhanced, even though it would take some years for the channel to pay its way. Demands followed from the ISBA that a proper separation should exist between a company's tariff for its two channels – a separation, let it be said, which excluded such advertiser benefits as annual volume discount!

Arising from this genuinely held concern on the part of the ISBA and of its constituent companies, the IBA introduced the Advertising Liaison Committee whose purpose was, and is, to act as a forum at which it is hoped differences between the members – the companies (ITCA), their customers (ISBA) and their agencies (IPA) – will be resolved. It has been described by a wag as a game played by dissenting adults. In reality the debate only flows in one direction, since the chair is held by the IBA who have a direct lien over ITCA but none over the other parties at the feast.

All monopolies are, of course, relative. This can be seen from the fact that ITV's share of display advertising is 40 per cent, whereas it is arguable that, given the billing of the ISBA and IPA, collectively or separately, and given their dominant role at the ALC, they have far greater power and influence over ITCA than ITCA has over them.

The reality is that each needs the other and that their common interests should be greater than their differences. Indeed, in all my twenty-five years at Granada I can recall very little serious conflict and a very high degree of consensus with clients and agencies alike. Most of the issues which apparently separate buyer and seller and which find their way on to the ALC agenda are associated, needless to say, with the effect of demand on supply. The ITA, and subsequently the IBA, have regarded 10 per cent, or six minutes of advertising in an hour of broadcasting, as palatable to the public – and the public have consistently confirmed that view.

After the oil crisis and its effect on forward planning, the television companies introduced pre-empt rates as a means of allowing demand to condition the price of television. One result of pre-empt rate cards – associated with the newly infinite flexibility of computers – was to allow buyers to leave their buying until the last minute. Pre-empt rate cards became a hot topic at ALC from which emerged a set of principles designed (by ISBA) to ensure that advertisers could elect to buy into the pre-empt structure at any level they wished, and that a company must be seen to use its best endeavours to sell all of its product.

At the same time the spectre of the 'equal-impact buyer' grew ever greater. This figure wants to buy, say, 350 ratings across the network, but because station A may have lower ratings than station B the buyer will need to invest in ten spots on station A and only eight spots on station B; he will spend more on ten spots than on eight, needless to say, and those extra two spots will harden the market on station A because of its fixed availability. Double jeopardy. So long as agencies buy on an equal-impact basis, therefore, relatively low ratings on a seven-day station would seem to benefit that company – an irony which is hard to reconcile with the constant demand from agencies for high ratings.

The direct consequence of this ever-increasing dilemma was 'share schemes' – hot topic number two. I was the first to publish a formal advertiser share scheme. My purpose was to make it possible to sell all of our airtime all of the time without running the risk of losing a share to another, more expensive, lower-rating station. We offered a substantial discount to anyone spending at a level equivalent to our share of ITV homes. No one can easily deny that a plethora of share schemes makes advertising planning inflexible, but, properly administered, they give optimum value while protecting the company's revenue base and avoiding the need to indulge in price manipulation. Other hot topics will no doubt arise – some will be resolved, others will simmer.

Meanwhile, the trend is towards better targeting; at last it addresses the subject of buying airtime which will deliver the right audience for the product and at the right price. Two factors have brought this about: easier access to BARB data and the huge range of programme genres available across our two commercial channels.

Buyers may continue to buy television by the yard, and the companies may continue to sell it that way – I hope not, because it is too valuable a commodity to be so poorly exchanged. Whether clients will allow or encourage their agencies to indulge in target buying has yet to be seen, but the benefits are obvious and the facilities exist. All it needs is initiative.

The Television Commercial: An Essay

DAVID BERNSTEIN

DAVID BERNSTEIN

David Bernstein describes himself as being as old as Mickey Mouse and a graduate of Oxford University. He is currently Chairman of The Creative Business, the international consultancy which he founded in 1972 after having been Creative Director of three major advertising agencies – McCann-Erickson, Garland-Compton and S.H. Benson.

He is a former President of the Advertising Creative Circle and received advertising's highest award, the Mackintosh Medal, in 1982. He is a broadcaster, speaker and author. His books include *Creative Advertising, Company Image and Reality* and the widely praised *Working for Customers*, written for the CBI.

In the sixties he wrote TV plays, one of which was interrupted by one of his commercials.

He is a governor of St Martin's School of Art and serves on the governing board of SHAPE, the charity which provides arts access to the disadvantaged

IN 1955 the 'great and the good' awaited the arrival of commercial television with considerable apprehension; the rest of us with impatience. Advertising, everybody thought, would change television. Advertising people, although they saw opportunities in the new medium, were far from optimistic. A few agencies had invested heavily. Most chose to wait and see. Advertising might change television, but it was inconceivable that television would change advertising.

One perceptive and cautious agency chairman advocated boycotting the new medium because there would be too great an awareness of advertising. He was worried about television's power, not to move merchandise, but to illuminate the industry itself. Television significantly increased both the public's awareness of the business and the advertising industry's perception of itself. Adbiz had arrived complete with celebrities, star salaries, glitzy award ceremonies, backstage gossip and dizzy movement of accounts and personalities.

Television makes things famous – people, places, brands, advertising. Today when people discuss advertising they generally mean TV – the commercial. Today's typical advertisement seems light years away from that of pre-1955. But equally it is very different from the advertisements that the anxious critics of ITV had forecast or the viewers of the US scene had witnessed.

Television changed the advertisement. The commercial considerably influenced the content and form of television itself. The commercial has changed our conception of the way we believe advertising works. And our experience with the commercial has changed the way we regard US advertising.

These are some of the themes I want to explore.

Roots

Sit and view an evening's commercials from 1955 and you would be struck by obvious differences: black-and-white; a greater proportion of longer time-lengths; middle-class actors, values and accents; a painstaking slowness in delivery and editing – spelling everything out; poor lighting. But one aspect I believe you would recognize – a high entertainment quotient.

The British commercial is a product of its prehistory. 'The embryo', to ruin Wordsworth, 'is father to the man'. In the fifties we looked to the USA for professional guidance. Broadcast advertising was an American invention. UK agencies studied US reels. If the agency was US-owned, producers and writers taught their British associates. But there was more to it than technique, particularly in the climate of the time. There was the *ethos* of the TV advertisement, and the British felt uneasy with it.

It is easy to dismiss this as part of the general British distaste for commercialism. Certainly the debates in Parliament and in the quality press betrayed an aversion to selling. But the more telling arguments concerned the conflict between the aims of the broadcasting system and those of the advertiser, and the associated effect upon the viewer.

US television was the bogey. It was, in fact, the only example to hand. US broadcasting companies were accused of giving up too much of their editorial birthright. 'The newspaper advertiser does not demand to come bobbing up in the middle of the first leader. But the television advertiser still comes bobbing up anywhere.'

In serious first leaders – and parliamentary debates – advertising was seen as the enemy of public service, undermining its standards and impartiality. Lord Reith said in the House of Lords in May 1952:

The Government are here on record to scuttle – a betrayal and a surrender. . . . Somebody introduced dog racing into England. . . and somebody introduced Christianity and printing and uses of electricity. And somebody introduced smallpox, bubonic plague and the Black Death. Somebody is minded now to introduce sponsored broadcasting into this country.

One evening, ten years later, Associated-Rediffusion transmitted Sophocles' *Electra* in full, in Greek. In 1984 the *Financial Times* wrote, 'It is arguable that Granada aims higher in terms of intellect and quality than the BBC.' But that was in the future. In the early fifties, advertisers and agencies were not only aware of the hostility towards US-style advertising, but to a large extent shared it.

The result of the great debates was a tribute to British compromise (than which there is no better). We had the ITA, later the IBA, with its clear functions. Contractors were kept on their toes. Advertising and editorial were kept firmly apart. Controls – indirectly Government controls – were introduced into advertising for the first time. And those controls have increased – and inspired controls in other media.

There would be no sponsorship. But then the US system was changing. Parliament did not know it at the time, but direct sponsorship would have to go. 'Spot' advertising on the UK model would be the rule. The change was a liberating experience. The producer could concentrate on the show and not the promotion and the pack shot.

So British TV started from a different point. No 'and now a word from our sponsor'. It gave the agency and the advertiser greater independence. They could be their own people. It helped us develop our own identities and more quickly.

The British difference

But there was another, even more fundamental, difference between the UK and the USA. In the USA, television and television advertising arrived together. In the UK, advertising arrived second. It was an interloper. The advertisement would not simply interrupt a programme, it would break an accepted habit.

How would people accept advertisements? Agency views differed. Views differed within agencies according to the attitudes of clients and the home base of the advertiser. Some held the opinion that an ad was an ad was an ad, irrespective of the medium. The purpose is to sell. Others felt irritation to be counter-productive. Entertainment to many was the key. But how could the entertainment be married to the product? If the experience of cinema advertising was any guide, then all we would have had to do was begin with some general non-commercial entertaining section and attach a commercial message at the end. Popular television programmes, perhaps, could be adapted and compressed in sixty seconds (ITA willing)? Conversely, if advertisements pretended to be anything but advertisements, would advertiser insincerity be worse than irritation?

Or perhaps there was a correlation between liking and buying? Would consumers buy out of gratitude? Phooey, said some. Yet. . . . Was there a way to *fuse* entertainment and selling? Could commercials find an entertaining way to sell?

And while we discussed these issues, studied US commercials and wrote pilot scripts, agency managements were deciding how to accommodate the new medium. Few embraced it. Many did not believe it would succeed. Although new appointments were made and external advisers were hired, there was considerable ambivalence. McCann-Erickson set up a TV operations board of ex-BBC and film professionals. Yet the television department was regarded as a detachable entity and based in a different building. It took three years for an agency chief to stand up at the Advertising Creative Circle and say that he thought commercial television was here to stay.

There was a feeling, too, in agency mainstreams that what these television people were doing was not real advertising. They were making cinema films about the clients' products for transmission on small screens to be viewed by a small minority of people in one area of the country. In some cases I feel sure that this view, leading in turn to an attitude of indifference, generated a period of benign neglect which allowed the pioneers to learn by doing and by making all sorts of mistakes and breakthroughs.

The 'real' advertising was happening elsewhere. Yet if you ask anyone over forty to recall pre-TV advertising, the responses reveal very little except the occasional poster. One executive who responded said, 'Was it really only Bisto and Guinness?' Of course, this is not to imply that only advertisements you can *remember* over thirty years later had any effect. The point is that television was the first truly intrusive advertising medium. Apart from cinema, it was the first with a captive audience. But in the cinema, ads don't interrupt the film. It was the *intrusiveness* of the television commercial which both attracted and worried the early practitioners of the art. Think of a pre-TV intrusive advertisement and you might hit upon the notorious black widow 'keep death off the roads' poster for road safety. But even outdoors you can avoid reading the advertisement. In television, at home in your chair, selective perception doesn't operate. The eye doesn't select. The mind doesn't choose. Whereas in the press the reader will be attracted by, or choose to read, those items and advertisements in which he is interested, once the television set is on and the programme has begun, the choosing is over. As a result, the viewer is subjected to advertisements for products in which he is not interested or, indeed, of which it would be impossible for him ever to be a consumer. The commercial changed advertising by making the public aware of products for which they had neither need nor interest. On television, everybody saw everything. Television became the first truly mass medium. It was the reaction of those people for whom the advertisement was not intended which, as much as anything, affected the continuing debate on television advertising and the professional attitude towards the nature of the commercial.

The development of a brand: *Fairy Liquid*
(Young & Rubicam and Grey Advertising).

The development of a brand: *Persil* (J Walter Thompson).

FACING PAGE:

The development of a brand: *Fry's Turkish Delight* (Foote Cone & Belding).

The development of a brand: *Oxo* 1955-1985 (Street and J Walter Thompson).

FACING PAGE:

The development of a brand: *Camay* 1956-1985 (Lambe & Robinson, Benton & Bowles and Grey Advertising).

Perfume worth
9 guineas an ounce

creamy fragrant camay WITH MOISTURISING CREAM

Soft lather.
Soft skin.

Camay. Altogether more alluring.

Katie Boyle's
Scrapbook

The Retailing Revolution 1955-1985

The changes in retailing which television advertising helped to accelerate are vividly illustrated by the astonishing growth of the importance and efficiency of the grocery multiples of which Sainsbury's is an outstanding example.

At the beginning of the thirty years some 54% of the grocery trade of Britain was in the hands of independent retailers who had not yet organised themselves into voluntary groups like Spar, Vivo, Centra, V.G. and Mace whose symbols were to become a familiar part of the High Street scene. The multiple grocers, by contrast, accounted for less than 22% of turnover in 1955 with a larger proportion of the trade going through the Co-ops.

By 1985 the position had been completely transformed. Over 70% of the grocery trade was being handled by the multiples a number of whom had been the subject of takeovers and mergers. In thirty years the Co-op's share of trade had halved while that of the independents had fallen even more to less than 15% of the total.

In 1955 counter service still dominated food retailing, even among the major multiples. At this stage Sainsbury's had only nine self-service stores out of a total of 257 and were employing 10,000* staff who were responsible for an annual turnover of just under £40,000,000. By 1985, 253 Sainsbury stores were self-service, 18 operated on a counter service basis while six SavaCentres (jointly owned with British Home Stores) and 23 home and garden centres (under the Homebase name) had developed out of the original grocery operation. In thirty years Sainsbury's staff had quadrupled to 40,000* and turnover had grown eighty times to over £3,000,000,000 putting the company in the front rank of British business. (*Full-time equivalent).

The small corner store, often operating as a family business without paid staff, continued to provided a valuable service to its customers even in the mid-eighties despite the rapidly declining importance of the independent sector of the grocery trade. Such shops survived because of an element of personal service and the willingness of the proprietor and his family to work long hours, including weekends, when the supermarkets were closed. But their range of merchandise was limited and prices noticeably higher than in the multiples who competed fiercely with one another not only in terms of price but in offering facilities like restaurants, in-store bakeries, car parking and consumer credit supported by a wide range of merchandise and ruthless stock control.

The independent grocery outlet benefited from manufacturers' television advertising. But, unlike the major multiples, it could not afford television advertising on its own account unless it belonged to a voluntary group of stores.

Sainsbury's (Bath) Sainsbury's supermarket in Green Park Road, Bath which opened in 1982 has over 12,500 square feet of sales area, 24 checkouts and parking spaces for 500 customers' cars. Like other supermarkets the store carries a range of non-food lines including electrical accessories, china, glass and kitchen equipment.

SavaCentre (Edinburgh) the impressive pedestrian approach and store entrance.

Homebase (Catford) Sainsbury's home and garden centre at Catford was the twentieth Homebase to be opened. The store, which is open seven days a week, is designed to meet the needs of the gardener and do-it-yourself enthusiast and carries over 15,000 product lines including tools, building materials, plumbing and central heating equipment, ironmongery and a wide range of shrubs, plants and garden materials.

Homebase (Hull) Like Catford the Hull Homebase is open seven days of the week and has an indoor and outdoor sales area of over 50,000 square feet.

Guinness 1985 'Pure Genius!' (Ogilvy & Mather).

Guinness 1980 (J Walter Thompson).

The hard sell

Ronnie Kirkwood believes that much early advertising was too intrusive and bad-mannered: 'loud-mouthed salesmen who confused shouting with communicating and bullying with persuading'. If they irritated the target market, what would they do to the uninterested?

For television was proving to be a powerful medium, a regular visitor into your home. Strange stories began to surface. Television personality John Slater was greeted by a total stranger asking him, 'How do you like my new wallpaper?' There *was* a face-to-face relationship with the viewer – in the viewer's living room. It *was* the next best thing to being there. There was every reason to regard the commercial as a surrogate personal sales pitch. The presenter commercial was undoubtedly a basic standard format. It was traditional television, an echo of the newsreader and station announcer. It was equally the huckster in the marketplace or the serious, sincere, professional adviser. It was, moreover, seemingly quite easy to write. It required a minimal set. It featured a person and a pack, perhaps with an insert, a chart or demonstration and a caption. The writer did not have to rely on complicated filming technique or, indeed, much help from outside. He could read it to his stopwatch. A further stimulus to the popularity of presenter commercials, of course, was US experience. In sponsored television, the presenter was the star of the show and the constraints of the production kept him in a simple set in medium close-up, looking at camera and pointing to the pack in his left hand. Ronald Reagan did it then. President Reagan did the same thing thirty years later.

Mind you, the pitchman could not do everything and certainly could not close the sale in thirty seconds, though many of them tried. And you could not question their enthusiasm. Companies were expected to be proud of their products in those days – particularly American companies. Today, pride is more often conveyed, rather than overtly expressed. I remember hearing about an Irishman in a group discussion who, when asked what he thought about a certain product, said, 'Well, the adver*tise*ments speak highly of it.' In the fifties, most of the ads did. Today, the viewer is expected to extract such information from the advertisement, rather than accept it pre-packed.

In thirty years the sell has gone from hard to soft. The communication model has gone from one-way to two-way and advertisements become more consumer- and less manufacturer-oriented. The television commercial – our experience with it against a particular background – has been responsible for this sea-change in advertising practice.

Birth pangs

It is 1955. You are an agency head. Television will happen. At least, it will start. The date is fixed: 22 September. You want to be on air that very night, for your client's sake if not for your own. What do you do? You try to interest the art directors and copywriters in this new medium. That should not be difficult. But the established members of the creative department aren't jumping. Too old to learn new tricks? A passing fad? Not mainstream? Maybe the younger people would be more adaptable? How about those with barely two years' experience and no fixed ideas? They may not be the most likely to succeed, but at least they would be least likely to fail. Then, of course, there must be people with relevant experience outside. *Some* relevant experience. So what do you do? Teach the experts advertising or the advertising people expertise? Of course, you try both. Maybe you can hire a film director or a TV producer or an ex-BBC executive, somebody with experience of cinema commercials or Radio Luxembourg?. . .

The experts proved a mixed blessing. What they could teach was soon learned, and not wholly applicable. Early commercials had too many words (the legacy of radio) and too many long shots (the legacy of cinema).

The same early but temporary use of outside talent was happening in the contracting companies. Getting on air and maintaining a schedule amidst difficulties and against odds meant that people were too busy *doing* to learn what it was they were doing. The flexible survived and got better. Those representing an earlier existence found themselves unwanted and looked for other jobs. . . .

The first commercials

This new product, ITV, had a rolling launch. It began with London. No test-market campaign had a more ostentatious or prestigious send-off. It went on air at 7.15 with Elgar's *Cockaigne* Overture played by Sir John Barbirolli and the Hallé Orchestra. ITV thus stressed its (eventual) regional nature with a midland composer's treatment of a London subject played by a northern orchestra.

Soon, according to Sir Brian Young, 'The public were fascinated by ITV's newscasters, cash quiz shows, American programmes and commercials.' The commercials were a novelty. More to the point, they were *part of* the totality of commercial telly – and seen to be.

Britain's first-ever television commercial, a 60-second spot for Gibbs' S R Toothpaste, was transmitted at 8.12 pm on 22 September 1955 in the first 'natural break' in *Channel Nine*, a star-studded variety show introduced by Jack Jackson

The first commercial was for Gibbs' SR toothpaste. It featured a tube of toothpaste, a block of ice and a commentary about its 'tingling fresh' qualities. It was perhaps somewhat symbolic, being frozen. Brian Palmer, who wrote it, freely admits that it was not a very television sort of ad. It was an adaptation of a press ad. 'I look at it now,' he says, 'as an illustrated lecture.' Also on the first night was a commercial for Crosse and Blackwell, featuring their '10 o'clock Tested' panel. It too was an adaptation of a press advertisement. It began by showing the viewer the press ad over a reader's shoulder, moving in and dissolving through to movement. The first Persil commercials were cartoon treatments of their posters – dancers and sailors in different shades of white. 'Persil washes whiter. That means cleaner.' Television was already a support medium.

Moreover, the medium had to utilize other media to establish itself. The devices of previous media are always utilized when a new medium starts: early television plays, for example, would close each act with a curtain, and early cinema films were photographed stage plays. So our early commercials were adapted press ads or cinema films and used *their* devices to position, give credence to, the incidents in the new medium. Many fifties' commercials showed too much reverence for the theatre's proscenium arch.

On the morning after the opening night, Bernard Levin wrote in the *Manchester Guardian*: 'I feel neither depraved nor uplifted by what I have seen. . . certainly the advertising has been entirely innocuous. I have already forgotten the name of the toothpaste.' Levin was judging British commercial television in the context of what US experience, direct or secondhand, had led him to believe. US observers, on the other hand, sensed the British difference immediately. 'The advertising was painless,' said the New York *Herald Tribune*. The *New York Post* described it as a 'paragon of phlegmatic British understatement and restraint', while the *New York Times* declared: 'The peace was wonderful.' And, above all, 'British advertisers are giving viewers credit for some intelligence and at least a bit of good taste,' the *Daily News* commented.

The hostility, the lessons of US television, the different circumstances of UK broadcasting and, perhaps, an inherent distaste for the blatantly commercial had shaped an attitude towards the television advertisement which, starting that first night, has prevailed to this day. We recognize that television is an entertainment and information medium, and ads are part of that totality. Ads will have to inform and entertain. Nobody spelled that out and not everybody believed it or practised it. Indeed, it would be wrong to suggest that there was a uniform approach to the commercial. The early months were marked by a variety of approaches reflecting different models of how advertising worked. There were thinly adapted radio and cinema ads, transplanted US commercials, mini-TV programmes, presenter sales pitches, documentaries, simple animation, unsophisticated jingles and occasional forays into experiment.

Time spots and admags

There were also some forays into the no-man's land between advertisement and editorial – time spots, for example. The advertiser could book the station clock and tie in his product with the time announcement. A time spot could appear either side of the station clock. 'Time to light a Red and White. Just the job for the man who inhales.' Samuel's tied in appropriately with their Ever-rite watches. Other punctual advertisers were Saxa Salt, Burberry's and Aspro. These time spots were regarded by the ITA as annoying and were abolished amongst a number of 'qualitative improvements' on 24 December 1960.

Abolished three years later, as a result of the Pilkington Report, was the advertising magazine. This had been created to encourage the smaller advertiser. It was a loose-story format centred upon, say, a pub (as was *Jim's Inn*) or a block of flats and featured in each episode a collection of products. The attraction was not so much the sales story of the product as the ingenuity of the scriptwriter in linking the diverse products and making them relevant to the storyline. Nevertheless, it was an inexpensive introduction to the medium and many creative and production people in television and advertising cut their teeth on admags.

Jim's Inn, the best-known of all advertising magazines, first appeared in the spring of 1957 and ran successfully for nearly 300 editions until admags were brought to an end by the Postmaster-General in March 1963. Its appeal relied on a strong and believable story-line, recognizable characters and the warm personality of the landlord, Jimmy Hanley himself. A wide variety of products ranging from the familiar to the outlandish were woven every week into a skilfully written script. Set in the fictitious village of Wembleham, *Jim's Inn* became very nearly as familiar to the public as the 'Rovers Return' or the 'Bull' at Ambridge

Advertisers could – and still can – advertise live. The opportunity to transmit a message – often simultaneously to several regions, live from an ITV studio – was rarely seized, and then chiefly by companies or brands in the news, such as petrol or tyre companies. They looked and sounded like news, and there was difficulty keeping their promotion hermetically sealed from real editorial.

The IBA became obsessive about separation. Its watchdog, as far as the agencies were concerned, was the ITCA copy committee, a self-regulatory body from the contractors themselves who made sure that the spirit as well as the letter of the IBA regulations was observed. They were particularly vigilant about implications that ITV programmes and/or those appearing in them were in any way associated with products, though that did not stop advertisers using BBC equivalents. Nevertheless, advertisers could associate with ITV programmes by advertising at fixed times. For example, Max Factor was a permanent fixture in the long-running *Sunday Night at the London Palladium*.

Agency producers kept a close watch on the television companies. Both sides were learning from each other. Granada set up their own training school, Viking Studios, near Earls Court. They trained their own people, but also clients and agency staff. As Sidney Bernstein put it, 'Later, when they went into the studio, at least they didn't feel lost.'

Advertising creative and production people had to learn the techniques of production and format drama, sitcom, variety, talking heads etc. It was easier than teaching outsiders advertising. Orson Welles has said that 'any intelligent person could learn the technique of film making in an afternoon'. Brian Palmer, however, recalls that every time you asked an expert a creative question you got a technical answer.

It was the era of jargon: language used as a professional barrier to entry. Scripts were written to reveal one's knowledge rather than to communicate an idea. Complicated scripts and elaborate storyboards were prepared. The storyboard was devised as a visual aid, but it became in some hands a blessed icon. 'The nearest thing to a real film is a real bloke acting it,' said Dennis Abey, producer of commercials and features.

A different medium

But what sort of medium was it? Visual, surely, we thought. And yet the press art directors were not all that keen. An aural medium? Up to a point. But surely not just radio with pictures? It was clearly a moving as opposed to a still medium. Movement – that was it.

But where had the art directors done movement before? Sandy McKendrick was one of the few who had done it. He had been an art director at JWT before going to Ealing Studios. At JWT he had done strip cartoons for Horlicks. At Ealing he practically invented the storyboard. Strip cartoons are, after all, cinematic – longshot, close-up, two-shot, reaction shot and so on.

Writers did better storyboards than the average art director, because, not being trained to draw, they indicated the barest essentials (such as stick men), which were easier to *move*. (I should mention that in those days art directors could draw. Indeed that was a *sine qua non* of the job. Today the skill is something of an optional extra – another result of television.)

Conversely, artists did better audio than the average copywriter because, not being trained to 'write,' they communicated colloquially. They wrote as they spoke. This also *moved*.

Was movement, then, the essential characteristic of the television commercial? Or was it rather movement through time? TV was a narrative medium. And who had experience of narrative? Certainly not the art director; more likely the writer. And though that did not automatically make him a screenwriter it put him in pole position relative to the art director – at least to begin with. As they worked, the creative people began to realize that television was more different than they had imagined. There were the obvious differences from press:

1 Press is static. TV moves. (You look at one. You watch the other.)
2 Press is silent. TV has sound, music, effects.
3 Press can be read. TV is heard – but can also be read (e.g. supers).
4 Press can't make the reader read. TV has a better chance of making the viewer view.
5 Press advertisements do not intrude. People need not read them. TV commercials intrude into an entertainment medium.

But there were other, less obvious, differences – differences related to the factor of *time*:

1 Press imposes no time limit on reading. TV imposes limits. If a point is missed the viewer can't go back.
2 Press can adjust the size of type to incorporate a long copy story or a text which may be read by the really interested. TV can seldom

CLIENT: Rowntree & Co. Ltd.
PRODUCT: Kit Kat
JOB NO: 85911A
TITLE: Public Garden
LENGTH: 15 secs
TYPE: Live Action
DATE: 1.4.64
1st TRANSMISSION: 17th July 1964

ARTISTS: Edward Waddy (Gardener);
Robert Lankasheer (Mate)
COMMENTATOR: Manning Wilson

VISION	SOUND

Open on C.U. of potted flowers in full bloom. Camera pans left, a thermos flask is seen standing beside an elderly gardener, who sits on a bench opening his lunch box.

1½ seconds silence
F/X: Atmosphere track
Gardener: So one day she says -

Cut to E.C.U. of lunch box as the lid is opened and the gardener's hands take out a Kit Kat bar, this is held in E.C.U. for a split second. Hands then begin to open the bar.

Gardener's Voice Over: try one of these. I'll give you a bit in a minute.

Cut to M.C.U. of gardener opening the Kit Kat bar.

Gardener: It goes down just right.

Cut to E.C.U. of Kit Kat bar separated from wrapper in gardener's hands.

Gardener's Voice Over: Something nice

Cut back to M.C.U. of gardener as he holds out a finger of Kit Kat to left of screen. Another man's hands take it from him.

to finish off with.

Cut to C.U. of his mate as he eats the Kit Kat.

Mate: Just the job!

End atmosphere track

Cut to pack shot. This is a packed lunch on table, sandwiches and apple with a Kit Kat in the foreground. The Kit Kat wrapper breaks itself and the bar animates out, snaps in two and remains in that position for a second then the action is reversed and the bar wraps itself back into the pack. Super: A Rowntree Product centre lower half of screen.

Commentator:
Pack a lunch

F/X: Snap

Pack a Kit Kat.

J.W.T. PRODUCER: Peter Madren
PRODUCTION COMPANY: Augusta
DIRECTOR: Pat Jackson
LIGHTING/CAMERAMAN: Stephen Dade

afford more than sixty-five words within thirty seconds. (Rushing the audio was TV's equivalent of reducing the type size. It rarely worked.)

3 Press allows the reader to come back to the advertisement when he so desires. TV does not.

4 Press allows the reader to use the advertisement. It is tangible and can become the reader's property. TV is ephemeral.

5 Press has no control over the order in which the advertisement is looked at. TV controls the order and the advertiser can thus tell a story the way he wants it told.

It was only when the real differences began to be appreciated that well-conceived and produced commercials became anything but an exception – around the early sixties. Till then we sought to apply advertising's rules, which were press-oriented, to the commercial.

The storyboard

One key difference – which has been touched on already – was the relation of the rough to the finished product. Whereas press roughs bear a close resemblance to the finished advertisements, TV scripts and storyboards are indications only. A television commercial relies on the contribution of several outside talents. A detailed script and storyboard religiously pursued downgrades the contribution of the executor, though such tactics were necessary in the early days when there were few outside production people who appreciated the advertising requirements of the commercial.

The storyboard differed from the press rough by being essentially an interim stage, a chrysalis. Preliminary work is done in one medium for eventual execution in another. A finished storyboard is a contradiction in terms. The main problem with early storyboards was that they were used at three different stages of a commercial's life, by people with different degrees of sophistication in the medium, for different purposes:

1 The writer and artist in creating the commercial.
2 The agency team in presenting the commercial.
3 The production team in shooting the commercial.

The Television Storyboard. A simplified post-production version of a TV storyboard for a 15-second commercial for Rowntree's **Kit Kat** made in 1964

It was an attempt to catch time on the wing. But often *rigor mortis* could set in once a piece of planned movement was fixed in a frame. A detailed storyboard was counter-productive. If the script called for a tree in a garden, the artist might show a larch in the garden of a suburban semi. A literal client would expect to see just that. The storyboard was a crutch. It was the best way of presenting visual narrative on paper, but we needed also to fight the passage of *audio* time. (The words 'video' and 'audio' were replacing vision and sound in our scripts. I personally welcomed the move, since *video* (I see) and *audio* (I hear) put the emphasis on the television audience, rather than on the advertiser.)

Audio was not spoken press copy. We had been told that by visiting Americans, but it was not till we started writing and producing commercials that we fully appreciated the difference. Adapting a novel or short story for television involves, according to Granada's Derek Granger, a 'radical reworking' of the original. To approximate the spirit of the original you have to start again. Press copy similarly had to be broken down, rearranged, put into bite-sized chunks. Redundancy had to be introduced (in other words, repetition of key words and the introduction of what, in press, would appear as padding). The narrative had to be built block by block. The compression which press can get away with, indeed lives by, confuses the ear. Each element of audio needs to have space to itself.

The learning process

In 1955 we learned all this by doing and failing and doing again. We were sailing uncharted waters and ignoring any charts on offer. It was too much fun. Thirty seconds was unknown territory. Our American friends worked in one-minute lengths with thirty-second cut-downs. We were originating in thirties and fifteens. If we were aping anybody, it was the programme people, the producer, the writer of drama and sitcom dialogue. We soon realized not only that sitcom writers had the luxury of thirty *minutes*, but that the shorthand of *their* dialogue had been fashioned over months, if not years. We had to construct our own narrative form.

There was an interrelation of word and picture. It was summed up first in the phrase, 'Say what you show; show what you say.' This was 0–level advice at best. It got us started, but not very far down the road. Vision and sound had to relate to each other. But identical messages meant that one of them was probably unnecessary. Show a

The manoeuvrable Triumph 'Herald'. When this commercial was made Standard-Triumph and Wolseley had not yet come together in the British Leyland Motor Corporation (BLMC) and a little gentle 'knocking' against a competitor was therefore considered permissible. The police Wolseley, featured in countless TV detective series, has given chase to the Triumph Herald which, with its exceptionally small turning circle, has been able to outwit its pursuers. Other effective demonstration commercials for the Herald showed the car climbing the steps of the Royal Albert Hall

bowl of soup and say 'This is a bowl of soup' and what do you have? Say 'This is a bowl of Heinz' and you go a bit further. Say 'What's this?' – better still 'not soup again!' and you might begin to create tension and attention. Sound could add to vision, vision to sound. Multiply, reinforce, contradict for effect, create drama. One of them might not be needed to do much at all.

We learned because we had to. From the beginning, the demands on advertising had been high because the demands of television itself had been high. TV encouraged advertising to surpass TV. If you are interrupting a story with a story of your own you had better make sure that your story is better than the one you are interrupting. Technique would help, of course. Cartoons, music, star presentation, puppets. . . and money. Advertisers were soon spending as much on thirty seconds as programme companies did on thirty minutes.

We learned the hard way, but behind us came what Harry McMahan called 'the tube-raised generation' who got it all through the pores. Kids who had grown up with the medium were writing for it, seemingly without effort. The first inkling I had that the art could be intuitive occurred when I gave a young girl a copy test in the late fifties. She wrote a fifteen-second commercial for an up-market cigarette. She described the action as follows:

1 A 707 is taking off.
2 We see the 'Fasten seat belts. No smoking' sign light up, then off.
3 We look along a row of seats at two men. The first is removing his seat belt. The second has already removed his and is taking out a packet of Benson and Hedges.
4 Close-up of hand holding pack and first man's hand taking a cigarette.

A special medium

We began to realize that TV was a special medium. The attitude shifted in two stages. First (and quickly) it became apparent that the ingredients of a press ad could not simply be transferred to the new medium. Literary copy and static pictures were not the stuff of television. The press ad had to be adapted.

The picture had to move. We had to learn the craft of making it move. Whereas the press ad selected *one* position of a subject, the commercial could alternate that view with the subject's view of, say, the product or a third person's view of both. That could be shot from above or below; close-up or from a distance; moving or still; going forward or sideways. It could be accompanied by effects to add realism, or suggest tangential thoughts or distant locations. There were dimensions that some of us had not realized. Whereas copy was copy, a script could be delivered by an actor in innumerable ways. Some of us froze at the choice. Others gorged themselves. The images communicated too much. We learned about distracting 'video vampires'. Music could give messages a shape, add value to words, deepen the emotion and the images. Music could create a mood. Above all, it could stay in the mind, bringing words and pictures with it. Like poetry, music could 'make meaning more meaningful'.

The press ad could come to life. The slogan could live. The promise could be seen happening. The press ad had 'before' and 'after'. Television could let you see the one *become* the other. 'Someone's Mum isn't using Persil,' said the press ad and the poster. Copy had to become audio. The commercial would show the mother and get behind the phrase. In 1958 the commercial stated, 'The world revolves around Mum.' Later on it would ask questions: 'What matters to a Mum?' and answer it in words and gestures and product in use. A boy or girl would talk about 'my Mum'. Lines became storylines. We were into narrative.

But this was still stage one, the shift from press to a television version of press. Press would remain the dominant medium for a decade. The prevalent advertising values were those which could be transmitted on the printed page. Only when brands were new to advertising or launched in a television area could television begin to lead.

Nevertheless television was already special. The media reps went about chanting, 'Sight, sound, motion.' For the first time people in the round, real life, the products themselves came into your living room. You could relate to them, compare yourself with them, their lives with your own. You could also discuss. Television is still the only advertising medium which respondents discuss while consuming the advertisement. ('Mrs Thompson up the road's got one of those. She wouldn't be without it.')

It wasn't radio with pictures. Add pictures to a good radio script and you distract. And though it might have been designed as a moving press ad, it was viewed in very different circumstances. A good press ad is a private communication with the reader in charge. He has chosen to read it and at his pace. When he wants to. Alone. Not in public simultaneously with millions of others at a pace dictated by the advertiser.

No, television was different. It could tell a story the way the advertiser wanted it told, at the time he wanted and to the audience he wanted. It could demonstrate. It could suggest. It could compare. It could ingratiate. It could leave lasting impressions – a picture, a phrase, a sound. And every commercial, no matter how short, was in fact a full page: the whole of the screen and the whole of the time one had bought.

And the viewer one had bought? The television commercial had made television a topic. The general public discussed the advertisements, then advertising itself. Advertising became more visible. Could the advertiser afford to ignore those viewers who saw the ad but weren't the target market? Ignore, bore, insult intelligence? (Did anybody criticize advertising for being patronizing *before* ITV?) For the first time advertising affected everybody.

TV focused attention on advertising and on commercialism. The television commercial is the ready-to-hand symbol of capitalism. Was it any wonder that some people became annoyed with ads, for example for products irrelevant to their needs or out of reach? The surprising thing is that, considering the noise from the anti-advertising lobby and the dire warnings of the 1954 debate, the hostility aroused by the real thing was not greater.

But the UK advertiser and agency never seem to forget that television is an entertainment medium. Perhaps they are viewers themselves. Entertainment entered advertising in 1955. It was initially scorned by the advertising purist and largely mishandled by the practitioners. Once the relationship of entertainment to selling was established, once a *modus vivendi* or, better still, a fusion was effected, then the purist began to change his mind not simply about the role of entertainment but, as we shall see later, the whole question of how advertising works.

And this was the second shift – television, not as a dependant of print, but as an advertising medium in its own right. Television was the most important change to take place in advertising this century. As David Ogilvy says, 'It is the most potent medium for selling most products.' But the manner in which television went about it was different, as were priorities. Or so it seemed to those brought up in the direct confrontational school of advertising and to those who followed the pattern set by US commercials.

Production values

The early British television commercial was harshly lit, two-dimensional, black-and-white. Subtlety was rare and difficult to achieve. The film technicians of the day were made aware of new demands. The advertising industry was beginning to change film production. It had to create new standards. Denis Auton, Creative Director of Young and Rubicam, surveyed the scene and asked why he couldn't get the effects on film which Irving Penn, for example, was achieving in stills photography. Why did black-and-white inevitably mean soot-and-whitewash?

Then a stills photographer, Keith Ewart, aided by JWT, turned to film production. Gaston Charpentier made a commercial for Gillette Wet Shave, with extreme close-ups of drops of water. James Garrett and others began to attract and encourage new talent in direction and lighting. Film editors began to understand the demands of the *advertisement*.

Then in 1969 came colour. The art director who had manifested little enthusiasm for monochrome packs began to show a considerable interest. Colour was something he knew about. No longer was the production company the sole repository of technical expertise. We began to hear the phrase 'production values'. Products – fashion, beauty, food – which had looked their best only in magazines could be shown to good advantage on the box. Colour communicated more. 'Appetite appeal' was now a television asset.

Colour came in. Advertising took off. So did production costs. What were we paying for? Give or take the odd rip-off – attention to detail. Television programme standards were no longer good enough. Television news standards were appropriate only when the product was making news. The television commercial was creating its own standard of television excellence. This attracted the features director. And feature films attracted the commercials director. Whereas the feature promised more scope, the commercial promised more money per foot of film. There was also the challenge of miniaturization, getting a message across and communicating the right feelings about the brand in thirty seconds.

Changing the 'grammar' of film

In 1955 sixty seconds was the norm. Most US commercials we had seen lasted a minute. We made thirty-second cutdowns but they were support; they fed off the minute version. There were seven-second spots but they were in effect posters. They could not tell a story.

Then financial pressures made thirty seconds the norm. We had to learn to use the advertising budget more cost-effectively. Maybe use a different medium altogether. Or use a separate medium complementarily: television for mood and drama, say, and press for the details. Or we could learn to use television itself more economically, to tell the story in a shorter time. There were the obvious means – speaking more quickly, undercranking, reducing the elements. Better still, you could cut corners in the narrative and hope that the viewer kept up with you. In 1955 we had cut our teeth on the established 'grammar of film'. A character could not move from A to B in other than real time unless a dissolve was interposed. You needed an establishing shot to show where you were before moving in (tracking rather than cutting) to a 'medium close-up'. It was laborious but, we thought, necessary. Everything had to be spelled out. And, because this was advertising, much of it had to be repeated.

By 1968 Persil were making commercials which owed nothing to press and used contemporary music and film techniques. Nevertheless the audio was still explicit. 'When your children go out you don't always go with them. Or do you?' The family's clothes washed in Persil by Mum go with them of course – as the script explains. Today that thought would be suggested rather than underlined.

When today, as a viewer, we say that old films are slow, the reason is that we have learned to do the work. We have learned the new grammar unconsciously, by watching television and particularly television commercials.

Whereas the press copywriter had communicated by what he physically wrote, the new breed of writer realized that the commercial communicated far more than what was written. Pictures lead. Words become comments. Information moved from the right-hand side of the script (audio) to the left (video). The 'how' was saying as much as the 'what'. And more people than ever before were contributing to the 'how'.

Is it too much of a simplification to say that, whereas the 1955 commercial would tell the viewer something, the 1985 commercial invites the viewer to learn something? Perhaps. There were interesting exceptions in the fifties, and there are still emphatic injunctions today. However, there is an undeniable swing from the overt advertisement – and not only on television. Participation presupposes an alert and knowledgeable viewer. It could be argued that if the viewer participates in – helps create – the ad he is more likely to recall it. He has been involved. Humour calls for involvement. Who likes to have a joke explained? We have to complete the *gestalt*, close the gap. The art of the comic is to judge the width of that gap. Too narrow and it isn't a joke. Too wide and there's no communication.

'Sch ... you know who!' Schweppes (now part of Cadbury Schweppes) was an imaginative user of television advertising from the start of the ITV service. Early campaigns featured the eccentric talents of Roland Emmett and Stephen Potter to the accompaniment of a voice-over from the company's Managing Director, Sir Frederick Hooper. The two later examples shown here made use of the entirely different approach of Benny Hill (as a West Country publican) and William Franklyn, well-known to viewers from such series as *Top Secret* and *Masterspy*. Franklyn appeared in a similarly mysterious role for Schweppes for nine years

Serve eggs...
save money

'olidays are Egg...aped

Commercials which demand viewer participation – by not spelling everything out – are, by definition, shorter and arguably more effective. Is the preponderance of humorous television commercials due to this fact? Not entirely, I would think. It is partly due to the advertiser's need not to disturb the 'ecology' of television, in other words the entertainment and information medium, and to the advertiser's need to be liked.

Critics say humour in advertising is counter-productive – for example when the viewer remembers the joke but not the brand. But failure to brand is a common malady and not exclusive to humour. What is being criticized is not humour, but bad advertising practice. Others believe there is nothing more boring than an old joke. Purely verbal humour (particularly the pun) has a limited lifespan. But the situation-comedy commercial bears constant repetition because the viewer enjoys anticipating and pre-empting the dénouement – Penelope Keith, for example, as the upper-class teacher at the finishing school in the Parker pen commercial; or the Smash Martians. And when the situation is locked into a phrase and the phrase is locked into the name of the brand, then humour is probably working harder than any traditional hard-sell form of advertising: 'Happiness is a cigar called Hamlet'; 'We're with the Woolwich'; 'Heineken refreshes the parts other beers cannot reach.' Phrases such as these are part of the economy of the television commercial. A single line can sum up and call to mind a complete commercial, even a complex sales argument.

Commercials show the way

The need for economy in programming did not bring equivalent pressures. For example, sitcoms did not go from thirty minutes to fifteen. Consequently, the advances in narrative technique occurred, not in programmes, but in commercials. Sam Rothenstein compares the minimal change in the opening titles of *Coronation Street* during its history with the major changes in commercials over the same period. Commercials directors learned their craft and took it to features. (Though very few moved into *television* direction – copywriters occasionally wrote for the box but few commercials directors were

---

The British Eggs Authority's award-winning campaigns to promote eggs proved outstandingly effective in the sixties with their use of children and stars such as Tony Hancock, *left*, and Bernard Miles. 'Look for the little lion!' was their slogan

interested.) Richard Lester made Beatles films which had the pace and techniques of TV ads. Adrian Lyne, Al Parker, Hugh Hudson, Ridley Scott and many more followed suit. The language of the cinema had been absorbed by the viewer. But the commercial should not take all the credit. The cinema itself fought back against the box. It endeavoured to provide what could not be seen at home: wide screen, 3-D, Cinemascope and a new form of narrative – fragmented, oblique, disjointed. There was two-way traffic. As Brian Tesler says, 'When I was a kid narrative on cinema was the same as narrative in books. No quick cuts. No disorientation.'

But commercials training bequeathed more than narrative form. It gave the narrative form new standards in lighting and composition. In *The Duellist* every frame is as beautifully shot as a commercial. Ridley Scott expended as much love and care on it as he had on Hovis.

The technique and discipline of the television commercial affected the BBC. Programmes rarely over-ran. The presentation was improved. The presenters became more approachable, achieved rapport with the viewers. Upcoming programmes were not mere statements but trailers, even ads.

Credits – opening and closing titles – adopted the commercial's techniques. Very soon commercials were providing the comedy writers with familiar material to refer to or parody. Later the pithy, punchy language of the commercials affected light entertainment – on all channels. Before ITV, comedy sketches lasted about six minutes. Commercials were accustoming the viewer to getting a message in twenty seconds, seven even. This inspired writers and comedians – Frost, the Two Ronnies, Lenny Henry, Dave Allen. The programmes became a series of commercial breaks.

But commercials were also accustoming the viewer to another world, providing goals for what we would now describe as the 'upwardly mobile'. These goals were achievable – we had Harold Macmillan's word for it. Other words marked the years – acquisitive, affluent, permissive. This other world, was it real? People behaved differently, especially children, and especially at mealtimes. Ketchup bottles always poured and never left a dark, sticky ring around the collar. Kitchens were tidy and enormous. And – Sam Rothenstein's particular favourite – milk bottles that were clearly three-quarters full were quite clean and shiny above the milk line. People did silly things – though never dangerous, or erotic, or unholy things. The ITCA saw to that. Keeping a few paces behind changing *mores*, this IBA watchdog eventually relaxed its rules on brassieres: they could be shown on plastic models. You could show a lavatory, but preferably not at mealtimes.

But realism was strangely absent. It was a largely middle-class world peopled by stereotypes, perhaps a collective self-image. Philip and Katie for Oxo (upper); Joan and Leslie Randall for Fairy Snow (lower). Maybe this world was real for other people? Or maybe the viewer was not meant to take the commercial literally? Fantasy and hyperbole had undeniable attractions for the advertiser. Not only did they provide exciting and different situations for the viewer (and allowed full scope to the creative people's imagination) but they rewrote the rules of debate between the advertiser and the ITCA.

Nobody was meant to *believe* that Camay would make you daily more lovely, or that Cadbury's Flake would provide quite that form of satisfaction, or that Fry's Turkish Delight had anything to do with the Sahara (even the geography was somewhat fanciful) or that there was a bank manager in your cupboard, a tiger in your tank, a white tornado in your cleaning liquid or a ring of confidence around your neck. . . . But the viewer was expected to believe the fundamental truth of the product – in other words that it delivered a more than adequate standard of performance. Not so much eastern promise as western premise.

Television in the early sixties was provoking criticism in two areas. The programmes were becoming more realistic. Jimmy Porter's influence hit the screen not long after Shaftesbury Avenue. Establishment (we hadn't heard that word much before) virtues were being attacked. Nothing was entirely sacred. Simultaneously advertisements were creating 'unrealistic desires and ambitions which can breed discontent and deaden our sense of responsibility for the real needs of the world'. While TV drama was showing us as we really were, the breaks conveyed for the most part fantasy, dream and luxury. Kitchen sink and Fairy Liquid.

But as long as Fairy Liquid kept its promise, did it matter? Hands that do dishes *could* be soft as your face. Eastern promise was as good a way as any to describe the sensation of eating Turkish Delight. The image was buttressed by the reality of the performance. The question wasn't so much 'Does the commercial honestly convey *information* about the brand's performance?' as 'Are the *values* conveyed by the commercial relevant to the performance of the brand?'

Brand values

The word, notice, was *brand*. Not product. Television became the prime vehicle for brand values. David Ogilvy, who popularized the idea of brand image in the early fifties (though he attributes the origin to Claude Hopkins some twenty years earlier) describes it as the personality of the brand. Advertising, though, was only one element of that personality. 'The personality of a product is an amalgam of many things. Its name, its packaging, its price, the style of its advertising and above all the nature of the product itself.' In product areas where differences are minimal and barely perceptible in blind test, the image is the distinguishing feature. As Ogilvy says, 'The brand image is 90 per cent of what the distiller has to sell.' All the more reason for the television advertiser to cultivate the image and maintain it.

Gradually it became apparent that the advertisement was not simply a component of Ogilvy's amalgam but an added value. The means by which the message is conveyed is saying as much, if not more, about the brand than the message itself. Advertisers realized they were transmitting covertly all sorts of ancillary and valuable signals. These, if made overt, might not have been accepted and certainly could not have been accommodated within the time-length of the commercial. Television in thirty seconds could not actually say much more than seventy words, whereas a full page in a tabloid newspaper could easily accommodate four hundred. Yet television could communicate feelings

'**Who likes Polo?**' By skilful direction and editing, Rowntree's Polo ('the mint with the hole') brought 'vox pop' interviews to a fine art. These commercials, never longer than 15 seconds, laid the foundation for a series of ingeniously zany campaigns using a variety of visual and verbal devices and a wide range of media

Regent Petrol. When the newly formed agency, Kingsley Manton and Palmer, made a successful pitch for the Regent account all the girls in their offices wore the Regent T-shirt to greet the client

Cadbury's Drinking Chocolate was the second commercial to be screened on opening night, 22 September 1955, and, like the first (for Gibbs' SR), was 60 seconds long

Chunky Dog Meat. Quaker Oats, makers of Chunky, used Liberal MP and bon viveur Clement Freud and his equally doleful-looking bloodhound, Henry, to sell Chunky in the sixties

and impressions, add dimension to a product presentation, depth to a product slogan.

Persil in the late seventies was communicating as much, if not more, by its style. The editing, the music, the casting. . . all were communicating bigness and confidence. 'Persil whiteness', thanks to what television had invested it with, had become what advertising people began to call a 'property'. A property is harder to define than to exemplify. It is a totality by which the brand's values are communicated. Like any good property, it should be built to last. And it can be developed. It may be a symbol (the Esso tiger) or a character (the Yorkie truck driver) or a slogan ('Setlers bring express relief') or a landscape (Birds Eye Country) or the Brooke Bond chimps.

And properties were part of the television offering to the viewer: familiar and recurring scenes, voices, incidents and phrases. Advertising on television was part of its content. The ads in this entertainment medium, whatever else they did, had to entertain. In press, ads could still merely inform.

How advertising works

Entertaining ads changed the way commentators looked upon the way advertising worked. No longer were ads meant to do things to respondents. Respondents were meant to do things *with* the advertising. When someone buys a packet of X he is associating himself with the values that that product's advertising represents. When he drives Y he is saying something about himself. When he buys a can of Z he is *drinking* the advertising. Advertising was not simply a means of highlighting the differences between brands. It became itself the difference.

And often production values *became* the product. Where will this lead? If products are distinguished only by the advertising, then technique will overcome ideas. It may sound old-fashioned, but I have grown up with two basic beliefs:

Left **The Bank Manager in the cupboard.** The clearing banks agreed in the early fifties not to embark on television advertising which they thought might prove expensive and self-cancelling. Although the Midland used TV to launch Gift Cheques in 1958 the ban was not lifted until the 'Big Five' (as they then were) began a joint television campaign in 1964 in which the bank manager, discovered in a cupboard, politely interrupted a number of family discussions about money matters. The campaign soon became part of popular culture and did much to bring the advantages of a bank account to a wider public. By the early seventies all the major banks were using television on their own account to promote a widening range of services

1   Advertising is about ideas. Ideas about products which motivate people towards purchase. Ideas which grow out of – and are inextricably linked to – those products.

2   A technique because it can *not* be inextricably linked to any one product is, at best, the means by which an idea is communicated. It is *not* the idea.

Our inventiveness, technical resources, wealth and variety of talent make London the (temporary?) creative capital of the television ad production world. Our features directors are more ready to do commercials, and our actors to appear in them. Production gloss and technical accomplishment can easily fool us into thinking we have an advertising idea. It is far more difficult to get away with that on posters. The poster is advertising's equivalent of the string quartet. Musicologists judge the worth of a serious composer by a string quartet because, whereas an orchestral piece can be carried by the fireworks of orchestration, the quartet reveals the bare idea and the thinking. How many television awards juries have honoured fireworks rather than advertising ideas? Not all, thank goodness. But when great advertising ideas *are* honoured, how soon after do the imitators swoop, adapting the idea, the solution to a specific problem, to other products. Yesterday's idea becomes today's technique becomes tomorrow's cliché.

Some great commercials were inexpensive to make: the Volkswagen snow plough, the Heineken video game, the Italian Teflon billposter. Inexpensive – but rich in an idea. Who was it who said: 'We haven't any money so we'll have to think'? I know who said this, however: 'There is an inherent drama in every product. Our No.1 job is to dig for it and capitalize on it.' It was Leo Burnett. The creative person's job is to look at the product continually anew – as if for the first time – and to communicate that insight.

Burnett was right. There *is* drama in every product. There is no greater *means* of conveying that drama than television. Yet television has been used less to dramatize a brand's virtues than to convey a brand's values. A medium which has brought news to our living room – flowing, like Lady Eden's Suez, all over the carpet – has been used infrequently to bring news from the advertiser. Retail stores; direct-response specialists; special offers; small local advertisers; large advertisers with a short-term promotion. . . all have used news in a tactical way. And videotape, which arrived in 1958, was taken up sparingly and grudgingly by the major advertisers. Agency producers

Don't forget the Fruit Gums, Mum! Yet another example of a television slogan which passed into the vernacular and helped to build the sales of a successful confectionery brand, Rowntree's Fruit Gums

and production company directors agree that video does not have the quality of film. It is ideal for post-production, as an editing tool. In finished commercials video is used tactically. It is regarded as suitable for documentaries and news, and unsuitable for creating and nurturing brand values. It has taken pop promos to reveal its potential. A combination of video and computer graphics is a magic box, permitting the film maker to create, in seconds, wondrous effects and titles which would have taken optical laboratories many days.

Equally the use of television, this most potent of media, to demonstrate a brand's tangible assets has surprised and disappointed those of us who awaited its arrival. 'Demonstration', said the American guru Harry McMahan, 'is television's long suit.' And the great TV demonstrations live in the memory – Band Aid's egg, Solvite's flying man, Everest Double Glazing's falling feather, Lego's kipper, Fiat's robots.

Changes

Television advertising has changed. From explicit to implicit; from right-hand side to left-hand side; from product attributes to brand values; from jingle to integrated music; from style-as-expression to style-as-content.

Television has changed advertising. The press advertisement is less verbal. It killed a whole school of copywriting – the leisurely, descriptive, somewhat self-indulgent, longish copy typified by Saxon Mills which spanned the Second World War. And when television became the lead medium – and the most fashionable – the art of copywriting fell into decline. There are few excellent press copywriters around under forty.

Many young writers who find scripting simple and natural find it hard and unnatural to write body copy. As a consequence press copy assumes the form of TV audio – short words, short sentences, short paragraphs; punctuation to aid the speaker rather than the reader. Mind you, the press itself apes and feeds off television. As Steven Foster says, 'Fleet Street's tabloids are carefully tuned to the expectations of a TV generation. In many cases they show positive attempts to re-create the effect of a television programme in print.'

The power of television is undeniable, but it can blind agency people to alternative solutions to a client problem. For twenty years now, for fast-moving package goods advertising has meant television. So the question asked of press is, 'Can it do what television can do?' The answer is probably not, though to look at much print advertising it seems, wrong-headedly, to be trying to. But is that the right question? Surely the challenge to each medium (television, radio, poster, press) is how can it exploit this particular strength to solve the advertiser's marketing communication problem? Always assuming, that is, that it can provide the appropriate audience at an appropriate price.

And till the advent of Channel Four, the television contractors didn't bother much about appropriate *audiences*. They were in the numbers business. Channel Four gave them the opportunity to target. Or rather the fact of minority viewing and complementarity made them consider not just cost-per-thousand, but cost-per-thousand *what?*

And the advent of cable, not to mention the possibility of the BBC taking commercials, makes targeting a practical proposition; while simultaneously satellite enables the global advertiser to address a whole continent simultaneously. The television commercial may change significantly as a result of this dual pressure. Broad brushstrokes on satellite and detail on cable?

Unless you are well into your fourth decade you can't imagine British television without advertising or advertising without television. It is a situation we take for granted. We have, in Milton Shulman's phrase, 'the least worst television in the world'. That goes for the programmes *and* the commercials. Indeed there is a spiritual union between the two, a tonal relationship between the programme material and the world of commercials which makes the literal separation (for all the IBA's efforts) almost impossible.

The quality and nature of our commercials which make them the envy of much of the western world, and which puzzle the Americans, are, I believe, the direct result of two factors above all others. They are the fears and hostility which preceded the arrival of Independent Television which gave us the system and heightened the sensibilities we enjoy today, and the early recognition that television is an entertainment and information medium and that advertisements are part of that totality.

We have chosen to have the least intrusive television advertising in the world. We now have a theory of how advertising may work which sits comfortably with it. Whether we have the most efficient television advertising in the world is another matter.

An Authority View 1

LORD AYLESTONE

LORD AYLESTONE

Lord Aylestone, then Herbert Bowden, entered Parliament as Labour Member for South Leicester after the General Election of 1945. Two years later he became interested in broadcasting matters for the first time on being appointed Parliamentary Private Secretary to the Postmaster-General, Wilfred Paling.

In 1949 he became a Government Whip and in 1955, following the return of a Conservative Government in 1951, he became Chief Opposition Whip.

When the Labour Party returned to office in 1964 he was appointed Lord President of the Council and Leader of the House of Commons, later becoming Secretary of State for Commonwealth Affairs in Harold Wilson's Government.

On his appointment as Chairman of the Independent Television Authority (as it then was) in succession to Lord Hill, who had been made Chairman of the BBC, he retired from the House of Commons. He took the title of Lord Aylestone from a district of his former Leicester constituency.

He presided over the Authority during a period of many far-reaching changes – the transfer of all television services from VHF to UHF, the introduction of colour and the coming of Independent Local Radio.

He retired from the IBA in 1975 and, returning to politics, he left the Labour Party to join the Social Democratic Party in 1981. Lord Aylestone was awarded the Gold Medal of the Royal Television Society in 1975

THE early autumn of 1967 was a particularly memorable time for me when I made an almost overnight move on 31 August from the office of Secretary of State for Commonwealth Affairs, with a place in the Cabinet, to my appointment on 1 September as Chairman of the Independent Television Authority. Admittedly, broadcasting was not completely unfamiliar to me since I had served for some time as Chairman of a Cabinet committee on the subject. But the move from Whitehall to the very different world of the Independent Television Authority in Brompton Road did mean a great change in my responsibilities, and I shall be eternally grateful to the Director-General, the late Sir Rober Fraser, who held my hand at that time. Hearing of my appointment, a jocular commentator remarked: 'You seem to have moved overnight from negotiating with Ian Smith in Rhodesia to dealing with Lew Grade in London.' Looking back, there is no doubt about which of those two gentlemen's company I preferred.

Some months earlier, while still under the chairmanship of Lord Hill of Luton, the Authority had reached a decision about the future shape of Independent Television and had announced the new franchises covering the whole of the United Kingdom. It had been decided that the fourteen existing companies were to be replaced by fifteen, with a completely new contractor covering Wales and part of the West Country. London was to be split differently, with a weekday company resulting from a 'shotgun marriage' of two existing companies, while another new contractor was appointed to cover London at the weekends.

I well recall one meeting of the Authority at which a name for the newly formed London weekday company was to be considered. After a great deal of deliberation the name 'Thames' was thought right, and the choice proved acceptable to the two somewhat unwilling partners to the marriage – both of whom, however, would have preferred to retain their single status. Some of the other companies whose functions and areas of operation had been altered found it difficult to understand why changes had been made at all, and inevitably there was bound to be a certain amount of unhappiness and disappointment. However, mine was not to reason why but to work and adopt the changed pattern. When I became Chairman of the ITA the basic decisions on the selection and appointment of the programme contractors for the new period had already been taken, but the resultant problems we all had to face were firmly on the plate of my colleagues and myself at the Authority.

Those companies whose contracts required changes had some difficult decisions to take in preparation for the new franchise period which was to begin at the end of July 1968. One company, Harlech TV – now more generally known as HTV – had reached an agreement with their predecessors, TWW, to take over some six months earlier in their area. I recall being present at HTV's studios in Cardiff on the day of the changeover, and it was not exactly an instant success. Wynford Vaughan-Thomas, then Harlech's Director of Programmes, and I sat together in the studios to see the first minutes on the air. Unfortunately, the opening scene on the screen showed nothing but cameras and crews with folk walking about in the studio. Something was obviously amiss, and in some embarrassment Vaughan-Thomas simply commented, 'Something is wrong,' and hurriedly left me while he went to investigate. On his return he said: 'I believe it was Bristol which was at fault – but at least the same thing happened to the BBC in the first minutes of BBC2.' Whether or not the blame lay with Bristol or Cardiff, matters were soon put right and HTV was successfully launched.

The main changeover elsewhere on the network took place as planned at the end of July, and went smoothly enough from the viewers' standpoint. But within the companies changes of personnel caused some difficulties.

My predecessor, Lord Hill, and his Authority colleagues had decided on a single programme journal for Independent Television, a proposal which inevitably presented some difficulties. Some of the companies had hitherto had a small programme journal of their own covering their area and, not unnaturally, were hesitant about giving it up. I recall taking a mock-up of the new *TV Times* to Belfast to try and bring Ulster TV into line. They were a little upset when I referred to their programme journal as 'rather like a Church magazine in comparison with the proposed *TV Times*'. I should think that by now, however, the programme companies are grateful for the Authority's insistence on one national programme journal able to contain their own regional programme information.

Following the Pilkington Report of 1962 the Government had decided that all television transmissions in Britain should move from the 405-line VHF standard into 625 lines in UHF, with the object of improving coverage and reception quality for viewers. This involved considerable changes at the transmitters and the introduction of numerous relay stations. The work involved was to take many years to complete and, lacking any real technical knowledge, I was grateful for the tremendous help given me by our Director of Engineering, the late Howard Steele, who had the ability of reducing the most difficult technical problems to 'child's guide' levels, which suited me. It was a thrilling experience when, as a result of an immense amount of careful work and planning, we were able to see ITV programmes on the air in colour for the first time in November 1969.

Some fifteen years earlier, when the Government of the day had decided to set up a second television service to be financed from advertising revenue, and to be in programme competition with the BBC, there was a great deal of opposition and many fears, as I well remember. One fear certainly prevalent in political circles at the time was that advertisers would be able to dictate the content of the programmes – a fear, I must admit, which I shared. In a very short while, however, both the politicians and the viewing public realized that these fears were unfounded. Many of the advertisements on the screen were to prove as popular as the programmes.

One important duty of the ITA was to examine and approve all advertisements before transmission. I recall sitting with the ITA's Advertising Control staff at one of their regular morning meetings when new advertisements were being previewed. It was noticeable that the majority were acceptable – some needed amendment but very few were rejected outright, because the advertising agencies had very rapidly learned what was likely to be acceptable. Over the years an advertising control system had been built up which, despite an occasional hiccup, worked very smoothly. In this important field of responsibility I was much indebted to Archie Graham, OBE, the Authority's Head of Advertising Control.

In July 1972 the ITA became the Independent Broadcasting Authority with the arrival on the scene of Independent Local Radio which, like television, was to be financed solely from advertising revenue. As in the case of television, the Authority was made responsible for control of the content of all radio advertisements broadcast by the Independent Local Radio stations.

Although not having personally taken part in the interviewing and selection of the television companies in 1967, my IBA colleagues and myself found we had a surfeit of interviewing the many applicants for the Independent Local Radio franchises. This process went on for many weeks, a task not made any easier by the high standard of preparation and presentation of the applications. I believe there were some sixty applications for the first nineteen stations. Public meetings were held in the areas which the stations were to cover, and small IBA committees did some preliminary sifting of applications locally. Interviewing was detailed and thorough, and we were greatly assisted in this task by the excellent briefings we were given by the IBA staff. Programme proposals were taken into consideration, as well as the applicants' ideas for local coverage.

Local as well as national news had to form an essential part of their proposed programme schedules. Above all, the Authority had to satisfy itself on the financial strength of the applicant consortia, bearing in mind the need for adequate finance in the run-up period as well as the initial months on the air.

Returning for a little light refreshment with my colleagues after having interviewed four or five applicants in a day, I remember remarking: 'I think we must feel as a young man does when looking for a bride with so many different attributes before him. He is confused and undecided, liking one lady's figure, another's voice, another's hair, another's personality.' The IBA's Director of Finance added: 'Don't forget her money, Chairman!'

We first went on the air experimentally in London, using a temporary aerial rigged between two tall chimneys at Lots Road power station. For some weeks we transmitted classical music all day and, when the two London ILR stations finally went on the air with normal transmissions, we received many complaints from listeners who said they preferred our classical music. Of course, most classical music was cheaper to use than more current compositions, for which we would have had to pay copyright fees. Those early days of Independent Local Radio were to prove difficult for some of the companies, as only a few were financially viable from their first days on the air.

Hearing the Independent Local Radio stations on the air at last was a great pleasure to me as I neared the end of my many happy years as Chairman of the IBA.

An Authority View 2

ANTHONY PRAGNELL

ANTHONY PRAGNELL

Anthony Pragnell joined the Home Civil Service in 1939 in the Inland Revenue. After war service as a navigator in the RAF, he rejoined the Civil Service, graduating in law at London University in 1949.

He joined the headquarters staff of the General Post Office in 1950 and was one of the first officials to be appointed to the newly formed ITA in August 1954. He became Secretary of the Authority a year later when broadcasting began.

For the next four years, until the appointment of Archie Graham in April 1959, Anthony Pragnell included advertising matters among his numerous responsibilities and was the first Secretary of the Advertising Advisory Committee. In 1961 he became Deputy Director-General of the Authority, responsible for administrative services, an appointment which he held until he retired in 1983.

After retirement, he became a Director of Channel Four Television and a Fellow of the European Institute for the Media at Manchester University. He is also a member of the Data Protection Tribunal

ANY chapter entitled 'An Authority View' in a general history of television advertising over the last thirty years could give the impression that the Authority (the ITA and then the IBA) has tended to have an opposing attitude on advertising to that of the television companies. Such an impression would be wrong. It has not proved a field of conflict between the Authority and the programme companies; and in the detailed procedures of day-to-day control of copy and the inclusion of advertising in the programmes there has probably been closer cooperation at executive level between the Authority and the companies than in any other aspect of the Authority's service.

However, in advertising as in other areas, the Authority has specific responsibilities under the governing statute. It has, therefore, had to be prepared from the start to take its own view on matters of advertising policy. In the earliest days that view had to be formed by the ITA itself, with the assistance of the Advertising Advisory Committee. Later, as the network of programme companies developed and the functions of selling advertisements and including them in the programmes became an important part of company operations, practices of consultation and cooperation grew up which have valuably assisted the Authority in the formation of policy. But it is worth recording that, whatever the weight or lightness of the Authority's regulatory touch may have seemed over the years, it has from the start been an essential feature of the governing statutes that specified programme and advertising responsibilities are placed directly on the Authority which, in turn, extends them to the television companies by means of the programme contracts.[1] In later sections of this chapter, therefore, the accounts of how various aspects of advertising control have developed are necessarily accounts of the views that the Authority has taken on the matters described, even though those views have also been shared by the programme companies.

The Authority's general approach

Before more detailed matters are dealt with, it will be useful to describe three important principles which have been central to the Authority's approach to advertising questions.

Separateness and distinctiveness of the advertising content

It is essential that the mix and content of the programmes should not be directly governed by advertising considerations. The proper form of advertising (subject to the statutorily limited and defined exceptions) is therefore 'spot' advertising. This must, in the words of the governing statutes from the Television Act 1954 onwards, be 'clearly distinguishable as such and recognisably separate from the rest of the programme'.[2] Furthermore, it should not be excessive in amount.[3]

Responsibility towards the public for advertising content

A television service which carries advertising has obligations to the public both of a general kind – to see mainly that categories and methods of advertising are not misleading or socially harmful – and of a more specific kind – to devise and effectively operate machinery which will apply the Authority's general obligations to individual advertisements. The framework within which the system must operate in all these matters is set out in the governing statute.[4] This makes the Authority ultimately responsible, but the means by which its obligations are discharged can properly, and in practice must, involve the cooperation of the television companies (who sell the advertising – see below) and indeed the advertisers and their agencies, for the interests and objectives of the different parties concerned in the preparation, purchase, selling and showing of advertising have much in common. In practice the cooperation of the television companies, as well as of the advertising business, owes as much to their own sense of responsibility as to any formal requirements.[5]

The selling of advertising

It is the job of the television companies, and not of the Authority, to sell the advertising which is shown on Independent Television.[6] Their income depends upon their ability to do so, and that income will govern the amount of money available for programming. So clear is the Act about the responsibility of the companies for selling the advertising that, while it gives the Authority the duty of approving the form and detail of rate cards, the fixing of the cost at which advertising time will be sold is the job of the programme companies.[7] This separation of powers has seemed to the Authority to be right: as the overall supervisory body, its ability to discharge its responsibility for programme quality and standards would be weakened if it also had responsibility, whether as a fixer of advertising rates or also as a seller of the time, for the financial fortunes of the system.[8]

Some historical background

As matters have developed over the last thirty years, advertising on Independent Television has become universally accepted as part of the national broadcasting scene and the early antipathy to its inclusion in the programmes has virtually disappeared. The idea that the advertising side might prove to be a relatively placid and ultimately non-controversial area is not one which would have been thought tenable during the period before Independent Television was set up. Much has been written about the genesis of the 1954 Television Act, drafted and eventually passed in the face of strong opposition in Parliament and elsewhere. But a reference to the discussions about advertising and its proper place in the system – about which much doubt was expressed – will not be out of place here.

Public debate had begun with the Beveridge Committee, whose report was published in January 1951.[9] The predominant view of that Committee had been in favour of the continuance of the BBC monopoly and against the introduction of broadcast advertising. But the view had not been unanimous. The powerful and eventually decisive minority report of Selwyn Lloyd is well remembered: it directly confronted the principle of the BBC monopoly and urged that competing bodies for radio and television should be set up, financed by carefully regulated advertising. It is less often recalled that a special note was appended to the Report by Lord Beveridge himself and by two other members of the Committee. They suggested that the ban on advertising might well be reconsidered, and they expressed regret that the issue of the acceptability of advertising as a source of broadcasting finance had not been fully explored. This last phrasing has an interesting ring to it in 1985, with the establishment of the Peacock Committee to consider a similar question with specific reference to the BBC.

During the next two-and-a-half years or so, during which a Labour Government was replaced by a Conservative one, opposition to the continuance of the BBC monopoly emerged as a coherent force to be reckoned with. The distinction between sponsorship and spot advertising was clarified, with the latter becoming progressively seen as the acceptable means of financing a self-supporting service.

The ascendancy of spot advertising was confirmed in the Government White Paper on Television Policy of November 1953,[10] and in the first Television Act.[11] The only exceptions were the permissibility of advertising magazines and features, which were seen as being essentially a series of spots strung together in discrete, and distinguishable, advertising periods, and very limited, and in practice rarely employed, exceptions from the no-sponsorship rule.[12]

Ministers were put under strong pressure during the 1954 parliamentary debates to include in the Act specific restrictions on television advertising. With great robustness, however, they held to the view that Parliament should lay down broad principles, should give certain reserve powers to ministers and should then leave it to the ITA, suitably advised, to control advertising. The only departures from this approach were the specific prohibitions on political and religious advertising or on any advertisement which related to any industrial dispute.[13]

A large responsibility and a wide discretion therefore rested with the first members of the ITA, who were appointed in August 1954, and with Sir Robert Fraser, the first Director-General, appointed soon afterwards. The ITA might have been forgiven if, given its public service role, its 'great and good' membership, the recent controversies and the hard things said about the likely results of complete advertising support (unique in Europe) for a major national service, it had been reserved in its approach to advertising questions.

But, in practice, the ITA saw no problems about the system's dependence on advertising for its livelihood. There was support for Fraser's bullish approach to advertising. He liked to refer to ITV as 'people's television', and he saw the advertising base of the service as an integral element in this concept. In his view, the need to earn advertising revenue, in order to be able to provide programmes of the quality and comprehensiveness which the Act required, was a means of ensuring that the service did not lose touch with the audience. He also saw a proper connection between the advertisers' desire to transmit their messages in association with successful programmes and the broadcasters' natural pride in their own work and their desire to have it widely seen. As the IBA under a successor Director-General was later to say to the Annan Committee: 'If the system failed to attract advertising revenue because insufficient people were watching, then it would lack the resources to produce good programming and would eventually collapse. Its feasibility rests on public approval. A commercial discipline from the outset put ITV in touch with popular style and taste.'

It is remarkable how many of the basic decisions taken in 1954 and 1955 have stood the test of time, subject only to some fine tuning. In only one field perhaps – that of the detailed day-to-day control of advertising content – have practices grown up which might be regarded as being of a totally different kind from anything that could have been foreseen in those early days.

This ability to maintain a consistent approach over the greater part of the advertising field is perhaps the more notable because many decisions had to be taken by the ITA before it had any picture of what television advertising in Britain was going to took like in practice. (I well remember waiting for that first Gibbs' SR advertisement to appear, and the immediate reaction of surprised approval when it came up on the screen.) Many of the decisions, too, were taken before programme contractors were securely in place. This meant that the ITA did not have, at the outset, the benefits of the consultative arrangements about advertising which were later to grow up with the companies.

Amount and distribution of advertising

This is an area where, with one important exception, the statutory requirements upon the Authority have not significantly altered since the Television Act of 1954. The one exception is that the original Act permitted – as had been foreshadowed in the 1953 White Paper – the inclusion of longer advertising items in the form of advertising magazines (covering a number of products) and features (covering the products of a single advertiser or those available in a single shop or location). These longer items were prohibited by the Television Act, 1963,[14] following the Report of the Pilkington Committee on Broadcasting. Twenty years or so later – although this was not evident at the time – they may be seen to have always been anomalous, if not aberrant, at least in a service which proved able to earn an adequate income from spot advertising alone.

The initial decision

One of the first papers on advertising put to the members of the Authority in the autumn of 1954 suggested that an advertising allowance of six minutes an hour for spot advertising would be a reasonable one, with the other, longer forms of advertising running free. Although this allowance has been proved by practice, the first of the justifications for it reads somewhat quaintly in 1985: US experience was called upon as evidence that more than 10 per cent advertising defeated its own object because of adverse public reaction. It was also pertinently pointed out – and it is still a valid consideration today – that, in the United Kingdom, an advertising-free service would always be available to people who were irritated by the advertising. It was suggested too that, while a lower quota than 10 per cent might endanger the commercial success of the new service, it was quite possible that some contractors would not want to show the full percentage – something which has never been the case.

Further refinements

The overall six-minutes-in-the-hour rule has survived until today, having withstood the scrutiny of several committees of inquiry. But in the light of experience it was to become apparent to the Authority, with no significant dissent from the programme companies, that an overall percentage was, on its own, an inadequate protection against the possible adverse effects of advertising. For it was clear that, whether or not the amount of time given to advertising in the programmes was, in the words of the Act, 'so great as to detract from the value of the programmes as a medium of information, education and entertainment',[15] the situation could not be appraised only by looking at the percentage over the day.

It was natural that advertisers and programme companies should want to place their commercials in the more popular evening hours, and the lack of any inner quota meant that, on some occasions, individual hours would carry well over six minutes in the hour, and the early introduction of schools and religious programmes facilitated this. This was because these categories of programmes were able to 'earn' advertising even though commercials could not be associated with them.

Trouble in The Times *and in the House*

As a first step towards remedying an excessive exposure of advertising in the evening hours, when most viewers were watching, in 1958 the ITA reached an agreement with the companies that no single clock hour should contain more than eight minutes of advertising.[16] But this did not satisfy the critics, drawn mainly from those who had opposed the whole advertising basis of ITV before it was set up. Controversy was opened in May 1959 with a letter to *The Times* from Herbert Morrison, complaining about the amount of advertising being shown in some individual clock hours. Morrison was not prepared to allow any flexibility – to accommodate, for instance, the fact that advertising breaks might fall awkwardly around the beginning and end of particular hours; nor was he prepared (and here he may have been on stronger ground) to accept that advertising magazines should not be taken account of for the purposes of the six-minute-in-the-hour rule or the eight-minutes-in-the-hour maximum.

Morrison's complaint brought a swift riposte from Robert Fraser, who called in aid a ministerial statement made during the parliamentary debates of 1954.[17] This had foreshadowed both a six-minutes-in-the-hour average for advertising and the exclusion of 'shoppers' guides' from it. Fraser pointed out that Herbert Morrison's appraisal of hourly amounts of advertising was not a valid one, since quite fortuitous placings of advertisements a few minutes on either side of the sixty-minute mark on the clock, which would mean little to the viewer, could give quirkish amounts in particular clock hours.

This robust and pragmatic defence did not prevent the attempted introduction in June 1959 of a Television (Limitation of Advertising) Bill under the ten-minute rule. This attempt was made by Herbert Morrison and five other Labour MPs who were hardened opponents of television advertising. The proposal was to limit advertising of all kinds to six minutes an hour, with no averaging allowed. The attempt failed. Unreasonable as the proposed limitation was in its inflexibility, it could well be that those of us in the Authority who tried to hold to the eight-minutes-in-the-hour maximum were misjudging – particularly with the continuance of advertising magazines – how much advertising the programmes and the audience could be expected to bear.

A final decision

The situation did, in fact, prove unstable, and the Authority received during the following year substantial evidence of public dissatisfaction with advertising exposure on ITV. This came as part of a regular Research Services survey commissioned by the ITA into public attitudes towards ITV. One such survey showed more than two-thirds of those sampled in April 1960 as expressing dissatisfaction – either that they liked a few advertisements but disliked most, or that they would prefer no advertising at all. This result compared with only half the sample expressing dissatisfaction in the same terms in a survey undertaken three years previously in 1957. The total generally liking advertising fell correspondingly from just under a half in 1957 to just under a third in 1960.

As a result, the Authority ruled that by the end of 1960 no clock hour should contain more than seven minutes of spot advertising. This final objective was reached by way of an interim limit of seven and a half minutes, operative from September 1960.

The decision to confine advertising to seven minutes in the clock hour meant that the system could go into the Pilkington phase with clear rules about the amount of advertising which could be defended as reasonable – with the exception, as it turned out, of the continued exclusion from the hourly maxima of shoppers' guides. Despite its critical attitude towards some other aspects of the ITA's stewardship, the Pilkington Committee gave the ITA a clean bill about the volume of spot advertising.[18] Since then the Authority's broad approach has not been seriously criticized.

A flexible approach in practice

The seven-minutes-in-the-hour maximum has always been applied with some flexibility, with the Authority being willing exceptionally to permit a transfer of advertising from one hour to another, or even on rare occasions from one day to another, if desirable in the interests of better programme presentation.

Two special exceptions

On two occasions, also, the Authority has been willing to allow a more extended departure from the normal arrangements, but in neither case has it permitted any departure from the overall six-minutes-per-hour average.

On the first occasion, the departure was to a significant extent in the interests of the advertisers. It occurred in the aftermath of the coal dispute of early 1972. Power cuts and transmission failures arising during the dispute had affected the broadcasting of advertisements and led to requests for deferment of advertising from companies and utilities, including suppliers of electrical and gas equipment, whose operations were being hit. In these exceptional circumstances the Authority agreed that, for six weeks after the dispute, in March and April up to seven-and-a-half minutes of advertising in the hour could be broadcast. In addition to the proviso that the six-minutes-per-hour daily average should be observed, it was a condition that there would be no increase in the number of intervals to accommodate advertising. The object in agreeing to these particular arrangements was to enable some of the backlog of advertising which had resulted from the dispute to be recovered, as well as to facilitate the early return to normal efficiency of industrial advertisers who were particularly vulnerable to the loss of television advertising at that particular time.

The second occasion was more extended, and the Authority's decision to allow a departure from the norm was primarily made in the interests of the service as a whole at a time when substantial new financial demands were being made upon it as a result of the introduction of Channel Four. During the first two years of that new service's transmissions, from November 1982 onwards, the Institute of Practitioners in Advertising were in dispute with Equity over the level of fees to be paid to actors for appearances in commercials on the new service. This led to a shortfall of advertising on the new channel with an adverse effect upon revenue. For the period of the dispute, which was not settled until the end of 1984, the Authority felt it proper to assist the ITV contractors, whose subscriptions to finance the new channel were at the start greatly in excess of the extra revenue earned from it, by allowing two minutes per day of off-peak time to be transferred into peak. There could thus be an excess over the normal seven-minutes-in-the-hour maximum, but the rule was that the two minutes should be evenly spread, with not more than one additional minute being shown in any single clock hour. The concession did not increase the total daily allowance of advertising. Although, in the event, there was no obvious harm to the look of the service and no adverse public reaction, the arrangements were not continued beyond the end of the dispute.

Arrangements for inserting and distributing advertisements in the programmes

The obligation on the Authority to ensure that the amount of advertising shown does not detract from the value of the programmes stands on its own in the Act. In practice, however, the point at which a particular amount of advertising detracts will depend to a large extent upon the way it is distributed over, and introduced into, the programmes. The Authority has therefore tended to look at all these matters together, as described below.

Natural breaks

The 1954 Act said (and this still remains the statutory provision) that 'advertising shall not be inserted otherwise than at the beginning or the end of the programme or in natural breaks therein'.[19] Natural breaks are nowhere specifically defined or described in the Act, and it has been left to the Authority to evolve its own conventions about how advertising could be introduced during the course of a programme. Again, as in other matters, a certain robust common sense was initially required, and there were plenty of people ready to pounce upon even the slightest apparent deviation from what was proper in this area.

The basic question to be confronted was how far it was possible for naturalness to be contrived. At one side of the spectrum was the stage convention of a play of two or three acts, of which any act other than the last would frequently end with the curtain being brought down at a point in the action which would leave the audience keen to know what was going to happen after the interval. Furthermore, acts would often be subdivided into scenes, which would, for example, mark the passage of time or a change of location requiring a change in setting. Obviously the translation of a stage play to television would provide natural breaks at the points where they would occur in the stage presentation.

But, at the other end of the spectrum, there was the cinema film which had no pre-existing breaks of this kind (or only one in the case of a very long film), and which, as producers and film enthusiasts often asserted, had been conceived as a continuous single piece. The Authority's line has been consistent in saying that it is still possible to discern points in films where, even if there were no advertising, interruptions in the continuity of the action occur – for instance where there is a clearly marked lapse of time in the action or a change of location.

This common-sense approach has also been applied to a question which caused much comment in the early days. The question was whether a break specially written into an original television programme could really be considered as natural or not. The Authority had little truck with scepticism on this matter. Just as it was appropriate for stage dramatists to divide their works into acts and scenes, so was it acceptable for people writing for television to divide their works into 'parts' (as the new medium described them), subject always to the end of a part corresponding to an interruption in the continuity.

The discussion about natural breaks in drama programmes, important as it was from the point of view of compliance with the Act, was largely an academic one from the audience's point of view. The public as a whole was little concerned. New types of programme such as *Robin Hood* and *Douglas Fairbanks Presents*, and imported items such as *I Love Lucy* and *Dragnet* fell neatly into segments in which advertising could be inserted without spoiling the audience's enjoyment of the programme. In more serious offerings the theatrical convention was readily accepted.

In the case of programmes other than dramatic ones, natural breaks may occur irrespective of any action by the programme company (for example, during the intervals of some sporting event) or may call for careful identification (for example, on a change of topic or exposition in a documentary or discussion programme).[20]

But it took some years for all members of the viewing audience to become attuned to the insertion of advertising within programmes. The Authority and the companies tended to concentrate their attentions on getting things right in drama and documentaries. It was, therefore, with somewhat wry amusement that in 1959 we read a piece in the *Manchester Guardian* by its then television reviewer, W.J. Weatherby. At a time when the critics of advertising on television were still primarily exercised about its appearance within drama, Weatherby surprisingly wrote that he found the regular inclusion of advertising excusable in plays when the subject was a thriller with exciting scenes, but that it was ludicrous in variety and similar programmes 'where it was not "natural" by any stretch of the imagination'.

Distribution rules

The ITA was already aware of the fact that breaks which were natural when taken individually might cease to appear so to the viewer if they occurred too frequently in relation to the nature of the surrounding programmes. By 1960 the Authority was able to describe to the Pilkington Committee a detailed set of rules about the distribution of advertising over the programmes.[21] These rules gave the number and length of breaks allowable in programmes of particular lengths. They were not in principle very different from those applicable in 1985, as they appear in Section 2 of the IBA's *Advertising Rules and Practices*. The main differences are that advertising is not now permitted within documentaries, plays or children's programmes if they last for less than half an hour. In the 1960s such insertions were permitted, subject to the overriding prohibition – which still applies – on internal breaks in programmes of less than twenty minutes. On the other hand, in 1960 advertising was not allowed in religious programmes or in news bulletins, or between national and local news bulletins when these were shown successively. The restriction on internal advertising in the news was lifted on the introduction of the half-hour *News at Ten* in 1967. This departure from past practice caused some eyebrows to be raised at ITN and elsewhere. But in the light of experience it came to be accepted that the break in the half-hour news did not detract from its value, and in fact provided an opportunity for the bulletin to 'turn the page', often allowing – depending upon the incidence of the news of the day – for a change of tone and pace. With the trend towards more news, and with the eventual introduction of a fifty-minute news programme four days a week on Channel Four, a prohibition of internal breaks would have been unreasonable. These breaks have proved a particular attraction to advertisers wanting to reach viewers in the business and professional categories.

There has also been a change in relation to advertising in religious programmes. In 1977, after the IBA had consulted the Central Religious Advisory Committee, the Home Secretary agreed to a proposal to allow the insertion of suitable advertising in religious programmes of more than half an hour in length, provided that these programmes were not broadcasts of religious services or were not otherwise of a devotional nature.

Since the crystallization in the early 1960s of detailed rules about the distribution of advertising – rules which have been subject to the relatively minor adaptations described above – the natural-break controversy has almost entirely disappeared. The Pilkington Committee accepted the internal break in principle, recommending merely tighter definition and control, while the Annan Committee took the whole question of advertising insertions in its stride, accepting the practice which had been evolved under the Authority's aegis as part of the accepted pattern of UK broadcasting, recommending only that the IBA should reduce the number of internal breaks in programmes where they were inappropriate.

Insulation of programmes from advertising

It should be mentioned briefly that the governing Acts have always contained provisions regarding the exclusion of advertising from certain categories of programme or for the insulation of some programmes from advertising.[22]

Such provisions are plainly of importance, and were considered particularly so in the 1950s; the notorious appearance, for example, of J. Fred Muggs, a chimpanzee, in commercials accompanying the US transmissions of the Coronation in 1953 was much called on during the 1954 parliamentary debates to support the need to protect certain types of programmes. The statutory provisions were originally valuable in alerting a new system to the need to exercise constant vigilance about the juxtaposition of programmes and advertising material. In practice they have not raised serious problems, and this has been due as much to the discretion and good sense of programme and advertising officers in the Authority and the companies as to the existence of formal rules.

Intervals between advertising periods

Similarly, there has always been provision for regulating the minimum interval between advertising periods. Under the present Act this is an optional power given to the Home Secretary, rather than a provision which is mandatory,[23] and the matter is not in fact the subject of any specific mention in the IBA's *Advertising Rules and Practices*.

Control of advertising content

It is in this field that the greatest development has taken place over the last thirty years, both in approach and in machinery. The following sections will deal mainly with the role and powers of the Advertising Advisory Committee (AAC); the *Principles for Television Advertising* (the predecessor of the IBA *Code of Advertising Standards and Practice*); and the Authority's approach to certain important categories of advertising.

The Advertising Advisory Committee, 1954-63

The first Television Act of 1954 unwittingly put the ITA in a somewhat false position over the control of advertising, although there is no record that the Authority or its staff at the time thought this fact important. The initially anomalous position was this: the power to make the major decisions about the standards of conduct to be adopted in the advertising of goods and services formally rested with the Advertising Advisory Committee rather than with the Authority. Apart from being given the duty of prohibiting religious and political advertising the Authority had four duties only in relation to the content of advertisements. It had to appoint an Advertising Advisory Committee.[24] It had, for all practical purposes, to comply and secure compliance with the recommendations of that Committee.[25] It had to consult with the Postmaster-General from time to time about the classes and descriptions of goods or services which must not be advertised and the methods of advertising which must not be employed.[26] Finally, it then had to carry out any directions which he gave about such matters.[27]

The Act itself, having given mandatory powers to the AAC, was not detailed in giving that Committee its terms of reference. These were stated to be 'to give advice to the Authority with a view to the exclusion of misleading advertisements. . . and otherwise as to the principles to be followed in connection with the advertisements included' in ITV programmes and the preparation of a code of standards of conduct in advertising.[28] A further clue – but no more – as to what the Committee was meant to concern itself with could be found in its required composition, which was to be 'representative of organisations, authorities and persons concerned with standards of conduct in the advertising of goods and services (including in particular the advertising of goods or services for medical or surgical purposes)'.[29]

The untidiness of the formal position was undoubtedly due to the approach, right in its essentials, adopted by ministers in relation to the initial legislation. On the one hand, they wanted to avoid hamstringing the Authority in advance with a number of detailed rules. Indeed, this would not have been feasible in legislation setting up an entirely new television service, the nature of whose operations in day-to-day practice could not be clearly foreseen. On the other hand, they wanted to reassure parliamentary and other critics that advertising would be responsibly handled and controlled. The ITA and its staff were not in fact dismayed by any formal ambivalence of their position, although they were later to represent to the Pilkington Committee that it was wrong in principle for the Authority to be subject to mandatory recommendations from an advisory committee.[30]

A key appointment, obviously, was going to be that of the AAC Chairman. The ITA was fortunate in being able to persuade Robert (R.A.) Bevan to be the first holder of this position. Bevan was chairman of S.H. Benson Ltd, one of the leading advertising agencies, a member of the Council of the Institute of Practitioners in Advertising (IPA) and later its President. Other members of the Committee, appointed in January 1955, were, in accordance with the Act's requirements, people nominated by the Ministry of Health, the British Medical Association (BMA), the British Dental Association (BDA), the Pharmaceutical Society, the British Code of Standards Committee (concerned with the voluntary control of medical advertising outside television), the Retail Trading Standards Association (RTSA), which was a national body of retailers and manufacturers designed to bring influence to bear against advertising, selling methods or trade descriptions which were likely to mislead the public, the Advertising Association, the IPA and the Incorporated Society of British Advertisers (ISBA). The AAC was a powerful and energetic committee, although originally perhaps more balanced towards professional than consumer interests – which nevertheless were not unrepresented, given the presence of the BMA, BDA, RTSA, Pharmaceutical Society, British Code of Standards Committee and Ministry of Health nominees.

The Principles for Television Advertising

Between January and March 1955, the AAC considered and approved for submission to the ITA, under the title *Principles for Television Advertising*, the code which the Act required. In the drafting of this document, full account was taken of the voluntary codes, existing or still in draft, applying to other media, and valuable expert assistance in details of the code was given by members of the Committee.

The code as submitted was then discussed with the Postmaster-General, as the Act required, so far as prohibitions on the advertising of particular goods and services and on the use of particular methods of advertising were concerned. He gave his approval and it was published in June 1955.[31] The document, though relatively short by today's standards, was nevertheless comprehensive in scope and skilful in picking up points likely to be of particular relevance to television.

It was in three parts. First came a statement of general and particular principles. The main general principle was that television advertising should be 'legal, clean, honest and truthful' and that standards applicable to it should take account of its greater intimacy within the home compared with other media. The particular principles related to such matters as the avoidance of false or misleading advertisements, guarantees, competitions and advertising in children's programmes. The second part of the document was an appendix which gave more detailed rules about specific classes and methods of advertising, including the advertising of medicines and treatments, and financial advertising. The third part of the document consisted of the British code of standards in relation to the advertising of medicines and treatments; this code was adopted in the *Principles* as the basic standard for Independent Television.

In the first volume of his history of Independent Television in Britain[32] Bernard Sendall says that the first code can only be described as a boldly liberal one. This is certainly true in relation to what it did not exclude or even restrict. For example, no specific reference of any limiting kind was made to tobacco or alcohol, even in connection with children's programmes. But in other less obvious ways the code was to be used to impose high standards of advertising from the very start of ITV transmissions. As with most codified rules, a measure of interpretation was found necessary. Thus even before the first transmissions had begun the AAC met to consider proposed scripts for a refreshing drink which, it was claimed, could speed recovery in illness. In the proposed advertising a nurse was to be shown. The question of principle which the AAC had to ask itself, quite apart from the validity of the claim made for the product, was whether the rules applicable to medicines should apply to products which were not medicines but which were put forward as being beneficial in illness. The Committee did, in fact, deal with this first borderline case *ad hoc* without giving a clear answer to the question of principle, but in early 1957 it took the view that it was permissible to advertise borderline products only in ways which would also be allowable in the advertising of medicines and treatments proper.

The AAC also took a strict line about advertisements for toothpastes which were thought to be making stronger claims that they would prevent tooth decay than could be conclusively proved from the evidence then available.

Betting advertising

For the purposes of this first code, the AAC deferred any recommendation about betting advertising, including football pools. Left to itself, the AAC would not at that point have wanted to prohibit this kind of advertising altogether. It was aware, however, that the ITA, although not unanimously, was not keen to have it on the screen. The Pool Promoters' Association conveniently announced that it wanted to wait and see, and did not propose to book time for football-pool advertising in the initial stages of ITV transmissions. The AAC was able, therefore, to defer a recommendation on betting as a whole.

The matter was left in abeyance until 1956 when some programme companies informed the Authority that, if allowed, they would want to take football-pool advertisements, but not other betting advertisements. Another company stated at that time that, as a matter of house policy, it would not wish to take betting advertising. After consideration of the matter at two meetings, the AAC agreed to recommend to the ITA that, subject to substantial restrictions on the time at which pools advertisements should be shown and on methods of presentation, football-pool advertising, but no other betting advertising, should be allowed.

A majority of the Authority remained opposed to football-pool advertising, and the ITA recognized that, if it wanted to secure a permanent prohibition on pools advertising, it would have no option but to approach the Postmaster-General and ask him to issue a directive. Before the Postmaster-General had been able to consider the issue fully matters took a new turn. The programme company which, it had been thought, did not want as a matter of policy to take any betting advertising, decided that, if permitted, it would show advertising from on-course bookmakers in and around broadcasts of race meetings. This would mean that the advertisements would be seen largely by people already interested in racing, and probably betting, and it could not be said that any undesirable stimulus was being given to betting activities. The company questioned the logic of the AAC being willing to sanction advertising for one form of betting (football pools) while refusing to do so for on-course bookmakers in association with racing transmissions. The company asked the Authority to agree to its making representations direct to the AAC. After hearing the views of the company, the AAC formed the opinion that, as a matter of both practice and justice, permission for other forms of betting advertising could not in the long run be withheld if football-pool advertising were allowed. Since it was not prepared to recommend the advertising of other forms of betting, its decision had to be that the existing prohibition on pools advertising should not be lifted. By this somewhat circuitous route, therefore, the ITA secured a prohibition on betting advertising of all kinds.

To complete the story of betting, advertising of which still remains prohibited, by 1970 the Authority had changed its mind and it then approached the Minister with a request for football-pool advertising to be permitted. This approach was unsuccessful, as was a subsequent one in 1983.

The Advertising Advisory Committee after Pilkington

In its evidence to the Pilkington Committee the Authority pointed out the disadvantages of it, as the responsible corporation, having to comply with the recommendations of advisory committees (there were two others, for religion and children, in addition to the AAC), however expert their specialist membership and however valued their advice to the Authority. The Pilkington Committee shared this view and thought that it was 'wrong in principle and contradictory in terms' that these committees' advice should be binding on the Authority. It recommended a change in the law.[33]

The Television Act, 1963 therefore contained amending provisions which retained the AAC as a body which the ITA was obliged to appoint and did not reduce its advisory functions. The Committee's obligation to prepare an advertising code and its power to make recommendations binding on the Authority were, however, removed. The duty in relation to the code was transferred to the Authority which was, and still is, obliged 'to draw up, and from time to time review, a code governing standards and practice in advertising and prescribing the advertisements and methods of advertising to be prohibited, or prohibited in particular circumstances'.[34] The AAC remained centrally concerned with this code in an advisory capacity, in that it was given the duty of keeping the code under review and of submitting to the Authority alterations which appeared desirable.[35]

The consumers' voice on the Advertising Advisory Committee

One of the criticisms made of the AAC around the time of the Pilkington Committee was that, while a range of professional advertising interests were represented, there was no specific consumer representation. This was not, in the ITA's view, wholly true of the initial membership for, as pointed out earlier, the BMA, BDA, RTSA, British Code of Standards Committee and Ministry of Health nominees could all be regarded, in part at least, as speaking as much for the public as for their organizations. Furthermore, by the time of Pilkington lay members had been appointed to the AAC from the ITA's Scottish and Northern Ireland Committees. The composition of the Committee had first been established in 1954, before the later full emergence of consumer bodies separate from organizations such as the Cooperative Movement, the National Council of Women and the National Federation of Women's Institutes, which had traditionally included the representation of the consumer among their aims and objects. The first Television Act had also clearly indicated that the AAC was to be representative of interests concerned with standards of advertising conduct, and these interests were, in fact, represented in a balanced way on the Committee. The Advertising Advisory Committee had acted with great effectiveness, and, as he is quoted as saying to the Pilkington Committee, Robert Fraser had been impressed with its 'consumer approach'. The Pilkington Committee did, however, decide to recommend that the consumer's voice should be specifically heard on the AAC, and the 1965 Act added 'the public as consumers' to the previous list of those who should be represented on it.[36] Whether or not the change was strictly warranted on the grounds which the Committee advanced is not a question for discussion here. What can be said, however, is that the AAC, with its new composition, has remained a valued part of the Authority's system of advertising control and that consumer members have played a full part in achieving this end. The practice of having an independent Chairman of the Committee has been particularly successful.[37]

Cigarette advertising

In the new 1963 legislation the obligation on the ITA to consult the Postmaster-General from time to time on prohibited categories and forms of advertising, and to carry out any directions from him, was unchanged.[38] The Postmaster-General did, in fact, exercise these powers in 1965 in a centrally important way when he prohibited cigarette advertising, in respect of which the ITA and the companies had progressively imposed stricter and stricter rules about timing and methods of presentation. There was some protest from ITV about this – the Authority felt that it was illogical and discriminatory to select the television medium as the only one subject to formal prohibition. But there is little doubt that, given the body of evidence which points to a link between smoking and ill-health, the ITV system can feel more comfortable in its mind at not showing this category of advertising, even though much of the money which would have been spent on television may merely have been transferred to other forms of advertising and promotion.

Financial advertising

This is another field in which the statutory link with the Postmaster-General and his successor ministers responsible for broadcasting policy has been of particular relevance. It has also been one in which the Authority has taken the lead, with the programme companies, in extending the scope of what may be advertised on television in ways which still leave the public protected. The first *Principles* permitted television to advertise invitations to invest only in a limited number of cases – UK Government and local-authority stocks, stocks of public corporations, National Savings Certificates, building societies, and the Post Office and Trustee Savings Banks.

Over the last thirty years the situation has changed radically. Investment facilities have, for example, been extended to authorized unit trusts and stockbrokers; prospectuses of listed companies and announcements of results may be advertised in approved forms; a wide range of insurance companies may advertise their services; approved lending and credit agencies may buy time; and a wide range of institutional and corporate advertising is now permissible. The extension of the scope of financial advertising has been accompanied by carefully defined rules about its form and content, as set out in the Code.[39] In the formulation of these rules, which have been seen as an integral accompaniment to the extension of the allowable range of financial advertising, the Authority and its legal advisers have always been in close and often complex consultation with Government departments and with the Stock Exchange and other representative City interests. The AAC has also been continuously involved with these developments.

All these increased opportunities in the financial field have benefited both the advertiser and the system. In 1984 financial advertising was to represent some 4–5 per cent of total television advertising revenue.[40]

Medicines and treatments

An area which, perhaps in contrast to financial advertising, was from the outset seen as being a likely major source of revenue was that of medicines and treatments. It was also one which was bound to be a controversial area, not only because of the emotiveness of 'patent medicine' advertising but also because of the proper desire of medical and consumer bodies to prevent people from undertaking self-medi-cation which might be useless, unnecessary or perhaps even harmful, particularly where the condition to be treated was one which ought to be dealt with professionally.

The early *Principles for Television Advertising* gave extended guid-ance about the advertising of medicines. This guidance incorporated, as already mentioned, the existing British Code of Standards. Reference has already been made to the early discussions about advertisements for borderline medical products possibly involving an impression of professional advice. In this and in other matters a body of case law was built up, much of which was incorporated progressively into the Code.

The importance of protecting the public generally in the advertising of medicines and treatments was recognized by the programme companies as much as by the Authority, and in 1959 the ITCA appointed the first medical consultant to assist their Copy Committee. He was followed by others in dentistry and specialized medical fields, and later by a veterinary expert. The ITA itself consulted the AAC in 1959 and again in 1960 to find out specifically whether individual members, or the bodies they represented, felt any concern about tele-vision advertising practices in the medical field. While members of the AAC had given detailed comments about certain techniques being used by advertisers in a few cases, there had been no criticism or disquiet about the general run of medical advertising. But these timely actions and the presence on the Authority's Advertising Advisory Committee of Sir Guy Dain, as BMA representative, as well as four other members particularly concerned with standards of conduct in the advertising of medical or surgical products, did not damp down the continued simmering criticism of television advertising. This came to a head early in 1961 when the BMA gave to the Pilkington Committee evidence which was highly critical of some medical advertising on television, and this was followed by a House of Lords debate initiated by Lord Taylor, raising similar points. In the light of these criticisms the ITA called for a full-scale review of all medical advertising and ruled that all such advertisements (instead of only those selected as raising possible doubts) should, in future, be referred to a professional consultant, who would be free, if he wished, to take a second opinion at the expense of the television companies. Detailed examination was made of thirteen advertisements to which Lord Taylor had specifically referred. Most of these were cleared, subject, in some cases, to modifications of copy, and two were considered, after rigorous review, to be unsuitable.[41] Even after more than twenty years, it is interesting to ask whether all this was much ado about nothing, or a true complaint against the Authority and the companies. The answer, as is often the case, is that it was probably a little of both, although on the specific cases the balance of advantage lay with ITV.

With the passing of the 1963 Act the position was, in any event, clarified. That Act made it a formal requirement that a medical advisory panel should be appointed with a wide remit covering advertisements for medicines and surgical treatments and appliances, toiletry products making medical or prophylactic claims, and veterinary products.[42] The ITA had two obligations in relation to this panel: the first was to consult it about the terms of the statutory advertising code, both when it was being drawn up and when it was being reviewed;[43] the second was to ensure that any advertisement falling within the panel's field should be referred to a member of the panel before it was first broadcast.[44] These strict requirements, already effectively in place before the Act confirmed them, have worked well for more than twenty years. The system has been fortunate in being able to appoint distinguished and authoritative members to the panel.[45]

Advertising and children

The 1955 edition of the *Principles* recognized, even before the programmes had begun, the sensitivity of this area. It concentrated on two central aspects. The first was the necessity of avoiding physical, mental or moral harm to children arising from advertising in association with a programme intended for them or which large numbers of them would be likely to see. The second was the avoidance of any method of advertising which took advantage of children's natural credulity and sense of loyalty. The wording of these principles, although now expanded, stands up well even today. Particular provisions giving effect to the two sets of principles were also included.

Over the years, the Authority has refined and strengthened all these provisions, and a special Appendix, 'Advertising and Children', forms part of the IBA code. For example, there is now a list of advertisements which, in the interests of children, must not be broadcast before 9 pm, and those for alcohol, tobacco and matches may not be broadcast during or immediately around children's programmes. A whole vein of control has been progressively introduced, designed to avoid children feeling let down by anything bought as a result of television advertising (the size and scale of a toy must, for instance, be shown, and demonstrations must not be misleading; and there must be an indication of the price, and information on whether or not batteries and accessories are included). Health and hygiene are also stated as matters to be safeguarded in television advertising: sweet eating throughout the day or at bedtime is not to be recommended, and sweets and snack foods are not to be seen as substitutes for proper meals.

Another aspect of present control looks at the portrayal of children in advertisements. The code provisions here refer to the law governing the employment of children in the production of advertisements. More extensively, they point to the importance of not showing children doing dangerous things in advertisements in case this leads to carelessness over child safety among the audience.

Apart from the provisions in the Code concerning the form, content and timing of advertising affecting children, the IBA's *Rules and Practices* are also relevant in prohibiting the inclusion of commercials within children's programmes of half-an-hour or less in length. A majority of the Annan Committee wanted no advertisements at all within or between programmes for children, and no advertisements promoting products or services of particular interest to children to be shown before 9 pm. Those members of the Committee who took this view, which was powerfully argued,[46] did so partly because of the effect on children's appreciation and enjoyment of the intrusion (as they saw it) of advertising, but mainly because of the danger of encouraging covetousness in children when they were immature in judgement. The

IBA did not accept these concerns as valid (nor did a minority of the Annan Committee). It did not believe that harm was being done, and it considered that trying to shield children from advertisements in the way proposed was an unrealistic aim when they saw so many of them elsewhere, including at other times on television. The IBA decided, however, to exclude advertising from what is in practice virtually all children's programmes, for very few of these last for more than half an hour.

In considering this whole field, the Authority has had to strike a proper balance. On the one hand, it must not be over-fussy and molly-coddling, and on the other it must not dismiss too lightly the fears of those who see problems, particularly at a time of recession and high unemployment, in television commending to and for children seemingly attractive products, often quite highly priced, which only some parents can reasonably afford. Toy advertising is particularly concentrated in the period before Christmas, and it is then that most representations on this subject are made to the Authority. The present rules, which contain many prohibitions, restrictions and exhortations, seem about as far as the IBA can reasonably go, short of the kind of blanket prohibition suggested by the Annan Committee. The subject will continue to be sensitive and controversial.

Television Advertisement Duty and the levy

Over the last thirty years, television advertising revenue, from less than £10,000,000 in the first full year, has grown to a 1985 figure of close on £1000 million a year. The amounts of advertising shown, which are recorded year by year in the Authority's Annual Report, have stood for the last five years at above an average of five-and-a-half minutes per hour for all broadcasting hours and at not less than seven minutes an hour in evening peaktime.

With only occasional dips in advertising revenue, the self-supporting IBA system has been a remarkable financial success. This was evident by the early 1960s, when the network of programme companies, although not the full population coverage of the system, was virtually completed. In 1961, for instance, the net annual revenue figure was around £70,000,000, and the ITA itself, in a paper to the Pilkington Committee dated October 1960, said that an income of the present size was 'bound to give rise to a level of profits quite without parallel in present times, for the cost of producing and operating the Independent Television service is estimated at not more than £25 millions a year'.[47]

Television Advertisement Duty

It was not surprising, therefore, that the Treasury's interest was stimulated. In fact the Chancellor of the Exchequer – who, ironically, was Selwyn Lloyd – announced in his Budget speech of April 1961 the imposition of an excise charge of 10 per cent (Television Advertisement Duty or TAD) – subsequently increased to 11 per cent – on all advertising on television from 1 May that year. This flat impost was severely criticized. The advertisers feared that it would be in large part passed on to them. The television companies objected to it because it was discriminatory and put at risk the existence of the smaller companies (three of whom, Border, Grampian and Westward, did not come on the air until 1961). The Authority saw the worst disadvantage of TAD as the fact that it jeopardized its policy of dispersing power in a federal network and of securing adequate finance for programmes. As it said in a memorandum of August 1961 to the Pilkington Committee (sent also to the Post Office for transmission to ministers):

From the point of view of the Authority's own plural policy, the duty is objectionable in that it hurts small companies more than large ones and could reduce the number of companies that either single or competitive services can securely sustain. It could also give rise to a situation where the economic survival of a programme company could be maintained only by limitation of expenditure, which would inevitably fall in large part on programmes and result in a reduction of programme standards.[48]

But the Authority did not feel able to assert that some form of special taxation on television was in principle wrong, given the prosperity of some of the larger companies (not wholly unmerited in view of the early risks which they had undertaken) and given also that the Government seemed so far unwilling to tackle high profitability by the introduction of a competing self-supporting service. In the ITA's view, however, if some form of taxation was to be levied on the system it should be through a graduated tax on profits.[49] This preferred system was not, however, to be achieved until 1974 when, as described later, a profit-based levy was first introduced.

A graduated revenue-based levy 1964–74

The first published version of what was to emerge as the Television Act of 1963 originally provided for a levy on profits. The details were not spelt out: the formulas for calculating the levy were to be settled by the Postmaster-General after consulting the Treasury and the Authority. To quote the subsequently deleted terms of the Bill, they were to be 'framed by reference, among other things, to the annual profits of the contractors'. The Authority was to be responsible for collection of the levy under suitable terms included in the programme contracts.

However, as soon as the Bill had been published the Government had a change of mind and altered the basis of levy from profits to turnover, although on a graduated basis. This arrangement came into operation in 1964, replacing TAD.[50]

The NBPI investigation, 1970

In practice the revenue-based levy proved unsatisfactory – its lack of sensitivity to fluctuations in the fortunes of programme companies required three changes of scale in the period 1969–71. In 1970 the Minister of Posts and Telecommunications referred the costs and revenues of the companies to the Prices and Incomes Board. The Board's report, made in October 1970,[51] confirmed the Authority's firmly held view that the revenue-based levy, despite its graduations, was unsatisfactory because it was a prior charge on spendable income, whatever profit or loss situation might result for a company. The report forecast a continuously worsening financial position for the television companies but said that, without the levy on revenue, profits would on average remain high in relation to profits in industry generally. It stopped short, however, of endorsing the Authority's views in favour of a profit-based levy.

A profit-based levy from 1974

Relief was, however, to come in the IBA Act of 1974. This introduced from that year a profit-based levy at the rate of 66.7 per cent after a free 'slice'.

One particular advantage of the profit-based levy has been its flexibility in coping with variations in the collective and individual fortunes of the television companies. It has so far been changed only once, in 1982, to meet the exceptional circumstances of the provision of finance to the Welsh fourth channel which the television companies have to contribute through their subscriptions, as they do to the national fourth channel. The change consisted of an increase in the free slice to £650,000 (previously £250,000) or 2.8 per cent (previously 2 per cent) of revenue, whichever was the greater. The 66.7 per cent levy above that was not altered.

Despite the advantages of a profit-based levy, there are those outside the ITV system who regard the high rate of the levy above the free slice as a disincentive to proper cost-consciousness on the part of the companies. The kind of argument advanced by such critics is that the effect of expenditure, when fed back into profits and when Corporation Tax is also taken into account, is to reduce them by under 20 per cent rather than by a more substantial proportion of such expenditure. The Authority itself has, however, to look to the quality of the service which the companies provide and favours a system which encourages expenditure on programmes. It has tended to feel, therefore, that any risk attached to a profit-based levy is well worth taking given the disadvantages of a purely revenue-based levy, as demonstrated at the end of the 1960s and in the early 1970s. It is not convinced, either, that a high rate of levy removes the normal commercial disciplines to the extent that critics assert. It is to be expected, also, that the second half of the 1980s may not provide such a steady growth in income as occurred in the previous decade.

The Authority and the advertiser

In this section, the Authority's relations *vis-à-vis* the advertisers and their agencies are dealt with under three separate headings.

The Authority and rate cards

The first Television Act and its successors have all made it clear that the Authority, while responsible for the form and detail of rate cards and for seeing that advertising is sold strictly in accordance with the published tariffs, has no responsibility for the commercial terms on which advertising is sold.[52] This is clearly a wise provision. The Authority is not the body which sells the advertising and therefore cannot have a 'feel' for the proper market rate which comes from selling advertising under highly competitive conditions. Inevitably, if the Authority were to set advertising rates, it would be taking crucial decisions which could affect the ability of the programme companies to comply with the IBA's expectations about the effort and resources to be put into programme production.

So clear is the distinction to the Authority about the responsibility for fixing rates that when, in 1967, the Government sought to control increases in advertising rates in pursuance of its prices and incomes policy, the Authority felt obliged to disclaim any obligation or capacity itself to impose such control. It was, however, glad to note that the television companies themselves cooperated in the observance of necessary price restraint.

International Wool Secretariat 'Mechanical Sheep' (Davidson Pearce).

Rowntree's Kit Kat 'Road Liners' (J Walter Thompson).

Paging the ORACLE (see page 211)

ORACLE, Independent Television's teletext system which makes use of the 'spare' field-blanking lines of the TV signal, was announced in April, 1973. Experimental transmissions began on 1st October, 1977 and it soon became apparent that the system's ability to update editorial material within minutes would provide advertisers with an important complementary medium even more topical and flexible than television itself.

Editorial and advertising pages on ORACLE can be rapidly accessed at any time during the broadcasting day by viewers whose sets are equipped with teletext decoders and advertisements can be booked to appear in full-page or fractional page form both nationally or by individual ITV region.

The ORACLE Index summary page.

An ORACLE full-page advertisement for *British Airways* flight arrivals.

Wines from Greece full page advertisement.

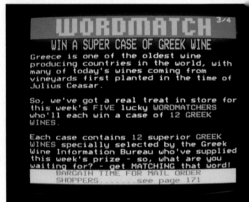

Wines from Greece competition advertisement.

The first paid-for advertisements were shown on ORACLE on 1st September, 1981 and four years later 2,800,000 homes were receiving the service with a daily 'page traffic' of nearly 2,000,000 viewers.

Financial Advertising

The successful joint campaign for the major clearing banks in 1964 ('the Bank Manager in the cupboard') was soon followed by separate campaigns on behalf of each of the 'Big Four'. By 1984 both Barclay's and the Midland, each spending over £5,000,000 a year on television, figured in the lists of 'Top Twenty' TV advertisers. The building societies and insurance companies had begun to use the medium extensively even earlier.

These stills are only a small selection of campaigns which have appeared since the coming of colour to ITV in 1969 and represent television's fastest-growing category of advertising.

General Accident – car park altercation between John Cleese and George A Cooper (Leo Burnett).

Woolwich Equitable Building Society 'We're with the Woolwich' (Ogilvy & Mather).

Commercial Union 'Bruno' (Doyle Dane Bernbach).

Lloyd's Bank Leo McKern (Lowe Howard-Spink).

Midland Bank 'Gryphon' (Allen Brady & Marsh).

Midland Bank 'Teamwork – motorcyclists' (Charles Barker).

TAMmeter 1955 the electro-mechanical device designed by Television Audience Measurement (TAM) to produce viewing data for the industry research service between 1955 and 1968. The TAMmeter was a domestic clock whose clock-work mechanism had been supplemented by a mains-powered electrical system for recording on metallized tape when the nearby TV set was 'on' and to which channel it was tuned. TAM field-workers called every week on each household on the viewing panel to collect the tapes together with the self-completion viewing diaries which recorded information on individual's viewing habits.

AGB Setmeter 1985 the compact design of the current Setmeter shows the results of advances in solid-state circuitry. The Setmeter uses an electronic digital display to show the time and also stores viewing information for the whole family. Recording tapes, diaries and visits by fieldworkers are no longer necessary. The Setmeter is 'scanned' every 24 hours via a telephone line and the accumulated date transferred direct to an AGB central computer.

AGB's Research Centre at West Gate, London, W5 where television data and other market research information are processed.

Top: Hovis 'Downhill Ride' (Collett Dickenson Pearce).

HOVIS – *'Farmhouse Kitchen'.* Some of the most memorable commercials ever seen on television were those for Hovis directed by Ridley Scott of which these are two superb examples – 'Farmhouse Kitchen' and 'Downhill Ride'. All relied on a painstakingly recreated evocation of childhood and the association of the brand with a simpler more kindly world to which present-day customers of a long-established product would respond. (Collett Dickenson Pearce & Partners).

IBM Personal Computers (Saatchi & Saatchi).

American Express based a campaign for their charge cards on a number of international celebrities, including Richard Branson of the Virgin group of companies (Ogilvy & Mather).

ICI 'The Pathfinders' the first of a series of highly effective corporate advertising campaigns (Ogilvy & Mather).

Shell shows restoration of the countryside after the construction of a major cross-country underground pipeline (Ogilvy & Mather).

Welsh Development Agency the first national Development Agency to use television (Waldron Allen Henry & Thompson).

Olympus Cameras 'David Bailey' (Collett Dickenson Pearce).

Ford Sierra launch commercial (Ogilvy & Mather).

As mentioned above, the Authority has, and accepts fully, the duty of seeing that advertising rate cards are adhered to and, as a related duty under the Act, of ensuring that in the acceptance of advertising there is no unreasonable discrimination either against or in favour of any particular advertiser.[53] The rules are well known to the programme companies' sales staffs, and few breaches of them have come to the notice of the Authority. However, in 1982, the Authority was informed – and a subsequent investigation confirmed – that a major network company had offered favourable and unpublished terms to advertising agencies which were prepared to guarantee to place with the company a certain proportion of expenditure in the area concerned. Although, both in relation to ITV's sales practices as a whole and in relation to the company's own record (which had been consistently of a high standard), this incident was exceptional, the Authority thought it proper to express its formal concern to the company and to make public that it had done so.[54]

Copy clearance

The practice of central examination and clearance of copy by the ITCA in the first instance, but in consultation with the ITA in cases causing any problems, and with the close involvement of the AAC in matters of general principle, grew up early in the life of ITV. In 1963 the existing procedures, but with a strengthening of the position of the ITA, were formalized in arrangements[55] which have continued virtually unchanged to the present time. Under these arrangements (which are more fully described elsewhere in this volume) the Authority's staff see scripts, comments by medical and other consultants, and finished commercials at the same time as the ITCA copy control organization. Necessary discussion can therefore take place, at the appropriate level, of any points of doubt before an advertisement is accepted for broadcasting. Alongside this day-to-day control machinery is the Joint Advertisement Control Committee, chaired by the Authority's senior advertising specialist, the Controller of Advertising. These arrangements provide for detailed discussions with advertisers or, as is most usual, advertising agencies, to be conducted usually by the programme companies and not by IBA staff.

Some ten years later the Annan Committee was to ask itself whether the IBA controlled advertising adequately. It reported that the ISBA and IPA, while agreeing that the system worked well, thought that the control mechanisms were very tough and the Authority somewhat legalistic in its approach. But the Committee said that this view failed to convince them and that, on the whole, the IBA's procedures stood up well to criticism and yet were not too onerous on the advertisers.[56] Those, both inside and outside the Authority, who have seen at first hand the approach to the control of advertising standards by, successively, Archie Graham, Peter Woodhouse and Harry Theobalds, are likely to regard the Annan appraisal as well merited.[57]

The Advertising Liaison Committee

The Authority's staff have always kept in close touch with advertisers and advertising agencies, informally through many personal contacts and more formally with the officers and staff of the two representative advertising bodies, the IPA and the ISBA, both of which have from the start nominated members to the Advertising Advisory Committee. Furthermore, the Authority has always given close attention to any representations from these bodies on aspects of its services.

During the public debate of the late 1970s about the future of IBA services, including a fourth channel, which led to the passing of the Broadcasting Act 1980, advertising policy questions came into prominence. The central advertising issue which emerged related to the sale of time on the fourth channel. The advertisers had primarily wanted a channel which would provide a genuinely competitive advertising market. This was not considered compatible with the kind of service which the Authority had advocated during the 1970s and which was envisaged by the Government in 1979. The Home Secretary pointed out in September 1979 to the Royal Television Society in Cambridge: 'Competitive advertising on the two channels would inevitably result in a move towards single-minded concentration on maximising the audience for programmes.'

The Broadcasting Act 1980, made clear that each television programme contractor would have the job of selling – and would retain the revenue from – advertising on the fourth channel in its own area, and during its contractual time when there was more than one contractor.[58] But within this system where no new advertising recipients were to be introduced, the option still existed for the companies to sell individually as in ITV, or set up a single selling organization for the new service throughout the country. A single selling organization would, of course, have acted on behalf of all the programme contractors, who would receive from it the net share of revenue appropriate to their contract area and hours of transmission.

In the event the Authority decided that separate selling should continue rather than insisting upon the setting up of a new selling organization. As it stated in a full statement of its Channel Four plans in November 1979,[59] it considered that a separate selling organization would produce only the appearance rather than the reality of competition, and would inevitably lead to higher costs and lower revenue for the system as a whole.

During all this debate, the Authority was in discussion with advertising interests who left the IBA in no doubt about their disappointment at the turn which events were taking and about their concern that the extension of the ITV television companies' advertising monopoly could lead to arbitrary conditions being imposed against advertisers. A particular worry, for instance, was that those selling television time might make it a condition of buying time on ITV that time should also be bought on Channel Four.

In order to meet the advertisers' concern on these and other matters by providing a forum for the discussion of issues of common interest, the Authority stated that an integral part of its plans for the fourth channel would be an Advertising Liaison Committee (ALC) with representatives at the highest levels from the ITV companies, the ISBA and the IPA. As the Authority pointed out in its November 1979 statement, such a joint body would be particularly valuable when the fourth channel came on the air; but it made clear that the ALC was also relevant to the existing Independent Television service.

The Advertising Liaison Committee was set up in 1980, with a composition which matches the Authority's expectations for it. The Committee is chaired by the Chairman of the IBA, with the Authority's representatives consisting of a member (George Russell from 1980), the Director-General and the Controller of Advertising. The two advertising bodies and the ITCA are represented by their presidents, chairmen, directors and members of their governing bodies.

The Committee has always met quarterly. The value and importance of the business discussed seem, to an outsider at least, to have fully warranted the establishment of a top-level forum. The IBA's Annual Reports present frank and informative accounts of the work of the Committee year by year.[60]

After five years' experience of the ALC, the conclusion must be that it has provided a valuable means of discussing matters among parties who, as the Committee's deliberations have shown, have an effective common interest in areas which had on occasion during the previous quarter of a century been too exclusively delimited.

Advertising on the new services

Channel Four

This service began broadcasting in November 1982. Reference has been made earlier to the dispute between the IPA and Equity which bedevilled the advertising elements in Channel Four in its first two years. The dispute not only harmed the revenue-earning capacity of the new channel but also, because advertising was not sold to the same extent throughout the country and because commercial breaks on a nationally distributed service could not easily be reduced, resulted in damaging effects upon the continuity and attractiveness of the new service in its early stages. The settlement of the dispute at the end of 1984 was, therefore, a welcome relief.

The advertisers' reservations about the possible linking of advertising bookings and sales procedures between the existing and the new services have already been mentioned. The Authority took account of this concern, which it regarded as proper, in the drafting of the new television programme contracts which were to apply from 1 January 1982. These contained a clear provision prohibiting any such linking without the agreement of the Authority. Without such agreement, tariffs and discounts had to be independent for each service and no term or obligation which related to the other channel could be imposed by a television company on advertisers or advertising agencies placing orders for advertising on either of the channels.

The Advertising Liaison Committee provided a means of discussing the practical application of these contractual provisions and the extent to which it was appropriate for the IBA to agree to any cross-linking of advertising on the two services. Joint rates and any form of conditional selling were not considered by the Authority as areas where any deviation from the strict terms of the contract was warranted. In the case of volume discounts, it was common ground between the television companies and the advertisers that it was fair for total expenditure across both channels to be aggregated, and the IBA itself saw no problem about allowing this.

There was, however, no such unanimity about share discounts. A share 'parity' discount was a common feature of television advertising marketing in ITV; it is granted to advertisers who reach agreement with a television company that a given proportion (normally the company's proportion of the total of homes covered nationally) of the advertiser's television expenditure will be spent with the company. The desirability or otherwise of such discounts is not a matter where the ISBA (who oppose them in principle) and the IPA (who recognize that they have a place, provided non-participants suffer no discrimination in their dealings with the television companies as sellers of advertising time, and provided that the television companies take a flexible attitude towards advertisers' marketing criteria) hold identical views. But the ISBA and IPA were at one in representing to the Authority that an advertiser's total expenditure across both ITV and Channel Four should not be aggregable for the purpose of share discounts. The ITCA, on the other hand, urged that they should be. The Authority decided that aggregation should be allowed, but did so only after obtaining assurances from the television companies that conditional selling, linking one service with the other, would not result. To the advertising interests the Authority gave an assurance that it would closely investigate any suggestion that conditional selling was being resorted to, and would keep the matter under review in the light of actual experience of Channel Four's operations. This was done, and in May 1984 the Authority announced its decision, following consultations with the ITCA and individual advertising interests and discussion at the ALC.[60] It was in favour of aggregable share discount schemes subject to strict conditions to avoid any suggestion of discrimination against advertisers not participating in the share discount scheme. Similar arrangements were agreed to cover the particular circumstances of London with its two television companies.[61]

As for other aspects of advertising on Channel Four the IBA decided, after consultation with advertising interests, that the existing *Advertising Rules and Practices*, into which flexibility had traditionally been built to meet particular programme circumstances, should generally apply to the new service. However, it indicated its willingness to consider allowing longer advertising breaks between Channel Four programmes and more – but shorter – breaks within those programmes. In practice this flexibility has not been used to any significant extent, although it remains available if the need arises. Channel Four's quarterly advertising break patterns are agreed with the Authority's Advertising Control Division. The existing copy control arrangements apply to advertising on Channel Four as to that on ITV.

Breakfast-time television

As with Channel Four, the IBA decided that the existing rules and practices should in principle apply to TV-am, but with reasonable flexibility to match the less formalized and more fragmented nature of breakfast-time programming. In practice this meant more frequent and shorter breaks than would normally occur elsewhere in ITV. Special arrangements, not in the event often used, were also laid on for the clearance of advertisements (by telephone with IBA and ITCA advertising-control executives) late at night for inclusion in the following morning's programmes.

Conclusion

After thirty years Independent Television remains the only large-scale European television service financed only by advertising. Apart from an initial loan, soon repaid, neither the Authority nor any programme company has received any assistance from public funds. In fact since 1960, in addition to normal taxation the ITV system has paid to the Exchequer, first in Television Advertisement Duty and then in levy, a total of some £700 million in special taxation. But the success of the advertising base of Independent Television must not be appraised primarily by financial criteria. Through the exercise of its statutory powers and with the cooperation of the television companies and the advertising business the Authority has shown that the savage beast of advertising which it was once feared would stalk through our living rooms can be domesticated. The Authority has been able to prove that a self-supporting television service can operate on equal terms of programme quality and public approval with a system financed from the licence fee. The continuance of what seems to be a proven basis for financing UK public-service television broadcasting – that of giving the BBC and ITV each an entirely separate source of finance – is a more open question in 1985 than it has been for the last thirty years. The success of the ITV system in that period will no doubt be a factor in the deliberation and debate on this question; equally, perhaps more important must be investigation of the effect on the entirely self-supporting ITV system if it has to compete with a BBC television system which has advertising as a supplementary source of finance.

References

1 See provisions throughout the Broadcasting Act 1981 (BA1981) which include the words 'it shall be the duty of the Authority' and, in particular, those about advertising in sections 8 and 9.
2 BA1981, schedule 2, paragraph 1 (1).
3 *Ibid*, schedule 2, paragraph 3.
4 *Ibid*, sections 8, 9 and 16.
5 See, for example, paragraph 77 of IBA Evidence to the Annan Committee on the Future of Broadcasting: September 1974.

6   BA1981, section 8 (1).

7   *Ibid*, schedule 2, paragraph 7 (1).

8   See, for example, paragraph 94 of IBA Annan Evidence.

9   Report of the Broadcasting Committee 1949, HMSO, Cmnd 8116 (Beveridge Committee).

10 HMSO, Cmnd 9005.

11 Television Act 1954, received Royal Assent 30 July 1954.

12 The no-sponsorship rule and its exceptions are now to be found, effectively unchanged in BA1981, section 8 (6) to 8 (8).

13 BA1981, schedule 2, paragraph 8.

14 Now BA1981, schedule 2, paragraphs 1 (2) and 1 (3).

15 *Ibid*, schedule 2, paragraph 3.

16 The emergence of the eight-minutes-in-the-hour rule, and subsequent changes, are fully described in the ITA's evidence to the Pilkington Committee, reprinted in Vol. 1, Appendix E (HMSO, Cmnd 1819) to the main Report as Paper 70 on p. 439.

17 David Gammans, Assistant Postmaster-General, House of Commons, 22 June 1954.

18 Report of the Committee on Broadcasting 1960, HMSO, Cmnd 1753, paragraph 228.

19 BA1981, schedule 2, paragraph 4.

20 The conventions about natural breaks, as they have developed, are now collated in section 4 of the IBA's *Advertising Rules and Practices*.

21 Pilkington Evidence (*op. cit.*, Paper 69, pp. 437–39).

22 BA1981, schedule 2, paragraph 5 (1).

23 *Ibid*, schedule 2, paragraph 5 (2).

24 Television Act 1954, section 8 (2) (b).

25 *Ibid*, section 8(2).

26 *Ibid*, section 4(5).

27 *Ibid*, section 4(5).

28 *Ibid*, section 8(2)(b).

29 *Ibid*, section 8(2)(b).

30 Pilkington Evidence (*op. cit.*), Paper 79, pp. 478-84.

31 This first edition of the *Principles* was published as an Appendix to the IBA's Annual Report 1954–55.

32 Bernard Sendall, *Independent Television in Britain*, Vol. 1, *Origin and Formulation, 1946–62*, Macmillan, 1982.

33 Report of the Committee on Broadcasting 1960, HMSO, Cmnd 1753, paragraph 644. In fact the Committee also recommended that the Authority should no longer be obliged to appoint the three hitherto mandatory committees. This later proposal was not adopted.

34 BA1981, section 9(1)(a).

35 *Ibid*, section 16(2)(b) and 16(3).

36 *Ibid*, section 16(2)(b)(ii).

37 Following the retirement of R.A. Bevan as Chairman in 1959, Mr Glanvill Benn, publisher and member of the Council of the Advertising

Association, was appointed. He was followed by Sir Daniel Jack (1964–68), Mr Samuel Howard (1968–76), Professor Royston Goode (1976–80) and Professor Aubrey Diamond 1980–).

38 BA1981, section 8 (5).

39 The rules about financial advertising are to be found in Appendix 2 of the IBA *Code of Advertising Standards and Practice*, 1985.

40 MEAL estimate for 1984.

41 An ITA Paper of July 1961 to the Pilkington Committee explaining the arrangements for the control of medical advertising was reprinted in Pilkington Evidence (*op. cit.*) as Paper 72, pp. 446–51 in shortened form. This excluded paragraphs dealing in detail with the thirteen specific cases.

42 BA1981, section 16(5).

43 *Ibid*, section 16(6).

44 *Ibid*, section 16(7).

45 The composition of the Medical Advisory Panel is given year by year in the Authority's Annual Report (see also Appendix 6).

46 Report of the Committee on the Future of Broadcasting, March 1977, HMSO, Cmnd 6753 (Annan Report), paragraphs 12, 9 and 12.10.

47 Pilkington Evidence (*op. cit.*), Paper 68, paragraph 5, p. 424.

48 *Ibid*, Paper 99, paragraph 10, p. 583.

49 *Ibid*, Paper 99, paragraph 17, p. 585.

50 Television Act 1964, section 13. For a full account of the events surrounding the Government's change of mind see Bernard Sendall, *Independent Television in Britain*, Vol. 2, *Expansion and Change, 1958–68*, Macmillan, 1983, ch. 23.

51 National Board for Prices and Incomes, Report 156, October 1970, HMSO, Cmnd 4524.

52 BA1981, schedule 2, paragraph 7 (1).

53 *Ibid*, schedule 2, paragraph 6.

54 IBA Annual Report 1982–83.

55 Under a provision in the Television Act 1963 (now section 9 of BA1981) the Authority was given direct responsibility for drawing up and reviewing a code of advertising standards (with the assistance of the AAC and the Panel of Medical Advisers under what is now section 16 of BA1981) and was given strict powers of direction *vis-à-vis* programme companies in securing compliance with the Code.

56 Annan Report (*op. cit*), paragraphs 12.17 and 12.18.

57 Graham was the Authority's Advertising Control Officer (later Head of Advertising Control) from 1959 to 1974, Woodhouse was Head of Advertising Control from 1974 to 1980, as was Theobalds (later Controller of Advertising) from 1980 onwards.

58 Now BA1981, section 13.

59 Appendix XIV to IBA Annual Report 1979–80.

60 IBA Public Statement, 22 May 1984.

61 IBA Public Statement, 20 July 1984.

A Medium
Built on Research

SIR BERNARD AUDLEY

SIR BERNARD AUDLEY

Sir Bernard Audley, Chairman of AGB Research plc, was educated at Wolstanton Grammar School, Staffordshire and Corpus Christi College, Oxford where he read modern languages. He served as a lieutenant in the King's Dragoon Guards in 1943–46 in Italy, Greece and the Middle East.

He was Assistant General Manager of Hulton Press from 1949 to 1957 and became Managing Director of Television Audience Measurement Ltd (TAM) in 1957. In 1962, together with Martin Maddan MP, Dick Gapper and Doug Brown he left to found AGB Research, now one of the most successful and fastest-growing British multinational companies.

The AGB group has become recognized as Europe's leading force in market research, information systems, marketing services and industrial/technical publications. The group is the only organization of its type to be quoted on the London Stock Exchange and is established in twenty-three countries throughout Europe, the Far East, Australasia and the United States.

Sir Bernard is Chairman of the Netherhall Trust, President of the Periodical Publishers' Association and Governor of Hong Kong College. He became a Freeman of the City of London in 1978 and a Liveryman of the Gold and Silver Wyredrawers in 1975. He was knighted for his services to the market research industry in 1985

T ELEVISION broadcasting and market research are near contemporaries. Both made their début in the thirties. Both achieved great technical and commercial progress in the first two postwar decades. Both now play a substantial part in the process of marketing consumer goods. Both face the pressures, and can exploit the opportunities, which arise from advances in communications technology. They are not, however, mere contemporaries following parallel life-paths. The marketing process of television, especially Independent Television, involves market research more intimately than does the marketing process of any other business. The unusual degree to which research is involved in the marketing process of Independent Television is largely explicable in terms of four factors.

The need for research in media

The need of any advertising medium to justify the charges it makes to its advertisers is fundamental. In other industries the function of research is, for the most part, confined to providing manufacturers and distributors with information for their own exclusive use about the acceptability of their goods and services to consumers and users. The advertising media use research for this purpose, too, as in the case of copy tests and programme research; but they also need it as a proof to their customers of the value of what they supply. This first and fundamental factor accounts, of course, only for that enhanced intimacy between marketing and research which is shared by all advertising media.

Why television differs from other media

Three other factors, historical, technical and practical, explain why Independent Television differs in this respect from the press and poster media. The historical factor is the habit, so to speak, which has resulted from Independent Television's original need for ammunition in its fight to enter the marketplace and later to reinforce its position there. This need persisted for the best part of a decade: the 1963 Television Act, which extended the life of the Independent Television Authority for twelve more years and thereby showed that the medium was here to stay, might perhaps be taken to mark the end of the need for ammunition. But by then the long-term value of research had been recognized and its various users had come to rely on it.

The technical factor is the feasibility of achieving, in the case of television, a more valid measure of exposure than is possible in the case of press or posters. The history of television audience research is dominated by the consequences of technical improvement for validity, speed of reporting and efficiency; and the trend continues. Finally, the practical factor is the usefulness of the research results, to which the number of media researchers employed by programme contractors, advertisers and advertising agencies bears witness.

Through its close and deep involvement in the marketing process, research has assisted the medium to establish and justify itself and has thereby contributed substantially, even fundamentally, to its success. The story of its contribution, which is as relevant to the annals of market research as it is to the celebration of ITV's thirtieth anniversary, and as interesting, it is to be hoped, to the general reader as it will be to those who have been associated with it personally, had best begin with a review of the various kinds of research involved and a more detailed explanation of the special place of audience measurement amongst them.

The main types of TV research

The central research function is the measurement of the audiences reached by both Independent and BBC television broadcasts. This measurement provides information about the numbers of homes and individuals viewing the various channels: by time, by programme and by commercial break. To achieve this it is necessary to collect data for each minute, which can be done accurately only by the use of recording devices to monitor all the TV sets in a representative sample of homes. The selection of such a sample depends on information obtainable only from two other kinds of research: boundary surveys to define the limits of the various television areas, and establishment surveys to determine the size and relevant characteristics of the population of each area. Although audience measurement is the central function of research, and must figure prominently in any account of research for Independent

Television, other kinds of research have also played an important part in the development and operation of the medium. They include the monitoring of the audience's appreciation of programmes; research into the recollection, appreciation and understanding of commercials for the purpose of testing their efficacy; and studies of the social effects of television. These other kinds of research will be described in more detail after the nature, purpose and history of television audience measurement have been considered.

How audience research is carried out

Audience measurement in Britain is currently carried out by AGB Research under contract to BARB, the Broadcasters' Audience Research Board. This body represents principally the Independent Television contractors and the BBC, but it also takes into consideration the interests of two other groups, the advertisers and the advertising agencies.

The system operated by AGB is based on a regionally organized sample of some three thousand homes. This sample comprises fourteen panels, one per TV area, each consisting of a number of homes selected and maintained so as to be representative of the area in terms of social class, age of housewife, size of household, and claimed weight of viewing, the major determinants of viewing particular programmes or at particular times. All the TV sets in a panel home are monitored by a detection unit which automatically registers the state of the set: whether it is on or off; if on, whether it is displaying pictures received directly off air or from a videocassette recorder; and if off-air, from which channel. Videocassette recorders are also monitored by detection units to obtain details of the channel recorded and used for playback. The detection unit receives statements from individuals, too, using a remote push-button handset, concerning when they begin or end a period of viewing. The detection units are continuously polled by a central meter, which stores the data until it is itself polled, once daily, by a minicomputer at AGB's operating centre.

Comprehensive results are published weekly, in two volumes. These contain estimates, for each TV area, of the size of each channel's audience, in terms of numbers and percentages of homes and individuals, by time, programme, commercial break and commercial. For relevant categories the cost-per-thousand of audience is also shown. The basic weekly reports are supplemented by a service which enables subscribers to receive by Viewdata, on any day, summary results for the previous day. A monthly report contains summaries which offer a broader view of trends.

These daily, weekly and monthly reports are available in common to all subscribers. Special analysis is also available exclusively to those subscribers who require it. A well-known and widely used type of special analysis shows, for a series of programmes or commercial spots, the cumulative number and proportion of homes or individuals reached at each stage in the series, and the number and proportion of homes and individuals receiving or seeing various numbers of items in the series.

The need for television audience research

Independent Television is an arena in which various contests take place. The programme contractors compete among themselves for advertising revenue, while the BBC competes with them for share of audience. The advertisers compete, one with another, for share of market. The advertising agencies compete for accounts.

The number of people watching any particular programme depends on its content, quality of production and time of transmission, but the overall size of the audience during an afternoon or evening depends also on the skills of the programme schedulers. A careful study of the programmes available to each channel and their likely audience appeal is essential. Research information consisting of ratings for homes and individuals, as well as the audience profile, are the tools of the programme scheduler's trade. An appropriate juxtaposition of programmes, taking into account their strengths and weaknesses, is essential if a channel is to be successful in the highly competitive world of television. The audience measurement system is used by the programme companies to demonstrate the value of their medium in justification of their rate cards. Such a demonstration is relevant to the use of the medium in general, as compared to the use of other media: press, posters, radio and cinema. Although the contractors' franchises are regional there is a degree of competition for advertising revenue, to the extent that part of it is disposable where best value for money can be obtained. The BBC, on the other hand, has its own need for information about its share of audience as a means of justifying its use of resources.

The advertisers put audience measurement to equally good account. They use it as a basis for planning advertising strategy, and for monitoring the performance of their advertising agencies and media independents. Conversely, the two latter need to demonstrate to their clients that their efficiency in time buying is as good as, if not better than, the value for money obtained by other advertisers from their agencies and media shops.

The television audience measurement system thus supports the mutual commercial activities of the suppliers and users of the television advertising medium. It referees the various concurrent contests in the arena.

How TV audience measurement has developed

Television audience measurement is now highly developed in Britain. In the thirty years of its existence it has achieved by stages earlier reporting and increased accuracy to such good effect that the systems on which it is based are being adopted or copied in many countries. This situation is the result of two factors. To some extent it has been stimulated by changes in the industry's circumstances and requirements, or at least to changes in the balance between them. To a greater extent, and more obviously, it has been both prompted and made possible by advances in electronic engineering, the technology of telecommunication and data processing. The history of the two factors, and their inter-relation, in the course of three decades, shows why Independent Television is a medium built on research. After thirty years of operation in Britain television advertising is now, and has been for many years, an accepted part of our way of life. Most evenings, at peak viewing time two-thirds or more of the population are watching television, over half of the viewers looking at programmes provided by the Independent contractors. At other times during the day the audience is smaller but tends to be more specific: housewives, perhaps, or children; or men with a particular interest in sport. These basic facts are common knowledge, taken for granted by all concerned.

It was not always so. Before it was accepted, Independent Television had to establish its credentials as an advertising medium. For example, when the ITV service opened in London in September 1955, fewer than 200,000 homes could receive it. In the course of the next six months the number more than tripled, to over 600,000. As the number of homes which could receive it grew, so did the medium's value to advertisers; but it had to be demonstrated. Information was therefore needed, not only about the number of homes capable of receiving Independent Television but also about the numbers and kinds of viewers it was reaching.

Managing the industry research service

The need for a research system for the medium was soon recognized. Within a few weeks of the opening of the London service a Steering Committee for audience research was inaugurated. It represented the Institute of Practitioners in Advertising (IPA), the Incorporated Society of British Advertisers (ISBA) and the programme companies, which were represented in due course by the Television Programme Contractors' Association (TPCA), later to become the Independent Television Companies' Association (ITCA). The Steering Committee was soon replaced by the Television Audience Research Advisory Committee (TARAC), to be superseded in turn by the Joint Industry Committee for Television Advertising Research (JICTAR), and more recently by the Broadcasters' Audience Research Board (BARB). Despite changes of composition and name the function of the research committees throughout has been to commission and supervise a single research system for the interested parties. Initially, agreement could not be reached. IPA and ISBA purchased information from the BBC. In March 1956 the Steering Committee placed a contract with Television Audience Measurement Ltd (TAM); but agreement was still not complete, because Granada appointed the A.C. Nielsen Co. to handle audience research in the North. This arrangement continued for three years, when Nielsen withdrew and took a financial interest in TAM, which retained the industry's audience research contract until 1968. In that year AGB Research secured the contract which it still operates.

Thus, after some initial hesitation, the industry settled on the system developed and offered by TAM. It had four components: boundary surveys, establishment surveys, ratings research and validation checks. All four continue to be relevant.

Boundary and establishment surveys

The regional basis of Independent Television has been a major factor in its development and in the associated research requirements. The first of these was to chart the geographical bounds of each contractor's franchise. This required boundary surveys, in which small geographically defined units, such as electoral wards, are examined by means of a sample survey to determine the proportion of TV homes which can receive the various relevant ITV channels. If the proportion exceeds an agreed value, originally 25 per cent but later reduced to 15 per cent, the unit is allocated to the area covered by the channel. Many units are thus allocated to more than one area, which accounts for the overlaps. All the homes in a unit are classified as part of the potential audience of the area to which the unit is allocated. The original need for boundary surveys is obvious. It may be less obvious that boundary surveys are also required when television transmitters are upgraded or reallocated, and when new ones are set up.

The boundaries of television areas determine the size and character of their potential audience in terms of both homes and individuals. Since these were not known in the detail required, especially because the number of homes with TV sets able to receive ITV was growing rapidly, surveys were needed. These were called establishment surveys, and information was collected from a sample of households. It included housewife's age, social class, normal weight of viewing, ability to receive adequate pictures from the various channels, age and sex of household members, and so on. These surveys were crucial in the early days because it was essential for the programme companies to demonstrate the growing size and composition of their potential audiences. Establishment surveys are still carried out to monitor population changes.

Representative samples

When the boundary of a TV area has been defined, and the size and profile of its potential audience are known, it is possible to select representative samples of homes in order to determine their viewing behaviour. There are various methods for collecting the requisite data: different samples of homes or individuals in each period, questioned about viewing during the last seven days, on the previous day, or at the moment of contact; or the same sample in all periods, in other words a panel, who record their viewing continuously or otherwise. The use of a panel has several advantages, particularly the possibility of analysing an individual's viewing over considerable periods of time. It was soon recognized, too, that if a panel is used it is possible to employ mechanical methods for recording the time of reception and the identity of the channel, and thereby to increase the accuracy of the measurement. There was, however, no practical method – nor is there yet one – of obtaining information about individuals' viewing without asking them to record it themselves. The audience measurement system was therefore designed to monitor TV sets mechanically and to obtain data on individuals' viewing by means of diaries.

Validation checks

Not unnaturally, the accuracy of audience estimates derived from the system was questioned by those who thought, or hoped, that they were too high or too low. There was thus a need for validation checks. These, too, can be implemented in various ways; the most convincing is the coincidental method, in which interviewers call on a sample of homes at predetermined times to discover what viewing is taking place at the moment of contact. Professor Maurice Kendall is still remembered for his contribution to the methodology of coincidental surveys. Many such were carried out, with the result that the meter/diary method gained general acceptance. Coincidental surveys are not often used these days, but are occasionally necessary for validating the introduction of new techniques, such as the replacement of diaries by the use of push-buttons or other electronic means of recording information on individuals.

The basic principles of audience measurement were soon established. Subsequent development has mainly concerned the type of equipment used and the resultant changes in the method of data retrieval. These, however, have been of considerable significance.

Methods of measurement

In the TAM system, channel identification was achieved by electro-mechanical sensing of the TV set's tuning apparatus. The state of the TV set – whether it was on or off, and if on, which channel it was receiving – was recorded by a clockwork meter using styluses to mark a moving band of heat-sensitive paper, as in meteorological recording devices. Individual household members recorded in a diary for each quarter-hour whether they were viewing or not, and on which set if there was more than one in the home.

Panel homes were visited every week by an interviewer whose duties were to extract the tapes, date and time them, adjust the clock as necessary, collect the diaries, maintain rapport with the housewife, and return the tapes and diaries to TAM's operating centre. Tapes and diaries were gathered by supervisors and transported by road or rail in order to minimize delay. At TAM's headquarters the meter tapes were decoded by a procedure consisting of manual winding-on and transcription into punched-card format. Data from the individuals' diaries were also transcribed to punched cards. This system enabled the production of weekly reports essentially similar to those produced now, although they were simpler and contained less detail.

The change since 1968

The conclusion of a contract period in 1968 gave the industry an opportunity to consider the possibility of using another system and another research company. AGB offered an alternative, technically more advanced, method of collecting the same range of data, and an enhancement of the weekly reports. The system allowed more accurate timing of TV set switching, return of tapes by post without need for interviewers' visits, and faster input of meter and diary data. The result was greater speed of reporting and cost-effectiveness. AGB's system was adopted.

The basis of these improvements was the Setmeter, an electromechanical event recorder in which time-stamped records of changes of reception state were recorded in binary-digital form on heat-sensitive paper tape. These records were machine-readable in a matter of seconds. The individuals' diaries were laid out in a mark-sensing format, so that they, too, were rapidly machine-readable. Apart from an improvement in the method of channel detection by sensing the local oscillator's frequency, this technical basis of the main industry-research service remained unchanged until 1984.

In the decade and a half which followed the award of the JICTAR contract to AGB, electronic technology continued to advance and the TV scene continued to change. AGB accordingly developed its techniques in three directions: to cope more efficiently with multi-set homes; to provide for the recording of individuals' data electronically; and to retrieve data from the panel home automatically. The last two of these are closely connected, since paper diaries cannot be retrieved by the modern apparatus of telecommunication.

In the 1968 system each TV set in a household was associated with one meter, whose functions were both to detect changes in the state of the TV set and to store records of them. A more efficient arrangement is to separate these functions, so that only one storage device is needed. This consideration led to a detection-unit-plus-meter design in which the electrical system of the panel home is used for communication between the detection unit and the meter. Alternative methods were developed for the electronic recording of data for individuals. An obvious possibility is the use of push-buttons on the detection unit, each allocated for use by one of the individuals in the panel home to indicate each time he or she starts or ceases to view the TV set. In these days of the remote control of television sets such a system might seem old-fashioned, but in any case would be less convenient to use than a push-button remote handset. Such a system was developed. So too was an alternative device, an electronic diary which panel members could use, with a light pen, to record their viewing in the same format as used in the paper diary. The industry's choice, in 1984, was the remote push-button method.

The most significant development was the method for retrieving data from panel homes automatically, by using a small computer to telephone them in the early hours of every morning. For this purpose the meter in each panel home is connected to the telephone. Complicated software in the meter and minicomputer enable them to recognize each other and inter-communicate without causing inconvenience to the panel home. The significance of this development, of course, is that it enables overnight ratings to be calculated – that is, results for the previous day. It would be unnecessary, and pointless, to present overnight results in the depth of detail appropriate to weekly reports; their value lies in their ability to provide rapid summary feedback, especially to the broadcasters' programme controllers. The development was implemented for private use by Thames Television in 1980.

After the audience research contract had been renewed several times, and the arrangements for sponsoring and supervising it had been changed by the replacement of JICTAR by BARB, AGB was reappointed to introduce and operate a new system from 1984. This involved the re-equipment of panel homes with apparatus embodying the developments for the more efficient monitoring of multi-set homes, electronic recording of individuals' viewing by means of a remote push-button handset, and automatic data retrieval by telephone. The scope of the detection units was extended to take account of the growing use of videocassette recorders.

Other forms of research in television

It is appropriate at this point to turn aside, for the moment, from the main type of research in order to consider other kinds of research which have played a part in the development of Independent Television. Since 1964 the Independent Broadcasting Authority (IBA), formerly the Independent Television Authority (ITA), has had a statutory duty to ascertain the state of public opinion about the programmes which it broadcasts. This is discharged by an annual survey covering opinions on such aspects of its output as the impartiality and quality of material, breadth of coverage and absence of offensive matter. It does not cover particular programmes. In response to the Pilkington Committee's report in 1962, which called for measurement of the quality of programmes as well as their acceptance as indicated by ratings, the IBA developed and implemented a continuous audience-appreciation system. This is based on samples of viewers, a panel in London, who use a diary to record their appreciation of programmes in terms of interest and enjoyment. The results, analysed by demographic groups, are distributed by the IBA to the programme companies. More recently BARB has initiated its own continuous audience appreciation system, very similar to that sponsored by the IBA although smaller in scale.

The audience appreciation research carried out for the IBA and for BARB relates to television programmes. It yields information about general levels of acceptability and provides feedback to those responsible for devising and producing particular programmes. Advertisers and agencies, however, require feedback at the level of advertising campaigns or particular advertisements, in order to monitor their impact in terms of being liked, being remembered and being understood. This calls for *ad hoc* research, commissioned by advertisers or agencies, to meet their particular requirements at the time. Some of this research involves quantitative studies, often these days mounted on omnibus surveys. Much qualitative research is also employed, usually based on group discussions, especially as a basis for the formulation of advertisements and particularly to ensure that adverse features are avoided.

Besides the obvious effects of television on the way people spend their time and on the form of their leisure pursuits, the medium has had profound and subtle social and psychological effects. Attitudes to society, public behaviour and ways in which public opinion is formed, to mention but a few, have changed under the influence of television. It has even been asserted recently that the mental processes by which information is taken in, stored and recalled, have changed under its influence. Many studies supported by the Independent Television industry have been, and continue to be, carried out. The earliest are perhaps more widely known, especially those of Himmelweit, *Television and the Child*, and Belson, *The Impact of Television*.

Finally, there is a panel-based continuous measurement of grocery and domestic products which is used, principally by advertisers and their agencies, to measure the performance of brands in the market. Its short title, TCA, conceals the connection with Independent Television of which its full name, Television Consumer Audit, is a reminder. It was originally sponsored by the Independent Television Companies as a service to their clients which would enable them to see, in terms of market share, the benefit of their investments in television advertising. The power of television advertising having been accepted, the TCA continues, its connection with Independent Television less evident but still important.

What lies ahead?

It is now difficult to imagine living in a developed economy without television advertising. It is here to stay, but the scene is changing rapidly. In conclusion, therefore, it is appropriate to touch briefly on what the future will bring. One of the effects of electronic technological advances is to increase competition for use of the television screen. Home computers and television games are popular and will compete more and more for screen time. So will cable television, which will increase the viewers' choice, and satellite transmissions from abroad. Fresh competitors will enter the arena, and their presence will compel adjustments in both methods of operation and forms of organization and association.

The same technological advances present a challenge to audience measurement. The proliferation of television channels will increase the difficulty of identifying the source of pictures and analysing the resulting information; and the increasing number of alternative uses of TV sets will add to the complexity of the monitoring equipment in panel homes.

Just as it is now difficult to imagine a world without television advertising, so it is difficult to envisage television advertising unsupported by research. It is a medium built on research, and such it is likely to remain.

TV Advertising and the Social Revolution

LORD BRIGGS

LORD BRIGGS

Asa Briggs, Lord Briggs of Lewes, has been Provost of Worcester College, Oxford since 1976. Before that he was for ten years Vice-Chancellor of the University of Sussex. He is well known as a social and cultural historian and is President of the Social History Society. His most comprehensive work in this field is his book *A Social History of England*, which appeared in 1983.

Lord Briggs has been particularly interested in the history of communications and has taken an active part in international as well as national conferences concerned with the past, present and future of broadcasting. He is the author of four volumes on *The History of the BBC*, of *Governing the BBC* and *The BBC, the First Fifty Years, a Short History*. He has been Director of Projects of the International Institute of Communications since its foundation, and he was a director of Southern Television from 1964 to 1981

THE word 'revolution' was used more often during and at the end of the Second World War than it was during the 1950s. Julian Huxley, for example, published in 1944 a volume of essays called *On Living in a Revolution* in which, following Peter Drucker, he hailed 'the end of economic man'. After the war, he wrote, people would not be willing to return to the world of 1939. Values had changed. So too had aspirations. Mark Abrams, a pioneer of social research, said much the same in his *Condition of the British People 1911–1945*, a concise study with a firm statistical base which was published in 1947.

Both Huxley and Abrams were thinking primarily of conscious and deliberate changes in the direction of public policy associated with the ideas of 'fair shares for all', political and economic planning and the welfare state. Yet such changes, exciting though they might appear to the politically active, were themselves associated in turn after 1945 with a continuing climate of austerity: 'shortages' and 'crises' were the two key words, queues the daily experience, 'spivs' the public villains. In retrospect, at least, there was to be a bigger social and cultural breakthrough during the late 1950s, although it was seldom called a 'revolution', since 'austerity', by then something of a bogey word, gave way to what soon came to be called, by contrast, 'affluence'. Most recent social historians would agree with Arthur Marwick's judgement in his *British Society Since 1945* that 'the upheavals of the 1960s were at least as great as those of the Second World War'.

There were many moralist critics of 'affluence', however, just as there were to be moralist critics of 'permissiveness', from J.B. Priestley on this side of the Atlantic to J.K. Galbraith on the other, with Priestley inventing the evocative new term 'Admass' on a return from the United States in 1954. Some social observers, when comparing conditions on the two sides of the Atlantic, pointed out rightly how relative British affluence was – they were right in both the short and long run – and how dangerous it was to overestimate its psychological and political consequences. They did not, however, dispute its influence on the current mood of society and on patterns of culture.

It was 'culture' which was beginning to be perceived of as a 'melting-pot culture', less dominated by 'standards' than the cultures of the past, more subject to the pressures of the topical, less controllable by 'the Establishment', another favourite term in the social criticism of the late 1950s. There were more 'sub-cultures', however, some unequivocally anti-Establishment, some even 'counter-cultures'. Entertainment figured more prominently in 'popular culture' than did information. 'Showbiz' no longer needed to be justified: its ramifications extended far beyond the stage or the screen. The 'media' were beginning to be thought of as such. In all of them 'news' and 'features' were more blurred than they had been. 'Gimmicks' proliferated. Both commodities and ideas were more expensively packaged.

Above all, perspectives were changing. 'Today' was coming into its own. The first day of Independent Television, Thursday, 22 September 1955 – 'This is IT! What will it look like?' asked *Picture Post* – came and went. 'It's going to be a wow,' Godfrey Winn prophesied. A pattern was soon set, metropolitan before it became provincial, with the advertisements quickly becoming as accepted a part of the daily repertoire as the alternative programmes themselves. There was little nostalgia then for the recent past, although the death of Winston Churchill in 1965 stirred it. Anthony Sampson, anatomist of the new Britain – his first *Anatomy* appeared in 1962 – could claim in 1965 that it was 'hard to recall what Britain was like before the first television toothpaste advertisement'. Few people cared.

In retrospect, the 'swinging' sixties were to stand out as *the* decade of hectic cultural and social change in contrast with the 'bleak' seventies and 'realistic' eighties, when the mood had changed again – and more than the mood – and when nostalgia had once more become fashionable. It is arguable, none the less, that the years since 1979, years of high unemployment, have been the most radical years of this century – with the Government refusing to seek consensus and attempting to lower inflation, to reshape the economy, to reduce the power of the trade unions, to refashion the welfare state, the proudest achievement of the 1940s, and, above all, to restructure individual motivations, wiping out, if possible, the experience of decades of twentieth-century history. There is certainly a sharp contrast in purpose and in style with the 1960s. 'Permissiveness' is officially out, although there is more drug-taking now than there was during the 1960s – and in a far broader span of the population.

In terms of the twentieth century as a whole, however, the sixties contrast also with the fifties, 'a decade of illusions', perhaps, but also a decade with what T.C. Worsley called at the time 'a new tone, desperate, savage, regretful at times, very funny'. This was not the tone, however, of 1951, at the opening of the decade, the year of the Festival of Britain which, within the space of a decade, was to stand out in Michael Frayn's words as 'the last and virtually the posthumous work of the Herbivore Britain of the BBC News, the Crown Film Unit, the sweet ration, Uncle Mac, Sylvia Peters . . .'.

From 1952 onwards Britain benefited from the growth in world trade and a marked improvement in the terms of trade, but in a society which had lived through seven years of incessant emphasis – necessary emphasis – on the export drive more attention was being paid at last to the domestic market. 'The miracle has happened,' wrote *The Economist* in June 1954, 'full employment without inflation.' The last rationing was abolished in that year, the year of the Television Act which broke the BBC's monopoly, and of the first mention in print of 'teddy boys'. Two years later, when it had already become clear that economic miracles did not last and that there would be continuing sterling crises, there were crises of other kinds in a period of continuing economic growth. The year of Suez and Hungary, 1956, saw also a remarkable domestic conjunction. An obvious decline in Britain's world power was accompanied by an equally obvious break in domestic behaviour, a break that was to become a breakthrough.

The great rock 'n' roll wave, which swept across the Atlantic, was not only totally transforming the world of sound but ushering in a wave of controversial new manners and styles. Young people, with more disposable income to play with than ever before, were in the vanguard, but they were not alone. Elvis Presley's *Heartbreak Hotel* was a new film of 1956 which appealed specifically to the young. John Osborne's *Look Back in Anger*, an 'overnight revolution', and Brendan Behan's *The Quare Fellow* were new plays with a different appeal to a more varied audience, ready to listen to authors bundled together somewhat indiscriminately as 'angry young men'. London was at the centre of the first change, although with the coming of the Beatles, who released their first Parlophone record six years later, Liverpool was to figure on the world map, trans-Atlantic 'showbiz' in reverse. There was an enhanced self-consciousness, an edge of violence, physical as well as verbal, with new body language. 'Everybody over twenty has passed through his teens,' wrote the *World's Press News*, 'but nobody over thirty has been a teenager.'

The youngest teenagers of 1956, when the wave began to be discussed, had been born in 1943, two years before the Second World War ended. They spent much of their income on records and accounted for over 40 per cent of the record market by the late 1950s. The transistor radio was made for them. Yet it was the power of television which received most attention during the late 1950s. The year the war ended, 1945, had been the year, too, of the Bomb, and during the 1950s, before the term 'bomb culture' had been invented – Jeff Nuttall's book with that title appeared in 1968 – it was fashionable to compare the effects of television on their (and their elders') lives with the effects of nuclear power, if not of the Bomb itself. Thus Lord De La Warr, who helped to pilot the 1954 Television Act through Parliament, claimed in 1959 that in discussing television they were dealing with a 'force' of 'almost equal importance to the future of mankind. . . as nuclear power'. Already in 1947 Grace Wyndham Goldie, a seasoned critic – and producer – had described television as 'a bomb about to burst': 'We have loosed upon the world forces which affect men's minds as powerfully, and possibly as dangerously, as the new weapons of war affect their bodies.'

In 1947 there were 14,560 television licences; in 1956, two years after the BBC's monopoly had been broken by Act of Parliament, there were 5,739,593. By 1961 there were 11,267,741, by 1965 13,253,045. There were then only 2,579,567 for sound radio only. Television by 1965 seemed with little dissent to be both the single biggest expression and the single biggest generator of 'change', the fashionable in-word. Its role in both respects was scrutinized far more systematically than the role of sound broadcasting had been in the 1920s. Another in-word was 'communications', and sociologists, most of whom leaned to the left, some to the 'New Left', were turning to the study of them. Raymond Williams followed up his *The Long Revolution* of 1961, which traced changing historical patterns of communications back to the eighteenth century, with a shorter Penguin Special called *Communications*. It was one of a popular series, *Britain in the Sixties*, and appeared one year before the first issue of *Private Eye*.

The subject of the first serious study of the psychological and social effects of television, Hilde Himmelweit's influential *Television and the Child*, published in 1958, fitted naturally into a pattern of continuing change. The children of the 1950s were the teenagers of the 1960s and are now in their thirties. Two years before Himmelweit wrote, the 'Toddlers' Truce', the hour of television silence between 6 and 7 pm, had been abandoned, and in 1964 the BBC was to jettison its *Children's*

Hour on sound after its audience had dwindled to twenty-five thousand. Uncles and aunts were out-of-date. There was never any agreement, however, on the effects of television on children and teenagers. 'Because there has been an impressive lack of agreement in this debate,' three American writers on the subject, Wilbur Schramm, Jack Lyle and Edwin Parker, concluded in 1961, 'the effect has been not so much to prove charges as to raise a series of disturbing questions' such as 'does television deepen the ignorance or broaden the knowledge of children, debase their tastes or teach them about life too early?' There was to be a similarly 'disturbing' effect when questions were raised about the impact of television on political behaviour. Trenaman and McQuail's *Television and the Political Image* (1961) was the first scholarly British study on this topic, which became a major theme in the days of student protest during the late 1960s and has continued as such through the 1970s and 1980s, with the spotlight on the continuing troubles in Northern Ireland. Trenaman and McQuail were concerned with an election – the 1959 General Election won by Harold Macmillan, when local audiences at political meetings had already dwindled. The continuing debate focused more on violence, however, than on passivity, for whatever else was to be reversed in the late 1970s the trend towards increased violence was not.

An early attempt was made by William Belson to answer all the basic questions about effects in his book *The Impact of Television* (1967). It included chapters on the effects of television on the interests and initiatives of viewers, on family life and 'sociability', and on the reading and buying of newspapers and magazines. There were arguments about all these too, particularly about the last, until the talk gave way, and then not completely, to arguments about the effects on television itself of cable and satellite.

By then, the concept of a 'communications revolution' was a cliché. The disappearance from the scene of familiar national newspapers and magazines during the 1960s seemed only one stage in it, and greater concentration of business power merely a prelude to a greater concentration on the future within a massive leisure complex. Competition from television – and with it erosion of press advertising profit margins – was only one factor in the story of newspapers and (increasingly specialized) magazines. Newsprint rationing ceased in 1959, and although television by then accounted for over one-fifth of all advertising and was universally considered to be the dominant display medium, the share of the press, including the provincial press, in advertising expenditure as a whole did not fall significantly between

1960 and 1979. Colour supplements, the first of them appearing in 1962, preceded colour television: in 1968 there were only 20,428 colour licences, although by 1972 the figure was 1,634,000.

Colour was a special technological bonus for the advertisers. It did not save the cinema, however. Cinema admissions had already fallen from 1585 million in 1945 to 501 million in 1960, and they were as low as 193 million in 1970. Bingo took the place of the cinema for a time – a cuckoo in the nest – but it, too, was to begin to go out of favour during the 1980s. Betting shops, however, were to stay; the Betting and Gambling Act of 1960 had legalized them. Already, three years earlier, to the horror even of some people in the business, Independent Television had for the first time presented the starting prices of races on the home screen. Within the expanding leisure complex, sport was to be transformed as much as men's and women's fashions or tourism, the latter, in particular, heavily dependent from the start on advertising. Sport was to become heavily dependent on business sponsorship too, while abolition of the maximum wage in soccer in 1962 was as much of a cultural landmark as the coming of rock 'n' roll. Pre-1955 sport or pre-1962 sport, even amateur sport, is even more different from post-1962 sport than pre-1955 BBC-monopoly broadcasting was different from Independent Television broadcasting.

While considered in retrospect as a central feature of the continuing 'social revolution', Independent Television in the first instance had to be related even at the time to the more general consumer boom which led into the 'swinging sixties'. Between 1955 and 1960 the proportion of the population using refrigerators rose from 6 to 16 per cent. The figures for washing machines were 25 to 44 per cent and for motor cars 18 to 32 per cent. Television advertising might be spurned at first by retailers – some large firms, otherwise in the vanguard of 'social revolution', like the John Lewis Partnership, avoided it altogether – yet retailers benefited substantially from its increasingly dominant role in the 'propaganda of commodities', as Christopher Lasch has called it. The marketing of food and drink, toothpaste and cleaning products was as conspicuous in the revolution – although less generally noticed by social historians – as consumer durables. Only tobacco has been widely noticed, and that because of the future ban.

Between 1956 and 1959 expenditure on television advertising more than quadrupled, in the latter year exceeding the total revenue of all the national and London evening papers, which itself had just reached a record peak. It was not only the volume of television advertising but its content and style, however, which captured public attention – the slogans, the jingles, the packs, the images, the straight caption, 'as advertised on TV', familiar outside the home. This was 'marketing' as distinct from 'selling', and it involved trying to have on hand and to make available 'what the consumer wants'.

'Won't it be nice when we have lovely lingerie *and* Lux to look after our pretty things?' newspaper advertisements, produced in the years of austerity, had asked. 'But while there is still no Lux', they added, 'and you have to wash treasured things with the soap or flakes available, do take extra care.' In fact, there was to be no return to the prewar age of Lux. Detergents, developed during the war as soap substitutes, saw to that. The consumer wanted them. And the washing machine, the television set, the refrigerator and the motor car were among the first consumer durables which every home came to feel that it needed. They were not just status symbols; they had obvious social use too, even if the use could carry with it social costs, as in the case of the motor car. As Harry Hopkins put it in his brilliant survey *The New Look* (1963), 'The kitchen, not long ago synonymous with woman's obligation, now became the shining badge of her triumph.' He wrote too soon to note that it was only for a time. Women's liberation, seldom out of the news in the late 1960s, did not stop at that point, although it never went so far as its most vigorous advocates demanded – or expected.

Much was made during the late 1950s and early 1960s, particularly in the pages of *The Economist*, of the erosion of the class system and of its political effects as a result of the consumer revolution, backed by television. The working class was ceasing to be working class, it claimed, and Conservatives were ceasing to be conservative. This was bourgeoisification or *embourgeoisement*, two of the most awkward of the current terms. The thesis was exaggerated, as sociologists such as David Lockwood and H.J. Goldthorpe showed at the time. Nor did class divisions disappear during the 1960s and 1970s. Much was to continue to be made of them by foreign observers, collecting impressions, fuzzy or acute, in media as different as *Pravda* and the *Wall Street Journal*; and Ivan Reid was to demonstrate their continuing relevance in his rigorously empirical *Social Class in Britain* (1977), in which he turned systematically to the statistics of birth and death, health, education and use of leisure.

There were many signs, however, from the late 1950s onwards that what Ernest Bevin had called 'poverty of desire' – in his view the worst form of poverty – was diminishing, that aspirations and expectations were rising, and that traditional distinctions in dress and food were far less important than they had been before 1939. There was new meaning in the differences that persisted, however, and advertising could make the most of them. Much was made by critics of its 'manipulative' aspects. It was better judged, however, as part of a new cultural (and economic) system.

In retrospect, it is perhaps more significant to focus on the changing world of the child, who was to grow up within a new pattern of material culture, than on the reactions of people who had grown up during the 1930s. Already children had been granted extra privileges in the age of austerity, of 'fair shares for all', even in relation to goods not rationed by the state. 'Unfortunately Cadbury's are only allowed the milk to make an extremely small quantity of (milk) chocolate,' ran an advertisement of 1947, 'so if you are lucky enough to get some, do save it for the children.' Ten years later, in their impressive survey of Bethnal Green, Peter Willmot and Michael Young quoted a young mother who reported, 'When I was a kid Dad always had the best of everything. Now it's the children.' When television entered this already changing world, children were ready for it. Indeed in 1955, before the coming of Independent Television, the BBC reported that among the five- to seven-year-old age group 85 per cent watched television daily: if there was no set in their home they found a home where there was one.

In 1961, 23.1 per cent of the population was aged fourteen or less, and they were now a distinct element in the new television audience, alarming many teachers who feared that the communications system would have – or already was having – a bigger impact on their attitudes than the educational system. This was the theme of an influential conference called 'Popular Culture and Personal Responsibility', organized by the National Union of Teachers in 1960. Among Hilde Himmelweit's research sample of children studied there was an average viewing time of just under two hours a day, but she included a whole chapter on 'addicts' also and noted cautiously: 'Side by side with a more cosy-going approach of life. . . we found evidence of a less strictly controlled and possibly less moralistic home atmosphere.'

It became fashionable during the 1960s to think of the population in terms of age groups rather than of income groups, and to identify a 'generation gap'; the gap seemed greatest in higher education, where the number of university students more than doubled in a decade. They received more attention, particularly from television, not when they were studying, but when they were drawn into 'student protest' during the late 1960s: the drama attracted and repelled. In retrospect, however, perhaps the most interesting feature in education in the longer period from the 1960s to the 1980s was the less dramatic but crucially important increase in the proportion of children attending comprehensive schools. In England it rose from 34.4 per cent in 1971 to 82.9 per cent in 1982, when the proportions for Scotland and Wales were as high as 96.3 and 96.2. The grammar school and all that it stood for was almost out, but the public schools survived.

Since between 1971 and 1981 the proportion of children under fifteen fell as a percentage of the population of working age, concern was increasingly focused less on the young than on the numbers of over sixty-fives, who increased by over two million during the same period. In the 1984 edition of *Social Trends*, an invaluable official publication which first appeared in 1970, the lead article, 'Changes in the Life Styles of the Elderly, 1959–1982', was written by Mark Abrams, who had surveyed the social scene forty years before, to support the case for changes in national policy.

The growth in possessions of the elderly since the 1950s had not lagged behind that of the population as a whole. More than half of them had a telephone, 'a rare piece of apparatus in the homes of elderly people in 1959'. The reason why, of course, was related to the changing family pattern. By the early 1980s only 10 per cent of elderly women were members of households that contained three or more persons, whereas in 1959 the proportion was 27 per cent. By then, too, only 2 per cent lived in a household where there was a child under the age of fifteen. Half-a-million more pensioners were by then living alone than in 1971.

Between 1959 and 1982 the size of the average household fell from 3.08 persons to 2.6 persons and, for all the vicissitudes in national economic (and political) circumstances, by 1983 97 per cent of households owned a television set, 59 per cent owned a car and 76 per cent had a telephone. There had been a remarkable increase in home-centred activities throughout the period as homes had become warmer and more comfortable (and garden centres had proliferated), and there was a corresponding increase in do-it-yourself, partly, of course, because getting others to do it for you became more expensive. The proportion of males carrying out DIY tasks rose from 55 per cent in 1959 to 81 per cent in 1982, and the proportion of females from 48 per cent to 60 per cent.

Television had been a harbinger of this shift, although figures for overall viewing in 1982 showed that people were spending rather less time viewing than they had done during the 1960s. There were other

Top left **The City of London** in the sixties outwardly continued to reflect traditional values which had changed little since the war. The bowler hat, dark suit and tightly rolled umbrella remained *de rigueur* yet there were already signs of a challenge to authority and of a widening generation gap. The contents bills of the two surviving evening newspapers mark the disappearance of the third London evening, *The Star*, which had closed at the beginning of the decade despite its circulation of nearly 750,000 copies a day

Left **Students of the Sixties.** These students could easily have been the offspring of the City businessmen seen emerging from the Bank Underground station. The sixties saw the appearance of hippies, 'flower power' and the 'beat generation', and signs of a decline of family and traditional *mores*. Respect for authority, the influence of formalized religion and the constraints of class structure were already beginning to break down

Above **Carnaby Street,** despite its close proximity to the more conventional Regent Street, became a centre for new trends in fashion and retailing in the sixties. It was an era of coffee shops, boutiques and wine bars and of the much shorter-lived flared jeans and miniskirts

pressures influencing the home by then, of course, including unemployment – the global figures would have been deemed intolerable in the 1950s, as would the figure of nearly 126,000 unemployed school leavers in 1983 – and the rise of the 'dual economy' outside the control of the nation's taxation system. By 1982, no less than 43 per cent of the nation's recognized labour force were women, and the number of part-time employees had risen during the previous ten years by 34 per cent. The state of the economy was being strongly influenced not only by cyclical but also by structural factors, for the technology of the workplace was now changing faster than the technology of the home.

Most of the distinctive features of British society in the late 1970s and early 1980s had not been consciously planned by Government. Indeed, the official emphasis by then, in complete contrast to that of the late 1940s, was on the operation of market forces. For an understanding of the new society it is necessary to consider together within the same analysis official statistics and official policies, and business and trade union statistics and strategies. Within this context Independent Television as a market research-oriented industry is perhaps more generally concerned with the 'social revolution' than any other 'industry', while its programme output continues to reflect and to direct change in ways in which there is no complete agreement within the industry itself. It recognizes continuities, of course, as well as changes. Thus, for Brian Palmer in 1980, what twenty-five years of Independent Television had proved was 'the infinite durability of a good advertising idea'.

Statistics collected by the Advertising Association cover global changes, for example those which relate advertising expenditures to Gross National Product and reveal that record expenditure on advertising in real terms reached its peak in 1973 on the eve of 'the time of troubles'. Such statistics obviously register 'the general health of the economy', as Harold Lind, retiring Director of Research at the Advertising Association, put it in 1977, when the optimistic mood of the 1960s had been dissipated – although by 1981 an *Economist* headline read 'Britain's media men smile into the slump.' 'In the long term,' it suggested, 'advertising may not suffer much even if there is a long recession. Its growth or otherwise seems to have little to do with the dynamism of the economy within which it is taking place.'

Other statistics collected by the Advertising Association make possible a deeper analysis. They include swings in expenditure not only on particular branded products but on whole 'macro' categories of retail items, and they seek to identify differences in the behaviour of social groups of people working and living in different parts of the country. The term 'general health of the economy' is too broad to cover this kind of analysis, which has to take account of long-term forces such as the rise of 'consumer protection', related, perhaps (after lags), to changes in the educational system as much as to media content, in addition to economic shifts such as the decline of key sectors of manufacturing industry or the expansion of financial services. It is fascinating to chart how during the 1970s and early 1980s many products began to be advertised widely on television for the first time.

Information from the Advertising Association, summarized in 1985 in its *Advertising Statistics Year Book*, can be supplemented by material derived from occasional surveys made by individual television companies, such as Rediffusion's economic and marketing studies, prepared in book form by George Murray in 1962 and in 1964, or the more specialized *The Uncommon Market*, published – by Thames Television – around 1975. The fact that Independent Television has been organized on a regional basis – with the regions acquiring more real importance in some respects to people living in them than the official and administrative divisions into which the country is divided – makes it possible to explore continuing regional differences statistically.

Social change takes place at different rates and within different frames in different parts of the country. It is not surprising, in consequence, that as the national economic situation deteriorated during the 1970s more attention began to be paid to geographical contrasts – north/south; east/west; metropolitan; urban/suburban/rural.

The Thames Television survey showed, for example, in a year of alarming inflation *and* unemployment – a combination which would have been considered extremely unlikely, if not impossible, before the 1970s – that the proportion of people in the AB socio-economic group was 14 per cent in the Thames area as against a national average of 12 per cent, and that the proportion of people in group DE was 28 per cent against 34 per cent; that weekly income and expenditure were significantly higher than in most other regions except that covered by Southern Television; that motor cars were owned in 62.8 per cent of the homes as against a national average of 57.9 per cent; and so on. Yet a higher proportion of families owned electric cookers and washing machines outside the Thames area: London, after all, was a centre of the restaurant and the launderette, not to speak of the biggest supermarkets, strategic agencies in the 'social revolution'. Of no less than 34 per cent of the nation's supermarkets of 8000 square feet or more, 103 were located in the Thames area by 1975 – with the

Midlands in this case coming second, with 18 per cent, 55 in all.

The background of continuing regional difference within what is often thought of in unsophisticated fashion as an undifferentiated national mass market with increasingly specialized smaller markets inside it (and since the 1970s a Common Market encompassing it) is the theme of D. Elliston Allen's pioneering little book *British Tastes: An Enquiry into the Likes and Dislikes of the Regional Consumer* (1968). Advertising research made it possible and it would be useful to have an up-to-date version of it.

The Thames survey statistics, like much advertising research, did not show variations within the Thames area itself, the kind of variations which continue to keep Britain a divided society even within the same geographical region. At the end of the 1970s Tower Hamlets, to take one example, had only half the GLC average of car owners, and within Tower Hamlets there were variations, too, with 77 per cent of the occupants of one small group of twenty-one houses not even possessing a hot-water supply. Social deprivation in Britain's inner cities in the 1980s remains a pressing national problem. Liverpool, in particular, now figures on a very different kind of social map from that of the 1960s. And everywhere there are still marked differences between those who hold mortgages and those who pay rents and, above all, between those who are employed and those who are unemployed.

If it is legitimate to talk of a 'social revolution' since the 1950s, it is apparent, therefore, firstly that it is an unfinished revolution and, secondly, that how it will continue in its later phases is itself a matter of debate. There is more than one option. For this reason sensitive social historians since the 1950s, in an age when futurology has risen, would have become almost as interested in the future as in the past. They appreciate, of course, how impossible it would have been to predict during the 1950s just what Britain would be like a full generation later.

Copy Controls
from Within

PETER WOODHOUSE

PETER WOODHOUSE

Educated at the City of London School and Peterhouse, Cambridge, Peter Woodhouse began his career as a barrister. After serving as a major in the Royal Marine Commandos during the Second World War he was appointed Legal Assistant to the City Remembrancer of the Corporation of London in 1949.

Eleven years later he became Secretary and Legal Officer of the Institute of Practitioners in Advertising, dealing with the problems of several hundred member agencies.

He left the IPA in 1969 to become Head of Copy Clearance of the ITCA and, working closely with the Copy Committee, the IBA and their consultants, was responsible for the pretransmission vetting of all television commercials.

In 1974 Peter Woodhouse succeeded Archie Graham as Head of Advertising Control of the Independent Broadcasting Authority which he left in 1981 to start his own business

Decisions! decisions!

'You bloody bastard,' said Kate, looking round the door.

Another copy control day begins.

'It's in the commercial for the new film *Death in Fragments* – the villain's throwing the hero down the cliff. We need a double-head, of course. The agency says it's not too violent but want to keep the audio. I've said "no" because of the language. But can we discuss "after 9 pm"?'

First decision needed.

From the inside, copy control is all about decisions – scores each day, thousands each year – decisions about the meaning of words and phrases, the implications of pictures, the performance of products, the availability of services, the fairness of comparisons. It is about checking facts, assessing evidence and reaching decisions about what can mislead, cause harm or give offence – decisions which will be fair to advertisers and acceptable to the public. It is about reaching them quickly to meet demanding transmission dates – yet making sure that debate and discussion can widen where necessary to take account of many viewpoints.

Consider, then, today's first decision. Important? Trivial? Censorious?

Death in Fragments is an action film, exciting, rough and tough. How best can the advertiser capture its flavour, be imaginative, dramatic, memorable, persuasive – all in twenty seconds? Isn't some hearty cursing justified? But what of those who dislike swearing, who fear to hear such language on the lips of their children? For them the blame for bad example will rest squarely on television advertising. Although only one influence among many, it would, as the identifiable influence in the home, be the prime target for their anger.

Few will know of Kate or any of those at IBA and ITCA responsible for copy controls. So before our day begins in earnest, we ought to find out why so many decisions are needed, who takes them and how.

Powers and duties

Every year many thousands of new television commercials are made – made by advertising agencies for their advertiser clients after much research, with great expertise and at considerable expense. So powerful are they with words, music, pictures, and colour that few advertisers serving mass markets can fail to use them. Each transmission is seen in the homes of millions of families – seen by young children, by impressionable teenagers and by men and women of all ages, of different races, cultures and opinions – often seen again and again over weeks or months.

As a previous chapter has shown, Parliament gave the ITA, as it was originally called, powers and duties to set advertising standards high enough to match the power of the medium. The ITA had to draw up and enforce a code of standards and to decide which classes and methods of advertising would be unacceptable and, in particular, to exclude any advertisement which might be likely to be misleading or offensive to public taste and decency. The ITA's decisions were made binding upon the programme companies.

Advertising under attack

As soon as ITV transmissions began, it became clear that there was much to learn and do before a system of control could be built which would gain public confidence. In fact, by a historical chance the new advertising medium was to grow up at a time when criticism of advertising was most fierce and vocal.

The end of the war had released a surge of idealism and aspirations for a fairer society. New ideas in politics and economics were being eagerly canvassed, and the foundations of the welfare state were being laid. Traditional establishment practices and moralities came under critical attack. Industry and commerce were seen to have far wider duties to the individual and to society than ever before. That the fostering of demand could automatically lead a nation to prosperity was no longer accepted. On the contrary, many took the view that the constant struggle for money to meet the demands of the advertisements would merely breed discontent. Indeed advertising, the outward and visible face of commerce, was often held up as the exploiter which for its own ends created anxiety and neurosis. The acquisitive society it fostered was denounced as the enemy of the 'good life'. Competition alone could not adequately protect the purchaser from inadequate and harmful products or deceptive practices. A new description of those in need of protection was coined. Soon 'the consumer' was a force in politics.

Although it was accepted that material desires did need to be fulfilled, they could only be properly satisfied if the consumer had an information service by which to choose wisely. Advertising, it was said, failed to provide it. Even if it told the truth, it was claimed that it told only part of the truth and displayed only the product's advantages. Some felt even more strongly that 'the major part of advertising is and always has been a campaign of exaggeration, half truths, intended ambiguities, direct lies and general deception'.[1]

British advertisers and agencies, too, were themselves largely inexperienced in the new medium. Unfortunately, this often led them to try to translate into film the style and content of their press campaigns. It was not long before it was apparent that persuasion which was subtle or amusing in print could become blatant or vulgar on television, and that enthusiastic self-praise and hyperbole could appear on the screen as a crude attempt to mislead.

Fear and suspicion about the role of advertising was further aroused in 1957 by Vance Packard's readable book *The Hidden Persuaders*. Its theme was that in America the use of mass psychoanalysis to guide campaigns of persuasion had become the basis of a multi-million dollar industry: 'Professional persuaders have seized upon it in their groping for more effective ways to sell their wares.'[2] Although based heavily on anecdote, the highly spiced examples were calculated to alarm: 'A Chicago advertising agency has been studying the housewife's menstrual cycle and its psychological concomitants to find the appeals that will become effective in selling her certain food products. . . the same agency has used psychiatric, probing techniques on little girls.'[3]

It became the vogue for intellectual critics, if not the man in the street, to submit commercials to Freudian analysis. Perhaps the greatest notoriety was achieved by Cadbury's Flake, as the pretty girl was seen, with loving anticipation, to unwrap the bar and place it ecstatically between her lips. It fell to an ITA Chairman, no less, robustly to play the defensive straight bat. 'If some people care to make a chocolate bar commercial into a blue movie – that's their problem.'[4]

Throughout the 1960s pressure to control and restrain advertising grew, led by opinion in the USA where Ralph Nader's famous duel with General Motors was followed by a whole series of specific challenges to the honesty of US advertising and sales practices.

The British Consumers' Association's magazine *Which?* on several occasions criticized television advertising for making viewers believe that the qualities of the advertised goods were superior to those of cheaper products when, according to *Which?*'s research, they were not. As an independent body *Which?* had great influence, although its testing methodology was sometimes challenged by advertisers.

A self-appointed political group, the Advertising Inquiry Council, was for some months active in seeking examples of misleading advertisements. It told the Pilkington Committee in oral evidence that 'it was its impression that from five to eight per cent of all advertisements on television were false or misleading', but did not define its allegations more closely to the Committee.[5] It was, however, vocal enough to influence the Labour party to set up a commission under Lord Reith, which was later to condemn advertising for creating an imbalance between the producer and consumer and recommend the establishment of a national consumers' authority with an income of millions to test products and investigate claims.

Response to challenge

Against this background those in Britain charged with the responsibility for television advertising were striving to meet this uniquely demanding challenge. They had quickly to recognize and define those areas in which the viewing public was vulnerable, and to create machinery to make sure that the necessary remedial rules and practices would be effectively enforced. All, however, was new. Apart from laying down broad general principles of honesty and decency, they could not anticipate the infinity of possible treatments which might be put forward by creative scriptwriting. All that could guide them was common sense and practical experience. Like common law the system had of necessity to be built pragmatically, case by case.

Public appraisals

The success of early controls over television advertising came to be assessed in 1962. After two years' detailed deliberation the Government's Committee on Consumer Protection, under the chairmanship of a distinguished lawyer, Sir Joseph Molony, made recommendations regarding new legislation and controls for the protection of consumers, which in 1968 were embodied in the Trade Descriptions Act. While it was to be a criminal offence to apply descriptions to goods which were misleading 'to a material degree', Molony agreed that no precise rules could be formulated to deal with those advertising techniques which had incurred most criticism – that is, vague claims for superiority, the singling out of features of spurious importance and emotional appeal. These were best dealt with by a code of general principles to be applied to the individual facts of each case, which was the approach already adopted for television.[6]

About emotional appeals in advertising – appeals to fears of being regarded as less than adequate, of falling behind in the race to emulate the Joneses, or worry lest your best friends won't tell you – it was impossible, agreed Molony, to generalize. Everyone had different personal convictions, related as much to wider conceptions of morality and taste as to the merits of the particular product or its advertised presentation.

What strikes one person as a gross offence against good taste will seem to another unexceptionable and to yet another as merely laughable. . . . Some will think that mother love or any other healthy human emotion can only be debased or weakened by its portrayal as part of an advertisement, others that it is reinforced by good example even when it is pictured with a commercial motive. . . . [7]

'Of such matters', the Committee said, confirming what ITCA and ITA already well knew, 'their assessment depends on opinion not fact and any attempt at exploitation or at control is circumscribed by the limits imposed by the composite of public opinion.'[8] Unfortunately, no help was forthcoming as to how to judge what that meant in practice!

The Pilkington Committee on Broadcasting reported shortly after Molony. Its report referred to a number of allegations about misleading advertising, but passed no judgements on them except to say that 'the benefit of the doubt should go to those who might be misled – the viewer'.[9] It did recommend, however, that the then ITA, as well as ITCA, should be directly involved in the day-to-day case-law decisions, and that the decisions should be fleshed out in a detailed and specific code. It also proposed that arrangements for obtaining specialist advice on medical advertisements should be made statutory. Concerning undesirable emotional appeals, Pilkington was of no greater help than Molony. It fell back on urging compliance with 'the spirit as well as the letter of the Code'.[10]

The two independent investigations had therefore recognized that the early controls were on the right lines. The pragmatic case-by-case approach was judged appropriate, but in need of greater consistency and professionalism.

These views were taken to heart, and from the mid-1960s resulted in a revision in the roles of ITCA and ITA in advertising control, in a more detailed code and in an increase in professionalism through staff and resources.

The role of the programme companies

Paradoxically, in the formative years it had been not the statutory body, the ITA, but the programme companies which had taken on the practical task of enforcing and interpreting the original *Principles for Television Advertising*. As with other media, advertising agencies contracted with individual television programme companies for the transmission of their advertisements – and it was convenient as well as logical for their legal agreements to include an undertaking to adhere to the *Principles for Television Advertising*. Within the process of accepting the advertisement, the programme company with which the booking was made could ensure that the advertisement had indeed fulfilled this condition. As advertisements were often to appear on a number of stations, the need to coordinate decisions on acceptability came to be undertaken by a committee of the Independent Television Companies' Association. That Advertisement Committee comprised representatives of all the programme companies. It later delegated copy-control functions to a small representative Copy Committee. Although after Pilkington the ITA (which became the IBA in 1972) took a direct rather than a supervisory role in making decisions on individual advertisements, the ITCA retained a parallel function – that of 'clearing' commercials for transmission.

The ITCA's motivation has always been different from, but complementary to, that of the IBA. Like other media owners, the television programme companies have a natural interest in the standards of the advertisements they accept. Any legitimate criticism affects their reputation as broadcasters. Failure to set proper standards diminishes the credibility of television advertising and thus devalues the television airtime they have for sale. Dissatisfaction with standards may lead to statutory requirements inhibiting the uses of the medium and restricting the categories of advertisements permitted, thus curtailing revenue.

Furthermore, the ITCA, in direct daily touch with the practical problems of advertisers and agencies, can provide a body of responsible opinion able to take these problems into account and represent them to the IBA. It can make restraints more palatable to advertisers by explaining fully why they are needed. It can help agencies by providing advice and constructive criticism at the early stages of campaign plans, and thus help to avoid costly hitches and last-minute problems when deadlines are vital. Indeed, the ITCA has issued a whole series of printed booklets called *Notes of Guidance* which explain and expand on the code. Where criticisms of advertising of a product category seem justified, it can explore and pave the way for code changes by drafting and discussing with advertisers practicable provisions. Conversely it can make a reasoned case for lifting restrictions where this seems justified in the light of changed circumstances and public opinion.

In 1970, for example, much emotion was generated by injuries suffered by children from fireworks on Guy Fawkes night. The fireworks manufacturers came under hostile attack from the media. The ITCA and ITA had seriously to consider whether they should continue to accept any advertising for fireworks. However, their positive suggestion to the Firework Manufacturers' Safety Association for their advertising to include care warnings grew into the Fireworks Code. This set out guidance on the safe use of fireworks and has since been referred to in all firework advertisements as well as in some of the numerous official public-service announcements issued by the Central Office of Information which are screened by the television companies without charge.

The ITCA's decisions were, in the early days of ITV, taken by the Heads of Sales of the programme companies, meeting frequently in the Advertisement and Copy Committees. The chairmen of these committees often spent many hours each week talking to advertisers and agencies about copy problems. Gradually, however, a highly professional and experienced permanent Copy Clearance staff was built up. Detailed records and files were established and consistency achieved in the application of the IBA code to different advertisers. The Copy Committee was thus able to meet less frequently and to concern itself only with the more difficult and disputed decisions and with code developments.

Who takes the decisions?

The system of copy clearance is simple. Agencies are asked to send the script of any proposed television advertisement to the ITCA so that it can be examined to see that it complies with the IBA code. If it does not seem to do so, the ITCA will discuss with the agency possible amendments which would make the script acceptable. When these are agreed, a revised script is submitted by the agency and the ITCA can then indicate officially that it is approved. The agency is then able to go confidently ahead with its production plan and make the film or videotape. It will know that it is using approved wording and, in addition, it has the benefit of official advice regarding the proposed visual content of the film. During these exchanges, the ITCA will have provided the IBA with a copy of every script, together with a note of any action proposed or advice given. In this way, and through telephone contact and meetings, the IBA is enabled to require additional matters to be dealt with before the ITCA gives the agency a decision on the acceptability of the script. If any differences of emphasis between the IBA and ITCA cannot be resolved informally, a Joint Advertisement Control Committee exists to explore the problems together.

Decisions begin with the ITCA's permanent staff. There are four copy groups, each of which deals with a quarter of the volume of business passing through the ITCA. Although there is some regular interchange, each copy group will service the same agencies for some time, so that the group heads and executives get to know their opposite numbers in the advertising agencies as well as the products they handle and the copy problems which have already been discussed and resolved. Much of the contact is informal by telephone or face-to-face at meetings.

The agencies know that with every script which makes a new claim, they will have to produce evidence or justification. Sometimes this is easy enough to assess, but it may be technical, scientific or medical. In these cases, the group will have it assessed by a member of the IBA's Medical Advisory Panel or by one or more expert consultants which the ITCA retains in many other fields, and arrangements can be made for the advertisers' experts to meet ITV's consultants. The group heads can refer matters of significance to a daily meeting of their colleagues held under the chairmanship of ITCA's Head of Copy Clearance. The other groups, for example, may need to know of a newly substantiated claim for a product improvement, as this advance may well affect existing or future claims of a competitor who is being serviced by another group. Difficult decisions can be made by the Head of Copy Clearance in the light of the experience of all the group heads.

Those cases on which an ITCA staff decision is not acceptable to advertisers are referred to the Copy Committee. The views of IBA's Advertising Control Officers are, of course, also being taken. This adds a further important dimension to the discussion. The sometimes difficult diplomatic task is to find a solution acceptable to the IBA, the ITCA, the agency and the advertiser. In seeking a mutually satisfactory outcome, discussions can widen to involve IBA's Controller of Advertising – perhaps using the more formal machinery of the Joint Advertisement Control Committee of which he is Chairman.

The IBA's Advertising Advisory Committee

Matters affecting the scope of, or amendment to, the IBA code itself are referred to the IBA's statutory Advertising Advisory Committee, on which serve representatives of the public as consumers, of medical and pharmaceutical interests, and of those in the business of advertising. The Chairman of the Copy Committee attends these meetings as an observer, as do the senior staff members of the professional bodies representing advertising agencies and advertisers – and their views can be invited.

At each of the Advisory Committee's meetings, a summary of all comments and complaints received from members of the public is considered. The Committee views commercials which are controversial and recent examples of advertisements in categories of special interest – such as those for, say, children's toys, alcoholic drinks or financial services.

After each of its meetings the Advisory Committee makes recommendations which are considered at the next session of the members of the IBA itself. The recommendations are, since Pilkington, no longer mandatory but carry much weight with the Authority. They may lead to formal proposals by the IBA to the Government for changes to be made to the code.

Consistency and change

From the original brief *Principles for Television Advertising* of 1955 has grown the detailed IBA *Code of Advertising Standards and Practice* which is recognized worldwide as covering all areas of likely concern. The particular categories of advertising to which the viewer may be particularly vulnerable, such as alcoholic drink, medicines and financial propositions, have been given specially detailed regulations, as has the whole area of advertising which may affect children.

Notwithstanding its detail, the code (like much law) often can do no more than state an intent. How any particular advertisement will be taken or understood by viewers, and whether it does or does not conform to the code's letter or spirit, must depend on the judgement of the code authorities at the time. While, in order to be fair, they will seek consistency and to follow precedent, there are perceptible tides of change over the years in line with corresponding change in what Molony called 'the composite of public opinion'.

Treatments once acceptable may a few years later, under the same code wording, well be unacceptable or vice versa. What was thought in the 1960s to be merely colourful hyperbole could well be regarded as grossly misleading in the eighties. Perhaps, however, such changes are most easily detected in the area of what, to quote the Broadcasting Acts, 'offends against good taste and decency'.[11] In 1959 the Copy Committee was ruling that 'real models wearing foundation garments should not show any movement if their flesh was visible'. Ten years later they could find 'probably acceptable' live models 'wearing girdles beneath gauzy robes with the wind disturbing the edges of the drapery'. But by 1979 no pain was experienced in the sight of nubile girls in the briefest of bras and panties curvaceously poling a raft down a river.

False teeth or lavatory pans, which could in earlier days not be shown without upsetting public sensibility, did not, when tentatively depicted several years later, raise any eyebrows. Today we can, without impediment, see dentures smiling at us from a bathroom tumbler or be taken on a visual trip right round the bend of our lavatory bowl – so long as it looks hygienic. But few of us today, however nostalgic, would need the comfort which the ITCA Chairman felt necessary to give members of the Townswomen's Guild in 1971. 'The girl who sets up house in a television commercial is never without her wedding ring. Have a close look and see!'[12]

Because of changes in the code and its interpretation over the years, and in the climate of public opinion which continues to inform such changes, it would be a mistake for this chapter to illustrate the working of copy controls by actual case histories. Any of the thousands of interesting examples of decision making recorded in the minutes of the IBA or ITCA could warrant a chapter to itself – such are the niceties of fact, language and visual treatment, and the pros and cons of debate.

But at the beginning of this chapter a typical day had just begun at the ITCA – let us imagine how it might continue. . . .

Action this day

9.10   Kate has gone to talk to the IBA and the advertising agency about possible timing restrictions to keep the commercial for *Death in*

Fragments away from children's viewing time – 9 pm is the accepted watershed for adult viewing. Strange how advertisements and programmes are judged by different standards – television programmes are invited into the home, advertisements are not. Once shown, a programme, even if disliked, will not be repeated, at least for a long time. An advertisement can be expected to appear again and again. A parson telephoned angrily about an advertisement for a razor blade which showed two young men gently boxing (to illustrate how smooth their cheeks were after a shave). 'Can we not', he cried, 'enjoy with our children the family film without being subjected to such examples of personal violence?' The film they watched with enjoyment was an Alistair Maclean thriller with thirteen violent deaths – including a transfixing with a harpoon!

A political view

Several letters arrive. The first complains of a commercial for holidays in South Africa. 'It's despicable', says the writer 'to help a Government which oppresses its people. It's misleading to show these scenes as only whites can enjoy them.' We must tell him that it's not a copy clearance function to apply political judgements – and that we did check that all the places and facilities shown in the commercial could be enjoyed by all races.

Doctors and dentists

The next letter comes from a member of the IBA's Medical Advisory Panel who writes to confirm that he is to retire soon. At our request he has consulted his colleagues on the Panel and they have selected a likely replacement – a leading consultant at a teaching hospital who they believe would not only be highly suitable but also willing to be available to us for advice when we need it. We shall ask for IBA approval – and after we have met our prospective new consultant informally to explain our needs and to get his consent, the IBA will send his name to the Royal College of Physicians and the Department of Health to see whether they, too, agree with our choice.

This Panel is of immense value. As early as 1959 it was evident that the ITCA needed specialist advice on claims for medicines, lotions and appliances and also on foods and drinks which referred to nourishment or health properties. It invited Dr A.H. Douthwaite, Senior Consulting Physician at Guy's Hospital, to become its adviser on general medical

371

matters and Dr Alastair Frazer, Professor of Medical Biochemistry and Pharmacology to oversee claims of nutrition. Other consultants were soon added to cover further specialized fields of medicine and dentistry. After Pilkington the Panel was given a statutory basis under the aegis of the IBA. Every new medical claim must be referred to a Panel member before it is accepted in a commercial. 'The aim of television medical advertising', said Lord Richardson, himself a member of the Panel, addressing the Royal Society of Medicine, 'is to strike the right balance between the public interest and legitimate self-medication, and great care and much expertise goes into doing it.'[13] Panel members are all eminent in their profession and their contribution is of great public service. It is with some amazement as well as gratitude that Copy Control staff recall, for example, the elegant, kindly and wise Sir Derrick Dunlop, the Chairman of the Committee on the Safety of Medicines, finding time amid his enormous responsibilities regularly to visit us to discuss advertising claims about the efficacy of cough mixtures or the speed of action of headache remedies.

Harmony in Europe

A third letter is from the IBA, enclosing the latest version of the EEC's draft *Directive on Misleading Advertising*. The Home Office has asked for comments within two weeks. There are clearly difficulties in seeking to reconcile the British system of pre-transmission approval of advertisements by a public broadcasting authority with some European concepts involving court-room procedures. A paper must be prepared for the Copy Committee this week so that it can give the IBA its views.

We have to think ahead to when cable and satellites will carry television advertising across national frontiers. Our system is internationally envied by many who find strictly legal solutions inflexible and court procedures expensive and subject to delay, and we must make sure that 'harmonization' does not, for us, involve a step back.

Closed circuit

9.45. Movement in the corridors indicates that the time has come for the 'closed circuit' viewing session. The little ITCA viewing theatre is full. Except for secretaries all the ITCA Copy Clearance staff are present facing a cinema screen and two large television monitors. We all have an annotated copy of the day's list of films and tapes to be viewed. This is the final stage of clearance, when we see the scripts that we have approved translated by the agencies and production teams into finished commercials. Do they follow the agreed wording? Has any visual action crept in during production which was not clear from the script? Have size, scale, performance become exaggerated or misleading? There is an air of expectation as the reel begins.

We are not the only viewers – simultaneously, and in their own offices, the advertising control staff of the IBA and the individual programme companies are also watching. This is a confidential land-line transmission for copy clearance purposes only – no members of the public or advertisers can watch. Indeed, confidentiality is a fundamental principle of copy clearance. It would be disastrous if future advertising plans and details of product changes could leak to competitors. Today there are forty commercials on the reel and we ask for a second showing of those about which any points are in doubt. In the early days the programme companies were actively involved in copy decisions. Nowadays they join the viewing session mainly so that they are aware of those which impose on any commercials timing separations from certain programmes, in order to avoid impressions of sponsorship.

A daily conference

10.15 The viewing ends. We meet to agree which commercials can now be approved as they stand and which, if any, need amendment. Such has been the care taken at the earlier script-approval stage that only one or two in every hundred finished commercials need change. Today one featuring a special price offer has explanatory wording overlaid – a 'super' – saying 'Offer ends 31 December.' We think, on balance, that the size of type is too small to be read easily on the home screen. We shall ask the agency to make the 'super' larger.

10.30 The IBA telephones. We confer and agree on conclusions reached this morning. The IBA has the final word if disagreements persist.

10.45 We tell our traffic staff to tell the programme companies that all but one of today's commercials are cleared for transmission. We learn that that particular one is due for first transmission tonight, as the sale begins tomorrow. We reconsider – we agree we can fairly allow today's transmissions to go out with the 'super' unamended – but only today's.

11.00 Mark's group wants our opinion on a videotape. It's an American commercial for a toy – a model battery-driven car – which is being redubbed with English soundtrack. 'Is it OK as it stands?' the agency asks. They have sent us a specimen toy. Several ITCA volunteers run it down the corridors. We look at the tape again. Can the real size be appreciated? Yes, a child is seen with it to give it scale. Does it work as shown? Yes, we've tried it. We agree it's OK if they add two big 'supers': 'Batteries not included' and 'Price around £7.'

The special part of the IBA code which deals with advertising and children has been constantly refined over the years to make sure children are not misled. Naturally there is a lot of toy advertising before Christmas and some critics claim that this can make children unhappy and parents upset. Neither the IBA nor ITCA have found evidence for this. Many of us are parents. We believe that children live in a real world and know that they cannot expect lots of expensive gifts at Christmas. Like the rest of us they like to dream and choose. And parents are usually quite robust enough to say 'No!' or 'Too expensive!' But we do insist on a price indication for each toy, so that Grandma will not have to go all the way to the shops before she finds out the price is beyond her means. Before inclusion the exact code amendment needed much discussion with the toy trade to ensure that it could work in practice, because the manufacturers who make and advertise toys do not control their retail prices in the shops.

11.45 Another script featuring children, this time for eggs, has come to Tom's group. 'Make sure they have a nourishing breakfast' is its theme, and a small boy is heard to say, 'I don't always eat all my school dinner, you know.' This we think is unacceptable. Children may get the idea that it's all right to leave their dinners uneaten if they've had a good breakfast. The agency disagrees – it is obvious that children cannot be expected always to eat everything offered at school. It is proper to remind parents of this. We shall ask the Copy Committee for its opinion.

12.00 A smell of cooking has pervaded the room. Steaming plates are brought in. Martin's group wants our opinion on a pie filling. 'You'll need a spoon for ordinary sloppy fillings,' says the script. 'Take a fork to ours.' We compare the product with two leading competitive brands. We find the word 'sloppy' disparaging and the product differences marginal. Amendments will be required, we decide.

The canteen staff has cooked for us a package convenience food – a curry. It smells great – even at this time of the morning. But no – it won't, we think, provide 'four generous helpings'.

12.10 The morning session goes on to cover a fluoride toothpaste claim put forward after extensive clinical trials assessed by our dental consultant, the Head of the School of Preventive Dentistry at a London teaching hospital; we shall need meetings with the advertiser and the consultant before any final script can be agreed.

12.20   Finally we learn of a new partwork publication which will, in monthly instalments, trace the history and effect of major philosophies and religions throughout history. Unless television is available for advertising, the advertiser will not proceed with plans to publish. The IBA, in consultation with the ITCA, will have to decide whether the partwork is 'directed to a religious end'. The Broadcasting Acts wisely forbid such advertising – and advertising directed to political ends, too.[14] Parliament concluded in the very beginning of ITV that it was wrong to allow time to be bought to influence opinions on such matters. We shall ask to see representative chapters, pictures and a list of contents, and find out whether the work is entirely a commercial venture. Will the intent or effect be to change opinion on religious matters?

We shall need the views of the Copy Committee, the IBA and probably of the IBA's legal advisers. Religious opinion has been upset in the past by the need to apply the law. Many thought it anomalous that an advertisement for the *New English Bible* had to be refused, while one for a partwork dealing with witchcraft and magic was accepted.

Many conversations

12.40   The meeting has gone on longer than usual. The group heads hurry back to their daily round of telephone calls and meetings and studying scripts. Nearly a hundred new scripts have been delivered, and preliminary views will be needed on every one before the day ends. Several urgent videotapes have come in for quick clearance. One is from a tabloid newspaper due on the air tonight. Its racy, spicy, sexy articles, if acted out on screen, can easily cause offence. The presenter's voice-over, packing into thirty seconds references to all the day's feature stories – plus some sensational nightie offers – is likely to become noisy and strident. This time several telephone calls, some indignation and a sense of humour get an acceptable solution.

A salesman calls

13.00   The Copy Committee Chairman has called to dispose of a long agenda over sandwiches and beer. He wants to inform himself about the many items which his Committee will have to consider tomorrow afternoon. The Chairman is experienced in copy problems, having served a number of years on the Committee. Committee and staff have a good working relationship based on mutual respect – official and commercial backgrounds complementing each other well.

It might be thought that, as salesmen, members of the Committee could be tempted to trim a possible adverse decision to avoid the possible loss to television of a valuable campaign. In fact, it is very rare for revenue to be at risk. Alternative creative approaches to copy can almost always be found. Furthermore television Heads of Sales of necessity have robust attitudes. Their daily discussions with agencies and advertisers over the sale of television time are likely to be far more abrasive than any difference over the acceptance of copy. The uncommercial IBA presence and overview is, however, a formal assurance of lack of bias if one is required. Indeed, it needs to be said that advertisers do not seek to apply commercial pressures. Television advertising is a small world, a professional world, where good reputations and trust are highly valued.

A matter of comparison

15.15   The Chairman stays to meet the marketing director of a large manufacturer of soaps and detergents with his agency counterpart. They have come, in strict confidence, to outline plans to launch a campaign for one of their major brands of washing powders which has been improved. They present to us technical evidence on the reformulation of the product, with the details of practical washing and wearing tests which have been carried out to measure the new product's performance against that of its competitors. They also outline the kind of copy approach and claims they will be making. This is a highly competitive field – the different manufacturers are constantly making improvements in a wide range of products and they need to communicate these to the public by making the strongest possible comparison in their advertising against those of their rivals and indeed against their own former brands. To this end testing is highly sophisticated – needing to take account of different fabrics, machines, water softness and temperatures, types of staining and soiling as well as variations in home-usage patterns. Any new claim which they can justify to us may well require us to obtain the adjustment of claims currently being made by rivals. Significant commercial benefits may hinge on the possible claims.

In the early days, advertising of washing products was the category most often criticized. It caused annoyance because of a great weight of seemingly unreal and exaggerated claims for superiority. 'Whiter than white' is still quoted as the archetypal meaningless slogan, probably unfairly if one looks at the astonishing differences between what used to be regarded by housewives as white and the whiteness now achieved by modern technology. Attempts at side-by-side comparisons of whiteness had to be forbidden as the limitations of the television screen could not provide a fair representation. Some comparisons were suspect because the test methodology was faulty in not measuring like against like.

Matters rapidly improved after the ITCA had appointed leading independent experts in detergency as consultants. In separate discussions with the manufacturers concerned, a set of test procedures were laid down to form a basis for the making of justified comparisons. Comparisons came to be more sensibly based on specific advantages under defined conditions rather than on generalized claims for overall superiority. It became the practice for the ITCA's consultants to make periodic visits to the manufacturers' development and testing laboratories and to keep broadly in touch with the current research aims of each. The meeting today will enable the ITCA to brief its consultant and to prepare for changed stances in the rival advertising campaigns.

To judge the justification of comparative claims is one of the most difficult of the ITCA's copy functions. While evidence submitted can be put to one or other of ITCA's specialized consultants and studied for flaws, there is always the danger that the research is incomplete or based on methodology which somehow favours the product concerned.

As all submissions are made to the ITCA in confidence, it obviously cannot invite a rival to comment on them. Only later, when the advertising has appeared, does a rival have the opportunity to rebut the claims. Such, however, is the care taken initially that it is rare for an objection to be sustained. There is no doubt, however, that the expert knowledge of competing manufacturers and their readiness to take issue with any advertising presentations that they find unfair does help the IBA and ITCA to eliminate possible misleading elements.

To see ourselves as others see us

16.15 Still with the Chairman, we visit the offices of a large advertising agency with an outstanding reputation for its creative work on television commercials. Over the past few months we have had tense exchanges as some people within the agency resent what seems to them to have been a narrow and over-sensitive attitude on our part. We give them a brief presentation on our role and function and then get down to specific criticisms. A failure to communicate fully the reasons for our decisions is at the root of some of the heat – and this criticism is dissipated by this opportunity to explain them. But not all of them accept the need to be as cautious as we are on matters of taste. 'Outdated Victorian attitudes. . . double standards. . . inconsistent with programme content. . . ,' they continue. 'Perhaps, but. . . ,' we rejoin. There are no winners, but personal confrontation does at least serve to put a human face to an imagined stony bureaucracy.

A round of final questions: 'What about complaints? How do you judge whether you have got things right or wrong?' Public reaction is the best indicator – and from time to time the IBA transmits announce-ments inviting viewers to comment. Each month about a hundred such comments and some complaints come in by letter or telephone. Most are reflections of personal likes and dislikes of the goods or services advertised, or the style of presentation of the advertisement. Some result from mishearing what has been said – or from mere suspicions that the claims cannot be substantiated.

Response to complaints

All these complaints are, of course, investigated and answered – usually by the IBA as the body statutorily responsible. A few are found to be justified, and the commercial has to be changed or withdrawn. A recent IBA Annual Report gives a typical year's total:

An airline omitted to add a 'two or more persons' qualification in a fare offer; a driving school commercial omitted a necessary copy detail; a dental fixative was felt, on review, to be slightly exaggerating the benefit; an umbrella 'New from America' was in fact made in the Far East and only marketed through a US company; a newspaper commercial led with a 'ban the bomb' story that was presented in a biased way; a Scottish magazine could not wholly substantiate its 'fastest selling' claim – although it subsequently did so; an electric typewriter offer did not include VAT in its price; an amusement park commercial mentioned two facilities that were not quite ready when the transmission started; a special telephone handset offer contained a legally-required superimposed reference that was not large enough to be read easily; and a computer system omitted to include mention of a monitor component that was a necessary adjunct and involved extra cash.[15]

In factual matters, of course, only one justified complaint is necessary for action to follow. Where more general offence or harm is alleged, some evidence of significant public affront is needed – but quite a small postbag of responsible opinion will sound warning signals at the IBA and ITCA. On rare occasions, the full planned programme of transmission of a commercial has had to be curtailed.

Sometimes remedial change is made with the full cooperation of the advertiser. The Central Office of Information, for example, made a public-service commercial to explain to young children the Green Cross Code. A 'Superman' hero 'kept watch' from on high, and if he saw children about to cross the road carelessly he would 'magic down' to chide them and see them safely across. However, a number of parents wrote to say that children were being deliberately careless so that 'Superman' would appear! A solution was quickly found by adding a final comment by 'Superman' – 'But I shan't be with *you* when *you* cross the road.'

There was a far less happy outcome to complaints about a Christmas advertisement of a large multiple store. To illustrate the wide range of goods on offer it chose the comedian, the late Tommy Cooper, as presenter. Dressed as a small boy, he was shown in Santa's Grotto in a department store. The store's Santa was seen pressing gifts on Tommy, who tried unsuccessfully to explain his preference for a football game. Santa took Tommy off-stage, but Tommy sneaked back alone and, playing to the audience, took the football game he wanted.

As soon as the commercial was shown there were telephone calls and letters from viewers who felt that Tommy's actions seemed to condone stealing. Three organizations in particular – the Oxford Street Association, the Association for the Prevention of Theft in Shops and the National Consumer Protection Council – referred indignantly to the growing problem of shoplifting, especially at Christmas. 'The fact that this shoplift appears to be fun makes it all the more reprehensible and can do nothing except encourage people, especially young children, to take advantage of situations in which they are not under scrutiny.'

The advertiser responded angrily that it was total nonsense to suggest that it would contemplate advocating shoplifting, and that the commercial would be seen by all responsible persons as a good-natured pantomime in Tommy Cooper's well-loved zany style. This, indeed, had been the impression of the ITCA and IBA staff when the commercial was accepted. There was, however, no ignoring the strength of feeling from responsible people that it could lead young people into harm and might contribute to a serious social problem. After a review which went as far as the IBA Director-General and Chairman, it was most reluctantly concluded that the commercial must be withdrawn.

Did the ITCA and IBA fail the advertiser by not having refused the commercial in the first place – or by not standing by its acceptance, once made? Perhaps – but without the benefit of hindsight an initial refusal would have seemed absurdly harsh, and later, in the light of informed criticism, continuation would have seemed irresponsible. Neither the IBA nor the ITCA present themselves as omnipotent, and both make it clear that an acceptance of an advertisement can never be unqualified. Nevertheless, such reversals are as painful as they are rare.

Research into attitudes to television advertising is regularly conducted by the IBA both generally and in relation to specific product fields. For example, public reactions to experimental campaigns for sanitary towels and tampons have been studied to determine whether, and under what restraints, this category may be acceptable. Similarly, the possibility of permitting advertising of contraceptives, strongly advocated by some on social grounds, but equally strongly rejected by others as offensive, has been studied.

At best, however, research results can give only the broadest guidance – if strong antipathy is shown by only a small percentage of a poll it has to be remembered that this, translated into numbers, amounts to hundreds of thousands of viewers.

18.00 We gratefully accept a drink from our hosts and go on talking and arguing about the permanently exciting world of advertising. And then this imaginary but typical ITCA day has ended.

On the train home, however, echoes of the last questions linger. 'Can the success of the copy control system be measured?' Probably only by asking another question. 'Does anyone give it much thought?'

Earlier we took a brief look at the concerns, the allegations, the criticisms put forward during ITV's early years, at the reservations of the sociologists, politicians and consumerists. They were once able to ask in all seriousness whether advertising would ever be an acceptable basis on which to support a respectable, successful public service of television. Now, advertising standards seldom make news. Most of the old fears have gone. Both the advertising business and the public are broadly content. The most recent independent inquiry, the Annan Committee, found that 'on the whole the procedures of the IBA for vetting advertisements stand up well to criticism and yet are not too onerous on the advertisers'[16] and in a major speech in 1985 Lord Whitelaw – a distinguished former Home Secretary – could deliver his conclusions on thirty years of Independent Television without once mentioning advertising standards.[17]

The future, especially the international future, will throw up new problems and challenges which will need to be faced squarely and without complacency, but today politicians and broadcasters can without reservation make plans for advertising to fund the next generation of national and international broadcasting services. From the inside copy controls will go on, day by day, as they have since 1955, testing the good judgement of those who impose them. If from the outside they can stay largely unnoticed, that will be a fair yardstick of their success.

References

1 A.S.T. Bester, *Advertising Reconsidered*, quoted by F.P. Bishop, *The Ethics of Advertising*, Robert Hale Ltd, 1949.
2 Vance Packard, *The Hidden Persuaders*, Longmans, Green and Co. Ltd, 1957, p.5.
3 *Ibid.*
4 Lord Aylestone, address to the Advertising Association, reported in *Campaign*, 16 July 1971.
5 Report of the Committee on Broadcasting 1960, HMSO, Cmnd 1753, para. 243.
6 Final Report of the Committee on Consumer Protection, HMSO, Cmnd 1781, para. 781.
7 *Ibid*, para. 778.
8 *Ibid*, para. 779.
9 Report of the Committee on Broadcasting 1960, HMSO, Cmnd 1753, para. 249.
10 *Ibid*, para. 255.
11 Independent Broadcasting Authority Act 1973, Section 4.
12 Lord Aylestone, 'Television and Public Taste', *ITA Notes*, May 1971.
13 Sir John Richardson Bt, MVO, MA, MD, FRCP, Symposium of the Royal Society of Medicine, *ITA Notes*, August 1969.
14 Independent Broadcasting Authority Act 1973, schedule 2, para. 3.
15 IBA Annual Report and Accounts 1983–84, p. 64.
16 Report of the Committee on the Future of Broadcasting, HMSO, Cmnd 6753, para. 12.17.
17 Lord Whitelaw, the Robert Fraser Lecture, 'Thirty Years of Independent Broadcasting', June 1985.

Commercial Production

JAMES GARRETT

JAMES GARRETT

James Garrett, Chairman of the group of companies bearing his name, received his early training in production with British Transport Films, which he joined in 1948. Six months before the start of Independent Television he joined a company specializing in the making of commercials for the new medium, and a year later moved to one of the largest of the commercial production houses – TVA (Television Advertising), a company making not only film commercials but also entire advertising magazines under contract to several of the ITV programme companies.

He left TVA in 1963 to set up James Garrett and Partners. The company has grown to such an extent that it today operates in the United States, Germany and South Africa in addition to the UK. Other companies have been formed in the James Garrett Group in the areas of industrial and scientific films and documentaries.

James Garrett has been an active member of the film industry trade union, the ACTT, of which he has been a Council member and Vice-President. He was also for a number of years Chairman of the advertising producers' trade association, the AFVPA.

He was adviser on television to the Conservative Party from 1969 to 1974

Everybody's somebody in the Royal Navy.

Royal Navy officers recruitment (Young & Rubicam).

Rowntrees Polo – the journeys of Marco Polo (J. Walter Thompson).

Bob Martin's 'Just like Eddie' (Waldron Allen Henry & Thompson)

Henkel Solvite (Bowden Dyble Hayes)

e development of a brand:
bonnet (Dorland Advertising).

'Happiness is a cigar called Hamlet'.

Hamlet Cigars 'Channel 5' (Collett Dickenson Pearce).

Hamlet Cigars motorcycle an sidecar (Collett Dickenson Pearce).

Krona Margarine Rene Cutforth in Australia (Davidson Pearce).

Coca-Cola 'I'd like to teach the world to sing' (McCann-Erickson).

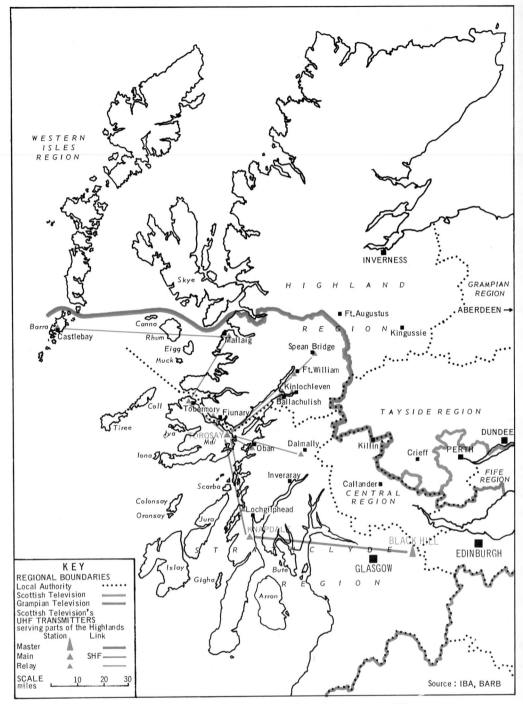

An example of transmitter and marketing boundaries (see page 152)

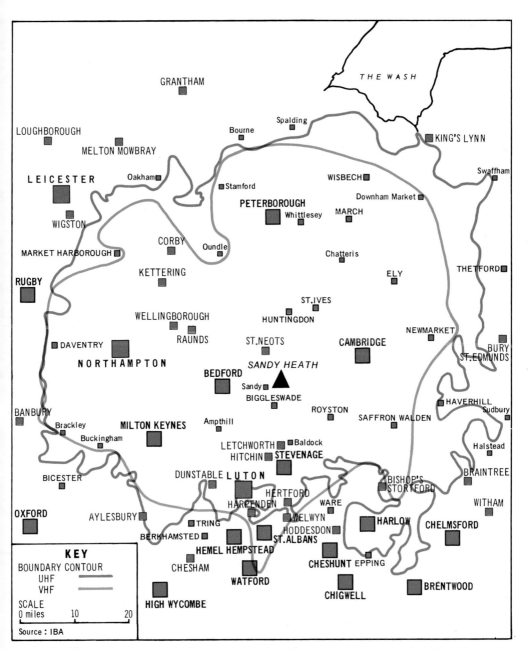

THE WASH

GRANTHAM

LOUGHBOROUGH
MELTON MOWBRAY
Bourne
Spalding
KING'S LYNN
LEICESTER
Oakham
Stamford
WISBECH
Swaffham
WIGSTON
Downham Market
PETERBOROUGH
Whittlesey
MARCH
MARKET HARBOROUGH
CORBY
Oundle
Chatteris
THETFORD
KETTERING
ELY
RUGBY
WELLINGBOROUGH
ST.IVES
NEWMARKET
DAVENTRY
RAUNDS
HUNTINGDON
ST.NEOTS
CAMBRIDGE
BURY ST.EDMUNDS
NORTHAMPTON
SANDY HEATH
BEDFORD
Sandy
BIGGLESWADE
ROYSTON
HAVERHILL
Sudbury
BANBURY
Brackley
MILTON KEYNES
Ampthill
SAFFRON WALDEN
Halstead
Buckingham
LETCHWORTH
Baldock
BRAINTREE
BICESTER
DUNSTABLE
HITCHIN
STEVENAGE
BISHOP'S STORTFORD
OXFORD
LUTON
HERTFORD
WARE
WITHAM
AYLESBURY
HARPENDEN
WELWYN
HARLOW
CHELMSFORD
TRING
HODDESDON
BERKHAMSTED
ST.ALBANS
HEMEL HEMPSTEAD
CHESHUNT
EPPING
CHESHAM
BRENTWOOD
WATFORD
CHIGWELL
HIGH WYCOMBE

KEY
BOUNDARY CONTOUR
UHF
VHF
SCALE
0 miles   10   20
Source : IBA

The difference between UHF and VHF coverage from the same site Note particularly the gains and losses of important marketing centres as a result of duplication of the service. The problem was vastly more complicated when VHF and UHF were radiated from different sites (see pages 112-113).

Channel 4 was introduced on 2 November 1982.

The launch of TV-am 1 February 1983.

ON a visit to New York some years ago, I came across a book which I thought might be of interest to a politician friend of mine. I brought it back, gave it to him and to my surprise he looked not at the flyleaf, not at the preface, but at the index. It was a salutary lesson on how the great and the good assess the interest to them of any publication. It's got nothing to do with the subject matter or the quality of the writing – it's to do with the number of references made to them personally between the covers.

So for those of you of like mind, you had better skip this chapter. The production of commercials over this last thirty years has been to do with people above everything else. But to have dwelt on the contribution, both positive and negative, of the hundreds of people who have strutted on our stage during that time would have been a distraction for you and a confusion for me. So the world I shall so subjectively present to you is devoid of names, corporate or individual. Yet, of course, there have been heroes galore, and I dedicate this chapter, for what that's worth, to all those who have worked, cared and contributed by thought, word and deed to create what I firmly believe to be the finest production business in the world.

The present has always been interesting and demanding, the future exciting, beckoning us into tomorrow with unrelenting persistence. As for the past – it's largely irrelevant. This is probably true of most other spheres of activity and endeavour, but I am sure that it is particularly true of the imprecise commercial world of advertising and for those of us who serve in it.

Having said that, we all inevitably have recourse to the past, for a variety of reasons and motives – precedence, reassurance, nostalgia – but we re-enter it with all the benefit of hindsight. We delve selectively, subjectively and usually secretively – and always from the inescapable reality of the present.

The idea of taking a backward somersault to 1955 and writing a mildly definitive account of the first thirty years of the production of commercial messages suddenly became very daunting – even more so when I discussed the proposition with surviving contemporaries and fellow contributors. For I found that we had all lived through a totally different thirty years and that our perspectives of that span of time were all quite different. Our memories depended on a number of factors – on where we came from in 1955, because inevitably we all came to television advertising from somewhere else; on how we had used the three decades or on how they had used us; on the pattern of our successes and our failures; and on how we had been judged by the people who were succeeding us.

We had only one thing in common – this totally different perception. It was as if we had been living in differing ages, but in practice we were all inhabiting the islands of our minds, part of the atoll of commercial television, but separated from each other by the seas of subjective recollection.

So I leave to others the facts and figures, the dates and data, the *post hoc* rationalization of those burgeoning years of a successful medium and take you on a conducted tour of my very own island.

In the beginning

When the definitive book on commercial lobbying in the twentieth century comes to be written, the success of the interests which caused commercial television to come into being might well be hailed as one of the greatest achievements for vested interest of that period. The commercial television medium was conceived as a vehicle for gain – carefully, skilfully lobbied into being by a strange hotchpotch of people who knew that, if it came to pass, there would be something, largely undefined, in it for them. There was no real public clamour for an alternative to the BBC's service. The 'demand' was very largely an invention of the self-interested.

Only a small minority of advertisers had any positive understanding of its potential, and most of those were American. As for the rest, their support, such as it was, stemmed as much from a dislike, hatred even, for the postwar, newsprint-rationed, arrogant newspapers and a longing for a means of cutting them down to size as from any real belief in their need for, or ability to exploit, a new medium.

As for the agencies, most of them were fearful of change and largely unconvinced either that the medium would be effective or even that it would last. There were exceptions, of course, but some agencies went to the lengths of employing expendable people so that when – when, not if – the experiment failed, the names of the 'specialists' could be expunged from the club, and the old membership left unscathed. A dweller on another island, who in 1955 managed a large agency, recalled to me that early in 1955 he held a meeting with all his clients to discuss the advisability of using the new medium. The debate centred around the proposition that the introduction of messages into the homes of the masses might create an over-awareness of advertising which would work against the established acceptance of it in other media. He and his colleagues obviously decided to brave the unknown, for that agency went on to be an early and notably successful proponent of television advertising.

So this was the climate in which we, the makers of messages, came into being. It was a hesitant experiment in an advertising society which was only just beginning to develop some commercial confidence and purpose after a long war and a socialist-dominated, austere, rationed decade.

There was an embryonic commercial production business which existed to provide messages for the infant screen advertising business, but it had neither the capacity nor the management intellect and interest to make it the natural rock upon which to build the new church. It was, after all, on the side of a different God who resided in the cinema. And television, once these people discovered that they could not extract some media-owning benefit from it, had no attraction purely as a source of low-cost production volume. But demand did produce supply – some of it provided by the wrong people for the wrong reasons, but some through sensible, intelligent effort to understand and to articulate the needs of a new, uncharted, largely inarticulate business.

Inevitably mistakes were made, the greatest of them being to turn to America for our precedents. We were, after all, only the second major society to introduce advertising on television, so there was nowhere else to look. But it is always a mistake to look westwards for any parallel in advertising and communications. No two societies in the world are wholly alike, and it has been proved foolish to try to transfer, intact, from one country to another any system or philosophy. The differences of culture, language, politics, history and economic circumstances between societies so outweigh the common factors – of product, advertiser, consumer, media and supplier that we seldom make the attempt. But America always tempts us for the obvious reasons that we appear to share a language and, more importantly, because it is the birthplace of so many of the products and services which we serve and sell. As a society, too, it has a marvellously blinkered missionary zeal and confidence which we British find conveniently, insidiously, attractive. The irony is that American television advertising was at that time in a state of transition anyway, with sponsored programming giving way to network-originated production and live commercials losing out to filmed spot commercials. So it was not, in practice, a very sound model.

So from America, and an America in a state of change, we borrowed ideas about the style and form of messages and confused ourselves with the irrelevance of excellently written sixty-second films when our mandate was largely confined to anything from seven to thirty seconds' length. Agencies introduced systems devised to serve the needs of another culture. We imported 'experts', many of whom hung on tenaciously to their jobs long after they had been found wanting. We also went to the French for style and taste, greener grass and better food. These and other mistakes were all good formative stuff. Lessons learned by trial and error, as long as they are identified quickly and consciously, are usually good and lasting ones. Out of that initial, mainly pre-start-up time we learned, or ought to have, that there are no absolute precedents to be found in other societies, that good and effective nationals seldom gravitate from primary to secondary markets for the right reasons, and that the creative product of one culture is, as often as not, unsuited to another.

There was one other inescapable reality which quite profoundly affected the coming into being of a commercial production business, and that was the antagonism towards television in general and commercials in particular which prevailed in the 'establishment' film industry. Everyone concerned with the so-called 'legitimate' feature-film world regarded this upstart new service – quite rightly as it transpires – as a very real threat to their already ailing cinema-entertainment business. This distrust, hatred even, manifested itself in a whole host of ways – and it is important to remember that in those days there were no great independent suppliers of equipment and other support services to whom we could turn. Studios, laboratories, equipment, people were, for the most part, financially, emotionally or morally, owned by, and committed to, a world that rejected commercial television and all its works.

So our world was one in which it was considered *infra dig* for feature film people to work on commercials, in which major film studios turned down our miserly one- or two-day bookings out of hand. Indeed, they had no means of accommodating us and, if they had, their prices would have been prohibitive. We found laboratories unwilling and probably unable to deal with the timescales of our needs and the short-footage nature of our end product, and we found performers of any note spurning the prospect of lending themselves to commercial messages. In a word, we were pariahs in the eyes of all the existing support facilities so essential to our work – support systems under-used and available to us in principle, and yet denied to us.

There was one important exception to all this, and that was the documentary arm of the industry. It had existed and evolved through sponsorship, sometimes oblique and obscure in purpose, but it provided at least one body of talented and skilled people, with resources to match, who understood and accepted that it was reasonable to receive money in return for producing a message with a commercial purpose. Admittedly, that message was usually thirty minutes and not thirty seconds long, but that Mammon was alive, well and not wholly undesirable as a next-door neighbour was not difficult for them to accept. So it was largely out of the documentary sponsored film world that our commercials-production industry was born. I am personally certain of this, because it was from its ranks in the form of the highly virtuous British Transport Films that I came to advertising production in June 1955, three months before the off.

In retrospect it was a very uncertain world, with no experts, no expertise, no confidence and no predictable future. Yet, thirty years ago, it was exciting, challenging, exacting and stimulating. It has been that way ever since, and I would not have missed the experience for the world.

Thirty years of change: the three stages

For me, the advertising-production business has been in a state of pretty constant change since its very beginning. There have been mildly stagnant patches, caused in the main by political and economic uncertainty, but they have been of surprisingly short duration and we have had nothing to parallel the lost creative decade that America experienced between 1970 and 1980, or the media stagnation endured for even longer by some of our European neighbours. Indeed, positive change has come about in Britain, induced quite often by forces and circumstances which in other societies would have decimated the medium and reversed rather than stimulated the growth and confidence of the production industry which serves it. We are indeed a perverse nation.

It is convenient to break up the thirty years into boxes, if only for narrative purposes, and in my subjective view three lines can be drawn through the period which mark the more discernible changes of purpose and direction. The first two are subdivisions of what I have called 'the first revolution' and the third, which we have just entered, I regard as the beginning of what will prove to be the second. My three stages along the thirty-year road are:

1 The first revolution – the growing-up years.
2 The coming-of-age period.
3 The second revolution – journey into the unknown.

The growing-up years, 1955 – 69

These were the formative years. During this time we moved from being a motley bunch of companies and individuals who came together to make commercials for the new medium by chance as much as anything else, and became a reasonably coherent, purposeful supplier business.

As I said earlier, in 1955 we all came from somewhere else and had been doing something else before we started working in advertising. The majority of us came to agency television departments and to production companies from documentary film-making. However, much recruitment took place, especially by agencies, from the remoter areas of the unemployed of the feature-film world, from the theatre, from commercial radio – from any area of activity concerned with entertainment or the making of messages. No one came from advertising itself for the obvious reason that there was no one qualified or confident enough to make that sort of move.

On the production-company side, we joined or reinforced specialist units which were started up by established major documentary companies as adjuncts to their existing business. Others of us became part of new companies which came into being specifically to service the new medium. It is worth recalling that very real investment was needed in the business at that time, and of an order which companies today neither volunteer nor are expected to make, to enter the list of suppliers.

Of course, investment – working capital – was essential because we ourselves had to provide for the needs of our business to a degree and in a way which subsequent changes to the fabric of the film industry have made unnecessary. We had, for instance, to own all our equipment and our studios, for our business was almost entirely studio-based throughout most of this period. We had an urgent need for people to carry out a whole host of new roles, so we started by sifting through the ranks of the unemployed to separate the employable from the unemployable. For although the hard core of our effective people came out of documentary films, we got saddled at the start with the feature-film union agreements — ironic in view of the fact that the industry had rejected us.

This meant that our cosy four-man documentary crews had to be augmented by a further eight people if we were to record sound, and all at feature film rates, so we had to find these extra numbers from somewhere. We had to discover by trial and error who could adjust to our time and length scales. We had to pick out people who could be effective by the hour and the day rather than by the week and the month. They also had to be mentally agile and flexible enough to think about, plan and especially edit more than one subject at a time. It was the time of the proliferating church hall/studio, when we would employ a cameraman because he owned equipment and not necessarily because he was a good photographer.

We had to educate laboratories not just to handle our work at all but to provide us with a service. Negative cutting, to take only one example, used to take days and we needed it done in hours. We had to invent or create recording and dubbing facilities which would work by the half-hour rather than by the day. And we had to develop our own machinery for casting and contracting artists since, with one or two exceptions, all this had to be done by the production house.

For many of these reasons the business was service-dominated, for while we were coming to terms with this new industry so too were the agencies and, most importantly, our mutual clients. We were all finding out what each of us wanted, who was or was not trustworthy, who cared, who delivered, who was prepared to invest in the future, and a whole host of other things as well. Understandably the emphasis was, first of all, on actually getting films made at all — frequently it was not 'alright on the night', and then on achieving standards of service and execution that were predictable.

This service domination resulted in the concentrating of production in those companies which owned facilities and services, and eight years after the start something like 70 per cent of the production volume was being contracted with, say, no more than twelve production companies. Most of these were owned (at arm's length) by old-established organiz-ations or by absentee shareholders who had started up production houses in 1955 purely as an investment.

The year 1963 was when change began to happen for me. It was then that I started my own production company and I went overnight from co-managing for my absentee landlords a facility-owning company – studios, dubbing theatre, equipment and, unbelievably, a hundred-plus people – to my own set-up. We had just six people, no bricks and mortar, no hardware, but a lot of hope and, on the surface anyway, great confidence that what I was doing represented the way in which the world was going.

So during the latter half of this first stage, the commercials business became a business in the true sense of the word and started developing the form which, in the main, it has today – an owner-operated, subjective, people-dominated service industry. In case this sounds as though I am suggesting that alone we did it, I should make it clear that our evolution must be viewed in the context of the agencies and their needs. We are, after all, gentlemen's gentlemen's gentlemen. It is our job to respond to our immediate client, the agency, and I have always believed that, while we are physically separate, for much the same reason that the agency is separate from the advertiser, we are in reality a logical extension of the agency's service to its client, the advertiser. If we are clever or lucky, or both, we will understand the form and the pace of agency evolution – anticipate it even, if the gods are kind – but the changes that happened to us were essentially advertiser- and agency-led. That, though, is someone else's story.

So what was happening in those first fourteen years? Well, admags came and went – those fifteen-minute programmes with ten minutes of advertising artificially woven into a narrative form. It was sad in a way, because they made it possible for certain kinds of advertisers and agencies to use the medium, sometimes very effectively. They were, I suppose – again with the benefit of hindsight – at times embarrassing but they were part of our past. Along with cigarette advertising, admags were the most obvious casualties of that period.

A very good and lasting production contract was thrashed out between agencies and producers which has proved to be a very fair and enduring basis for the business conducted between us. The rules and conditions, worked out so laboriously nearly thirty years ago, were equitable and gave proper recognition to the partnership that is the essence of our association. It is probably too British to work in other societies, but it has served us all well more as a code of practice than as a legal document, and long may it last. Its existence and its observance, particularly in spirit, have been of extraordinary significance in fashioning the form of our business as it exists today, and have contributed in no small measure to its vitality and probity.

The recruitment of talent became a positive process rather than a negative one. New sources of directors were tapped, first from television, then from feature films where pretentious resistance to the idea of directing commercials was broken down by the investments of vision and money, by one agency in particular. Stills photographers joined the ranks of the commercials makers and, finally, respected agency creative people who were the first television generation and had lived with and developed an understanding of the medium from early adolescence. We were also growing our own first generation of skills in other craft areas – in the camera, editing and art departments – the new first-generation people who would contribute so effectively to the next phase. Performing talent relented, too, perhaps encouraged by the reputations and skills of directors who had come to our table, and actors and actresses from all strata of their profession started to endorse products at a price – always at a price.

In case this sounds like a world made up entirely of live-action production, it would be right and proper to record that from the very inception of commercial television the cartoonists, the animators, served the system well. In many ways, perhaps because they were already members of a cottage industry who came together from time to time to make a long film and then dispersed again, their individualism manifested itself earlier. From the very beginning good and effective animation commercials were flowing from both established and new companies. The early arrival of a small number of trans-Atlantic cousins gave a boost to our indigenous talent and, throughout the whole span of thirty years, animation in Britain has rightly earned a reputation for design innovation and advertising purpose. Perhaps it has something to do with the nature and form of animation, but it has always seemed to me the least self-indulgent and wasteful way of conveying advertising purpose. From 1955 to the present day some of the campaigns most indelibly stamped on my mind owe their memorability for me to the pen rather than the camera.

This whole process of evolution was aided by the break-up of the smokestacks of the feature-film industry. As many of the major studios were sold off and the makers of such longer films that were made discovered the virtues of location shoots and four-wall studios, so there came into being effective, flexible, independent suppliers of all those services that had been denied us in the early days. They included equipment-hire firms; independent set-construction services; new, untied studio space; specialist editing houses; new sound companies, many of them inspired into being by advertising production – all of them receptive to the nature and needs of our business. Even the film laboratories in their hour of need and declining feature-film volume started to recognize our virtue – or was it our worth?

So change was happening, positive change, aided and encouraged by similar evolutionary changes in client companies and agencies. Television advertising was the common denominator in the rise or decline of advertisers as companies and as individuals, in the market share of brands, in the growth or failure of old agencies and in the emergence of the new. Change – television-led change – was a rampant force in advertising, and to accelerate it along came colour.

The coming-of-age period, 1969–81

This has been easily the most formative and interesting period of the whole three decades. It is again impossible to write about evolution and change in my world without some reference to the general climate in which we operated and to the changes which took place in advertising – changes that are still going on – because we are the by-product of the business of advertising – not a profession but a business. Just as it adapts and evolves to meet the changing needs of the clients in a modern society, so too do we.

It is not for symbolic reasons that I have taken the arrival of colour as a turning-point in our business. It crystallized and accelerated processes which had of course been going on over the earlier phase, but its advent marked the start of a period which produced some fairly fundamental shifts in our social, political and economic worlds. All of these contributed to a decade which transformed many aspects of the way in which the communications business functions.

During this time we saw Britain's hesitant entry into Europe; long, bewildering periods of inflation; wild fluctuations in exchange rates; at least three quite fundamental changes in political management; the continued decline of our old industrial base; and the consequent rise in imported products of all kinds. These changes were accompanied by the growth of retail advertising and, in fact, the 'retailization' of all advertising resulting from economic pressures and decline; the upsurge of consumerism; a drift towards greater regulation; the increasing influence of marketing and research; and the spread of the cult of multinationalism and protectionism. It was a period of new attitudes, sometimes reinforced by the authority of law, towards the way in which the labouring agency is deemed worthy of its hire. The passing or assimilation of some of the postwar-wearied older agencies and the coming into being of the new ones, with their rather different philosophies and contemporary ethics, and the growing practice among agencies to go public, brought with it different motivations and radically altered their decision-making processes. And, of course, there was the firm establishing of a new scale of values for talent of all kinds within the agency system and its resultant tendency to disturb the economic ecology of the service business as a whole. With these forces at work in our society over the twelve-year period from 1969, it is small wonder that the production business changed, happily very largely for the better.

The first fourteen years had put us into pretty good shape and we adjusted quickly to the demands and needs of the changing world in which we served. As none of these shifts was planned or predicted, even by the most prescient of agency managements, it meant that all we could do was to follow and adapt as quickly as we could. In truth, we were all too happy to do so. Innovation and leadership are difficult to establish and sustain and, like the people we serve, if only on a microcosmic scale, our business is on the whole seriously under-managed, and those of us who succeed do so, initially anyway, through chemical accident rather than by some grand, well-thought-through, long-term plan. So following – always, I hope, constructively – is inevitably less exacting than leading.

But to return to colour. . . its advent triggered off one of the most significant changes of the period, for it resulted in agency control of the production of the message shifting decisively from the Television Department to the Creative Department. Until then, the agency tele-vision experts had managed to perpetuate the myth that the production of messages was far too complicated and important to be entrusted to the people who created them. The wholesale introduction of colour changed all that, since the new and relevant values in film production were ones which had traditionally been the preserve of the creative departments in the areas of print. So authority shifted quite drama-tically and quickly to writers and art directors.

One of the most important results was the introduction of fashion into the production business. Up to then, those of us who were deemed virtuous were judged by different criteria and, while these were not wholly superseded by the new order, a new permissiveness strode into the marketplace – again not, perhaps, by chance in view of what was going on in the world at large. Judgements and choice were arrived at by different people in different ways at a different cost to the advertiser.

It was the arrival of colour which triggered off the escalation of production costs. 'Colour '69', the BBTA conference held in January 1969, was designed to promote the advent of colour to the advertiser, to suggest to him the benefits that he would derive from it and, in part anyway, to reassure him that colour messages would not be inordinately expensive. At that conference the great and the good of the agency and production-company world made some predictions about the effect of colour on production costs.

Using as a basis for those prognostications the purely mathematical translation to colour rates of black-and-white film stock and processing, with a bit more added for extra lighting costs and wardrobe and a little bit more for luck, I seem to remember that we predicted with some confidence that the cost increase would be of the order of 25 per cent. Prices prevailing then were, for a thirty-second black-and-white commercial, on average £1800 – the production-house price to the agency. In 1955 the figure had probably been around £500. So in the first fourteen years, production costs had risen by between 300 and 400 per cent. One year later, in 1970, the cost of the average thirty-second commercial in colour had rocketed to over £3300, an increase near to 75 per cent.

Then during the seventies inflation in various degrees of severity came into the equation. To some extent it camouflaged the fundamental shift in production values and their true cost which had taken place over the previous fifteen years. This shift had a profound effect on the production business, in a world concerned with fashion, form, content and difference for difference's sake, sometimes to the exclusion of advertising purpose. It produced a business which is largely director/talent-led and fashion-conscious, in which cost is secondary to creative quality and form, which become an end in themselves.

Fashion has had at least one negative effect on the structure of the business because fashionability has, by very definition, the implication of transience. The lifespan of production companies has always been short. There is something about living by the day and the week rather than by the year which heightens the stresses and strains which occur in any group of disparate people. The factor of fashion, superimposed on business inherently frail in fabric and shallow of foundation, tended, over this period, to shorten the life expectancy of most companies, particularly the high fashion-based ones. Happily, however, the musical-chairs aspect of the process has caused very little real harm to the purpose of our business or, more fortunately, so far anyway, no very profound financial embarrassment to the world that we supply. On balance, this phase has resulted in this advertising society having at its disposal arguably the best production service in the world and one which is the envy of most other markets.

For this age has produced a whole generation of new and highly skilled talent. Happily anchored in the lee of advertising at a time when feature film-making was in the doldrums, and growth and opportunity in domestic television seemed to have evaporated, this new generation accepted that there was no place to go. They took optimum advantage of the chance to work regularly for a business which was prepared to put a premium on excellence and technical innovation. Over the period, advertising looked more and more to the world at large for inspiration and example, and grew to mirror, more immediately than ever before, trends and fashions with which viewing audiences were ready and willing to identify. All this proved attractive and valuable to our production people since it was, by chance rather than design, putting them in fine fettle to compete in the wider world outside the cloisters of advertising.

It was a phase when talent, home-grown and much of it – on the director side – drawn from advertising itself, became predictably available and the partnership, conspiracy even, between the creatively talented people in agencies and production companies was truly cemented. Scripts were written, not for clients, but for directors, or for execution in a form or style which it was known that the production business could deliver.

While this was a time of much indulgence and the end, in individual cases, did not always justify the means, I would confirm my contention that advertising in general benefited from the process. While the advertiser, sometimes unwittingly, has paid a very high premium for excellence, he has in return been rewarded with the massive bonus of the highest level of viewer acceptance of advertising achieved anywhere in the world. This stemmed from the fact that, right from the start of commercial television, he accepted that he was an uninvited visitor in people's homes; if they were to let him in at all, or to let him return regularly, then he had better behave politely, quietly and entertainingly. To those who were successful the prizes were often glittering.

So have they been for the elitist group of directors and technicians who were spawned in this period. The more adventurous and talented of them have gravitated into the world of entertainment production where their contemporary talents and skills have been harnessed to fill the sterile void of new people which America in particular faced throughout the seventies. Others, less adventurous perhaps, or less talented, now travel the world, the new missionaries or – better still – mercenaries, peddling our society's excellence to the creatively underdeveloped advertising communities that still abound.

I believe this period to be over, and while, somewhat forlornly, efforts are made to recapture the glory that was Rome, bands of the deprived – agency and production folk alike – comb our land looking for clones of lost heroes, hoping that perhaps by putting a high value on newcomers, they will somehow endow them with the talents of the old. The times, they are a-changing. We must recognize the change and work out how to turn it to the advantage of all of us who work in advertising.

The second revolution, c.1982 onwards

I have called the present period 'the second revolution' because that, I believe, is exactly the phase that we have entered. Most of us who came at a relatively early age into television advertising have been unbelievably lucky. We have had the almost unique career benefit of being in at the beginning of something totally new and then of growing up with it over thirty years. All we had to do was to accommodate perfectly natural change and predictable growth and to prevail in a business which in media value has grown from less than £10 million in Year One to something approaching £1000 million in Year Thirty.

For us in production, it has meant being part of a business which has grown from zero to perhaps £100 million over the same period. We have had it good – all of us – and very few of us have contributed materially to that growth. It has happened in spite of us. We have kept pace with it and developed alongside it but it has been virtually unstoppable organic growth of the most astonishing kind.

This luck of ours has been made even greater by the fact that, for most of this time, advertisers and agencies have been dealing essentially with a medium stagnant in form, give or take a station or two. For those of us who make the messages, the tools that we have been using have also remained largely unchanged, except for minor refinements in film-stock quality, lens definition, the design of lights, and camera and camera-related technology.

We have only had to deal with growth – not change. But change is again upon us, and not just in one area but across the board. In some ways, it's a bit like 1955 all over again. I have taken the year 1982 as the symbolic start of the second revolution because it heralded the arrival in our own marketplace of the new outlets for messages. They were, of course, breakfast-time television and Channel Four, both perfectly logical additions to the existing order but symbolic of media change. At roughly the same time the proportion of commercials which achieved their finished state on videotape rather than film – albeit most of them were originally shot on film – broke the 50 per cent barrier.

But what makes the present so fascinating is that on three major fronts – the dissemination of marketing messages, the nature of the form of those messages and the means by which they are recorded – we are faced with the prospect of tackling the new unknown. In all three areas, opportunities already exist which have been identified but not harnessed, or which perhaps already exist but are as yet unperceived. Technology, which used to follow our needs, is, for the first time in our lives, running ahead of our ability to understand and control it. And we are not dealing with quantum leaps which, having been made, result in set circumstances which we can analyse and with which we can come to terms at our leisure. We are suddenly engulfed in the process of change, ongoing change, at a time when the routine demands of the present are more exacting and energy-consuming than they have ever been before.

So, as the first thirty years comes to an end, we find ourselves firmly clinging to our past achievements, our known skills, and looking to our old gods for help and comfort. But in this new age the answers will not be found in the past. We who produce messages must turn to the people we traditionally serve for example and purpose, in the confidence that they will be forthcoming.

In facing up to this new revolution, we will have no excuses this time around about the technical resources available to us. Massive independent investment has been made in all the latest electronic hardware and the capacity and servicing systems existing in forms relevant to our business, supported by excellent specialist technicians. The onus is on us to make the running.

But the speed with which change has come upon us has left us a little breathless, and in some areas we are lagging behind its advance. On the media side, we see direct-advertiser money seeping away through new advertising vehicles which might well have been identified and encompassed by our traditional servicing system. We see commercials crossing frontiers which have not been conceived for that purpose. We are conscious of the fact that new media outlets such as cable are being neglected or ill-used.

Then there is the question of the new technologies of production, proliferating kaleidoscopically, as ordinary mortals, agency creative and production people, steeped in the values and the limitations of film over decades, strive to understand and employ this embarrassment of complex new riches. At this time we are struggling in the slipstream of technology's remorseless advance. We are using the new toys expensively and a little aimlessly. Creative work is being injected with electronic devices, often as a sleight-of-hand alternative to advertising purpose. Decision-making mechanisms designed for the technology of film are being applied to sophisticated and expensive new forms of message recording, which can result in the misuse of both time and money. We are, of course, learning as we go along – advertiser, agency and production company – at the moment often by default, trial and error and not necessarily through an awareness of the need to accommodate change. That will come.

The climate in which we producers are trading is also altering. The head is taking over from the heart, whether it be in the ranks of the advertiser demanding greater accountability from all his suppliers, agency and production company alike, or in the agencies, many of whom are now as openly committed to making money as to making messages – all perfectly reasonable, desirable even, if that is the way of the world, but certainly different.

We are (and will probably remain) a largely 'people' business, so now perhaps is the time to remind ourselves that we have been spoilt, over the last fifteen years in particular, because if people wanted to learn the trade of production, particularly film production, they really had to sit at the feet of advertising to do it. We got, and for a valuable span of time kept in the service of production, the very best emergent talent. As I said earlier, the drift away of that generation is well under way, and a void is beginning to develop in our supply pool – for a very good reason.

So much programme material is being generated now in Britain for consumption both here and abroad that emergent aspiring talent of all sorts no longer needs to consider spending time in the making of advertising messages as a fundamental part of the apprenticeship process. He/she can go straight from wherever it was that people came to us previously into other, more satisfying, job areas of production; so a very real fear is that we run the risk of becoming, as we were thirty years ago, a kind of repository for people who are not quite good enough to do anything else. We won't let it happen, of course, but in the future good people will need different arguments and incentives to make commercials, and it is in the interests of all of us to make sure that they are forthcoming. As the new attitudes become clear, we shall, in our chameleon-like way, adjust to them. Part of that adjustment process will be concerned with finding the right people for new or changing jobs – just as it was in 1955.

The shock of the new and its effects are not confined to our own narrow world of advertising production, and, as ever, we are only one link in a very long chain. But when the dust settles or at least clears, when major multinational clients have combined with other major multinational clients, when international agencies have merged and merged again, when the form of new messages, whether they span the world or repose within a videocassette, are conceived, we who produce commercials must be able to make those new messages in the right form, for the right price and with the right people, much as we have tried to do for the last thirty years.

So what's new?

The Effect of Television on Marketing

SIR RONALD HALSTEAD

SIR RONALD HALSTEAD

Sir Ronald Halstead was educated at Lancaster Royal Grammar School and Queens' College, Cambridge where he read natural sciences and gained an athletics 'blue'. He is a fellow of the Royal Society of Chemistry, the British Institute of Management and the Institute of Marketing. He has been awarded an honorary doctorate of Reading University and an honorary fellowship of Queens' College, Cambridge.

Sir Ronald was awarded the CBE for services to the food industry in 1976 and knighted in June 1985.

He joined the Beecham Group in 1954 and spent many years with the company in the United States becoming President of Beecham Research Laboratories Inc., the company formed to manufacture and market the new penicillins in the USA.

Sir Ronald returned to the UK in 1964 and was appointed to the Beecham group board in the same year. He was Chairman and Chief Executive of the group from July 1984 to November 1985 having previously been Managing Director (Consumer Products).

He is currently a governor of Ashridge Management College and a council member of the universities of Reading and Buckingham. He is Deputy Chairman of the British Steel Corporation and a director of American Cyanamid and of the Davy Corporation. He holds numerous other advisory appointments on various Government and industrial bodies. Sir Ronald is a former President of the ISBA and a past Vice-Chairman of the Advertising Association

T HE central theme which I want to explore is the learning process which has taken place over the last thirty years as marketers and the ITV companies have adapted their operations to fit each other's requirements more effectively. The interaction between these two groups – roughly, the buyers and sellers of television time – has been complex, and the business situation has changed considerably, but there is not the slightest doubt in my mind that the one certain and constant factor has been a major gain, directly to the good conduct of business in this country, and indirectly to the great benefit of the consumer.

What ITV has to offer its advertisers has obviously changed to some extent with changing circumstances – the growth in ITV set penetration from a few hundred thousand to virtually total coverage; the changes in the rules governing advertising; the immense strides made in the application of research to campaign planning; the rapid introduction of colour from 1969; improvements in television reception; and so on. But what matter above all are the opportunities for new marketing thinking which ITV opened up.

Television is often referred to as an educational medium, usually in contrast to its commercial functions. The thesis of this chapter is that its commercial functions have in themselves been highly educational, and that there are still many lessons which need to be learned if British industry is to continue to benefit fully from the medium's possibilities.

What television offered the marketer

We tend to forget what economic and social conditions were like thirty years ago. It takes a considerable conscious effort, even for those of us old enough to have been active in business in 1955, to recollect the business climate in Britain at that time, and particularly the rudimentary state of marketing. This was hardly surprising since in the previous fifteen years we had been through a war, followed by a decade of postwar austerity, during which the only problem for industry had been to produce. Just about anything which could be made and was not exported could be sold on the home market. Muscles which are not used suffer from atrophy, and this happened to the marketing function in many UK companies. It affected Beecham less than most of its rivals, but that was mainly because of the qualities of its Chairman, the remarkable H.G. Lazell.

I became aware of the difference between marketing in Britain and the USA when I went over to America in 1955 to help run the Beecham business there, and I took the opportunity to study marketing at the same time. In the USA the battle for sales was at full pitch, with television already ousting radio as the dominant medium for fast-moving consumer goods. But what particularly impressed me were the immense efforts put into marketing by American companies, and the almost total orientation of their activities in that direction. Americans had taken to heart Adam Smith's dictum that the end of production is consumption, and they made sure that their efforts were directed towards finding out what the consumer wanted, providing it, and then making sure that he (or more often she) knew it was there. It sounds simple, and although many years of experience have taught me that it is not as easy as it looks, one thing I know with absolute certainty is that, while you may not succeed even if you try, you will certainly never succeed if you don't try; and in 1955 most British firms, at least in as far as their domestic activities were concerned, were so production-oriented that they hardly interested themselves in marketing at all.

When I returned to Britain in 1960, I found a very different situation. By then, at least in the FMCG sector, British sales techniques had begun to catch up with those used in America, and in some ways had even improved on them. This is not to say that the general climate for marketing in Britain was as good as that in the USA – far from it. But the change was nevertheless striking, and the question is: to what extent could this be ascribed to the introduction of ITV?

Clearly there were many factors involved in the growth of marketing consciousness among British businessmen in the second half of the fifties. The era of shortages and rationing came to an end, and the consuming public began once more to have a choice. As the need to market one's products became greater, opportunities also grew. Newsprint rationing was abolished, thus ending the state of affairs which had severely reduced advertising in the popular newspapers and magazines, the only mass-advertising media in Britain before the creation of ITV. By the end of the fifties, press competition for advertising was intense, and advertisers were able to take advantage of circulations far higher than they are today.

Nevertheless, I have no doubt that the introduction of ITV was the most important single factor in bringing the marketing revolution to many major sectors of British industry. Television advertising provided many benefits for the advertiser, but by far the most important was the ability to communicate directly with a mass housewife audience. It is difficult to explain to marketers today who have grown up with television just what a change this was. Before television, advertisements could be expected to reach a mass audience. The *News of the World* and *Radio Times* both had circulations of around eight million, and the leading women's weeklies not far off four million. But as we discovered soon after the introduction of television, advertisements in the new medium had far greater immediacy and certainty of impact. By 1960 the most popular ITV programmes were being seen by over 40 per cent of all housewives, and that was at a time when only about half the households in Britain had a set capable of receiving ITV. For the first time ever, British advertisers had the ability to talk directly to a mass housewife audience in their own homes – and not only to talk, but to present moving pictures (although in monochrome), an immensely powerful combination. The most advanced marketing companies in the country had learned how to adapt their strategies to this new medium, and it completely changed their perspectives.

For the manufacturer of fast-moving consumer products relations with the retail trade are crucial, since the retail trade is the principal channel by which his goods can reach the public. Probably even prewar, and certainly in the bleak period of the forties and early fifties, the basic link between manufacturer and retailer was a large number of salesmen whose job was to make sure that their company's products were bought by the retailer, kept in stock, and (a very important point) displayed prominently and if possible promoted at the point of sale. This may not seem very different from the present position, but it was – mainly because in the early fifties tightly controlled multiple chains did not exist, and the basic sales unit for packaged goods was the small counter-service grocery shop. All of this, along with the disruptions caused by wartime and postwar rationing, made national brands difficult and labour-intensive to maintain. If this was true for a well-established brand, it was even truer for any attempt at a new product introducing a major launch. This necessarily slowed down product development in Britain and made competition sluggish.

The evidence that it was ITV which had the largest impact on changing this situation is very strong and very simple. By the early sixties, an increasing proportion of above-the-line advertising expenditure by FMCG manufacturers went on television. In some cases all their expenditure went to this medium, and even where some press coverage was maintained it was rarely significant. This was not due to any warmth of affection between the buyers and sellers of television time. It was based simply on the power of experience. Television worked, and as a result we were able to organize our selling efforts far more effectively than before.

To give just a few examples from Beecham, we can look at three brands which were well established long before ITV appeared – Macleans Toothpaste, Lucozade and Ribena. All three had excellent retail distribution and a loyal following, but the arrival of ITV opened up great opportunities both for the brands themselves and for the wider markets of which they were part. Many more people became immediately aware of their merits. The advertising themes were not necessarily new, but their impact certainly was. Toothpaste is perhaps the most obvious example. In the fifties over a third of the adult population never cleaned their teeth at all (and that, for the benefit of any incredulous readers, excludes those with dentures). I believe that television commercials from toothpaste manufacturers did more to reduce that figure than all the advice from the medical, dental and educational professions put together. Of course, for a brand to succeed it had to do more than merely wait for an increase in the size of the market. It had to sell itself, and also ensure that it kept abreast of technological improvement – again extremely important for toothpaste, where better formulations appear with considerable frequency. Furthermore, the impact of television commercials on the public was not a nine-day wonder. It may be that the first commercials had particular power because they were so new, but the magic continues. In the last ten years we have launched many new brands in a variety of countries, and, wherever practicable, the bases for these launches have been sustained television campaigns. The worldwide success of Aquafresh toothpaste is a good example of the continuing potency of the medium.

One of the by-products of the way in which ITV was introduced turned out to be extremely helpful for marketing purposes. This was the regionalization of Independent Television. The immediate effect of this was to cause a major restructuring of the advertiser's company planning, distribution networks and sales forces to fit in with the largely arbitrary regions formed by the siting and power of ITV's transmitters. This took a little time, but it was largely completed by the early sixties, by which time marketing men had stopped talking about conventional population regions and talked in terms of ITV areas instead. When this change had been made, we all had an immensely powerful tool to help in general selling, new product launches and test marketing. It was possible as never before to concentrate resources and sales techniques in a particular area, knowing that they could be supported by well-targeted advertising (give or take the odd overlap between viewers within adjacent areas). The relatively small size of the UK and its heavy population concentrations allow this system to work particularly well in the interests of the marketers.

Perhaps the relationship between manufacturers and ITV companies in activities such as test marketing helps to explain a fact which is unique to the United Kingdom. This is the degree of interest shown by the television companies in market research and the level of cooperation between the buyers and sellers of TV time. The best-known result of this cooperation was JICTAR (the Joint Industry Committee for Television Advertising Research), which was established in 1957 to formalize relations between the television companies and advertisers and their agencies to ensure that audience research was acceptable to all parties. Such cooperation had, however, started years before, in the very early days of ITV, and continues still, although JICTAR has now changed to BARB (Broadcasters' Audience Research Board), with the introduction of the BBC into the same measurement system. Naturally, there have occasionally been tensions between buyers and sellers in the committees controlling audience research, but in research terms the results have been of high quality, as is shown by the far better information that companies in the UK possess about the audiences for their commercials than do similar firms in the USA. Analyses of the coverage of a given campaign and the number of times an advertisement has been seen have become a highly developed science in Britain.

The research interests of the television companies have not been confined simply to the measurement of the viewing audience. In the mid-sixties they helped to finance and establish the TCA (Television Consumer Audit), which gave extensive and rapid information about the purchasers of packaged goods and provided the data for all TV areas in Great Britain. This has been important to manufacturers, supplying information about customer loyalty and brand switching which can be expensive to obtain elsewhere. I am sure it has also proved of benefit to the television companies as it made it easier for the buyers of television time to test scientifically the effectiveness of their advertising campaigns area by area. A strong case can be made that research in the packaged-goods area is stronger in the UK than anywhere else in the world and, if so, one should not underestimate the part played in this by the television companies themselves. From its beginnings in 1955, ITV had achieved coverage of about two-thirds of all households by the early sixties, 90 per cent by the end of that decade, and 97 per cent today. The ITV share of viewing has also fluctuated considerably, rising to about 70 per cent in the early sixties, falling to 50 per cent as the BBC fought back through the later sixties and seventies, and now (with Channel Four) rising to 55 per cent. Obviously advertisers and their agencies have a deep interest in audience movements of this type, but they are not central to my theme here. Suffice to say that ITV remains by far the most important mass medium in Britain, especially as its rivals in the popular press have almost all seen their circulations shrink in the past thirty years.

Technological change has made some impact in the television/advertiser relationship, although perhaps less than is often suggested. A most important change was the introduction of colour, which is now possessed by more than 80 per cent of all households. This widened the scope of advertising and heightened even more the verisimilitude of the products being shown. The same is true of the great improvement in the quality of sets and transmitters, all helping to give a better standard of reproduction for advertisements, and instant pack recognition as well. Similarly, the introduction of Channel Four in 1982 provided opportunities for more specialized advertisers, and for supporting campaigns aimed primarily at the larger ITV audience.

How advertisers grasped the TV opportunity

The introduction of ITV was a major event in the world of British marketing, but the surprising fact remains that after the astonishing, rapid success of its first few years, there was more than a decade in which television obtained a relatively static share of total advertising expenditure and in which advertising's share of real resources remained unchanged. This can be seen in Table 1. Between 1956 and 1960, display advertising (which is the relevant sector for consideration) increased its share of consumer expenditure by more than a third – a rate of growth unparalleled before or since. This was not entirely due to television – the ending of newsprint rationing had something to do with it – but obviously TV advertising was the major engine behind the growth, as is evidenced by the fact that by 1960 television accounted for almost 30 per cent of display advertising and 22 per cent of all advertising.

	TABLE I: ADVERTISING AND THE ECONOMY 1954–83	
	Advertising as % of consumer expenditure	TV as % of advertising
1954	1.30	—
1955	1.35	1
1956	1.44	6
1957	1.53	13
1958	1.63	19
1959	1.71	21
1960	1.91	22
1961	1.90	25
1962	1.84	25
1963	1.84	25
1964	1.93	25
1965	1.90	26
1966	1.84	26
1967	1.80	27
1968	1.85	26
1969	1.87	24
1970	1.74	23
1971	1.66	24
1972	1.76	25
1973	1.91	24
1974	1.72	23
1975	1.50	24
1976	1.59	26
1977	1.75	27
1978	1.86	26
1979	1.82	22*
1980	1.88	27
1981	1.85	29
1982	1.87	30
1983	1.96	31

* ITV strike   Source: Advertising Association

Thereafter the pace of expansion slowed dramatically, came to a halt and then went into reverse for all three elements – the share of TV in display, the share of display in total advertising and the ratio of total advertising to consumers' expenditure. These trends in turn did not show any long-term change until the second half of the seventies, when again all three moved in the opposite direction, with TV, display advertising and total advertising all rising.

By 1960, companies in all sectors of what we can loosely call the packaged-goods business had been converted to the value of television advertising. As far as they were concerned it had become the norm, and their whole marketing strategy became increasingly adapted to its central role. Of course, this does not mean that all marketing expenditures went on that medium, although most above-the-line spending did. For many brands, at least some of the time, below-the-line expenditure also flourished (most people who were around at the time remember the famous plastic daffodil promotion run by Procter and Gamble). But even such campaigns as this, although carried out at store level, often in cooperation with the multiple sector which was just beginning to expand, were also tied in with major TV advertising campaigns publicizing such a promotion – a technique that has been repeated with more or less variation ever since.

At that time, the packaged grocery sector and a few closely related areas (for instance the sellers of household durables such as Hoover) were very much the exceptions as far as British industry was concerned. They were also the exceptions (or one might even say pariahs) in relation to establishment opinion. One has only to read the report of the Pilkington Committee, which sat during the early sixties, to see how much hatred and contempt ITV generated among the 'great and the good'. It goes beyond my province to diagnose why such attitudes should be so prevalent among members of the British establishment, compounded as they are of a detestation of the culture which ordinary people enjoy and a dislike of selling in any form. Whatever the cause, I am certain that one of their effects has been to make Britain very much poorer and less competitive than our natural abilities should have allowed; and it is relevant to my theme insofar as I believe that much of this overt dislike of ITV spilled over from the academic and professional world into that of business.

I cannot prove it, but this seems to me perhaps the most probable explanation for the long period of stagnation in ITV revenue which followed its initial explosive take-off. During the sixties and early seventies, television's advertising base hardly increased at all, and in fact it could be argued that the banning of cigarette advertising in 1965 did more to reduce demand for the medium than new types of business brought in for the rest of the decade. Thus the link between the packaged-goods sector and television became ever closer with a result which may well have harmed both parties.

The harm to television can be seen relatively clearly from Table 2. Between 1963 and 1973, the real cost-per-thousand of TV advertisements fell by 9 per cent, over a period when the number of TV licences increased by almost 50 per cent, and colour TV sets from none to over three million. Simple economics explains the reason for this fall. The supply of airtime is virtually fixed, since there is a legal limit on the number of advertising minutes permitted per hour, and the amount of peaktime advertising – which from the point of view of advertisers seeking a mass market is what really matters – is determined by the length of the peaktime segment. Thus the price depends almost totally on demand, and with demand static (or falling) during the sixties and early seventies it is hardly surprising that the price of TV time should also fall.

TABLE 2: CHANGE IN TV RATES (CPT) 1963–83 (CONSTANT PRICE)

	TV
1963–73	−9
1973–83	+32

Source: Advertising Association

It is less clear why the arrangement should have drawbacks for advertisers, and indeed, from the standpoint of the present situation, this may well look like a golden age. However, many advertisers of packaged goods appeared to take TV advertising increasingly for granted. It was naturally something they approved of and wanted to engage in, but perhaps the generation of marketing managers in the early seventies was less enchanted with advertising in general and TV advertising in particular than their predecessors had been ten years earlier. This meant that if times became hard and the packaged-goods manufacturers felt themselves under pressure a number of them might regard their television budgets as relatively expendable; and if that happened ITV in general looked highly vulnerable.

In fact, by the early seventies the packaged-grocery industry was under very severe pressure. The main cause was the growth of the multiple grocery sector which, from very small beginnings in the mid-fifties had acquired, on TCA definitions, about 50 per cent of grocery turnover by 1973 (see Table 3). This gave the grocery sector the muscle, which they naturally used, to extract better deals from their suppliers. One of the casualties of this struggle was television advertising. The pressure was always on the manufacturer to take money out of his advertising budget and put it into trade discounts. When the economy as a whole was doing relatively well, manufacturers could usually meet the requirements of the grocery trade without cutting back savagely on their TV advertising, although they certainly did not expand it very much. But when times were bad, advertising could suffer very heavily, as is shown by the fall of TV rates in real terms of 25 per cent between 1973 and 1975. I believe that nearly all the firms which cut back on their advertising came to regret it, as the market share of retailers' own brands increased.

TABLE 3: % OF GROCERY TURNOVER			
	1961**	1973**	1973*	1983*
Multiples	27	48	51	73
Co-ops	20	13	20	15
Independents	53	39	29	12

** DTI   * AGB TCA

By 1975 it was possible, and indeed fashionable, to produce a very gloomy prognosis for the future of ITV revenue. With a base extremely dependent on the manufacturers of packaged goods, who were in turn suffering ever more external pressure, it was not difficult to construct a scenario of ITV in secular decline for the foreseeable future. Of course, we now all know that such forecasts have been proved wildly wrong. To return to Table 2, the ten 'lean' years when ITV rates fell in real terms were replaced by ten 'fat' ones when they outpaced inflation by 32 per cent. It is important to establish why this should have been so, particularly as I believe it casts light on one of the most important effects of television on British marketing.

The key change which took place in the second half of the seventies was the rapid increase in the number of industries which came to accept that they would benefit from TV advertising. One may debate exactly when the change took place for different industries, and even point to the fact that most of them had dabbled in TV advertising earlier. Nevertheless, no one can deny that the spread of advertising on TV widened considerably between the early seventies and the early eighties (see Table 4). The table itself probably underrates the degree of change, since even among the 'consumables' category a number of new types of product have entered over the past few years.

TABLE 4: CHANGE IN TV REVENUE BASE 1973–84

	% of TV revenue	
	1973	1983
Consumables	70	50
Durables	14	20
Financial	1	5
Services	6	8
Retail	4	6
Others	5	11

Source: Advertising Association/MEAL

In the mid-seventies, among the most important new entrants to TV advertising were the grocery multiples themselves. After several years of avoiding the use of TV advertising on their own account, a number of leading multiples began to advertise around the middle of the seventies; this reached its peak with the famous Tesco 'Checkout' campaign in 1977, when a leading multiple used TV as a deliberate marketing tool to change its image with the public, at a time when it dropped the use of trading stamps and compensated by heavy price cutting. Subsequently all the major grocery multiples have used TV advertising as an integral part of their marketing strategy. The general growth in the market share of the multiple sector cannot be ascribed entirely to TV, but I think the remarkable growth over the last eight years in the share of the top three groups (Sainsbury, Tesco and Asda) largely can be. Television has also spearheaded a change in retailer policy, from 'pile it high, sell it cheap' to value for money based on quality, range, freshness and service – thereby helping to repair margins which had been reduced by the excesses of price competition.

For the revenue of ITV, perhaps the most significant change has been the growth in financial advertising. This increased from 1 per cent to 5 per cent of total TV advertising expenditure between 1973 and 1983, and with it have come major changes both in public use of financial institutions (the large growth in the ownership of bank and building-society accounts, and the explosive growth in credit-card ownership) and also in the approach of many City institutions to marketing in general and TV advertising in particular. The full extent of this has probably not yet been seen, but it is likely to become increasingly important as a younger generation weaned on TV advertising takes over control of financial institutions.

I cannot discuss here the many other growth areas in TV advertising – cars, leisure and local advertising, for example – but it is significant that hardly any area which has once moved into TV advertising seems ready to reduce its reliance on the medium. Table 5 shows that even the consumables sector, whose share of TV advertising fell from 70 per cent to 50 per cent, is spending as high a proportion as ever of its total advertising budget on TV. All other sectors have significantly increased the share of their advertising devoted to this medium. Nor is there any reason to doubt that this process will continue. There has been a continual stream of new categories advertising on television, and with the development of Channel Four, with its relatively low rates and specialized audiences, the incentive for new types of advertising to move to television is likely to grow even more.

TABLE 5: RELIANCE ON TV ADVERTISING 1973–83

| | *TV as % of ad expenditure* | |
	1973	1983
Consumables	69	74
Durables	33	43
Financial	4	25
Services	31	41
Retail	14	22

Source: Advertising Association/MEAL

The rapid increase in TV rates between 1973 and 1983 is shown in Table 2. Clearly in one sense it resulted from an excess of demand over supply, but it is important to understand where the supply shortage manifests itself. At first sight one might imagine that the establishment of Channel Four and TV-am, which came close to doubling the number of advertising minutes available, would have provided a solution to the demand for extra advertising time created by the new TV advertisers. But this is not so, for a reason which emphasizes my original observation about the particular benefit of television advertising to marketers. ITV provided the marketer with access to the mass market as no medium had done before. This was the case in 1960 and, in spite of all the changes since then, it is still the case.

Channel Four is not intended to attract mass audiences. Even less can mass audiences be expected from the newer media – cable and satellite – which, whenever they achieve significant penetration (and I am not holding my breath waiting), are still almost certain to remain very much minority media. Thus we are left with the likelihood that the real cost of TV advertising time will continue to increase, as the immense value of TV advertising, and particularly peak-hour advertising, become more widely recognized.

Can marketing get more out of television?

The rigid legal restrictions under which Independent Television operates are now creating problems for marketers which are almost certain to get worse; and the most serious of these problems is the limitation on the amount of advertising time in peak hours which are those of most value to many marketing companies. As more advertisers compete for this limited period there is no alternative but to ration by price – hence the rapid real increase in TV advertising rates over the past decade. This is now beginning to prove a severe marketing deterrent. The packaged-goods companies in general are spending more than they ever did on TV but are receiving less, in terms of time and audience impact, than they have ever done. Thus, having shown marketers the promised land of highly effective communication with a mass audience, ITV is now in danger of barring our entry with an ever-rising rate card.

There are several ways of tackling this problem, one of which would be to allow an increase in the amount of peaktime advertising currently permitted. The real answer, however, would be the creation of a further commercial channel which would obviously help advertisers by strengthening competition for their custom. Consumers, too, would benefit from greater competition, as they always do. It would even be good for the ITV·companies, though they may not be prepared to admit it. The longer they are in a position to allocate peaktime slots to supplicant advertisers, the blunter their own marketing edge is bound to be.

The Agency Viewpoint 1: Birth Pangs

WINSTON FLETCHER

WINSTON FLETCHER

Winston Fletcher went into advertising after leaving Cambridge in 1959 and spending a year wandering about the world on a creative-writing scholarship. He joined Ogilvy and Mather as a trainee copywriter and then moved to Sharp's Advertising, where he became a director of the agency at the age of twenty-five. Four years later he became Deputy Managing Director of a new, small agency called MCR Advertising, and then set up his own – Fletcher Shelton Delaney – in 1974. In 1979 Fletcher Shelton Delaney was sold to Ted Bates Inc., the second largest agency in the world. Three years later Winston Fletcher became Chairman and Chief Executive of Ted Bates's UK operation, with a turnover of some £70,000,000.

Early in 1985 he left Ted Bates to become Chairman and partner in a new creative agency, Delaney Fletcher Delaney. He is currently Chairman of the AA's Public Action Group, and is on the Council and Executive Committee of the IPA. He writes incessantly on advertising matters for the national and trade press and is the author of five books: *The Admakers, Teach Yourself Advertising, Meetings, Meetings, Commercial Breaks* and *Safer Efficiency*

ENTERING advertising as a novitiate in the late 1950s I watched the birth of television advertising like a child watching a revolution through a curtained window: I could see lots of frenetic activity but had no idea what it all meant.

I joined Mather and Crowther (now Ogilvy and Mather) as a fledgling copywriter, and part of my training comprised a day's stint in the newly formed television producers' department. Mather's had cleverly bought in its neophyte TV producers from the BBC – but from sound radio. Less than astonishingly, these chaps were obsessed with the technicalities of producing splendidly sophisticated soundtracks. I was shown, and utterly baffled by, perplexing diagrams and graphs which purported to explain the mysteries of sound reproduction on film.

Even in my innocent ignorance, I had dark suspicions that television was more concerned with pictures than with sound, but it seemed impertinent to point this out to the pedagogic luminaries who knew so much about wavelengths and decibels, so I listened intently if uncomprehendingly.

That they were genuine experts – even if in the wrong discipline – became more evident when I moved from Mather's, one of London's largest agencies, to Robert Sharp and Partners, then one of London's smallest. Sharp's was a young, dynamic, creative hotshop, which at that time meant that the bulk of its advertising ran in the press rather than on television.

Sharp's realized that, in order to win the major clients to which it aspired, the agency would need to establish its ability to create and produce brilliant television advertisements. It was thus faced with a classic chicken-and-egg dilemma: how to prove it could make dazzling commercials when it had no commercials to make.

The explosive growth of television advertising, and the dearth of people with experience of the medium, had forced Mather and Crowther to recruit BBC sound producers. Other large agencies had roped in people from the movies, from the USA, from the theatre and from photography. Such agencies had lots of television commercials to be made and real jobs to offer. Robert Sharp's, like most other small agencies at the time, had neither.

Sharp's, often radical in its approach to management problems, decided to grow its own talent. First it employed a stunningly pretty young girl with great style and flair; she proved better as a model than as a producer and soon decided that appearing in commercials was much more amusing than making them.

Moving on quickly, a theatrical set designer was recruited. Set designs being inherently static and television inherently mobile, her experience proved even less relevant than that of the BBC sound producers. Still casting around for a solution to the intractable problem, Sharp's resorted to a device it had used successfully on other occasions: it ran a recruitment advertisement in the form of a quiz. The quiz questions were designed (or anyway intended) to identify applicants without experience but with the right abilities.

On this occasion, inexplicably, easily the best response came from a Frenchman living in Paris, who was working in finance but wanted to get into advertising. The directors of Sharp's flew to Paris, were impressed by his intelligence, enthusiasm and drive, and promptly recruited him to work in partnership with the set designer.

By now, Sharp's had become involved in making commercials for its recently acquired major clients, and it cannot be said that the bizarre duo of set designer and French finance man was an awe-inspiring success. They quit, and for a couple of months I found myself – with, you will by now have gathered, less than minuscule knowledge of what the hell I was doing – producing my own commercials. As a result I was wined and dined enthusiastically by all the commercial production companies who had heard on the 35mm grapevine that I was certain to be Sharp's next television producer.

I was so incompetent at the job that my tenure as locum was merci-fully brief. Instead, necessity being the mother of invention, Sharp's tried again. After a few months' training, a Cambridge graduate with great visual talent was thrown into the job and made a fair fist of it – though by this time the commercial production companies had sufficient experience to make commercials more or less on their own, with a little agency guidance, if necessary.

Soon the agency world was flooded with experienced and competent TV producers, and nobody would dream of recruiting sound producers or set designers ever again. The birth pangs were over, though the frenetic activity lingers on.

The Agency Viewpoint 2

JOHN HOBSON

JOHN HOBSON

Educated at Rugby and King's College, Cambridge, John Hobson began his advertising career at the London Press Exchange in 1930.

In 1945 he joined Colman, Prentis and Varley as Assistant Managing Director and ten years later, in the year Independent Television opened, he left to found John Hobson and Partners, which in 1959 merged with Ted Bates of New York to become Hobson Bates.

As Chairman and Managing Director of the British company John Hobson held a number of important industry appointments including those of President of the IPA and of the European Association of Advertising Agencies. He became Chairman of the Advertising Association during an important period of its development and played a leading part in setting up the levy to finance the self-regulatory advertising control system operated by the ASA and the CAP Committee.

At a much earlier stage he pioneered the introduction and development of the Hulton Readership Survey from 1949 onwards.

John Hobson is currently Honorary President of Ted Bates Limited

THERE is all too little documentation about the agency view on the beginnings of commercial television. Apart from some conversations with a few others who were around thirty years ago, in writing this piece I have to rely on personal recollections and opinions. Inevitably therefore it becomes somewhat one-sided, personalized and lacking in the historian's objectivity, and consists of rather disjointed reflections on various aspects of the story. Only some names stand out in my memory while others to whom equal (or more) credit belongs may be left out; if so they must forgive me.

The beginning

In 1951 and 1952, with a Conservative Government now in power, a second television service to compete with the BBC became a real possibility. The motivations of the different groups concerned were, of course, mixed. Those in the Conservative party who supported and lobbied for it were out to frustrate the monoply power of the BBC as much as they wanted to offer the public an alternative service. Their opponents were equally determined to conserve the Reithian values of the BBC and keep it from becoming popularized. The would-be and potential contractors, noting the US experience, were certainly expecting to make money but they were also looking forward to the creative opportunities of making new (and different) programmes and utilizing new and eager talent. The advertisers, also working on US experience, welcomed an additional and more powerful medium for selling their goods.

To the agencies, television offered a brave new world with great creative opportunities, new strength to the power of advertising and marketing, and – hopefully – a splendid additional source of turnover and profit. John Rodgers of J. Walter Thompson was very active in the parliamentary lobby and a committee of six, representing the six leading agencies, was formed under Bobby Bevan of Benson's to meet every week to formulate plans and policies. Norman Collins was involved for the prospective TV contractors, and Selwyn Lloyd led the parliamentary battle.

The agencies drew up a code of conduct for the new medium, using the new International Chamber of Commerce code as a model, and they opted for spot advertising as opposed to the American form of sponsorship. When the 1954 Television Act was being debated in Parliament these dispositions proved to be a powerful help and a safeguard. At the time Colman, Prentis and Varley was the agency handling the Conservative party account and its Chairman, the late Arthur Varley, was prominent in fostering the lobby within the Tory party. I remember that I myself, within CPV, was extremely worried about these developments because, being concerned for the general image of advertising, I feared it would not be improved when beamed into the public's living rooms. I could not have been more wrong.

So the Television Act was passed, the contractors were appointed, Robert Fraser was made Director-General of the ITA and the agencies readied themselves for the start in the autumn of 1955. But agency reaction was by no means unanimous. While some were enthusiastic about the future potential of the medium others, including some major agencies such as the London Press Exchange and Mather and Crowther, thought it would be a nine days' wonder. These attitudes governed the dispositions that each agency made to service the medium. Some went into it with eagerness, such as J. Walter Thompson who set up a small studio of their own where creative people could learn about commercials and actually practise making them. The less enthusiastic carefully segregated their television staff from their main business activities (so as to be able to drop them with the minimum of disruption when the nine days' wonder flopped) and in so doing stored up immense trouble for themselves.

A new agency learns the power of TV

I opened my new agency, John Hobson and Partners, almost on the same day that Independent Television opened in London, and we soon came to the conclusion that it was a medium to be reckoned with. I was fortunate in having with me John Metcalf, whose breadth of vision and creative talent rapidly absorbed the character of TV advertising. He masterminded commercials for Cadbury's and for our Sunfresh client, both of which conclusively proved television's sales power. As a result, when in April 1956 (at a time when the contractors had been losing money steadily) Cecil King, Chairman of the *Daily Mirror* group, asked me over lunch whether he should take up the Associated News-papers shares in ATV, I firmly encouraged him to do so. He bought the shares that afternoon, a critical development in the whole system because it saved ATV and gave it much-needed financial leeway.

Later Cecil King sent Ellis Birk to find out what he could do for *me*. Like a fool I did not ask him to allot me some shares in ATV, but I did ask whether my agency could have the *Daily Mirror* account. We did a splendid series of commercials for them, held the account for some six or seven years, launched the *Sun* for them under the guidance of Hugh Cudlipp and took ourselves into the 1960s in fine fettle. It was Cecil King, too, who also introduced me to the ATV account which led much later to the Granada business and later still to Scottish Television. Our experience in handling programme company accounts gave us an invaluable insight into the problems of the contractors.

Meanwhile the medium was progressing by leaps and bounds, despite the heavy financial losses of the original contractors. The Midlands station sarted in February 1956 and the North of England service in May. On opening night there were well under 200,000 homes with sets capable of receiving the new channel. In 1956 this figure rose to over 500,000. A year later it was just on 3,000,000, and twenty years later it had reached 19,000,000 homes and 97 per cent coverage.

Audience research

The agencies were now well satisfied with the power of the medium which rapdily took over from print and formed 85–90 per cent of a typical large agency's budget. In this context the development of research into television coverage became all-important. Clients naturally wanted to know the coverage their campaigns were getting. The first step was to take the BBC's aided-recall research, but this only lasted a few months. Later we at JHP carried out for our client, Granada, the Granada Viewership Survey based on the readership survey structure (which I had introduced in the original Hulton Read-ership Surveys) and using aided-recall techniques. But it was not long before the meter systems promoted by TAM and Nielsen superseded this form of research after a fascinating battle between the two. I personally became involved in this battle because I had known both Pat Napier of Nielsen's and Bedford Attwood of TAM for a long time. I saw a lot of both as my home happened to be situated between the two.

The joint decision and finance of the IPA, the ISBA and the

programme companies favoured TAM, which then became the established system. Some years later AGB won the contract from TAM and this situation still exists under the BARB system for both BBC and ITV.

New heads of media departments

The new measurements of media performance created completely new problems for agency media departments. Previously there had been measurements, first by circulation and later by readership, of the average potential coverage given by a medium which was based on research of a few weeks' duration. Now for the first time there were figures of actual audience coverage achieved (subject to normal margins of error) each and every day for each station for every programme and commercial break. The ratings therefore not only gave guidance on what times to book, but afterwards showed the audience achieved, which enabled a cost calculation to be made of the value delivered by the agency's campaign schedule. Agencies were now far more under the scrutiny of their clients concerning the efficiency of their media operation. Before the Second World War media buying was very largely a matter of cut rates negotiated over a drink in the Salisbury bar. Now it began to involve sophisticated computer-based calculations. My agency set up a subsidiary, Tempo, to undertake these assignments. Others made similar arrangements or bought computer time from us or from one of the other computer bureaux. When accounts were shared with a number of agencies, the results of media buying in terms of value delivered became matters of critical importance.

However, the media picture did not stand still. When AGB was awarded the industry research contract it set up its own computer system to provide agencies with the rapid data-processing service they needed. During the seventies the balance swung away from the planning of television schedules to the actual buying of television time. An element of planning was still always there because, with the greater detail of audience figures, it became possible to target campaigns more precisely. Channel switching became easier for the viewer, so that the earlier concentration on family groups was replaced by targeting on types of viewer.

Further influences which had a heavy impact on an agency's organization were the excess demand for the medium and the resultant proliferation of pre-empt rates. The net effect of all these developments on agency media departments was that they became adept at wheeling and dealing, at making last-minute bookings based on the latest available audience ratings, and at gaining by 'money dealings' what they might lose on media planning. Discounts on top rates could be as high as 70 per cent if the wheeling and dealing were successful, and the fact that one person's discount was another's premium was just too bad. Of course the game was being played in Monopoly values. One never knew the extent to which the client's target market was accurately represented by the audience research figures, but everyone seemed (and seems) satisfied with the game as played. Needless to say, the media function in the agency became very important, and the specialized media independents who began to appear in the seventies played a valuable part in servicing those agencies not equipped to handle so complicated a task.

The effect of Television Advertisement Duty

In 1961 Television Advertisement Duty of 10 per cent (later raised to 11 per cent) was imposed by the Government. Thus 15 per cent commission on 100 was reduced to 15 per cent on 90 or 13.5 per cent – a serious blow to agency profitability, which tended to run at no more than 2–2.5 per cent of total turnover. Some agencies were able to redress the loss by making special arrangements with their clients, but for many agencies the loss was a real one. The opportunity to retrieve this situation came with the new Television Act of 1964 when TAD was replaced by the Exchequer levy, which was applied to the net advertising receipts of the contractors.

Agencies learn to love TV

During the 1960s television gradually became the dominant medium in British advertising. The agencies loved its creative opportunities. Its coverage by 1970 had extended to over 90 per cent of the homes in the country, and its impact on clients' marketing had been proved over and over again. Its catchphrases and personalities had become familar in every home. The agency view was that for normal brand advertising it beat all other media and that any product which needed demonstration of its benefit (or working) had to have television. Print media were relegated to a supporting role, used only when the details of the product or an offer were so complicated that they needed explanation at length. In the average agency handling consumer products, television was given 85–90 per cent of the budget.

The marketing impact of TV

Another new consequence of television, of which the agencies and their clients were quick to take advantage, was the facility to run regional marketing campaigns. Most new brands were now given a small-scale test in a minor television area such as Tyne Tees, Border or even the Channel Islands. The acceptance of the product was closely monitored and its regional sales figures multiplied up to represent a national campaign. Any faults and misunderstandings arising from the commercial itself could be discovered and rectified. The regional breakdown of the national total also provided a means of handling smaller budgets which could not afford the necessary frequency of transmission for a nationwide campaign. These developments are now taken for granted and are in universal use, but over the 1960s they were virgin territory calling on agency skills and initiatives for exploration. Regional tests in other media were never as satisfactory because local print media had a different impact, character and cost element from national media.

One of the problems which caused the burning of much midnight oil and the furrowing of many brows was how to dispose of the sequence of spots in a campaign. Was it better to have high frequency for short bursts or to use the drip-drip disposition of less frequent spots over the whole period? I am not sure that the problem has ever been solved, but it is a typical example of the new questions the agencies were called upon to sort out and, if possible, answer. Most agencies were quick to recognize that the coming of television had created a brand new tempo of marketing and, of course, the big and sophisticated advertisers quickly saw what was happening. In the days of print media before the war it took months to get a new product noticed, tried and established. It involved the use of half or full pages in newspapers of broadsheet size. The written word was far less powerful than audio-visual communication, even before TV turned to colour. Television produced more impact more rapidly; new products could establish themselves in weeks rather than months; regional testing via television could provide quick guidance and safeguards.

Marketing became a new source of strength to those agencies which, like my own, claimed a special competence in its skills. Naturally this phase did not last long. The major advertisers developed their own internal marketing expertise and specialized departments for the purpose, but they expected their agencies to talk the same language and to make a positive marketing contribution. As a result, the marketing departments of the agencies became of the greatest importance. In many cases it was men and women with a marketing background, rather than those from the creative side, who were to become agency chief executives.

How agency creative organization changed

Looking back, however, I believe that while the media and marketing sides of the agency changed under the impact of television the greatest change was in the creative organization. It was a process of evolution rather than some instant dramatic swing. It began in the period of preparation for television when, looking ahead, the big agencies, especially those with American connections, began to equip themselves with people who could tackle the creative and mechanical problems of the new medium.

All sorts of people with some vague association with, or reputation in, the cinema, theatre, BBC television and trans-Atlantic television were enlisted to add to the almost non-existent stock of expert personnel. Second-line American TV people, who could not make the grade over there, came to Britain and were welcomed with open arms. The typical art directors of the print era found it hard to adapt; they were used to dealing in static visuals. I remember in one case the art director could not outline the visual movement without drawing his characters in a sequence of small movements like an animated cartoon.

The balance swung at this stage to the writers, because the nature of the television commercial is a brief story with the character of a narrative with a beginning, middle and end. Being a narrative medium it was more in the area of those who, like copywriters, were expert in handling words. And out of the words the visual element grew. This still left plenty of scope for creative visual treatments, but the starting point was the words.

While agency personnel slowly learned the skills of creating a commercial, there was no one in the agencies who knew how to make one. The production companies such as Television Advertising (TVA, which later became James Garrett and Partners) stepped into the picture. It was they who organized the actors and the studios, arranged for the jingles, hired the voices-over. But there was a need for a link between the agency and the production company, and this link man had to have enough expertise to supervise the production company's activities. So there grew up a new breed of agency man – the producer. He was perhaps the only element of completely new personnel which came into the agency with the advent of television.

American experience and examples were not altogether helpful. For one thing, the US media had grown up on sponsored programmes with live presenters interposed. The changeover to spots was only coming slowly in the States. Again, the hammer-blow commercials of agency men such as Rosser Reeves were not considered suitable for the British public who, it was thought, would not welcome this degree of hard sell in their living rooms. On the other hand, the delightful and light-hearted treatments of the French, such as André Sarrut, which inferred the selling message rather than being explicit about it, were considered too remote.

Development of the agency creative structure

So the British agencies developed their own style of commercial treatment and, I believe, after seeing so many American and French commercials on the box, that the British style was more acceptable and more effective with the British viewer than any other. At its best, this style identified the product's salient consumer benefit and demonstrated it in human terms.

Agency organization for creative work was divided between those agencies which worked in large departments and those which, like my own, operated in groups of two people – a writer and an art director. For a long phase the writer dominated, but more recently the art director has developed more power. Personally, I think this was a mistake in that it moved the TV commercial away from the product selling a message towards visual excitement, sometimes extravagant and distracting. In *Reality in Advertising* Rosser Reeves has a chapter on 'vampire video' – the dominance of the extraneous video element which can distract the mind from the selling story. And the fault can be seen in only too many current commercials which nevertheless win awards and enchant the clients. No names, no pack drill. Not that one would want to revert to a Reevesian hard sell, but I believe it is perfectly possible to convey the USP in vivid, human and pleasant fashion without extravagant visual treatment.

Those agencies which in the early stages – especially those which believed television to be a nine days' wonder – hived off the whole television operation into subsidiary companies or departments. They thereby created astonishing difficulties for themselves because the later dominance of television meant that the television tail wagged the agency dog. But mainly the television function – whether executive, media or creative – evolved as an integral part of the whole agency performance. The development of the TV medium, moreover, offered a unique opportunity for small creative groups to set up on their own and gradually challenge the larger units. This was more especially so when the medium began to focus on viewer types rather than on the whole family, so that the more specialized creative units could concentrate their talents on a fashion, cosmetic or other particular target.

Finally, there have been the inevitable hiccups in the structural development of television in which the agencies have been on the whole the passive bystanders. The arrival of the second ITV channel was not all that the agencies wanted; they would have preferred an entirely new set of contractors, but William Whitelaw had made up his mind. The battle with Equity over the rates paid to Channel Four artists, now fortunately more or less settled, caused the agencies acute problems for two years. Various strikes have taken place in the medium, some more damaging than others, causing the agencies short-term loss of revenue. But such interruptions have never resulted in any setback to the long-term development of the medium.

Plus ça change

Looking back on over fifty years in the agency business, I am constantly struck by the fact that, although so many peripheral factors have changed, the basic character of agency life is much the same as in 1930 when I first joined the London Press Exchange. The same battles rage between the executive and the creative side; the media departments are still wheeling and dealing, though in different ways; the clients still seem to prefer the agencies with creative notability to those which concentrate on the marketing and selling theme; there is still no recognition that a brilliant presentation of the wrong selling story is much worse than a straightforward rendering of the right one.

And the takeover by television has not changed any of this. Television has revolutionized agency creativity and agency finances; it has produced a fundamental change in marketing for both clients and agencies. It has introduced a more human and acceptable face to advertising among the general public. And, on balance, it has given the advertising agency an improved status in the community.

The Agency Viewpoint 3

TIM BELL

TIM BELL

After a career in the media planning and buying side of the advertising business with Colman Prentis and Varley, Hobson Bates and Geers Gross, Tim Bell, along with the Saatchi brothers, founded the Saatchi and Saatchi agency in 1970.

As Managing Director he orchestrated the merger with Garland-Compton in 1974 and then, as International Chairman, he took Saatchi and Saatchi into its position as the first British worldwide agency network when the Compton group was acquired in 1981.

He successfully ran the General Election campaign for the Conservative Party in 1979 and again in 1983. More recently he has been special adviser to Ian MacGregor throughout the coal strike.

Tim Bell is currently Group Chief Executive of Lowe Howard-Spink and Bell plc

O N 22 September 1955 there took place in some 170,000 homes in the London area an event of such magnitude that it was deemed necessary, in retaliation, to kill off one of the most loved characters of the day. For sixty seconds, those comparatively few people who had new televisions clustered round their sets and watched a black-and-white commercial for Gibbs' SR toothpaste – the first advertisement to appear on Britain's new commercial channel. Such was the anticipation of this event that the BBC, while publicly pooh-poohing the idea that a commercial channel could ever work in this country, chose – of course totally coincidentally – the night of its starting to kill off Grace Archer in its long-running radio soap opera, which at that time had an audience of over eight million.

It was extraordinary that the BBC should be so worried about commercial television when no one who was anyone gave it a chance of succeeding. Indeed, the first stations – A-R and ABC (later to be called ATV) made enormous losses in their first year and everyone said that that proved the point. Commercial television was too 'American'; the British people wouldn't take to it; they wouldn't want their programmes interrupted by ads; and it would never be as good as the BBC. Such was the conventional wisdom of the time.

They were in for a shock. In the last thirty years, principally because of the choice the new channel brought and the competition it created, television has transformed British life and the role of advertising agencies in that national life. It has changed what we know of the world and how we perceive it. It has changed our leisure time and how we use it. It has changed what we spend and how we spend it. It hasn't killed the art of conversation – merely changed its content. What factory teabreak, office-canteen lunch or school playtime of the fifties took place without someone mentioning *Take Your Pick* or *Robin Hood, Wagon Train* or *Double Your Money?*

Nowadays the topic would be *Minder, The Price is Right* or *Game for a Laugh* (or their latest favourite commercial) – but they are talked about just the same. And when you look at the success of *Coronation*

Street, which has been watched by a quarter of the entire population for most of those thirty years, you can't help thinking that the man who killed Grace Archer was right after all.

But, just as extraordinary as the BBC's reaction at the time, is the fact that, despite the changes in the last thirty years and for all the billions of pounds spent on them, we still don't agree on what a good television advertisement is, how much it should cost, or really what it does.

Not that that particularly concerned the advertising industry in 1955. If the nation had woken up to the powerful force that television could be in its life at the time of the Coronation in 1953, the advertising industry was still slumbering quietly. Newsprint rationing had not yet been abolished and media buyers were still adapting to a world where they no longer had to bribe Fleet Street's advertisement managers with cases of champagne to make room for their ads. The boot, or in this instance bottle, was only just beginning to be on the other foot. Harold Macmillan was not yet Prime Minister. The nation had not yet had it so good. Nor had it had Suez. The world had just lost Stalin, but not yet got Sputnik. And I was still at school. It was still the old world; the old Britain. And thus it was very much the old guard who initially came to run the new companies on the commercial channel. Magazine men were recruited wholesale to manage the programme side – the sales side were all ex-army officers and posh graduates. They seemed very smooth by comparison with their bawdy, boozy counterparts on newspapers, but few of them seemed to have any sense of what was to come, any vision of the potential they were dealing with.

The feeling at first, even among those whose job it was to make or place television ads, was that television had always been without ads, so we didn't really need them now. Consequently those early efforts, while the network was still coming into being, had a reputation for being irritating and boring, for shouting at you. And, of course they suffered for being in black-and-white. Many of them, too, were originally press ads merely 'done again' for television. Of course, there were exceptions in the early years. We can all remember 'Don't forget the fruit gums, Mum,' 'Too-good-to-hurry mints' and 'You'll wonder where the yellow went . . .'. But, by and large, old habits died hard. However, when in 1959 my mother decided she did not want me hanging around at home and sent me off to the Stella Fisher Employment Agency in Fleet Street to get myself a job, and I came back with a choice of three interviews – one in publishing, one in insurance and one with ABC Television – I had no hesitation in going for the last.

It was my generation who could, almost unconsciously, see the power of television and, by inference, the power of advertising in it. Soon we were flocking into almost any post we could find in either industry. As in the computer industry of the last ten years, the young generation knew just as much as the old guard but had no preconceptions to hamper them and infinite energy to boost them.

The fact that I saw myself, the day I presented myself to ABC, as a star in the making – an actor or a producer – not, as it turned out, the lad shifting the bits of cardboard on the big board in the advertising department, was neither here nor there. But it led to my joining CPV a couple of years later.

It was the generation who entered advertising in the late fifties and early sixties who transformed not only television advertising but, in doing so, the agencies themselves. Television advertising has come to change the structure of agencies, their role, profitability and their impact – both internally and externally. It has transformed a product's relationship with its consumer so that they can become intimate friends. A man can now love his car, a woman her washing-up liquid. It has so speeded the learning curve that new ideas are felt to be needed almost before the current one has been exposed. A campaign that was schemed in the fifties to last three years would now run through the same number of ads in three months. And most important of all, it has somehow managed to bring together, in virtual harmony, the entrepreneurs who are the life blood of our society and the technicians and mechanics who create order from chaos and make great ideas bear fruit.

But I wonder just how much the impact of this change is yet understood. Let's look again at the advertising industry that the public saw the day when it watched Gibbs' SR strut its stuff as the standard-bearer of TV ads. It saw an industry which hadn't a clue what television could do. Amazingly, it was an industry which, while it was happy to copy American methods, turned its back on the lessons that the Americans were learning about television.

Between 1955 and 1960 companies began to work on commercials, almost all of them completely adopting the advice and techniques – if not the actual transmission – of US ads. A huge percentage of those ads were for soap and detergents – a situation which, like the advertising for those products itself, has not changed all that much in thirty years.

We learned magic phrases such as vampire video, side-by-side comparison, slice of life, testimony and product demonstration, but all were virtually devoid of creativity. And in consequence the commercials which appeared so bored and irritated the viewer that TV advertising became the butt of both the comedians' sarcasm and the critics' indignation.

The most significant change in the agencies was the arrival of the new generation of men and women in key management roles. People under thirty-five started to hold down very senior jobs. Visualizers became art directors, copywriters doubled as scriptwriters, and the television producer was invented. In the media departments TV buyers emerged young and dominant compared to old, tired, heavy-drinking press buyers. And because there were choices to be made, media planners were invented; most importantly, agency finances were massively enhanced. After all, TV advertising was as much an extra exposure as an expensive activity. The most significant TV campaign was the launch of Babycham on television, using André Sarrut's brilliant animation. This campaign remains forever living proof that television advertising works and contains within it the proof that consumer habits can change if properly persuaded.

At that time young women were rarely seen in public houses or if they were they did not know what to drink. Babycham, the brilliant creation of Francis Showering, offered them a drink which neither overpowered them with volume like a half of bitter nor overpowered them with alcohol like a gin and orange. With the simple catchphrase 'I'd love a Babycham' Showering and Jack Wynne-Williams (whose advertising agency was responsible) enabled girls to know what to drink and what to enjoy. The drink truly became 'champagne for the masses', as its creator had intended. In later years, under bad advertising management, the brand became 'cheap champagne' or an 'aid to seduction', but now, with the help of Saatchi and Saatchi, it has become again pre-eminent as a sort of slightly alcoholic Coca-Cola.

By the time the TV network was fully formed in 1961–62 British agencies had at last started to originate work, and some great campaigns appeared both creatively and in terms of the techniques of TV advertising. In my time at CPV I remember particularly Sunblest with Sammy and Susie, Army recruitment using two-and-a-half-minute commercials after the news, and, most particularly, the conversion of smelly old Mr Therm to modern clean high-speed gas. There was, of course, still cigarette advertising until 1965, and at one extreme I remember the Gold Box Benson and Hedges advertising created by Alan Waldie while at CDP under Frank Lowe, which was not only brilliantly conceived but brilliantly received; at the other, I remember a commercial for Players featuring Stanley Matthews and captioned 'from one great player to another'. Sadly, both extremes still exist even after twenty-five years of experience.

As we entered the sixties the industry, both agencies and TV contractors, began to add to the statutory controls by voluntary control as history has shown all this had done is postpone the inevitable and set the standards for the next legal tranche of impediments on the freedom to advertise – a strategy of damage which seems to me to wrongly delay coming to terms with the inevitable. Although the American agencies were beginning to dominate the British scene, some great work was done in the sixties, particularly using animation. I well remember the Esso 'Blee Dooler', who became a national figure selling that unlikely product, paraffin. Sydney and Albert recast man as a dog's best friend, and of course the Homepride Flour Grader produced a great new agency in Geers Gross, a figure for the whole nation to love, and a new brand leader in the flour market. Schweppes became 'Sch . . . you know who' and Watney's Red Barrel led the new revolution. Great catchphrases were created in 'I'm only here for the beer' and 'Nice one, Cyril,' although I am not sure that great things happened to the sale of Double Diamond and Wonderloaf. On the boring and irritating side (known euphemistically as hard sell) Mars bars, Whiskas and Chum began to dominate our screens. I have always believed that this and detergent advertising rely heavily on expenditure to achieve their effect. I dread to think how much we might have consumed if this advertising had contained a compelling idea creatively executed – maybe no more, but at least we could have enjoyed doing it. I always remember a UK head of Procter and Gamble telling me that it was only when he got letters begging him to stop his advertising that he knew that it was working.

There was little or no car advertising in the sixties, due to the secret cartel agreement between the manufacturers, and virtually no spirit advertising for the same reason. Our screens were filled with food and packaged-goods advertising, most of which was highly unmemorable and uninspiring. We were all awaiting the seventies, when the creative revolution would be unleashed ten years after the one in the USA and yet become much more significant in its long-lasting effect. It has always fascinated me that the US agencies which dominated British advertising in the sixties never imported the good work being done in their home country to the colonial outpost of the UK, but perhaps that is the reason. In the seventies all this changed, the two key factors being the starting up of Saatchi and Saatchi and the emergence of CDP

Right The **Health Education Council** were responsible for a number of hard-hitting commercials in the anti-smoking campaign which appeared on television and in the cinema

Opposite, top **Players Cigarettes**. This was one of the first campaigns to come under the ITA's 'qualitative' restrictions in 1962 before the Minister of Health's total ban on cigarette advertising three years later. Over one hundred Players commercials had to be taken off the air

Capstan Cigarettes used slogans like 'made to make friends' and 'let Capstan take the strain' and showed young people enjoying the product in relaxed outdoor settings

Opposite, second from the bottom **Strand Cigarettes**. Although the Strand 'lonely man' commercials are still remembered after more than twenty years they failed to establish the brand among smokers. But actor Terence Brook and the 'Lonely Man' theme music by Cliff Adams became famous

Opposite **Benson and Hedges Cigarettes**. The commercials for B and H Special Filter were much admired for casting, direction and the Jacques Loussier arrangements of the music of J. S. Bach. The campaign featured actors like Peter Sellers, Dudley Moore, Terry-Thomas and Eric Sykes

1st Man: How d'you mean she's horrible?

2nd Man: Her hair smells. Her clothes smell. Her breath . . .

. . . it's like kissing an old ashtray

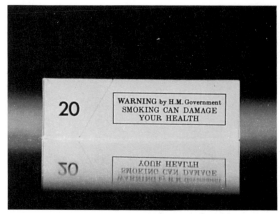

Sometimes it isn't only your health that cigarettes damage.

Players Cigarettes
Capstan Cigarettes

Strand Cigarettes
Benson and Hedges Cigarettes

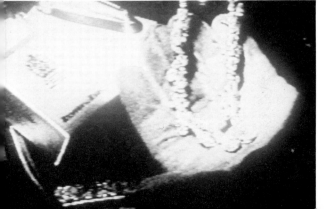

as the pre-eminent creative force. Both were television-led, and both still in one form or another (Frank Lowe, who led CDP in the seventies, is now LHS) dominating today's television advertising. These two, together with BMP, have made a lasting change to TV advertising from which the industry will not revert.

Through the sixties I had worked my way up from a TV buyer at CPV, through Media Group Head at Hobson Bates, to Media Director at Geers Gross. Then in 1970 Charles Saatchi rang me up and said: 'I hear you're the best media man in Britain, why don't you join us?' He was starting an agency – there were to be only nine of us, we only had two accounts and he was only twenty-six (I was twenty-eight and Maurice was twenty-four.) It was a massive leap in the dark – but he had done the pregnant-man ad and I thought that was the best ad I had ever seen, so I said yes.

One of the accounts was Jaffa oranges – the Citrus Marketing Board of Israel – and we came up with the line 'The chosen fruit,' but the IBA banned it because they thought it would stir up racial hatred. The other account was the Health Education Council and its anti-smoking campaign, which is what first got the Saatchi name known. It was the first time anyone had really done attitude-change advertising. In the wake of the Royal College of Physicians' report which linked lung cancer and smoking, Saatchi's launched the campaign with a commercial which intercut lemmings leaping off a cliff and commuters smoking as they crossed Waterloo Bridge; the voice-over said: 'There's a strange Arctic rodent called the lemming which every year throws itself off a cliff. It's as though it wanted to die. Every year in Britain thousands of men and women smoke cigarettes. It's as though they want to die. . . .'

It was the making of Saatchi's, because the controversy got them talked about in the national press – something which happened more and more as the years went on until the agency itself became a household word as none had before. There was a terrific series of ads – the quizmaster saying that if you smoke forty cigarettes a day you could win a case of chronic bronchitis, the line 'It smells like you're kissing an old ashtray', and every ad got talked about.

At the same time we were learning about attitude and behaviour changing. Three lessons emerged: first, to go for the young. It was too late to try to stop people who smoked heavily – the habit was entrenched. So it was decided to concentrate instead on stopping people from starting. Second was the consonance/dissonance model, which is a fundamental principle of communication. If somebody smokes and

Esso Blue Paraffin used an appealing north country cartoon character, the 'Esso Blee Dooler', in a series of telephone misunderstandings

enjoys it, that is consonance; if they smoke knowing that they might die, that is dissonance. So the purpose of the campaign was to shift them from consonance to dissonance. Of course they would try escape routes – like they could be run over by a bus – but we aimed to shut them off.

The most powerful of these ads, which actually resulted in a major behavioural change, showed a baby in an incubator surrounded by doctors and nurses. One doctor was saying, 'Poor thing. It's so weak because the mother smoked during pregnancy.' That really did shake women up.

The third thing we learned was latitude-of-acceptance theory, which is that a communication can be critically affected by the communicator. The same words in two different people's mouths can have a totally different effect. It was found that non-smokers telling smokers not to smoke got you nowhere. Smokers said these people didn't understand. Lapsed non-smokers were used; they were much better able to communicate – even to children who hadn't yet started.

Thus by 1978 the wheel had turned a full 180 degrees from Stanley Matthews and a footballer was used yet again – but this time it was John Hollins saying that if he had smoked he would never have played for England. He was a non-smoker, but it worked because he was a footballer. We had started off by saying that it you smoke you'll get lung cancer, and ended up by saying that if you smoke you won't be fit and your breath will smell. You would have thought that the greater impact would have been the threat of lung cancer, but it wasn't. We found that young people don't think about death – it is too far away. Young people don't die – only the old do. But being fit like John Hollins, or appearing unattractive to the opposite sex because you smell like an old ashtray, really does matter.

Although we were working to stop people smoking, I had worked on cigarette ads before – and Saatchi's now have Silk Cut. I didn't, and still don't, see any problem about this. In fact I still don't think cigarette ads should have been banned from television. Advertising is, in part, advocacy, and a society where all sides of an argument are expressed and people are allowed to make up their own minds is far better than a totalitarian one which tries to censor opinions. I think it would have been a fairer way to treat people to have allowed cigarette ads to go on, though maybe with a levy on them to finance some of the anti-smoking ads. To allow them in the press and on posters and not on TV is ludicrous.

Ironically, having the HEC accounts held Saatchi's back in a way, because people said that while they could do dramatic work for attitude-changing and Government campaigns, the same approach would not work for products. It was not until 1974, when Saatchi's bought Garland-Compton and got Procter and Gamble and Rowntree's and then won the Schweppes business, that things began to change for them.

The decade was full of surprises for the industry as a whole. Who could have foretold, for example, that the controversy over cigarette advertising and the restrictions on it would lead directly to one of the finest campaigns we have seen on television – Hamlet cigars? It was a campaign, incidentally, which if it were starting today would not get within a million miles of our television screens. The story of Hamlet is one of the remarkable successes of TV advertising. For a start, cigar advertising only came about because we weren't allowed to advertise cigarettes, but we could advertise pipe tobacco and cigars – the RCP study had not been so harsh about them. What the manufacturers immediately did was to call their tobacco by the name of their ciga-

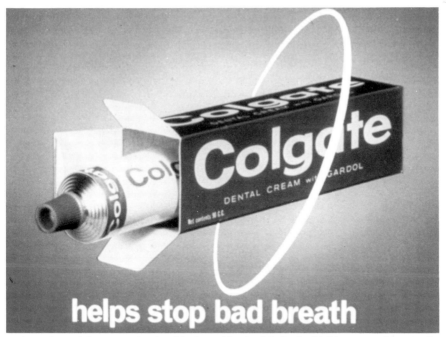

Colgate Dental Cream maintained its brand leadership in the highly competitive tooth-paste market with its 'invisible protective shield' and later the Colgate 'ring of confidence'

rettes. So Benson and Hedges introduced Mellow Flake, and would have a big B and H logo on the screen, making it effectively cigarette advertising.

Tim Warrener, who worked at CDP, wrote the line while travelling on top of a bus one night – 'Happiness is a cigar called Hamlet.' Thus Hamlet's advertising is the closest thing to promoting a drug that there has ever been, because what it does is show people experiencing a disaster – then they light a cigar and the disaster doesn't matter. It isn't that the disaster is averted – it's that they don't care any more. The absolute definition of a drug – the whole point of a drug – is that it lifts you out of your environment and enables you to be euphoric. And the line automatically implies that if you smoke a cigar you will be happy.

The only reason it is still allowed to run is that it was done fifteen years ago. The authorities argue that it doesn't matter because it's established. If you've passed it once, how do you unpass it? It is very much the same with Heineken – that campaign too would never now get through. It implies a beneficial property to the beer which the code says you are not allowed to do.

447

The two campaigns are, of course, saved by their sense of humour. In the sixties there was a famous campaign for Silvikrin which featured a really good-looking guy with a fantastic car and great clothes and a terrific girl, and it encouraged all the kids to put Silvikrin on their hair because it would make them successful. We are not allowed to do that any more. The code has tightened up every year since it started. We are implying that non-physical benefit results from consumption of the product.

The ultimate irony is, however, that the two most famous campaigns of the seventies and eighties are Hamlet and Heineken, yet tobacco and drink are the most highly controlled areas of advertising. I believe the message is that Hamlet and Heineken are probably the greatest pieces of advertising written since 1970 because they are in areas where the code is extremely prohibitive. When you get yourself trapped and you're not allowed to say all the conventional things, your imagination starts to work overtime and genuine creativity results.

There were three agencies who really influenced the seventies: CDP, Saatchi's and Boase Massimi Pollit. BMP's most famous campaign was the Martians for Cadbury's Smash. Incidentally, it took quite a lot for them to talk the client out of saying 'For Mash get Cadbury's Smash', which would have ruined the whole effect. Up against Smash was a similar product launched by Mars – called Wonder Mash. If ever there was a lesson to be learned about TV advertising it was in the battle between these two products. Smash used an out-of-this-world scenario with Martians and humour and a clever line at the end, but with a serious message that it was easier than boiling potatoes and crushing them. Wonder Mash went on about the granules in the bag and how it turned into mashed potato and the technology that was involved – it was the first commercial example of accelerated freeze-drying. Wonder Mash lost, because it wasn't about being right, it was all about hearts and minds. There is no doubt that Wonder Mash was logically correct and absolutely communicated the product's benefit, but nobody liked it as much as Smash, despite the fact that frequently Wonder Mash was cheaper.

Examples like that occur all the way through advertising history. Homepride flour versus McDougall's was another. McDougall's did advertising saying that their flour would rise and make wonderful light pastry and cakes and so on, and Homepride had little men in bowler hats jumping in bags and knocking lumps out. Homepride won, but don't misunderstand me – in both cases they were good products and they had product advantages.

Lego. The Danish construction toy, Lego, was successfully launched in Britain by its agency, TBWA. The commercials went on to win several major awards

From the explosion of TV advertising in the 1970s we began to learn, or relearn, many of the fundamentals of our trade. Three lessons in particular stand out: first, that TV advertising specifically lowers the price of goods, because it increases the volume of sales, from which comes increased productivity, which means the cost of goods goes down, which means the cost to the consumer goes down. Second, it forces the competition to produce better products. Razor blades have developed from the old Gillette blue disposables and non-disposables, double-sided and stainless steel, all because the competition is advertising. All the flour is now ready-sieved.

The third thing it does is to make people aware very quickly of new products and new product ideas, and that means it speeds up the whole learning curve. How long would it take, without television advertising, for people to discover the numerous soft drinks that exist or the variety of babies' nappies? What is more, because of the speed with which you can bring products to the market you can correspondingly quickly move on to the next technology. The learning curve of the manufacturer is thus speeded up and, in order to get an edge, he keeps on trying to develop a better product.

We also learned a lot more about target marketing in the seventies, particularly when aiming at the young. Saatchi's produced the classic Brutus jeans campaign, where the David Dundas backing track went to No.1. If you're aiming at fourteen- to eighteen-year-old kids and you can pitch a song that will go into the pop charts, there is absolutely no doubt that you have correctly aimed at your audience. In fact, the Brutus jeans story was a tremendous success because up until then Levi's had always had a huge brand share with all the others on a tiny percentage. Then in one year Brutus got about 18 per cent of the market. Another interesting development which emerged was the use of voice-over artists. Bill Mitchell's deep dark voice became well known, as did Orson Welles doing Carlsberg. We started to get very famous voices, and it became a great thing to try to get a well-known name to do voice-overs and to appear on screen in commercials as 'actors in a play'. It really started at the end of the sixties – Eric Sykes and Peter Sellers were both in the Benson and Hedges Gold Box commercials. Then, about the mid-seventies, David Bailey was used to do Olympus cameras. A famous campaign for Texaco had Morecambe and Wise. People were paid huge sums of money, not as presenters but as actors in a play. The reason wasn't primarily because they were famous, it was because they were good actors. The reason Orson Welles was used as a voice-over was because of his consummate ability to deliver a line. It wasn't actually because his voice was famous – though that helped – but he could deliver the line better than ordinary voice-over artists.

Not only did the seventies see an explosion in *how* things were advertised – but also in *what* was advertised. Newspapers came on to TV after the *Sun* was launched. It had enormous TV expenditure, doing almost live commercials with a bloke rushing on and saying, 'This week in the *Sun*.' It was a different commercial each weekend, and it built the paper into something bigger than the *Mirror*. My favourite was 'Pussy Week' in the *Sun* (for cats) – how on earth they got away with it, I don't know. That was done by Hobson Bates originally, and it was really the brainchild of a Media Director called John Hughes, who convinced Sir Larry Lamb that terrific media expenditure on TV would result in huge sales gains. I think they drew the line at 'Tiny Tits Week', though – for bird fanciers.

Another great media success was *Cosmopolitan*, which was Saatchi's in the early seventies. There was a commercial with little vignettes of a man and a girl. The man would say, 'Where did you learn to cook like that?' And she would say, '*Cosmopolitan*, page 48.' Then 'Where did you learn to dress like that?' And so on. It ended up with a couple lying in bed. The guy turned the light on and looked at the girl quizzically, and she said, '*Cosmopolitan*, page 107.' In the original script he had said, 'Where did you learn to do that?' and the IBA took the words out. But of course it didn't make any difference – living proof that some of these things in the code are justice being seen to be done rather than justice being done.

Car advertisements also came onto television – another example of TV benefiting society at large. Datsun arrived from Japan and broke the agreement between Ford, Vauxhall, Chrysler and British Leyland never to advertise. The interesting point is that their success forced all the car manufacturers into improving the quality of their cars because they were suddenly confronted with Japanese cars that had all the extras free – alloy wheels, fitted radios and so on. What is more, they were lower-priced, so British companies had to produce smaller cars at lower prices with all the extras on – the proof of advertising having the effect of forcing down the price of goods.

We also saw a change from ads for package goods being the biggest to retailers becoming the biggest advertisers. Now we have massive expenditure by people such as Sainsbury's, Tesco, Woolworth's and MFI, and the money that would have been spent on advertising a brand of biscuits is actually given in discounts to the retailer, who then advertises the product in his own campaigns on TV.

There are two reasons why the major retailers have chosen to advertise. First, they have realized that they can get people to come in and buy more by telling them these goods are available. Second, they have realized that by creating an image for their stores – by positioning themselves as to the kind of retailer they are – they also influence people's purchasing positions. Now you get dual purchasers asking themselves: 'What shall I buy?' – and 'Where shall I buy it?' What the retailers have also done now is move it around, so that 'Where shall I buy?' comes first. And the manufacturers have had to give in, because the retailer is in control of the situation.

Towards the end of the seventies corporate advertising came along in a big way – although ICI were the first to run a corporate campaign, with 'The Pathfinders' and 'Ideas in Action', the one with the most impact was Dunlop, which Saatchi's did. It showed a girl playing tennis with all the things Dunlop made disappearing, to the line 'Imagine how much you would miss Dunlop.'

BP decided they wanted to separate themselves from the criticism of multinational oil companies which were under a cloud because of the oil crisis in 1974, and Saatchi's handled that campaign, too. The irony was that they spent millions of pounds saying 'BP – Britain at its best' – when if they had never changed their name from British Petroleum to BP they wouldn't have had to point out to people that they were British.

All sorts of other developments took place in the 1970s. The awards system grew tremendously. It became important to win a Lion d'Or at Cannes, and so on. That is what really started the debate raging about what constitutes good TV advertising. There is a great divide in the industry between those people who say commercials that win awards are written for the benefit of other people in the industry – that they are elitist, self-adulatory and nothing to do with selling products – and those who say that ads that don't win awards are boring: they may sell products but they don't capture the imagination, they don't have any warmth.

What we do know after all this is that you cannot write advertising to a formula. You have got to use your imagination, and you have to tackle each opportunity with the maximum amount of creativity. If there were a formula you would be able to apply it, but there isn't one, so therefore – after thirty years – there is no method. Good television advertising requires imagination, creativity and strict discipline: discipline to be single-minded. Great advertising is essentially single-minded. It says: 'Buy this product and this will be the benefit.' Offer more than one benefit and you will confuse people – or they might not want some of what you offer.

There have been some marvellous joys during these years. People with small budgets have outsold people with big budgets simply because their advertising was more competitive. Homepride knocked lumps out of McDougall's. Brutus took the pants off Levi's. Heineken got Carlsberg in a froth without ever outspending them.

We've come a long way since Gibbs' SR, and we've learned a lot – even if we still can't agree what a good ad is, how much it should cost, or exactly what it does. If I had to pick the best campaign from all those years I think it would be Heineken. The best individual ad was, I think, the Fiat robot commercial. Overnight it made cars made by robots better than those made by men.

But my favourite commercial – nothing to do with whether it sold or not – was one that JWT did for Guinness. It showed a toucan sitting on a perch and a man standing in front of it saying: 'Don't forget the Guinness. Don't forget the Guinness.' And the toucan is just looking at him while he goes on and on. Then the door opens, his wife comes in and the toucan says, 'Bad news Mrs Harris. Your husband's turned into a parrot.'

I have a feeling that history will judge the good ads of the era as being those which managed to avoid Mr Harris's fate.

GLOSSARY OF ABBREVIATIONS

Editor's Note

All the abbreviations used in this book are included in the Glossary. So are many others which have gained currency in the period 1955–85 in the fields of advertising and broadcasting. Both are bedevilled with many hundreds of abbreviations which can baffle even the initiated and there is a need for a key to an esoteric language whose vocabulary is constantly on the increase.

Nevertheless, the list does not claim to be completely exhaustive. Nor can it ever be. Committees change their functions, and even their titles; they frequently spawn working parties and divide, as if by binary fission, before they finally disappear. Who now remembers WOPAC or DIMRASC, which once absorbed so much time and paper?

Where possible, I have given a few lines of explanation as to the origins and intended purpose of many of the organizations listed, but I would be grateful to learn of any glaring errors or omissions.

Finally, I have reluctantly decided to omit the initials of all advertising agencies, even those long-established and well-known. To have included a limited number would have been invidious while those accidentally or deliberately ignored would have had justifiable cause for complaint. Besides, advertising agencies have a habit of forming and of devouring one another with even greater rapidity than trade unions and broadcasting organizations.

AA	*Advertising Association* Representative body of British advertising founded in 1926.
AAC	*Advertising Advisory Committee* Set up under the Television Act 1954 to advise the ITA (now IBA) on the principles to be followed in the acceptance of all television advertising.
AAPA	*Advertising Agencies Production Association* Formed in 1963 to foster better standards of reproduction processes used in advertising.

ABC   *American Broadcasting Company* (US).
Associated British Cinemas.
Associated Broadcasting Company Successor to ABDC (qv) later named ATV (qv).
Audit Bureau of Circulations Formed in 1931 to certify accuracy of media circulation figures.
Australian Broadcasting Commission.

ABDC   *Associated Broadcasting Development Company* Fore-runner to ABC (qv) later named ATV (qv).

ABMRC   *Association of British Market Research Companies*

ABPC   *Associated British Picture Corporation* Parent of ABC Television, original programme contractor for the weekends in the Midlands and North.

ABPI   *Association of the British Pharmaceutical Industry* Formed in 1930 to represent the industry and to ensure that medicines of the highest quality are readily available for human and animal needs.

ABS   *Association of Broadcasting Staff* Replaced BBC Staff Association and included some IBA staff.

ABTA   *Association of British Travel Agents* Formed in 1950 to represent travel agents and tour operators.

ABU   *Asia-Pacific Broadcasting Union* Association of national broadcasting organizations in the Asia and Pacific areas.

ACC   *Associated Communications Corporation* Successor to ATV (qv).

ACORN   *A Classification of Residential Neighbourhoods.*

ACP   *American College of Physicians.*

ACR   *Automatic Cassette Recording.*

ACT   *Association of Cine-Technicians* Trade union formed 1933.
Advance Corporation Tax.

ACTT   *Association of Cinematograph Television and Allied Technicians* Replaced ACT (qv) in 1956.

ADA   *American Dental Association.*

AFPA   *Advertising Film Producers Association.*

AFVPA   *Advertising Film and Videotape Producers Association* Formed in 1979 (replacing AFPA) to represent the interests of producers of commercials on film and videotape.

AGB   *Audits of Great Britain (originally Audley, Gapper and Brown).*

AI   *Airtime International* Sales representation company for overseas radio and television stations. Wholly owned subsidiary of Scottish Television.

Appreciation Index Qualitative method of audience measurement by which programmes are 'scored' 0–100.

AIC   *Associated Industrial Consultants* Management consultancy company which devised first booking system for TV commercials.

Advertising Inquiry Council An unofficial group of MPs and others formed in the 1960s.

AIP   *Association of Independent Producers* Established in 1976 to represent the interests of the producers of films for the cinema and television.

AIRC   *Association of Independent Radio Contractors* Formed 1973 to represent interests of ILR (qv) companies.

ALC   *Advertising Liaison Committee* IBA committee established in 1980 to foster relationships, in which the Authority staff would be involved, between ITV programme companies and advertisers and agencies.

AM   *Amplitude Modulation* The original method of transmitting speech and music on a carrier wave. Used for long, medium and short-wave broadcasting.

AMI   *Association of Media Independents* Formed in 1981 to represent the interests of independent media specialists.

AMMC   *Audience Measurement Management Committee* Sub-committee of BARB (qv) dealing with quantitative measurement of the TV audience.

AMPS   *All Media and Products Survey.*

AMSO   *Association of Market Survey Organisations.*

ANG   *Associated Newspapers Group.*

A-R   *Associated-Rediffusion* Original London weekday television programme contractor.

ARMC   *Audience Reaction Management Committee* Sub-committee of BARB (qv) dealing with qualitative measurement of the TV audience.

ASA   *Advertising Standards Authority* Self-regulatory body set up by the advertising industry in 1962 to oversee advertising in all non-broadcast media.

ASBOF   *Advertising Standards Board of Finance* The organization which provides funds for the ASA (qv) and the CAP Committee (qv) through a levy of 0.1 per cent on the cost of non-broadcast advertisements.

ASH   *Action on Smoking and Health* Formed in 1971 to investigate damage to health caused by smoking and to promote action against the habit.

ASL   *Audience Selection Limited.*

ASLEF   *Associated Society of Locomotive Engineers and Firemen.*

ASFP   *Association of Specialised Film Producers.*

AS-SCC   *Advertising Sub-committee of the SCC* (qv) The principal forum for discussion of advertising matters between the Authority and the programme companies 1955–1964. Replaced by the JACC (qv).

ATV   *Associated TeleVision* Successor to ABDC and ABC (qv). First programme contractor for weekends in London and weekdays in the Midlands appointed in 1954. Later programme company all week in the Midlands until the end of 1981, when a reconstituted company, Central Television, assumed responsibility for the new dual regions of East and West Midlands.

AURA   *Association of Users of Research Agencies.*

BAFTA   *British Academy of Film and Television Arts.*

BARB   *Broadcasters' Audience Research Board* Joint body formed in 1980 by the BBC and ITCA (qv) to commission audience research.

BBC   *British Broadcasting Corporation* The UK licence fee-supported broadcasting organization established by Royal Charter in 1926 as successor to the British Broadcasting Company.

BBTA   *British Bureau of Television Advertising* Non-profit-making company set up in 1966 by the ITV companies to promote the use of television advertising.

BCU   *Big close-up.*

BDA   *British Dental Association.*

BDHO   *Broadcasting Department of the Home Office* Responsible for broadcasting matters since March 1974.

BDMA   *British Direct Marketing Association.*

BDMAA   *British Direct Mail Advertising Association.*

BET   *British Electric Traction Company* Parent company of A–R (qv)

BETA   *Broadcasting and Entertainment Trades Alliance* Non-performance trade union formed by the amalgamation in 1984 between ABS (qv) and NATTKE (qv).

BFI   *British Film Institute* Founded in 1933 to encourage the art and appreciation of film. Incorporates the National Film Theatre and National Film Archive.

BFPA   *British Film Producers Association.*

BFTPA   *British Film and Television Producers Association* Trade and employers association formed by the BFPA in 1973.

BISFA   *British Industrial and Scientific Films Association.*

BMA   *British Medical Association.*

BMRB   *British Market Research Bureau.*

BPO   *British Post Office* Government department originally responsible for posts and telecommunications. Under the British Telecommunications Act 1981 the Post Office retained responsibility only for postal and Girobank services.

BREMA   *British Radio Equipment Manufacturers Association.*

BRTA   *British Regional Television Association* Association of the ten regional ITV companies.

BRS   *Broadcast Relay Service Limited* The Rediffusion group of companies.

BRW   *British Relay Wireless.*

BSAVA   *British Small Animals Veterinary Association.*

BSI   *British Standards Institution* Formed in 1901 to establish national standards for industrial and commercial products.

BT   *British Telecommunications* Public limited company formed in 1984 to provide telecommunications and data-processing services.

BVA   *British Veterinary Association.*
British Videogram Association Represents the interests (particularly in the field of copyright) of British producers and distributors of pre-recorded videocassettes and discs.

CA   *Cable Authority* Established under the Cable and Broadcasting Act 1984 to promote, license and establish cable programme services.
Consumers Association Formed in 1956 to improve the standards of goods and services on sale to the public and to publish the magazine *Which?*.

CAA   *Cinema Advertising Association.*

CAAC   *Central Appeals Advisory Committee* Established jointly by the BBC and IBA to advise on the allocation of broadcast time for charitable appeals.

CAM   *Communication Advertising and Marketing Education Foundation* Financed by the advertising industry to promote education in advertising and marketing and to award certificates and diplomas.

CAP   *British Code of Advertising Practice* The code of standards and practice governing all non-broadcast media administered by the CAP Committee under the supervision of the ASA (qv).

CATCH   *Chief Assistant Television Contracts and Hearings* Senior member of the IBA staff responsible for processing applications for ITV contracts and arranging public consultations.

CATV   *Community Antenna Television* The use of a single master antenna (aerial) for programmes distributed by a local cable system, for example, in a large block of flats.

CBC   *Canadian Broadcasting Corporation.*

CBI   *Confederation of British Industry* Founded in 1956 to promote the interests and efficiency of British industry. Successor to the FBI (qv).

CBS   *Columbia Broadcasting System* (US).

CCIR   *Comité Consultatif International des Radio- communications.*

CCU   *Camera control unit.*

CEA   *Cinematograph Exhibitors Association* Established in 1912 to represent the interests of cinema owners and exhibitors.

CEEFAX   *See facts* BBC teletext system.

CNN   *Cable News Network* (US).

CoI   *Central Office of Information* Government service department producing information, advertising and publicity material for other UK government departments.

CP(M)   *Counter Products (Marketing).*

CPT   *Cost-per-thousand.*

CRAC   *Central Religious Advisory Committee* Committee representative of religious thought in Britain which advises both the BBC and the IBA. (See also CAAC.)

CRS   *Central Rediffusion Services.*

	Cooperative Retail Society.
CSA	*Creative Services Association.*
CSO	*Colour Separation Overlay* The use of electronic techniques to insert a picture against a plain background. Known as 'Chromakey' in ITV.
CTA	*Cable Television Association* Represents the interests of companies providing cable television services.
CTBF	*Cinematograph and Television Benevolent Fund.*
CTS	*Central Independent Television Advertising Sales* Body set up by a number of programme companies to promote advertising on ITV in Europe.
CU	*Close-up.*
D and AD	*Designers and Art Directors Association* (also known as DADA).
DBS	*Direct Broadcasting by Satellite* The transmission of television or radio programmes via a geostationary artificial earth satellite at sufficient power to permit reception via small 'dish' aerials which are of less than about 1-metre diameter.
DEA	*Department of Economic Affairs.*
DEP	*Department of Employment and Productivity.*
Db	*Decibel.*
DG	*Director-General.*
DHSS	*Department of Health and Social Security.*
DRASC	*Direct Response Advertising Sub-committee* Sub-committee of the ITCA Marketing Committee dealing with direct response and cash-with-order advertising.
DSIR	*Department of Scientific and Industrial Research.*
DTI	*Department of Trade and Industry.*
EAAA	*European Association of Advertising Agencies* Founded in 1960 to maintain and raise standards of service among European advertising agencies and foster competition.
EAN	*European Article Numbering* System of bar-coding for laser-scanning at the point-of-sale.
EAT	*European Advertising Tripartite.*
EBU	*European Broadcasting Union* Association of national broadcasting organizations established in 1950 to promote the interests of broadcasting cooperation and programme exchange.
ECS	*European Communications Satellite.*
ECU	*Extreme close-up.*

EETPU	*Electrical Electronic Telecommunications and Plumbing Union.*
EFP	*Electronic Field Production* The making of programmes on location using one or more electronic TV cameras and the use of videotape recording for editing.
EFTA	*European Free Trade Area* Group of seven European countries promoting mutual trading arrangements outside the original EEC.
EGTA	*European Group of Television Advertising* Established in 1970 to exchange information on advertising and media research and to study developments in the electronic media.
EIU	*Economist Intelligence Unit.*
ELDO	*European Launcher and Development Organisation.*
EMS	*Enhanced Measurement System* The new system of television audience measurement introduced in 1984 based on push-button meters and data retrieval by telephone line.
ENG	*Electronic News Gathering.*
EPOS	*Electronic Point-of-Sale* Laser-scanning of bar codes at the point-of-sale to record product sales information.
ESA	*European Space Agency.*
ESOMAR	*European Society for Opinion Surveys and Market Research* Founded in 1948 to promote the use of marketing and social research and to foster the highest professional standards.
ETU	*Electrical Trades Union* Now EETPU (qv).
FBI	*Federation of British Industries* Now the CBI (qv).
FBU	*Federation of Broadcasting Unions.*
FCC	*Federal Communications Commission* (US).
FDA	*Food and Drug Administration* (US).
FM	*Frequency Modulation* A method of transmitting speech and music on a carrier wave by varying its frequency rather than its amplitude (cf. AM). Also used for VHF sound and DBS television (qv). Uses more of the frequency spectrum than AM transmission.
FMCG	*Fast-moving consumer goods.*
FMF	*Food Manufacturers Federation.*
FPA	*Film Producers Association.*
FPG	*Film Purchasing Group.*
FS	*Fixed Spot.*

FTC	*Federal Trade Commission* (US).
FVO	*Female voice-over.*
FX	*Effects.*
GARC	*Guaranteed Audience Rate Card* Original method of publication of GHI and GHR rates (qv) in which the total audience and/or cost-per-thousand (qv) delivered to the advertiser are guaranteed.
GDP	*Gross Domestic Product.*
GHI	*Guaranteed Home Impressions* (or *Impacts*).
GHR	*Guaranteed Homes Ratings.*
GHz	*Giga Hertz* = 1000MHz (qv).
GNP	*Gross National Product.*
GPO	*General Post Office.*
HAC	*Head of Advertising Control* Senior member of the IBA staff responsible to the Director-General for all advertising matters. Appointment was retitled Controller of Advertising.
HBO	*Home Box Office* (US).
HDTV	*High Definition Television.*
HEC	*Health Education Council* Established in 1968 with members appointed by the Secretary of State for Social Services to act as the national centre for health education, information and publicity.
HOTA	*Heads of Television Association* Consists of Heads of Television of advertising agencies.
HPS	*Head of Programme Services* Senior member of IBA staff.
HTV	*Harlech Television* The name of the company was changed in April 1970 to HTV.
Hz	*Hertz* Unit of frequency equal to 1 cycle per second.
IAA	*International Advertising Association* Founded in 1938 to advance the general level of advertising and marketing efficiency.
IBA	*Independent Broadcasting Authority* The name adopted by the Independent Television Authority from 12 July 1972 when the Authority became responsible for ILR (qv). The public authority responsible for broadcasting services financed by the sale of advertising time.
IBC	*International Broadcasting Convention.*
IBiol	*Institute of Biology.*
ICC	*International Chamber of Commerce* Founded in 1920

	with national committees in many countries to represent the views of those with interests in international business.
IEE	*Institution of Electrical Engineers* Founded in 1871.
IFST	*Institute of Food Science and Technology.*
IGD	*Institute of Grocery Distribution.*
ILR	*Independent Local Radio* Collective title for independent local radio stations appointed and supervised by the IBA (qv) and financed by the sale of advertising time.
IMSM	*Institute of Marketing and Sales Management* Formerly the Incorporated Sales Managers Association (1921–61) now known as Institute of Marketing.
InstM	*Institute of Marketing* Professional body which replaced IMSM (qv) in 1968.
IOJ	*Institute of Journalists* Founded in 1890.
IPA	*Institute of Practitioners in Advertising* Founded in 1917 as the Association of British Advertising Agencies with both personal and corporate membership. Formerly the Institute of Incorporated Practitioners in Advertising (IIPA).
IPPA	*Independent Programme Producers Association* Formed in 1981 to represent the interests of British independent programme producers.
ISBA	*Incorporated Society of British Advertisers* Established in 1900 to represent and foster the interests of British advertisers.
ISP	*Institute of Sales Promotion.*
ITA	*Independent Television Authority* Public authority set up by the Television Act 1954 to provide a national television service financed by the sale of advertising time. Replaced in 1972 by the IBA (qv).
ITAP	*Information Technology Advisory Panel* Government body formed in June 1981 to advise the Cabinet (through the Minister for Information Technology) on matters of information technology.
ITC	*International Television Corporation.*
ITCA	*Independent Television Companies Association* Trade association formed in May 1958 to replace the TPCA (qv).
ITN	*Independent Television News* Company formed in May 1955, and owned by all ITV companies, which provides daily news programmes for ITV and Channel Four.

ITP	*Independent Television Publications* Company owned by all programme contractors which publishes *TV Times* and other publications.
ITV	*Independent Television* Collective title for service provided by the programme contractors under the IBA (qv).
IWMA	*Institute of Weights and Measures Administration.*
JACC	*Joint Advertisement Control Committee* A committee under the chairmanship of the IBA's Controller of Advertising formed in 1964 at which problems of advertising control are discussed by the IBA and ITCA.
JICTAR	*Joint Industry Committee for Television Advertising Research* Committee representative of advertisers, agencies and programme companies formed in 1960 to replace TARAC (qv). Now itself replaced by BARB (qv).
kHz	*Kilo Hertz* = 1000Hz (qv).
KRS	*Kinematograph Renters Society.*
LS	*Long shot.*
LWT	*London Weekend Television.*
MAP	*Medical Advisory Panel* Group of consultants appointed by the ITCA (qv) and given statutory powers in 1964 to advise the Authority on general and specialized medical matters, including veterinary science, in the acceptance of all advertisements relating to health and nutrition.
MAS	*Marketing Advisory Services.*
MBS	*Mutual Broadcasting System* (US).
MCA	*Music Corporation of America* (US).
MCPS	*Mechanical Copyright Protection Society.*
MCU	*Medium close-up.*
MEAL	*Media Expenditure Analysis Limited.*
MHz	*Mega Hertz* = 1000kHz (qv).
MIS	*Marketing Intelligence Services.*
MoI	*Ministry of Information* Wartime forerunner of the CoI (qv) of which Sir Robert Fraser, the first Director-General of the ITA (qv), was Controller of Production.
MORI	*Marketing and Opinion Research International.*
MRG	*Media Research Group.*
MRS	*Market Research Society.*
MS	*Medium shot.*
μV/m	*Microvolts per metre.* Measurement of signal strength.

MVO   *Male voice-over.*

NAB   *National Association of Broadcasters* (US).

NABS   *National Advertising Benevolent Society.*

NARAL   *Net Advertisement Revenue (or Receipts) After Levy.*

NARBL   *Net Advertisement Revenue (or Receipts) Before Levy.*

NATSOPA   *National Society of Operative Printers Graphical and Media Personnel.*

NATTKE   *National Association of Television Theatrical and Kine Employees.*

NBC   *National Broadcasting Company* (US).

NBPI   *National Board for Prices and Incomes.*

NCC   *National Consumer Council* Independent body established in 1975 and supported by Government grant to safeguard the interests of consumers.

NCW   *National Council of Women* Established in 1895 to promote the participation of women in public life.

NFT   *National Film Theatre.*

NFWI   *National Federation of Women's Institutes.*

NGA   *National Graphical Association.*

NOP   *National Opinion Polls.*

NOSC   *Network Operational Sub-committee* Group formed by ITV programme companies sales, presentation and traffic staffs to coordinate programme timings and placing of commercial breaks on all stations.

NPA   *Newpaper Publishers' Association* Founded in 1906 (as the Newspaper Proprietors' Association) to represent the interests of national morning and Sunday newspapers.

NPC   *Network Programme Committee.*

NPD   *New Product Development.*

NRS   *National Readership Survey.*

NS   *Newspaper Society* Formed in 1906 to represent the interests of local and regional newspapers.

NTI   *Nielsen Television Index.*

NTSC   *National Television Systems Committee* (US) Formed in early 1950s, it agreed and developed the US colour TV system based on 525 lines and 60Hz. Used in Japan and a few other countries. The remainder preferred the 50Hz PAL and SECAM (qv) systems.

NUJ   *National Union of Journalists.*

OOV   *Out of vision.*

OPCS   *Office of Population Censuses and Surveys* Government body controlling the registration of births, marriages and deaths and undertaking periodic population censuses. It was formed by the merger in 1970 of the General Register Office and the Government Social Survey Department.

ORACLE   *Optional Reception of Announcements by Coded Line Electronics* The teletext service developed by the IBA in 1972-73 and used for the transmission of editorial and advertising material on ITV and Channel Four.

OTC   *Over the counter* Most frequently applied to remedies for self-medication as opposed to prescription medicines.

OTS   *Opportunities to see.*
Orbital Test Satellite Experimental low-power test satellite launched in May 1978.

PA   *Production Assistant.*

PAC   *Public Accounts Committee.*

PAGB   *Proprietary Association of Great Britain* Formed in 1919 to represent the interests of the manufacturers of medicines sold to the public without prescription.

PAL   *Phase Alternation Line* Colour-television system used in the UK and many other 50Hz countries (but not France or the USSR).

PAS   *Public Attitude Surveys.*

PBS   *Public Broadcasting System* (US). Non-commercial TV network in the USA.

PCG   *Programme Controllers Group.*

PI   *Per item* System of charging for television airtime on the basis of number of items sold as a result of the advertising campaign.

PIB   *Prices and Incomes Board.*

PMG   *Postmaster-General* Government minister responsible until 1969 for posts and telecommunications.

PPA   *Periodical Publishers' (formerly Proprietors') Association.*
Pool Promoters Association.

PPC   *Programme Policy Committee* Committee consisting of Chief Executives of all ITV companies chaired by the Chairman of the Authority.

PRS   *Performing Right Society* Formed in 1914 to collect royalties for public performance (including broadcasting) of copyright music on behalf of composers, publishers and authors.

PS	*Pharmaceutical Society of Great Britain* Founded in 1841 to promote pharmacy and pharmaceutical education.
R and D	*Research and development.*
RAI	*Radiotelevisione Italiana* Italy's public broadcasting service.
RAL	*Retail Audits Limited.*
RBL	*Research Bureau Limited.*
RCA	*Radio Corporation of America* (US).
RCGP	*Royal College of General Practitioners.*
RCOG	*Royal College of Obstetricians and Gynaecologists.*
RCP	*Royal College of Physicians.*
RCS	*Royal College of Surgeons.*
RCVS	*Royal College of Veterinary Surgeons.*
RDU	*Remote Detection Unit* Audience measurement device capable of measuring viewing on up to four TV sets in one home, storing information temporarily and transmitting it for central computer processing by telephone line.
RECMF	*Radio and Electrical Component Manufacturers Federation.*
RIC	*Radio Industry Council* Established in 1914 to coordinate the interests of the electronics industry in the consumer sector.
	Radio Industries Club.
	Royal Institute of Chemistry.
RO	*Regional Officer* Member of IBA staff responsible for liaison with ITV and ILR companies in designated areas.
ROD	*Run-of-the-day.*
ROM	*Run-of-the-month.*
ROW	*Run-of-the-week.*
RPI	*Retail Prices Index.*
RSA	*Relay Services Association.*
	Royal Society of Arts.
RSGB	*Research Surveys of Great Britain.*
RTE	*Radio Telefís Eireann* Broadcasting service of the Republic of Ireland.
RTS	*Royal Television Society* Formed in 1927 as the Television Society to foster the arts and sciences of television.
RTSA	*Retail Trading Standards Association* An association of retailers and manufacturers to promote high standards in advertising and sales practices.
	Radio Television and Screen Advertising Sub-committee

	A sub-committee of the ISBA (qv) dealing with questions of radio, television and cinema advertising affecting advertisers.
S4C	*Sianel Pedwar Cymru (Welsh fourth channel)* Television service for Wales established under the Broadcasting Act 1980 and controlled by the Welsh Fourth Channel Authority.
SAA	*Screen Advertising Association.*
SAWA	*Screen Advertising World Association.*
SBB	*Satellite Broadcasting Board.*
SCC	*Standing Consultative Committee* Principal committee for consultation between the IBA (qv) and the programme companies on major policy matters. Chaired by the Director-General of the Authority.
SCNI	*Select Committee on Nationalized Industries.*
SDNS	*Scottish Daily Newspaper Society.*
SECAM	*Sequentiale Couleur à Mémoire* Colour television system adopted by a number of countries notably France and the USSR.
SET	*Selective Employment Tax.*
SFPA	*Specialised Film Producers Association.*
SFTA	*Society of Film and Television Arts.*
SFX	*Sound effects.*
SHEU	*Scottish Health Education Unit.*
SHF	*Super High Frequency* 3000-30000mHz (i.e. 3–30gHz). Used for terrestrial microwave links and for satellite transmissions.
SIA	*Storage Instantaneous Audimeter* Equipment devised by the A. C. Nielsen Company for recording and temporarily storing in-home viewing information for automatic retrieval by telephone line and computer analysis.
SLADE	*Society of Lithographic Artists Designers and Engravers.*
SMATV	*Satellite Master Antenna Television* Small cable distribution system receiving its signal from a satellite via a dish aerial usually 1.8 to 3 metres in diameter.
SMPTE	*Society of Motion Picture and Television Engineers* (US).
SOGAT 82	*Society of Graphical and Allied Trades.*
STAGS	*Scottish Television and Grampian Sales* Joint sales company for STV (qv) and Grampian which operated from 1970 until 1981.
STV	*Scottish Television.*

TABS	*Television Advertising Bureau Surveys.*
TAC	*Television Advisory Committee* Appointed to advise the Government through the Minister concerned (PMG or Home Secretary) on matters affecting television.
	Tobacco Advisory Council A committee of the major tobacco manufacturers under an independent Chairman formed in 1940 as the TMSC (qv).
TAD	*Television Advertisement Duty* An excise duty on all television advertisements applied from 1 May 1961 at the rate of 10 per cent. Increased to 11 per cent from July 1961 and replaced by Exchequer levy from 1964 on revenue and later profits.
TAM	*Television Audience Measurement Limited* Supplier of industry audience measurement service from 1955 to 1968.
TAPE	*Television Audience Programme Evaluation* System of prediction of audiences to television programmes devised by the advertising agency, Masius Wynne-Williams.
TARAC	*Television Audience Research Advisory Committee* Committee of programme companies, advertisers and agencies responsible for planning and controlling television audience measurement prior to the formation of JICTAR (qv).
TC	*Till countermanded (or cancelled).*
TCA	*Television Consumer Audit* Regular in-home audit of products advertised on television set up by programme companies in 1962 originally in the Midlands and extended to London and the North in 1963 using AGB (qv) research facilities. Later extended nationally.
TEN	*The Entertainment Network* Early UK cable service.
TFVA	*Television Film and Video Association.*
TGI	*Target Group Index* Method of assessing large national research sample of individuals by marketing characteristics operated by BMRB (qv).
TIE	*Television International Enterprises.*
TMC	*The Movie Channel* (US).
TMSC	*Tobacco Manufacturers Standing Committee* Forerunner of the TAC (qv).
TOM	*Television Output Monitor.*
TPA	*Television Press Agency.*
TPCA	*Television Programme Contractors' Association* Fore-

runner of ITCA (qv).

TRC	*Tobacco Research Council.*
TRI	*Television Reporters International.*
TRIC	*Television Radio Industries Club.*
TS-SCC	*Technical Sub-Committee of the SCC* (qv) Principal forum for discussion of engineering matters between the IBA and the programme companies.
TSW	*Television South West.*
TTI	*Thames Television International.*
	Thomson Television International.
TTT	*Tyne Tees Television.*
TVA	*Television Advertising Limited.*
TVB	*Television Bureau* (US).
TVI	*Television International.*
TVR	*Television Rating.*
TVS	*Television South.*
TWW	*Television Wales and West of England.*
TXN	*Transmission.*
UHF	*Ultra High Frequency* 300-300mHz which includes Bands IV (470-582mHz) and V (614-854mHz) in which all UK terrestrial television broadcasting takes place.
USP	*Unique selling proposition.*
VCR	*Videocassette recorder.*
VHF	*Very High Frequency* 30-300mHz including Band I (41-68 mHz) and Band III (174-216mHz) used in the UK until early 1985 for 405-line black-and-white television. Band II (88-108mHz) is used for VHF/FM stereo-sound services.
VHS	*Video home system.*
VO	*Voice-over.*
VT	*Videotape.*
VTR	*Videotape recording.*
WARC	*World Administrative Radio Conference.*
WTV	*Westward Television.*
WWN	*Wales West and North Television (Teledu Cymru).*

Appendices

APPENDIX A

THE IBA CODE OF ADVERTISING STANDARDS AND PRACTICES, 1985

FOREWORD

The Broadcasting Act 1981 makes it the statutory duty of the Independent Broadcasting Authority:

(a) to draw up, and from time to time review, a Code governing standards and practice in advertising and prescribing the advertisements and methods of advertising to be prohibited or prohibited in particular circumstances; and

(b) to secure compliance with the Code.

It follows from these statutory provisions that the Authority, a public board, is one of the country's official instruments of consumer protection. The controls involve the examination of all television and local sound broadcasting advertisements, including the bases of claims and demonstrations, before they are accepted for broadcasting.

The rules about advertising govern all advertising on Independent Television and Independent Local Radio until further notice. In drawing up this Code the Authority has consulted the Advertising Advisory Committee and the members of the Medical Advisory Panel appointed in accordance with the Broadcasting Act 1981.

Under the Act the Authority must consult the Home Secretary about the classes and descriptions of advertisements which must not be broadcast and the methods of advertising which must not be employed, and carry out any directions he may give them in these respects. The Authority has consulted the Home Secretary on the rules here published.

It should be noted that the Broadcasting Act 1981 expressly reserves the right of the Authority to impose requirements as to advertisements and methods of advertising which go beyond the requirements imposed by this Code. The methods of control open to the Authority include powers to give directions as to the exclusion not only of classes and descriptions of advertisments but of individual advertisements – either in general or in particular circumstances.

The programme companies, too, may in certain circumstances impose stricter standards than those here laid down – a right comparable to the recognised right of those responsible for other advertising media to reject any advertisements they wish. Notes of Guidance for advertisers and advertising agencies on the working of the control system and on specific areas of advertising are issued for television by the Independent Television Companies Association and for radio and and ORACLE teletext by the IBA itself.

THE IBA CODE OF ADVERTISING STANDARDS AND PRACTICE

Preamble

1   The general principle which will govern all broadcast advertising is that it should be legal, decent, honest and truthful. It is recognised that this principle is not peculiar to broadcasting, but is one which applies to all reputable advertising in other media in this country. Nevertheless, broadcasting, and particularly television, because of its greater intimacy within the home, gives rise to problems which do not necessarily occur in other media and it is essential to maintain a consistently high quality of broadcast advertising.

2   Advertisements must comply in every respect with the law, common or statute.

3   The detailed rules set out below are intended to be applied in the spirit as well as the letter and should be taken as laying down the minimum standards to be observed.

4   The word 'advertisement' has the meaning implicit in the Broadcasting Act 1981, i.e. any item of publicity inserted in the programmes broadcast by the Authority in consideration of payment to a programme contractor or to the Authority.

5   Programme independence

No advertisement may include anything that states, suggests or implies, or could reasonably be taken to state, suggest or imply, that any part of any programme broadcast by the Authority has been supplied or suggested by any advertiser.

6   Identification of advertisements

An advertisement must be clearly distinguishable as such and recognisably separate from the programmes. In particular.

(a) Situations and performances reminiscent of programmes must not be used in such a way as to blur the distinction between programmes and advertisements. In marginal cases the acceptance of an advertisement having such themes may depend upon some positive introductory indication that this is an advertiser's announcement.

(b) The expression 'News Flash' must not be used as an introduction to an advertisement even if preceded by an advertiser's name.

7   Rules 5 and 6 do not prohibit the inclusion of an advertisement by reason only of the fact that it is related in subject matter to an adjacent programme – e.g. advertisements for farm products and fertilisers in intervals around a farming programme. It is also acceptable for an advertisement to announce the direct and significant contribution of an advertiser's products to performances in events that have been broadcast – e.g. motor races or rallies. Normally, however, no reference to a programme is acceptable in an advertisement.

8   'Subliminal' advertising
No television advertisement may include any technical device which, by using images of very brief duration or by any other means, exploits the possibility of conveying a message to, or otherwise influencing the minds of, members of an audience without their being aware, or fully aware, of what has been done.

9   Politics, industrial and public controversy
No advertisement may be inserted by or on behalf of any body, the objects whereof are wholly or mainly of a political nature, and no advertisement may be directed towards any political end. No advertisement may have any relation to any industrial dispute. No advertisement may show partiality as respects matters of political or industrial controversy or relating to current public policy.

10   Religion
No advertisement may be inserted by or on behalf of any body, the objects of which are wholly or mainly of a religious nature, and no advertisement may be directed towards any religious end.

11   Charities
No advertisement may give publicity to the needs or objects of any association or organisation conducted for charitable or benevolent purposes.
(*This does not preclude advertisements which are confined to the giving of necessary details of flag days, fêtes, lotteries permitted under the Lotteries and Amusements Act 1976*, other events organised by such associations or organisations or publications of general interest.*)

---

*This Act does not extend to Northern Ireland

12 Good taste
No advertisement should offend against good taste or decency or be offensive to public feeling.

13 Protection of privacy and exploitation of the individual
Individual living persons should not normally be portrayed or referred to in advertisements without their permission. However, reference to living persons may normally be made in advertisements for books, films, radio or television programmes, newspapers, magazines, etc., which feature the persons referred to in the advertisement provided it is not offensive or defamatory.

14 Gifts or prizes
No advertisement may include an offer of any prize or gift of significant value, being a prize or gift which is available only to television viewers or radio listeners or in relation to which any advantage is given to viewers or listeners.

15 Stridency
Audible matter in advertisements must not be excessively noisy or strident.

16 Appeals to fear
Advertisements must not without justifiable reason play on fear.

17 Superstition   No radio or television advertisement should exploit the superstitious.

18 Unacceptable products or services
Advertisements for products or services coming within the recognised character of, or specifically concerned with, the following are not acceptable:
(a) breath-testing devices and products which purport to mask the effects of alcohol;
(b) matrimonial agencies and correspondence clubs;
(c) fortune-tellers and the like;
(d) undertake or others associated with death or burial;
(e) organisations/companies/persons seeking to advertise for the purpose of giving betting tips;
(f) betting (including pools); (*This does not preclude lotteries permitted under the Lotteries and Amusements Act 1976* but such advertisements shall be limited to an announcement of the event and necessary details.*)

*This Act does not extend to Northern Ireland

(g) cigarettes and cigarette tobacco;
(h) private investigation agencies;
(i) privately owned advisory services related to personal or consumer problems.

Note: An advertisement for an acceptable product or service may be unacceptable should it seem to the Authority that its main purpose would be to publicise indirectly the unacceptable product.

19 Trade Descriptions and claims

Advertisements must comply with the provisions of the Trade Descriptions Acts. No advertisement may contain any descriptions, claims or illustrations which directly or by implication mislead about the product or service advertised or about its suitability for the purpose recommended. In particular:

(a) *Special claims* No advertisement shall contain any reference which is likely to lead the public to assume that the product advertised, or an ingredient, has some special property or quality which is incapable of being established.

(b) *Scientific terms and statistics* Scientific terms, statistics, quotations from technical literature and the like must be used with a proper sense of responsibility to the ordinary viewer or listener. Irrelevant data and scientific jargon must not be used to make claims appear to have a scientific basis they do not possess. Statistics of limited validity should not be presented in such a way as to make it appear that they are, universally true.

Advertisers and their agencies must be prepared to produce evidence to substantiate any descriptions claims or illustrations.

20 Price claims

Advertisements indicating price comparisons or reductions must comply with the Trade Descriptions Acts, Price Marking (Bargain Offers) Order and succeeding legislation. Visual and verbal presentations of actual and comparative prices and cost must be accurate and incapable of misleading by undue emphasis or distortion.

21 Comparisons

Advertisements containing comparisons with other advertisers, or other products, are permissible in the interest of vigorous competition and public information, provided they comply with the terms of this section and the next following section of the Code.

All comparative advertisements should respect the principles of fair competition and should be so designed that there is no likelihood of the consumer being misled as a result of the comparison, either about the product advertised or that with which it is compared.

The subject matter of a comparison should not be chosen in such a way as to confer an artificial advantage upon the advertiser.

Points of comparison should be based on facts which can be substantiated and should not be unfairly selected. In particular:

(a) The basis of comparison should be the same for all the products being compared and should be clearly stated in the advertisement so that it can be seen that like is being compared with like.
(b) Where items are listed and compared with those of competitors products, the list should be complete or else the advertisement should make clear that the items are only a selection.

22   Denigration
Advertisements should not unfairly attack or discredit other products, advertisers or advertisements directly or by implication.

23   Reproduction techniques
It is accepted that on television the technical limitations of photography can lead to difficulties in securing a faithful portrayal of a subject, and that the use of special techniques or substitute materials may be necessary to overcome these difficulties. These techniques must not be abused; no advertisement in which they have been used will be acceptable, unless the resultant picture presents a fair and reasonable impression of the product or its effects and is not such as to mislead. Unacceptable devices include, for example, the use of glass or plastic sheeting to simulate the effects of floor or furniture polishes.

24   Testimonials
Testimonials must be genuine and must not be used in a manner likely to mislead. Advertisers and their agencies must produce evidence in support of any testimonial and any claims therein.

25   Guarantees
No advertisement may contain the words 'guarantee' or 'guaranteed', 'warranty' or 'warranted', or words having the same meaning, unless the full terms of the guarantee are available for inspection by the Authority and are clearly set out in the advertisement or are made available to the purchaser in writing at the point of sale or with the goods. In all cases, the terms must include details of the remedial action open to the purchaser. No advertisement may contain a direct or implied reference to a guarantee which purports to take away or diminish the statutory or common law rights of a purchaser.

26 Inertia selling

No advertisement will be accepted from advertisers who send the goods advertised, or additional goods, without authority from the recipient.

27 Imitation

Any imitation likely to mislead television viewers, even though it is not of such a kind as to give rise to a legal action for infringement of copyright or for 'passing off', must be avoided.

28 Use of the word 'free'

Advertisements must not describe goods or samples as 'free' unless the goods or samples are supplied at no cost or no extra cost (other than actual postage or carriage) to the recipient. A trial may be described as 'free' although the customer is expected to pay the cost of returning the goods, provided that the advertisement makes clear the customer's obligation to do so.

29 Competitions

Advertisements inviting the public to take part in competitions where allowable under the Broadcasting Act 1981 and Part III of the Lotteries and Amusements Act 1976* (which normally requires the presence of an element of skill) shall be accepted only if arrangements have been made for prospective entrants to obtain printed details of the conditions governing the competition, the announcements of results and the distribution of prizes. Any special conditions governing entry to the competition must be given in the advertisement.

30 Homework schemes

Fullest particulars of any schemes must be supplied and where it is proposed to make a charge for the raw materials or components and where the advertiser offers to buy back the goods made by the home-worker, the advertisement is not acceptable.

31 Instructional courses

Advertisements offering courses of instruction in trades or subjects leading up to professional or technical examinations must not imply the promise of employment or exaggerate the opportunity of employment or remuneration alleged to be open to those taking such courses; neither should they offer unrecognised 'degrees' or qualifications. Advertisements by correspondence schools and colleges will normally be accepted only from those granted accreditation by the Council for the Accreditation of Correspondence Colleges.

---

*This Act does not extend to Northern Ireland

32 Mail Order advertising

(1) Advertisements for goods offered by Mail Order will not be accepted unless:

(a) arrangements have been made for enquirers to be informed by the programme company concerned of the name and full address of the advertiser if this not given in the advertisement;

(b) adequate arrangements exist at that address for enquiries to be handled by a responsible person available on the premises during normal business hours;

(c) samples of the goods advertised are made available there for public inspection;

(d) an undertaking has been received from the advertiser that money will be refunded in full to buyers who can show justifiable cause for dissatisfaction with their purchases or with delay in delivery; and

(e) if required, arrangements are made for an approved independent organisation to receive and hold monies forwarded by television or radio respondents until it has been certified that the goods have been despatched.

(2) Advertisers who offer goods by Mail Order must be prepared to meet any reasonable demand created by their advertising, and should be prepared to demonstrate, or where practicable to supply samples of the goods advertised, to the Authority or to the programme companies to whom their advertisements are submitted.

33 Direct sale advertising

Direct sale advertising is that placed by the advertiser with the intention that the article or services advertised, or some other articles or services, shall be sold or provided at the home of the person responding to the advertisement. Where it is the intention of the advertiser to send a representative to call on persons responding to the advertisement, such fact must be apparent from the advertisement or from the particulars subsequently supplied and the respondent must be given an adequate opportunity of refusing any call.

Direct sale advertisements are not acceptable without adequate assurances from the advertiser and his advertising agency:

(a) that the articles advertised will be supplied at the price stated in the advertisement within a reasonable time from stocks sufficient to meet potential demand; and

(b) that sales representatives when calling upon persons responding to the advertisement will demonstrate and make available for sale the articles advertised.

It will be taken as *prima facie* evidence of misleading and unacceptable 'bait' advertising for the purpose of 'switch selling' if an advertiser's salesmen seriously disparage or belittle the cheaper article advertised or report unreasonable delays in obtaining delivery or otherwise put difficulties in the way of its purchase.

34 Alcoholic drink

(a) Liquor advertising may not be addressed particularly to the young and no one associated with drinking in an advertisement should seem to be younger than about 25. Children may not be seen or heard in an advertisement for an alcoholic drink.

(b) No liquor advertisement may feature any personality whose example young people are likely to follow.

(c) Advertisements may not imply that drinking is essential to social success or acceptance or that refusal is a sign of weakness.

(d) Advertisements must not feature or foster immoderate drinking. This applies to the quantity of drink being consumed in the advertisement and to the act of drinking portrayed. References to buying of rounds of drinks are not acceptable.

(e) Advertisements must not claim that alcohol has therapeutic qualities nor offer it expressly as a stimulant, sedative or tranquilliser. While advertisements may refer to refreshment after physical performance, they must not give any impression that performance can be improved by drink.

(f) Advertisements should not place undue emphasis on the alcoholic strength of drinks.

(g) Nothing in an advertisement may link drinking with driving or with the use of potentially dangerous machinery.

(h) No liquor advertisement may publicise a competition.

(i) Advertisements must neither claim nor suggest that any drink can contribute towards sexual success.

(j) Advertisements must not suggest that regular solitary drinking is acceptable.

(k) Treatments featuring special daring or toughness must not be used in a way which is likely to associate the act of drinking with masculinity.

35 Advertising and children

Particular care should be taken over advertising that is likely to be seen or heard by large numbers of children and advertisements in which children are to be employed. More detailed guidance is given in Appendix 1.

36 Financial advertising

Subject to the generality of the Code, financial advertising is governed by the rules set out in Appendix 2.

37 Advertising of medicines and treatments
Within the generality of the Code the advertising of medicines and treatments is subject to the detailed rules given in Appendix 3.

APPENDIX 1 · ADVERTISING AND CHILDREN

1 The child audience

No product or service may be advertised, and no method of advertising may be used, in association with a programme intended for children or which large numbers of children are likely to see or hear, which might result in harm to them physically, mentally or morally, and no method of advertising may be employed which takes advantage of the natural credulity and sense of loyalty of children. Children's ability to distinguish between fact and fantasy will vary according to their age and individual personality. With this in mind, no unreasonable expectation of performance of toys and games must be simulated by the excessive use of imaginary backgrounds or special effects. In particular:

(a) No advertisements which encourages children to enter strange places or to converse with strangers in an effort to collect coupons, wrappers, labels, etc., is allowed. The details of any collecting scheme must be submitted for investigation to ensure that the scheme contains no element of danger to children.

(b) Advertisements must not directly urge children to purchase or to ask their parents or others to make enquiries or purchases.

(c) No advertisement for a commercial product or service is allowed if it contains any appeal to children which suggests in any way that unless the children themselves buy or encourage other people to buy the product or service they will be failing in some duty or lacking in loyalty towards some person or organisation whether that person or organisation is the one making the appeal or not.

(d) No advertisement is allowed which leads children to believe that if they do not own the product advertised they will be inferior in some way to other children or that they are liable to be held in contempt or ridicule for not owning it.

(e) No advertisement dealing with the activities of a club is allowed without the submission of satisfactory evidence that the club is carefully supervised in the matter of the behaviour of the children and the company they keep and that there is no suggestion of the club being a secret society.

(f) If there is to be a reference to a competition for children in an advertisement, the published rules must be submitted for approval before the advertisement can be accepted. The value of the prizes and the chances of winning one must not be exaggerated.

(g) Advertisements for toys, games and other products of interest to children must not mislead, taking into account the child's immaturity of judgement and experience. In particular:

(i) the true scale of the product must be made easy to judge, preferably by showing it in relation to some common object by which its size and scale can be judged. In any demonstration it must be made clear whether the toy is made to move mechanically or through manual operation;

(ii) treatments which reflect the toy or game seen in action through the child's eyes or in which real-life counterparts of a toy are seen working must be used with due restraint. There must be no confusion as to the noise produced by the toy – e.g. a toy racing car and its real-life counterpart;

(iii) where advertisements show results from a drawing, construction, craft or modelling toy or kit, the results shown must be reasonably attainable by the average child and ease of assembly must not be exaggerated.

(h) Cartoon characters and puppets featured in ITV or BBC children's programmes must not expressly recommend products or services of special interest to children or be shown using the product. This prohibition does not extend to public service advertisements nor to cartoon characters or puppets especially created for advertisements.

(i) Advertisements which invite respondents to purchase products by mail or telephone must not be addressed to children. Advertisements which invite respondents to purchase, by mail or telephone, products of particular interest to children, must not be transmitted until after 9 p.m. This paragraph does not apply to advertisements which merely invite respondents to apply by mail or freephone for free brochures, leaflets, etc.

2   Restrictions on times of transmissions

(a) Advertisements for the following must not be transmitted during children's programmes or in the advertisement breaks immediately before or after them – alcoholic drinks and liqueur chocolates, cigars, tobacco and matches.

(b) Advertisements for medicines specially formulated for children must not be transmitted on television before 9 pm.* This restriction also applies to advertisements in which children are seen taking any medicine or in which its suitability for children is specially emphasised.

(c) Advertisements for matches being promoted by means of premium gifts of any kind must not be transmitted on television before 9 p.m.* and such advertisements must be clearly addressed to adults.

(d) Advertisements which feature personalities associated with ITV or BBC children's programmes and which promote products or services of special interest to children must not be transmitted on television until after 9 pm.*

(e) Advertisements which contain treatments which might alarm or frighten children will be the subject of appropriate restrictions on times of transmission.

(f) Products or services not of brand interest to children which however feature promotions of interest to children must not normally be transmitted on television until after 9 pm.*

3 Prices

Advertisements for toys, games and similar products must include an indication of their price. When parts, accessories or batteries which a child might reasonably suppose to be part of a normal purchase are available only at extra cost, this must be made clear. The cost must not be minimised by the use of words such as 'only' or 'just'.

4 Health and hygiene

Advertisements shall not encourage persistent sweet eating throughout the day nor the eating of sweet, sticky foods at bed-time. Advertisements for confectionery or snack foods shall not suggest that such products may be substituted for proper meals.

5 The child in advertisements

The participation of children in advertisements is subject to the following conditions:

(a) *Employment* It should be noted that the conditions under which children are employed in the making of advertisements are governed by certain provisions of the Children and Young Persons Act 1933 (Scotland 1937) and the Act of 1963; the Education Acts 1944 to 1948; the Children (Performances) Regulations 1968; and the appropriate by-laws made by Local Authorities in pursuance of these Acts.

(b) *Contributions to safety* Any situations in which children are to be seen or heard in advertisements should be carefully considered from the point of view of safety. In particular:

(i) children should not appear to be unattended in street scenes unless they are obviously old enough to be responsible for their own safety; should not be shown playing in the road, unless it is clearly shown to be a play-street or other safe area; should not be shown stepping carelessly off the pavement or crossing the road without due care; in busy street scenes should be seen to use pedestrian crossings in crossing the road; and should be otherwise seen in general, as pedestrians or cyclists, to behave in accordance with the Highway Code.

*On radio acceptable time segments on weekdays are 9 am–12 noon, 2–4 pm, 9 pm–6.30 am and at weekends and during school holidays 9 pm–6.30 am.

(ii) children should not be seen leaning dangerously out of windows or over bridges, or climbing dangerous cliffs;

(iii) small children should not be shown climbing up to high shelves or reaching up to take things from a table above their heads;

(iv) medicines, disinfectants, antiseptics and caustic substances must not be shown within reach of children without close parental supervision, nor should children be shown using these products in any way;

(v) children must not be shown using matches or any gas, paraffin, petrol, mechanical or mains-powered appliance which could lead to their suffering burns, electrical shock or other injury;

(vi) children must not be shown driving or riding on agricultural machines (including tractor-drawn carts or implements): scenes of this kind could encourage contravention of the Agriculture (Safety, Health and Welfare Provisions) Act 1956;

(vii) an open fire in a domestic scene in an advertisement must always have a fireguard clearly visible if a child is included in the scene.

(c) *Good manners and behaviour* Children in advertisements should be reasonably well-mannered and well-behaved.

6 Children as presenters
Children must not be used formally to present products or services which they could not be expected to buy themselves, nor must they make in relation to any product or service, significant comments on characteristics on which they cannot be expected to have direct knowledge.

7 Testimonials
Children must not be used to give formalised personal testimony. This will not, however, normally preclude children giving spontaneous comments on matters in which they would have an obvious natural interest.

APPENDIX 2 · FINANCIAL ADVERTISING

PART A · FACILITIES

1 Investment and savings
The following investment and saving facilities may be advertised:

(a) investment in British Government stocks, Savings Certificates and Premium Bonds, stocks of public boards and nationalised industries and Local Government stocks and deposit facilities in the United Kingdom, Isle of Man and the Channel Islands;

(b) deposit or share accounts with building societies designated under Section 1 of the House Purchase and Housing Act 1959;

(c) such facilities provided by the National Savings Bank, National Giro Bank, Trustee Savings Banks and recognised banks and licensed institutions within the meaning of the Banking Act 1979;

Note: acceptance is subject to any regulations made under section 34 of the Banking Act 1979

(d) savings facilities, guaranteed by the national governments of EEC countries, in currencies other than sterling, provided that a warning statement is included as to the effects of the value of the savings of exchange rate fluctuations;

(e) Unit Trusts authorised as such by the Department of Trade;

(f) the services of the Stock Exchange and Member Firms.

2 Prospectuses

Advertisements announcing the publication of a company prospectus which contains an application form, offering to the public shares or debentures to be listed on the Stock Exchange, may be accepted provided that:

(i) the text of the advertisement has been submitted to the Stock Exchange through the usual channels;

(ii) the form and content of the advertisement has been submitted to the Authority;

(iii) there have been supplied to the Authority such certificates as it may require from the issuing bank or brokers to the offer and the directors of the company in relation to the advertisement.

The Authority will require a certificate from the issuing bank or brokers concerned to the effect that the advertisement is accurate and not misleading and may, if it thinks fit, require in addition a certificate from the directors of the company covering such matters as the Authority may consider appropriate.

3 Insurance

Life and Endowment facilities, including linked life assurance schemes, annuities, retirement and sickness insurance, etc., may be advertised normally only by members of the Life Offices' Association, the Industrial Life Offices' Association, the Associated Scottish Life Offices' Association, the Linked Life Assurance Group and by registered friendly societies which are members of the Association of Collecting Friendly Societies, National Conference of Friendly Societies, National Union of Holloway Societies or Association of Deposit Societies.

General insurance cover (e.g. for motor, household, fire and personal injury) may normally be advertised only by members of the British Insurance Association and of Lloyd's underwriting syndicates.

Insurance brokerage services may normally be advertised only by brokers registered under the Insurance Brokers (Registration) Act 1977 or bodies corporate enrolled under the Act.

4   Lending and credit

The advertising of mortgage, other lending facilities and credit services is acceptable from:

(a) Government and local government agencies;
(b) building societies;
(c) insurance companies;
(d) registered Friendly Societies;
(e) those persons and bodies granted a licence under the terms of the Consumer Credit Act 1974.

5   Financial publications

Advertisements for publications, including periodicals and books, on investments and other financial matters must make no recommendation on any specific investment offer. Advertisements for subscription services must be in general terms and make no reference to any specific investment offer.

6   Corporate advertising

Advertisements giving a general picture of a company or group of companies may include a background of financial information provided such information does not appear designed to enhance the financial reputation of the company or group, or any associated company, in the minds of investors. Up-to-date information regarding turnover and capital expenditure (but not changes therein) may be included, but profit figures, references to distributions to shareholders and quotations from chairmen's statements and similar documents are not permitted. Availability of the annual report may also be mentioned.

Financial information included in such advertisements must not mislead by exaggeration, omission or selectivity. A recent annual report and accounts (or, in the case of a listed company, a statement of results) which verifies such information must be made available to the Authority.

7   Announcement of results

Advertisements of the results of companies whose shares are listed on the Stock Exchange may be accepted, provided that no such advertisement may give or imply more information than was released by the company to the Stock Exchange, and the form and content of such advertisements have been submitted to the Authority. Information included in such advertisements must not present the company in terms which may mislead by exaggeration, omission or selectivity. Reference must be made to availability of the full published statement of the results.

Note: A corporate advertisement or an announcement of results may be unacceptable should it seem to the Authority to have the effect of publicising indirectly any financial facility which may not be advertised under other provisions of the appendix.

8 Commodity investment
The advertising of commodity investment is not acceptable.

PART B · ADVERTISING CONTENT

Within the generality of the Independent Broadcasting Code of Advertising Standards and Practice, the following rules set out the minimum requirements to be observed in all advertisements offering services and facilities of a financial nature:

1 Advertisements must comply with all relevant legal requirements (see Appendix 4(b) for a list of relevant statutes affecting financial advertisements).

2 No advertisement is acceptable which directly or indirectly invites the remittance of money direct to the advertiser or any other person without further formality.

3 Advertisements must present the financial offer or service in terms which do not mislead, whether by exaggeration, omission, or in any other way. In particular:

(a) *Tax benefits* References to income tax and other tax benefits must be properly qualified to show what they mean in practice and to make it clear, where appropriate, that the full advantage may only be received by those paying income tax at the full standard rate.

(b) *Interest on savings and investments* References to interest payable on savings and investment must be stated clearly and be factually correct at the time of the transmission of the advertisement. Calculations of interest must not be based on unstated factors (e.g. minimum sum deposited, minimum deposit period, or minimum period of notice for withdrawal) which might affect the sum received by individuals or be capable of misunderstanding in any other way. It should be clear whether the interest is gross or net of tax. Interest rates related to variables (e.g. Bank of England rate) must be so described.

(c) *Interest on credit loans and hire* All advertisements for credit in any form, including loans and hire purchase and those concerned with hire transactions, must comply strictly with the requirements of the Consumer Credit Act 1974 and the Regulations made under it.

(d) *Rates of growth or return on Unit Trusts* No advertisement referring directly or indirectly to benefits to be derived from a purchase of units may state or imply that they are other than a medium to long-term investment. There may be no projection of specific rates of growth or returns and no implications that past performance will inevitably be repeated. All references to past achievements or future possibilities must be qualified by a clear and unambiguous reference to the fact that the price of units and the income from them may go down as well as up.

Note: Written confirmation will be required that the material text of any proposed advertisement for a unit trust has the approval of the trustee

(e) *Insurance premiums and cover* References to rates and conditions in connection with insurance must not be inaccurate or misleading, and in specifying rates of premium or cover there must be no misleading omission of conditions.

In life insurance advertising, references to specific sums assured or guaranteed bonuses must be accompanied by all relevant qualifying conditions – e.g. age and sex of the assured at the outset of the policy, period of policy and amount and number of premiums payable. In references to 'with profit' policies and bonuses there must be no implication that past performance will inevitably be repeated.

In advertisements for linked life assurance schemes any reference to a specific maturity value, unless guaranteed, must be qualified by reference to the variables which might affect the quoted figure. Advertisements must also contain clear and unambiguous reference to the fact that the value of assets can move both down and up. All insurance advertisements must comply in every respect with the Insurance Companies Act 1974 and the Regulations made under it.

(f) *Advertising by member firms of the Stock Exchange* Advertisements by Member Firms of the Stock Exchange must comply in every respect with the Stock Exchange rules and Code of Conduct, and written confirmation will be required that the text of any proposed advertisement has the approval of the Stock Exchange. Advertisements must not contain any investment recommendation or comment on individual securities.

(g) *Presenters in advertisements for investments and savings* No one may appear to give independent professional or personal advice on any investment or savings offer. Although artists and other celebrities may act in advertisements, they may not lend their personal authority nor the authority of their TV or film characters to the advertising message.

Note: Full and detailed information will be required in connection with any financial offer or service to be advertised on television.

488

APPENDIX 3 · THE ADVERTISING OF MEDICINES AND TREATMENTS

INTRODUCTORY

The proper use of medicines requires great care in their advertising. Such precautions should ensure that products or treatments for which health claims are made should advertise in compliance with the spirit and details of the Code.

Section 16 of the Broadcasting Act 1981 requires that:

(5) The Authority shall, after consultation with such professional organisations as the Secretary of State may require and such other bodies or persons as the Authority think fit, appoint, or arrange for the assistance of, a medical advisory panel to give advice to the Authority as to –

(a) advertisements for medicines and medical and surgical treatments and appliances;
(b) advertisements for toilet products which include claims as to the therapeutic or prophylactic effects of the products;
(c) advertisements for medicines and medical and surgical treatments for veterinary purposes, and such other advertisements as the Authority may think fit to refer to the panel.

(6) The Authority shall consult the panel before drawing up the Code under Section 9 and in the course of any review of that Code.

(7) The Authority shall ensure that, before the first occasion on which they broadcast an advertisement which in their opinion falls under paragraph (a), (b) or (c) of subsection (5) of this section, the advertisement is, in accordance with arrangements approved by the Authority, referred to a member or members of the panel for advice.

Under the provisions of the Act, a Medical Advisory Panel representative of both general and specialist medicine has been appointed and its advice is obtained before the first occasion on which an advertisement involving any matter of health or nutrition is broadcast.

With the introduction of new and changed products, the diverse licensing requirements of the Medicines Act 1968 and developments in medical opinion in respect of particular products reflected in advice from the Medical Advisory Panel, the Code cannot provide a complete conspectus of the pre-publication requirements of the Authority in relation to particular products or classes of products.

As a result of advice received from the Medical Advisory Panel, however, detailed advice on particular products can be given to advertisers by the TV and Radio programme companies' organisations. Reference should also be made to the British Code of Advertising Practice which establishes detailed minimum standards which have been adopted by media including the Independent Television and ILR companies.

The general principles governing advertising of medicines and treatments on ITV and ILR are set out below:

1   Medicines Act 1968

All advertisements for products subject to licensing under the Medicines Act 1968 shall comply with the requirements of the Act and any conditions contained in the product licence.

2   Unacceptable products or services

Advertisements for products or services coming within the recognised character of, or specifically concerned with, the following are not acceptable:

(a) contraceptives – this does not preclude advertising of approved family planning services;
(b) smoking cures;
(c) products for treatment of alcoholism;
(d) clinics for the treatment of hair and scalp;
(e) products for the treatment of haemorrhoids;
(f) pregnancy testing services;
(g) hypnosis, hypnotherapy, psychology, psychoanalysis or psychiatry.

3   Impressions of professional advice and support

The following are not allowable:

(a) presentations of doctors, dentists, veterinary surgeons, pharmaceutical chemists, nurses, midwives, etc. which give the impression of professional advice or recommendations;
(b) statements giving the impression of professional advice or recommendation by persons who appear in the advertisements and who are presented, either directly or by implication, as being qualified to give such advice or recommendation. To avoid misunderstanding about the status of the presenter of a medicine or treatment, it may be necessary to establish positively in the course of an advertisement that the presenter is not a professionally qualified adviser; and
(c) references to approval of, or preference for, the product or its ingredients or their use by the medical or veterinary professions.

4   Establishments offering slimming treatments

Advertisements of establishments which offer or provide treatment aimed at the achievement of weight loss or figure control will be accepted only if:

(a) such treatments are based upon dietary control, the availability of which is referred to in the advertisement;

(b) in the opinion of the Medical Advisory Panel such treatments are likely to be effective and will not lead to harm, and any claims made are justified;

(c) any financial and other contractual conditions are made available in writing to respondents prior to commitment.

5 Celebrity testimonials and presentations

No advertisement for a medicine or treatment may include a testimonial or be presented by a person well-known in public life, sport, entertainment, etc.

6 Cure

No advertisement shall employ any words, phrases, or illustrations which claim or imply the cure of any ailment, illness or disease, as distinct from the relief of its symptoms.

7 Diagnosis, prescriptions or treatment by correspondence

No advertisement shall contain any offer to diagnose, advise, prescribe or treat by correspondence.

8 Appeals to fear or exploitation of credulity

No advertisement shall cause those who see it unwarranted anxiety lest they are suffering (or may, without responding to the advertiser's offer, suffer) from any disease or condition of ill health; or falsely suggest that any product is necessary for the maintenance of health or the retention of physical or mental capacities, whether by people in general or by particular groups.

9 Conditions requiring medical attention

No advertisement shall offer any product for a condition which needs the attention of a registered medical or other qualified practitioner. (This does not preclude advertisements for spectacles and contact lenses.)

10 Tonic

The use of this expression is not acceptable in advertisements for medicines or treatments or products for which medical or health claims are made.

11 Encouragement of excess

No advertisements shall encourage, directly or indirectly, indiscriminate, unnecessary or excessive use of products within the scope of this section of the Code.

12 Exaggeration

No advertisement shall make exaggerated claims, in particular through the selection of testimonials or other evidence unrepresentative of a product's effectiveness, or by claiming that it possesses some special property or quality which is incapable of being established.

13 Vitamins

No advertisements shall state or imply that good health is likely to be endangered because people do not supplement their diets with vitamins. The Medical Advisory Panel may be prepared to accept restrained advertisements for vitamin products related to the dietary requirements of growing children, pregnant or lactating mothers or elderly people.

14 Analgesics

It is accepted that the relief of pain, such as a headache, may consequently ease tension. But no simple or compound analgesic shall be advertised for the direct relief of tension. In such advertisements there must be no reference to depression.

15 Refund of money

No advertisement shall contain any offer to refund money to dissatisfied users of any product within the scope of this section, other than appliances or therapeutic clothing.

16 Safety and protection of children

No advertisement shall encourage the adoption of any unsafe practices especially by children.

17 Competitions

Advertisements shall not contain any reference to a prize competition or similar scheme.

Appendix 4 · Statutes Affecting Broadcast Advertising

The following statutes and regulations made under them are among those which may restrict, control or otherwise affect broadcast advertising or should be particularly noted.

(a) *General*

Accommodation Agencies Act 1953; Adoption Act 1976 (Section 58); Betting, Gaming and Lotteries Act 1963, (Sections 10 and 22); Broadcasting Act 1981; Cancer Act 1939 (Section 4); Children and Young Persons (Harmful Publications) Act 1955; Children and Young Persons Act 1933 (Scotland 1937); Children and Young Persons Act 1963 (including the Children (Performances) Regulations 1968); Children Act 1958 (Section 37)

Civil Aviation (Air Travel Organisers Licensing) Regulations 1972; Consumer Safety Act 1978; Copyright Act 1956; Cream Regulations 1970; Defamation Act 1952; Education Acts 1944–81; Employment Agencies Act 1973; Energy Act 1976 (Section 15); Fair Employment (Northern Ireland) Act 1976; Fair Trading Act 1973; Food Act 1984; Gaming Act 1968; Geneva Conventions Act 1957 (Section 6); Hearing Aid Council Act 1968; Labelling of Food Regulations 1984; London Cab Act 1968, 1973; Lotteries and Amusements Act 1976; Margarine Regulations 1967; Marine etc. Broadcasting (Offences) Act 1967; Medicines Act 1968 and Regulations; Opticians Act 1958; Price Marking (Bargain Offers) Order 1979; Race Relations Act 1976; Registered Designs Act 1949; Sale of Goods Act 1979; Sex Discrimination Act 1975; Shops Act 1950; Telecommunications Apparatus (Advertisements) Order 1982; Trade Descriptions Act 1968, 1972; Trade Descriptions (Origin Marking) (Miscellaneous Goods) Order 1981; Trade Marks Act 1938; Trading Stamps Act 1964; Unsolicited Goods and Services Act 1971, 1975; Venereal Diseases Act 1917; Weights and Measures Act 1963 to 1979 and Regulations

(b) *Financial*

Banking Act 1979; Building Societies Act 1962 (Sections 14, 48 and 51, and Schedule 2); Building Societies Act (N.I.) 1964 (Sections 7, 8, and 11); Channel Islands Act 1967; Companies Acts 1948 to 1981; Companies Act (N.I.) 1960; Consumer Credit Act 1974 and Regulations; Depositors and Investors (Prevention of Fraud) (Jersey) Law 1967, and the Depositors and Investors (Prevention of Fraud) (General Provisions) (Jersey) Order 1980; House Purchase and Housing Act 1959 (Section 1); Insurance Brokers (Registration) Act 1977; Insurance Companies Acts 1974, 1981; Insurance Companies Act (N.I.) 1968; Industrial and Provident Societies Act 1965; Prevention of Fraud (Investment) Act 1940, 1958; Protection of Depositors and Prevention of Fraud (Amendment) (Bailiwick of Guernsey) Law 1970; Trustee Savings Banks Act 1969.

APPENDIX B

PART I

TELEVISION ACT, 1954

Second schedule: Rules as to advertisements

1 The advertisements must be clearly distinguishable as such and recognisably separate from the rest of the programme.

2 The amount of time given to advertising in the programmes shall not be so great as to detract from the value of the programmes as a medium of entertainment, instruction and information.

3 Advertisements shall not be inserted otherwise than at the beginning or the end of the programme or in natural breaks therein and rules (to be agreed upon from time to time between the Authority and the Postmaster-General, or settled by the Postmaster-General in default of such agreement) shall be observed –

(a) as to the interval which must elapse between any two periods given over to advertisements,

(b) as to the classes of broadcasts (which shall in particular include the broadcast of any religious service) in which advertisements may not be inserted, and the interval which must elapse between any such broadcast and any previous or subsequent period given over to advertisements

4 In the acceptance of advertisements, there must be no unreasonable discrimination either against or in favour of any particular advertiser.

5 The charges to be made by any programme contractor for advertisements shall be in accordance with tariffs fixed by him from time to time, being tariffs drawn up in such detail and published in such form and manner as the Authority may determine.

Any such tariffs may make provision for different circumstances and, in particular, may provide, in such detail as the Authority may determine, for the making, in special circumstances, of additional special charges.

6   No advertisement shall be permitted which is inserted by or on behalf of any body the objects whereof are wholly or mainly of a religious or political nature, and no advertisement shall be permitted which is directed towards any religious or political end or has any relation to any industrial dispute.

7   If, in the case of any of the television broadcasting stations used by the Authority, there appears to the Authority to be a sufficient local demand to justify that course, provision shall be made for a reasonable allocation of time for local advertisements, of which a suitable proportion shall be short local advertisements.

BROADCASTING ACT 1981

Second Schedule: Rules as to advertisements

1   (1) The advertisements must be clearly distinguishable as such and recognisably separate from the rest of the programme.

(2) Successive advertisements must be recognisably separate.

(3) Advertisements must not be arranged or presented in such a way that any separate advertisement appears to be part of a continuous feature.

(4) Audible matter in advertisements must not be excessively noisy or strident

2   The standards and practice to be observed in carrying out the requirements of the preceding paragraph shall be such as the Authority may determine either generally or in particular cases.

3   The amount of time given to advertising in the programmes shall not be so great as to detract from the value of the programmes as a medium of information, education, and entertainment.

4   Advertisements shall not be inserted otherwise than at the beginning or the end of the programme or in natural breaks therein.

5   (1) Rules (to be agreed upon from time to time between the Authority and the Secretary of State, or settled by the Secretary of State in default of such agreement) shall be observed as to the classes of broadcasts (which shall in particular include the broadcast of any religious service) in which advertisements may not be inserted, and the interval which must elapse between any such broadcast and any previous or subsequent period given over to advertisements.

(2) The Secretary of State may, after consultation with the Authority, impose rules as to the minimum interval which must elapse between any two periods given over to advertisements, and the rules may make provision for different circumstances.

6   In the acceptance of advertisements there must be no unreasonable discrimination either against or in favour of any particular advertiser.

7   (1) The charges made by any programme contractor for advertisements shall be in accordance with tariffs fixed by him from time to time, being tariffs drawn up in such detail and published in such form and manner as the Authority may determine.

(2) Any such tariffs may make provision for different circumstances, and, in particular, may provide, in such detail as the Authority may determine, for the making, in special circumstances, of additional special charges.

8   No advertisements shall be permitted which is inserted by or on behalf of any body whose objects are wholly or mainly of a religious or political nature, and no advertisements shall be permitted which is directed towards any religious or political end or has any relation to any industrial dispute.

9   If, in the case of any of the stations used by the Authority, there appears to the Authority to be a sufficient local demand to justify that course, provision shall be made for a reasonable allocation of time for local advertisements, of which a suitable proportion shall be short local advertisements.

PART II

Section 4(6) of the Television Act, 1954 – the famous 'no-sponsorship' clause which was to present the Authority and its lawyers with some problems of interpretation.

6   Nothing shall be included in any programmes broadcast by the Authority, whether in an advertisement or not, which states, suggests or implies, or could reasonably be taken to state, suggest or imply, that any part of any programme broadcast by the Authority which is not an advertisement has been supplied or suggested by any advertiser; and, except as an advertisement, nothing shall be included in any programme broadcast by the Authority which could reasonably be supposed to have been included therein in return for payment or other valuable consideration to the relevant programme contractor or the Authority:

Provided that nothing in this subsection shall be construed as prohibiting the inclusion, in any part of a programme broadcast by the Authority which is not an advertisement, of any of the following matters, that is to say:

(a) items designed to give publicity to the needs or objects of any association or organisation conducted for charitable or benevolent purposes;

(b) review of literary, artistic or other publications or productions, including current entertainments;

(c) items consisting of factual portrayals of doings, happenings, places or things, being items which in the opinion of the Authority are proper for inclusion by reason of their intrinsic interest or instructiveness and do not comprise an undue element of advertisement;

(d) announcements of the place of any performance included in the programme, or of the name and description of the persons concerned as performers or otherwise in any such performance, announcements of the number and description of any record so included, and acknowledgements of any permission granted in respect of any such performance, persons or record;

(e) such other matters (if any) as may be prescribed by regulations made by the Postmaster-General by statutory instrument after consultation with the Authority,

or as prohibiting the inclusion of an advertisement in any programme broadcast by the Authority by reason only of the fact that it is related in subject-matter to any part of that programme which is not an advertisement.

APPENDIX C

MINISTERIAL RESPONSIBILITY FOR BROADCASTING

Postmaster-General

1951–1955	Earl De La Warr
1955–1957	Dr Charles Hill
1957–1964	Reginald Bevins
1964–1966	Anthony Wedgwood Benn
1966–1968	Edward Short
1968	Roy Mason
1968	John Stonehouse

Minister of Posts & Telecommunications

1968–1970	John Stonehouse
1970–1972	Christopher Chataway
1972–1974	Sir John Eden
1974	Anthony Wedgwood Benn

Home Secretary

1974–1976	Roy Jenkins
1976–1979	Merlyn Rees
1979–1983	William Whitelaw
1983–1985	Leon Brittan
1985–	Douglas Hurd

APPENDIX D

INDEPENDENT TELEVISION AUTHORITY (INDEPENDENT BROADCASTING AUTHORITY FROM JULY 1972)

Chairman

1954–1957	Sir Kenneth Clark
1957–1963	Sir Ivone Kirkpatrick
1962–1963	Sir John Carmichael (Acting Chairman)
1963–1967	Lord Hill
1967–1975	Lord Aylestone
1975–1981	Lady Plowden
1981–	Lord Thomson of Monifieth

Director-General

1954–1970	Sir Robert Fraser
1970–1982	Sir Brian Young
1982–	John Whitney

Advertising Advisory Committee

Chairman

1955–1959	Robert A. Bevan
1959–1962	E. Glanvill Benn
1962–1965	Sir Daniel Jack
1965–1976	Samuel Howard
1976–1980	Professor Royston Goode
1980–	Professor Aubrey Diamond

Advertising Control

1955–1959	Anthony Pragnell (Secretary of the Authority)
1959–1974	Archie Graham (Head of Advertising Control)
1974–1981	Peter Woodhouse (Head of Advertising Control)
1981–	Harry Theobalds (Controller of Advertising)

APPENDIX E

INDEPENDENT TELEVISION AUTHORITY

Advertising Advisory Committee 1956

Chairman

Robert A. Bevan OBE, Member of Council, Institute of Practitioners in
 Advertising

Members
F. W. Adams BSc FPS ARIC, Pharmaceutical Society of Great Britain
L. G. Anderson DVM MRCVS, Royal College of Veterinary Surgeons
Humphrey Chilton, Incorporated Society of British Advertisers
Dr H. Guy Dain MD FRCS LRCP, British Medical Association
Roger Diplock, Director, Retail Trading Standards Association
Janet Hauff, Ministry of Health
Leslie W. Needham, Code of Standards Committee on the Advertising of
 Medicines and Treatments
James O'Connor ACIS, Institute of Practitioners in Advertising
George Pope, Advertising Association
Leslie Room, Director-General, Advertising Association
W. Stewart Ross FDSRCS, British Dental Association
Alan Whitworth, OBE, Director, Incorporated Society of British
 Advertisers

*Prior to the Television Act of 1963 the officials of the advertising trade
bodies – the AA, IPA and ISBA – were all members of the Committee in
their own right. From 1963 onwards however they attended its meetings
as observers. At the same time the Chairman of the AAC was required to
be independent of all advertising interests and the public as consumers
were represented on the Committee.*

APPENDIX F

INDEPENDENT BROADCASTING AUTHORITY

Advertising Advisory Committee 1985

Independent Chairman

Professor Aubrey Diamond LLM, Director, Institute of Advanced Legal Studies, University of London.

The Public as Consumers

Anne Harris CBE, Former Chairman, National Federation of Women's Institutes

Mrs Adrian Secker, Manager of a Barnardo's school for girls and Governor of an ILEA school for boys. Former Chairman Independent Local Advisory Committee for London.

Ramindar Singh, Member, National Consumer Council

Advertising Interests

Anthony Bracking, Chairman, Code of Advertising Practice Committee.

Eric Burleton, Director, Allan Brady & Marsh, Chairman, Advertising Controls Group, Institute of Practitioner in Advertising.

Dr Gordon Fryers MD MRCP, Consultant Director of Medical Affairs, Proprietary Association of Great Britain.

Ron Gray, Chairman, Lever Brothers.

Medical Interests

John Ferguson, Secretary and Registrar, Pharmaceutical Society of Great Britain.

Professor J. P. Quilliam DSc FRCP, Professor of Pharmacology, University of London.

Observers

Kenneth Miles, Director, ISBA
Neil Welling, Chairman, ITCA Copy Committee.
David Wheeler, Director, IPA.

APPENDIX G

INDEPENDENT TELEVISION AUTHORITY

Medical Advisory Panel 1964

Dr A. H. Douthwaite MD FRCP
Professor Sir Derrick Dunlop BA MD FRCP
Sir John Richardson MVO MA MD FRCP
Professor R. D. Emslie MSc BDS FDS
Professor Alastair Frazer CBE DSc MD PhD BS FRCP
Brian Singleton MRCVS
Dr K. A. Williams BSc PhD MInstPet AInstP FRIC

Second Opinion Specialists

Dr Philip Evans MD MSc FRCP
T. L. T. Lewis FRCS FRCOG
Ian Robin MA FRCS
Dr Peter Smith MD MRCP

INDEPENDENT BROADCASTING AUTHORITY

Medical Advisory Panel 1985

Sir Richard Bayliss KCVO MD FRCP
Dr P. A. Emerson MA MD FRCP FACP
Professor R. D. Emslie MSc BDS FDS
Dr Philip Evans CBE MD MSc FRCP
Dorothy Hollingsworth OBE BSc FRIC FIFST FIBiol
Professor H. Keen MDS FRCP
T. L. T. Lewis FRCS FRCOG
Dr Michael Linnett OBE MB FRCGP
Ian Robin MA FRCS LRCP
Brian Singleton CBE FRCVS
Dr Peter Smith MD BS FRCP

APPENDIX H

PRINCIPLES GOVERNING THE SALE OF TELEVISION AIR TIME

1   In order to keep the television medium competitive with other media, it is a major responsibility of the sales departments of the ITV programme contractors to give the best possible value to advertisers.

2   All contractors should make available for purchase, and use their best endeavours to sell, at published rates the maximum permitted commercial time. Decisions about programming schedules, programming hours and the removal of breaks from particular programmes are a matter for agreement between the IBA and the ITV contractors; these decisions are not and should not be influenced by any consideration of the possibility that a diminution of advertising time will harden advertising rates.

3   The contractors recognise an advertiser's freedom to allocate his budgets in accordance with his own marketing policy rather than a pre-determined allocation by region. The fact that an advertiser chooses not to participate in an incentive or share scheme should not affect his ability to buy any particular available air time at any published rate.

4   Pre-empt arrangements should be operated efficiently and in a fair and reasonable manner by the contractors. Subject to availability, advertisers should have the right to select at what level they enter the pre-empt structure but this should not preclude contractors from advising on the element of risk foreseen. There should be adequate cut-off points to avoid last minute pre-emption without notice.

5   Because of the many pressures that advertisers have to face in their normal business activities, the contractors should allow the maximum possible freedom of cancellation or alteration of schedules. It is, however, recognised that instances may occur when contractors should be recompensed for disruption to their business caused by cancellations. Where they do apply penalties or refuse cancellations, contractors should notify advertisers in writing, with reasons when appropriate.

6   Unless there is a particular need for confidentiality, contractors should promptly and regularly supply such information about the medium as will

enable judgements to be made of the television air time market area by area.

7   ITCA and/or the contractors should give ISBA (representing advertisers) and IPA (representing agencies) the earliest possible notice of any significant change in terms and conditions or in the structure of rate cards which may be contemplated, and thus an opportunity to express views and to comment.

8   The above principles will be the subject of discussion and review from time to time by the Advertising Liaison Committee.

As a result of over a year's discussions between the Authority, the programme companies, advertisers and agencies the Principles Governing the Sale of Airtime were hammered out clause by clause at the ALC. They were issued in January 1982.

APPENDIX J

INDEPENDENT TELEVISION AREAS AND PROGRAMME COMPANIES

I *The Major Companies*

Area	Programme company	Contract	On air
London	Associated-Rediffusion (A–R) (later Rediffusion Television)	Weekdays	September, 1955–July, 1968

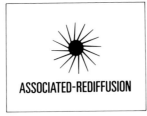

	Associated TeleVision (ATV)	Weekends	September, 1955–July, 1968

	Thames Television	Weekdays	July, 1968–

London Weekend
Television (LWT)

Weekends   July, 1968–

Midlands   Associated TeleVision
(ATV)

Weekdays   February, 1956 –
July, 1968
All Week   July, 1968 –
December, 1981

ABC Television

Weekends   February, 1956 –
July, 1968

*East &
West
Midlands

Central Television

All Week   January, 1982–

* Dual Region

| North of England | Granada Television | Weekdays | May, 1956 – July, 1968 |

| | ABC Television | Weekends | May, 1956 – July, 1968 |

| **North-West England | Granada Television | All Week | July, 1968 – |

| Yorkshire | Yorkshire Television | All Week | July, 1968 – |

** Originally *Lancashire*

II *The Regional Companies*

Central   Scottish Television   All Week   August, 1957 –
Scotland

*Wales &   Television Wales & West All Week   January, 1958 –
West of   (TWW)   May, 1968
England

Harlech Television (HTV)All Week   May, 1968 –

South of   Southern Television   All Week   August, 1958 –
England   December, 1981

* Dual Region

**South &
South-
East
England*

Television South (TVS)

All Week

January, 1982 –

*North-
East
England*

Tyne Tees Television
(TTT)

All Week

January, 1959 –

*East of
England*

Anglia Television

All Week

October, 1959 –

*Northern
Ireland*

Ulster Television

All Week

October, 1959 –

*South-
West
England*

Westward Television

All Week

April, 1961 –
August, 1981

* Dual Region

	Television South West (TSW)	All Week	August, 1981 –

The Borders	Border Television	All Week	September, 1961 –

**North Scotland	Grampian Television	All Week	September, 1961 –

West & North Wales	Wales West and North (WWN)	All Week	September, 1962 – December, 1963

Channel Islands	Channel Television	All Week	September, 1962 –

** Originally *North-East Scotland*

National  All Week   November, 1982–

National  All Week   February, 1983–

APPENDIX K

INDEPENDENT TELEVISION ADVERTISING REVENUE

Year	Revenue	Change
1956	£13,024,000	—
1957	£31,986,000	+145.6%
1958	£48,671,000	+52.2%
1959	£58,359,000	+19.9%
1960	£76,960,000	+31.9%
1961	£93,276,000	+21.2%
1962	£99,794,000	+7.0%
1963	£62,931,783	—
1964	£74,433,162	+18.3%
1965	£82,840,106	+11.3%
1966	£85,825,169	+3.4%
1967	£91,776,136	+6.9
1968	£98,758,870	+7.8%
1969	£97,539,737	−1.2%
1970	£94,742,339	−2.9%
1971	£108,633,692	+14.7%
1972	£134,161,914	+23.4%
1973	£160,830,730	+19.9%
1974	£149,244,563	−7.2%
1975	£176,532,201	+18.3%
1976	£230,806,620	+30.7%
1977	£299,886,549	+29.9%
1978	£363,004,836	+21.0%
1979	£346,795,579	−4.5%
1980	£529,311,243	+52.6%
1981	£611,236,286	+15.5%
1982	£697,079,051	+14.1%
1983	£824,310,721	+18.5%
1984	£912,265,807	+10.7%
1985	£982,603,315	+7.7%

The figures for the period 1956–1962 were estimated by Media Records Ltd on the basis of monitors' reports which were checked against each station's transmission logs.

The figures for the period 1963–1985 are those issued by the ITCA and are net after payment of all commissions and discounts but before the deduction of Exchequer levy. None of the above figures includes the cost of commercial production (which a number of other estimates include) and the foregoing totals are not therefore comparable with, for example, the figures issued by the Advertising Association.

APPENDIX L

Sources of Television Advertising Expenditure 1968–1984

	1968			1969		
	TV Exenditure £000s	TV as % of TV and Press	TV % Profile	TV Exenditure £000s	TV as % of TV and Press	TV % Profile
Agriculture & horticulture	478	14	0.35	339	7	0.
Charity & educational	1570	11	0.11	179	11	0.
Drink	9,338	58	6.79	10,085	58	7.
Entertainment	254	6	0·19	356	8	0
Financial	903	5	0·66	1,008	5	0·
Food	54,873	86	39·88	58,726	85	41·
Government & service	1,087	15	0·79	2,289	23	1·
Holidays, travel & transport	1,731	17	1·26	2,698	21	1·
Household appliances	4,435	35	3·22	3,868	30	2·
Household equipment	2,645	24	1·92	2,223	20	1·
Household stores	23,322	85	16·95	23,299	83	16.
Institutional & industrial	1,504	22	1·09	1,172	13	0·
Leisure equipment	1,562	26	1·14	1,756	28	1·
Motors	4,898	31	3·56	4,818	27	3·
Office equipment	24,900	1	0·02	127,200	6	0·
Pharmaceutical	4,320	43	3·14	4,363	40	3
Publishing	3,594	50	2·61	4,388	52	3·
Retail stores & mail order	2,026	10	1·47	2,366	10	1
Tobacco	2,911	21	2·12	2,361	16	1·
Toiletries & cosmetics	11,641	58	8·46	10,761	56	7
Wearing apparel	3,656	30	2·66	3,428	26	2·
Local advertisers	2,222	100	1·61	2,455	88	1
Total TV	137,589	47	100·00	143,074	45	100·

Source: MEAL Digest. *Not strictly comparable due to change in data base.

	1970			1971			1972			1973		
	TV Exenditure £000s	TV as % of TV and Press	TV % Profile	TV Exenditure £000s	TV as % of TV and Press	TV % Profile	TV Exenditure £000s	TV as % of TV and Press	TV % Profile	TV Exenditure £000s	TV as % of TV and Press	TV % Profile
	281	6	0.19	392	7	0.24	491	8	0.24	507	13*	0.23
	31	2	0.02	19	1	0.01	56	3	0.03	47	3	0.02
	,066	64	8.37	15,126	68	9·10	17,943	70	8·60	20,165	67	8·96
	329	9	0·23	668	17	0·40	1,064	20	0·51	1,712	25	0·76
	671	4	0·47	755	3	0·45	1,128	3	0·54	1,598	5	0·71
	,203	85	39·00	64,018	86	38·53	79,346	90	38·05	78,604	88	34·94
	,443	22	1·70	3,865	30	2·33	3,801	29	1·82	5,141	31	2·29
	,643	24	2·53	4,274	25	2·57	5,227	28	2·51	5,413	28	2·41
	,483	37	3·11	5,589	44	3·36	8,333	52	4·00	6,187	43	2·75
	,975	19	1·37	3,536	30	2·13	4,794	34	2·30	5,537	32	2·46
	,023	84	15·98	24,485	86	14·74	27,445	86	13·16	28,077	86	12·48
	910	10	0·63	853	10	0·51	801	8	0·38	1,111	9	0·49
	,469	33	1·71	2,498	29	1·50	4,207	35	2·02	7,842	39	3·49
	,944	24	2·74	3,456	22	2·08	5,557	26	2·67	7,004	29	3·11
	15	1	0·01	179	6	0·11	118	4	0·06	233	9	0·10
	,153	47	3·58	5,609	49	3·38	6,300	49	3·02	7,469	52	3·32
	,385	50	3·04	5,479	51	3·30	7,274	55	3·49	7,188	55	3·20
	,561	12	1·78	3,865	14	2·33	5,968	15	2·86	7,545	15	3·35
	,960	22	2·05	3,462	22	2·08	4,321	24	2·07	4,714	25	2·09
	,844	58	7·52	12,355	59	7·44	17,841	66	8·56	21,990	67	9·77
	,156	27	2·19	3,093	29	1·86	3,610	33	1·73	3,592	36	1·60
	,563	85	1·78	2,578	83	1·55	2,880	80	1·38	3,305	86	1·47
	,117	46	100·00	166,161	48	100·00	208,516	49	100·00	224,990	48	100·00

	1974			1975		
	TV Exenditure £000s	TV as % of TV and Press	TV % Profile	TV Exenditure £000s	TV as % of TV and Press	TV % Profile
Agriculture & horticulture	418	10	0·19	479·0	10	0
Charity & educational	65	3	0·03	18·0	1	0
Drink	20,973	67	9·41	28,130	72	9
Entertainment	2,300	31	1·03	2,989·0	35	1
Financial	2,933	10	1.32	4,879·0	16	1
Food	72,084	85	32·35	86,776	87	30
Government services	5,727	34	2·57	6,573·0	39	2
Holidays, travel & transport	5,628	27	2·53	7,289·0	31	2
Household appliances	5,964	44	2·68	8,285·0	45	2
Household equipment	5,013	29	2·25	6,973·0	34	2
Household stores	23,524	85	10·56	22,676	83	7
Institutional & industrial	1,133	8	0·51	2,597·0	17	0
Leisure equipment	8,672	40	3·89	12,619	48	4
Motors	4,034	20	1·81	10,118	33	3
Office equipment	248	10	0·11	450.0	15	0
Pharmaceutical	8,342	57	3·74	9,629·0	61	3
Publishing	8,500	59	3·81	8,223·0	57	2
Retail stores & mail order	11,414	19	5·12	20,779	25	7
Tobacco	4,788	26	2·15	5,708·0	28	2
Toiletries & cosmetics	23,317	69	10·47	27,037	70	9
Wearing apparel	2,807	32	1·26	5,247·0	44	1
Local advertisers	4,889	95	2·19	7,147·0	100	2
Total TV expenditure	**222,780**	**48**	**100·00**	**284,621**	**51**	**100**

Source: MEAL

	1976			1977			1978			1979	
TV Exenditure £000s	TV as % of TV and Press	TV % Profile	TV Exenditure £000s	TV as % of TV and Press	TV % Profile	TV Exenditure £000s	TV as % of TV and Press	TV % Profile	TV Exenditure £000s	TV as % of TV and Press	TV % Profile
,217	22	0·34	1,500	23	0·35	1042	15	0·21	1,100	13·1	0·27
46	2	0·01	18	1	0·00	12	3	0·00	129	2·6	0·03
,282	72	9·07	36,812	73	8·61	40,773	70	8·39	38,461	63·4	9·32
,509	37	0·99	4574	39	1·07	6,950	43	1·43	6,457	39·7	1·57
,295	17	1·77	9,801	20	2·29	11,983	20	2·47	11,432	16·1	2·77
,158	87	28·99	123,064	86	28·77	136,462	86	28·08	106,413	77·9	25·79
,054	41	1·98	7,866	41	1·84	12,493	41	2·57	11,231	36·4	2·72
,803	28	2·19	8,430	26	1·97	13,220	32	2·72	15·742	31·2	3·82
,707	52	3·57	18,746	56	4·38	20,128	51	4·16	14,523	42·2	3·52
,509	39	2·95	12,844	39	3·00	11,677	31	2·40	11,342	26·0	2·75
,209	86	8·21	33878	83	7·92	39,267	84	8·08	31,065	76·3	7·53
,862	24	1·37	7,875	29	1·84	8,394	27	1·73	4,718	15·3	1·14
,185	53	4·55	22,969	52	5·37	29,762	54	6·12	31,007	48·7	7·52
,760	35	3·87	16·684	33	3·90	22,222	36	4·57	20,389	28·4	4·94
24·0	16	0·45	784·0	17	0·18	63490	11	0·13	285	4·3	0·07
,501	62	3·51	13,572	59	3·17	14,850	58	3·06	14·503	53·9	3·52
,728	61	3·02	13,890	62	3·25	16,676	61	3·43	11,135	42·9	2·70
,595	25	7·48	35,372	27	8·27	34,233	22	7·04	29,127	17·0	7·06
,259	17	1·48	5,682	18	1·33	5,075	21	1·04	4,490	14·8	1·09
,432	73	9·68	34,693	68	8·11	36,253	66	7·46	30,129	54·8	7·30
,603	53	2·14	7,590	47	1·77	7,553	42	1·55	5,548	29·3	1·34
,523	100	2·68	11,047	100	2·58	16,238	100	3·34	13,325	100·0	3·23
,763	52	100·00	427,710	51	100,00	485,997	50	100·00	412,550	40·7	100·00

Source: MEAL

	1980			1981		
	TV Exenditure £000s	TV as % of TV and Press	TV % Profile	TV Exenditure £000s	TV as % of TV and Press	
Agriculture & horticulture	3,042	24·6	0·40	4,488	29·9	
Charity & educational	61	1·0	0·01	498	6·2	
Drink	66,652	73·8	8·74	81,780	77·3	
Entertainment	13,481	54·4	1·77	16,372	55·9	
Financial	22,947	25·0	3·01	37,083	28·0	
Food	205,517	87·6	26·95	281,680	90·8	2
Government & service	21,887	50·0	2·87	23,435	46·9	
Holidays, travel & transport	21,530	30·6	2·82	33,000	35·6	
Household appliances	29,163	52·8	3·83	43,694	61·0	
Household equipment	18,065	31·5	2·37	22,810	35·7	
Household stores	62,770	83·4	8·23	80,007	86·7	
Institutional & industrial	11,127	26·5	1·46	16,816	34·0	
Leisure equipment	50,677	60·2	6·65	67,396	61·7	
Motors	42,411	35·8	5·56	46,702	37·8	
Office equipment	1,319	12·7	0·17	2,289	13·4	
Pharmaceutical	23,172	64·8	3·04	30,764	68·2	
Publishing	24,937	61·1	3·27	36,220	65·0	
Retail stores & mail order	46,544	21·5	6·11	68,794	25·5	
Tobacco	7,114	14·2	0·93	9,419	20·3	
Toiletries & cosmetics	48,139	67·1	6·31	63,453	71·1	
Wearing apparel	12,515	47·1	1·64	13,879	48·4	
Local advertisers	29,457	100·0	3·86	43,993	100·0	
Total TV Expenditure	762,530	51·3	100·00	1.024	55·4	10

1982			1983			1984		
TV Exenditure £000s	TV as % of TV and Press	TV % Profile	TV Exenditure £000s	TV as % of TV and Press	TV % Profile	TV Exenditure £000s	TV as % of TV and Press	TV % Profile
8,331	42·9	0·58	9,716	45·6	0·55	11,594	48·3	0·67
971	10·5	0·07	426	4·1	0·03	85	0·8	*
107,458	80·8	7·52	143,925	84·3	8·19	141,831	82·8	8·23
18,872	56·3	1·32	25,280	60·3	1·44	26,161	53·9	1·52
59,856	36·5	4·19	86,089	38·3	4·90	77,765	31·3	4·51
379,580	93·3	26·54	437,862	93·4	24·92	428,166	90·6	24·86
31,632	48·0	2·21	52,091	56·1	2·97	50,438	51·9	2·93
49,123	40·7	3·44	72,983	49·3	4·15	54,923	41·1	3·19
71,094	69·6	4·97	79,119	70·5	4·50	74·671	68·0	4·34
24,658	35·0	1·72	35,143	43·0	2·00	34,106	38·7	1·98
105,893	89·8	7·41	135,888	90·6	7·74	133,959	91·1	7·78
26,413	41·5	1·85	33,961	47·6	1·93	42,279	47·9	2·45
108,708	69·4	7·60	114,087	67·9	6·49	78,661	56·5	4·57
70,607	43·9	4·94	87,675	45·7	4·99	90,821	43·3	6·27
6,631	24·3	0·46	13,123	30·0	0·75	33,839	45·3	1·96
46,921	74·0	3·28	48,198	68·8	2·74	47,189	69·4	2·74
42,385	67·6	2·96	48,447	71·7	2·76	56,188	69·7	3·26
85,666	29·1	5·99	107,348	33·3	6·11	111,736	32·0	6·49
13,128	22·2	0·92	15,093	23·6	0·86	15,637	26·4	0·91
85,269	74·8	5·96	104,923	77·1	5·97	98,084	74·3	5·69
21,480	56·8	1·50	18,357	50·9	1·05	14,258	42·4	0·83
65,278	100·0	4·57	87,123	100·0	4·96	99,980	100·0	5·80
1,430	60·9	100·00	1,756	63·2	100·00	1,722	59·7	100·00

APPENDIX M
TOP TWENTY TELEVISION ADVERTISING SPENDERS BY BRAND

	1970 Brand	£000s	TV as % of TV & Press		1980 Brand	£000s	TV as % of
1.	Radiant	1397	93·9	1.	Dulux Paint	4050	84·
2.	Ariel	1320	97·9	2.	Woolco/Woolworth	4037	54·
3.	Weetabix	1221	97·9	3.	Guinness Bottled, Canned & Draught	3880	87·
4.	Kellogg's Corn Flakes	1144	96·5	4.	Midland Bank	3232	72·
5.	Persil	1107	99·9	5.	Post Office Internat. Direct Dialling	3119	99·
6.	Daz	1091	98·0	6.	Milk Mktg. Board Milk	2812	81·
7.	Maxwell House Coffee Granules	940	93·3	7.	Nescafe Coffee	2670	90·
8.	Elec. Council Home Heat	876	97·0	8.	The Sun	2622	100·
9.	Blue Band Margarine	862	99·0	9.	Asda	2589	45·
10.	Stork Margarine	844	93·2	10.	Whiskas Supermeat	2586	100·
11.	Oxo Range	834	99·9	11.	British Airways Airline	2518	66·
12.	Fairy Liquid	811	100·0	12.	Co-op	2411	27·
13.	Milk Mktg. Board Milk	796	72·4	13.	Boots Store	2380	31·
14.	Guinness Bottled	747	80·6	14.	Martini Range	2353	100.·
15.	Shell Petrol	693	90·7	15.	Weetabix	2336	97·
16.	Omo Biological	632	100·0	16.	Crown Plus 2 Paint	2313	91·
17.	Palmolive Liquid	621	99·7	17.	Esso Corporate	2301	99·
18.	Nat. Dairy Council Milk	618	82·4	18.	Fairy Liquid	2290	99·
19.	Double Diamond Bottled	599	99·2	19.	Kellogg's Corn Flakes	2261	92·
20.	Gillette Platinum Razor Blades	592	86·8	20.	Castrol GTX	2256	90·

1984		
Brand	£000s	TV as % of TV & Press
British Telecom Corporate	14,507	90·3
Bold 3 Automatic Powder	9313	100·0
British Telecom Call Stimulation	9294	99·8
Whiskas Supermeat	8728	95·3
Woolco/Woolworth	8539	83·1
Ariel Automatic Powder	8402	100.0
Nescafe Coffee	7340	93·7
Dulux Paint	6966	91·5
Allied Carpet Curtain Store	6537	81·9
McDonalds	6207	96·9
Fairy Liquid	6200	100·0
Dpt. of Trade & Ind. British Telecom Shares	6145	64·8
Asda	6114	45·4
Nat. Diary Council Milk	6037	87·2
Kellogg's Corn Flakes	5906	100·0
Barclays Bank	5774	90·2
Midland Bank	5740	65·1
Castrol GTX	5397	88·0
Mars Twix	5204	100·1
Carling Black Label Lager Canned & Draught	5173	99·1

This analysis is not produced annually but shows at gross card rates (before commission and discounts) the annual expenditure of the top twenty spending brands on television in the three years – 1970, 1980 and 1984.

Because the data are derived from monitors' reports, verified by the transmission logs of the programme companies, accurate comparison cannot be made with contractors' net revenue figures.

But the three tables are useful in showing the proportions of expenditure obtained by television in comparison with advertisers' total outlay on press & TV in three selected years. In addition, the figures reveal the changing nature of television advertising over a fourteen-year period.

INDEX

Page numbers in **bold** refer to illustrations and captions

Index

List of Maps and Diagrams

Colour Pages